Reading Wittgenstein
with Anscombe,
Going On to Ethics

# Reading Wittgenstein
# with Anscombe,
# Going On to Ethics

## CORA DIAMOND

Harvard University Press

Cambridge, Massachusetts    London, England

2019

First printing

*Library of Congress Cataloging-in-Publication Data*

Names: Diamond, Cora, author.
Title: Reading Wittgenstein with Anscombe, going on to ethics / Cora Diamond.
Description: Cambridge, Massachusetts : Harvard University Press, 2019. |
Includes bibliographical references and index.
Identifiers: LCCN 2017055588 | ISBN 9780674051683 (cloth)
Subjects: LCSH: Wittgenstein, Ludwig, 1889–1951. | Anscombe, G. E. M.
(Gertrude Elizabeth Margaret) | Language and languages—Philosophy. | Ethics. | Truth.
Classification: LCC B3376.W564 D5198 2019 | DDC 192—dc23 LC record available
at https://lccn.loc.gov/2017055588

# Contents

Reading Wittgenstein
with Anscombe,
Going On to Ethics

# Introduction

~

I learned to read Wittgenstein by reading the *Tractatus* with Anscombe's *Introduction to Wittgenstein's Tractatus*. This was in 1965; and in the years since then, reading Wittgenstein has frequently brought me back to reading him with her *Introduction*. "Finding One's Way into the *Tractatus*," which I have put first in Part I of this volume, is not the earliest of the essays here, but it starts where I started on Wittgenstein, with the whole of Anscombe's *Introduction*.

The three parts of this volume are put together in somewhat different ways. The essays in Part I were written between 1998 and 2009, and are concerned with an overlapping range of issues. They were written independently and are not directly related to each other, apart from my taking up in Essay 3 something wrongheaded that I said about Anscombe in Essay 1. Essay 1 was originally published as a review of Anscombe's book on the *Tractatus* when it was reprinted in 2000, and it introduces many of the questions taken up elsewhere in this volume. One topic of the essays in Part I is Anscombe's view of philosophical clarification and its relation to Wittgenstein's understanding of philosophical method. These essays are in different ways also concerned with Anscombe's exposition of Wittgenstein's account of propositions and her criticisms of it. The Introduction to Part I is about how my disagreements with Anscombe, in the essays of Part I, come out of my understanding of Wittgenstein's unRussellianism, which is different from her understanding. The essays in Part II came out of my reading of the post-humous collection of Anscombe's papers, *From Plato to Wittgenstein*. Those papers led me to feel the force of questions that I had not seen before—questions about the place, in Wittgenstein's thought and Anscombe's, of propositions that can only be true. The two essays in Part II are descendants of a single essay, written in 2013, when I first became aware of those questions. The Introduction to Part II sets out those questions, explains the relation of the two essays in Part II to each other and to Essay 2, and explores further some of the issues that come up in Part II. In 2014, when both of those essays were about to appear, I was invited to give a talk at the Jowett Society in Oxford. I wanted to go on from the topics in the two essays to consider their relation to ethics and in particular to some of the questions that David Wiggins had raised about truth in ethics. But in order to put all those things into a talk, I had to summarize some of the material in the essays that appear here in Part II. Essay 6 is a version of the Jowett talk, and it can be read independently of the Part II essays, since it contains a summary of some of their main points. During the discussion after the Jowett talk, questions came up about the dispute between Wiggins and Bernard Williams about truth in ethics and about the nineteenth-century de-bate about slavery, which was important in Wiggins's argument. That discussion, then, forms the background to Essay 7, which focuses on the dispute between Wiggins and Williams in relation to the debate about slavery. The essays in Part III can be read independently of the rest of the book. The Introduction to Part III explains the background to those essays, considers their relation to Wittgenstein's later thinking, and explores further some of the questions that are only just touched on in the essays themselves.

In describing the three parts of this volume, I have set out features of each part and some of the differences between the parts. But the book has a unity that comes out in the concluding section of Essay 5: "In reading Wittgenstein and Anscombe, we can see them thinking about *thinking*, and about the ways we may respond to thinking that has mis-carried or gone astray." That gets at a theme of the entire collection. Right at the beginning of the *Tractatus*, in the preface, Wittgenstein had made the link between thinking about thought, and responding, or trying to respond, to misunderstandings and confusions. In the Introduction to each of the parts of this collection, I have tried to show how the essays in that part take us to questions about thinking and its limits, and about how we may respond to thinking that has miscarried or gone wrong or got derailed. A further kind of connection is explored in Essays 5, 6, and 7. I suggest there that we might take *responding to thought that has gone wrong* to be part of the job of thinking, part of its *ergon*, and that we might pick up also an idea of Aristotle's that is important for Anscombe—namely, the connection between *thinking truly* and the *business of thinking being done well*.

When Anscombe was writing her *Introduction*, the *Tractatus* was generally read as expressing a form of empiricism. Thus J. O. Urmson (1956), in his account of the development of philosophical analysis, treats the *Tractatus* as belonging, along with Russell's atomism, in the philosophical tradition associated with Hume. One of Anscombe's main aims in her book was to make clear how the *Tractatus* should *not* be read: as the work of "a latter-day Hume." She believed that Wittgenstein's genuine accomplishments in the *Tractatus* could be understood only if we broke with the assumptions that had so far shaped how the book was read and how its significance was understood. Anscombe wanted to put the book into a quite different sort of philosophical context—a context within which the *questions* with which Wittgenstein was concerned were clearly in view, as they had not been. She argued that we could not have in focus the questions that mattered to him while the book was taken to express a form of empiricism, distinctive mainly in its logical rigor and technical sophistication.

So Anscombe was reading Wittgenstein *against* the way he was read at the time she was writing. But she was, in the Wittgenstein book as in her other work, writing *against* the analytic philosophy of her time in other ways as well. And this was frequently central in her approach to the history of philosophy. Her work is a great contribution to what Myles Burnyeat has spoken of as "the history of philosophy done philosophically."[1] Her doing of the history of philosophy philosophically, as a doing of it *against* the way philosophy was done by her contemporaries, can be seen equally strikingly in her writings about Hume and Aristotle. When Bernard Williams set out the contrast between the activities of

---

1. Burnyeat 2006, xiii.

the historian of ideas, who might be writing about some philosopher, and the activities of someone doing history of philosophy in his sense, he spoke of them as distinguished by their different "directions of attention." The historian of ideas, concerned with a philosopher, "looks sideways to the context" in which the philosopher wrote, in order to explain what he was up to in saying what he did, while the attention of the historian of philosophy, in Williams's sense of the term, "is more concerned to relate a philosopher's conception to present problems," to *our* problems, and to consider also his subsequent influence on the course of philosophy. But this is importantly different from what Anscombe wanted to do. As she engaged in *the history of philosophy done philosophically,* she was especially concerned with the ways in which our contemporary assumptions shaped what we took the problems to be.[2] She was not, though, concerned simply to put us in touch with earlier ideas about what philosophical problems were worth considering. The *philosophy* of her history of philosophy lies in part in making alive and significant problems that are not our problems, not what we have taken to be our problems—also in making clear what kind of demands on philosophical thinking-through such problems can make, also in making clear what the thinking-through of those problems can achieve. I have especially in mind here two remarkable chapters of her book on the *Tractatus,* the chapters on negation. The two-chapter sequence begins with the setting out of some questions about negation and about the truth-functional combination of propositions. These are questions which she takes to be capable of striking us as questions, but which do not depend on our having "empiricist or idealist preconceptions" about what we ought to be concerned with in philosophy.[3] In the course of the two chapters, Anscombe sets out the *Tractatus* conception of propositions as pictures in such a way as to enable readers to be "struck even to the point of conviction" by the account. Her exposition is thus meant to be

2. But see also Adrian Moore's expression of Williams's later view, in which the kind of contribution the history of philosophy can make is that of bringing into view and questioning the assumptions underlying contemporary debates. (For Moore's statement, see Williams 2006, ix.)

3. See Anscombe 1963a, *An Introduction to Wittgenstein's Tractatus,* 2nd ed. [hereafter cited as *IWT*], 12–13, 51, and 53.

*philosophical*: it is meant to show how the analogy with pictures makes intelligible the logical character of propositions (*IWT*, 71); and it is also history of philosophy: it is meant to make clear what is at the heart of the *Tractatus*. Those two chapters are also the heart of her book as a doing of the history of philosophy philosophically. And also as the doing of philosophy *against* the shared preconceptions of the time: it is this in its total freedom from what Anscombe took to be "empiricist and idealist preconceptions."

Because this is a collection of essays on topics that are closely related to each other, it has been difficult to avoid some repetition. I have taken out things in some essays that are said better in one of the others. But I have also wanted to leave the individual essays so that they are understandable on their own; and I have wanted to leave Part III so that it could be read without reference back to the essays in Part II. The introductions to each of the three parts of the volume are meant to be readable either before or after the essays in that part, and do not presuppose that readers are already familiar with the examples discussed in those essays. All this has led to some unavoidable repetition. And, further, there are passages in Anscombe's book to which I have come back several times—including, for example, her remarks about "Red is a color" and about "'Someone' is not the name of someone." What Anscombe says about them has significant connections with much else in her book. Thinking about what she had said—and then coming back to it and thinking about it again—helped me to see where I disagree with her, and why I think there are tensions in her views. Reading Wittgenstein with Anscombe has meant never being sure I've seen to the bottom of the questions.

This is not a volume about "the resolute reading" of the *Tractatus*, although the issues that are connected with that reading do come up, especially in the discussions of "Red is a color" in the Introduction to Part I and in Essays 1 and 3. My disagreement with Anscombe about statements of that sort reflects a resolute reading of Wittgenstein on nonsense. One relatively minor change in my views about such issues is that I think the image of the "frame" of the *Tractatus* turned out to be unhelpful.

I have made some changes in all the previously published essays, but the changes in the three earliest essays are more substantial.

# Wittgenstein, Anscombe, and the Activity of Philosophy

## INTRODUCTION

### 1.

Although Anscombe's *Introduction to Wittgenstein's Tractatus* is a wonderful book, I disagree with Anscombe about a good number of things. This introduction is about the disagreements that emerge in Part I, and about the unRussellian character of the *Tractatus*. It is not a very introductory introduction, and can be read instead as an afterword to the three essays in Part I. The first section is about unRussellianism, and in the following sections I look at my disagreements with Anscombe in Essays 3, 2, and 1.

I start with something from Essay 3—the significance of Frege for reading the *Tractatus*, and what Anscombe says about it. Here I want to approach in a different way the questions Anscombe raises. This will lead me to a point from which I can address the main ways I disagree with Anscombe in Part I. My reading of the *Tractatus* is, like hers, unRussellian, but my understanding of the unRussellianism of the *Tractatus* is different from hers—and that, I think, is the source of my disagreements with her. But in trying to work out, for this introduction, how to present my disagreements with her, I realized that there is a further disagreement, not touched on in any of the essays collected here. Anscombe wrote that "Wittgenstein's conception of 'sense' may be called the same as Frege's, if we are careful to add that Wittgenstein had different *theses* about it" (*IWT*, 17). She does take seriously the importance for Wittgenstein of the connection between his conception of sense and the *directionality* of sense (about which, more below); but in writing this introduction, I've come to think that she underestimates the significance of directionality for Wittgenstein's conception of sense. She did not see, I think, what a profound difference from Frege's conception it marks. Wittgenstein did not modify Frege's conception of sense, nor did he have different theses about it. He started from a Russellian conception of sense (articulated by Russell in his account of asymmetrical relations), and transformed it radically, winding up with something altogether different from anything in Frege or Russell.[1] Writing this introduction has made me realize anew how deep the questions are that one gets into as one reads and thinks about Wittgenstein with Anscombe.

In discussing Frege and Wittgenstein here, I generally use the word "proposition" as the translation of "Satz." In passages that are specifically about Anscombe, I follow as far as possible her use of "sentence" and "proposition." For more about the use of "Satz" in the *Tractatus*, see Essay 4.

At the beginning of her book, Anscombe said that "almost all that has been published about [Wittgenstein's *Tractatus*] has been wildly irrelevant"; and she added that if this irrelevance has had any single cause, it is "the neglect of Frege and of the new direction that he gave to philosophy." She then set out what she took to be distinctive in Frege's sort of approach to philosophy, and how "empiricist and idealist preconceptions" get in the way of understanding such an approach. She also explained how she took Frege's approach to be significantly different from that of Russell. In Essay 3, I argued that her account is puzzling, especially in her treatment of the contrast between Frege and Russell. But my claim was that she was anyway *right* in thinking that

---

1. My disagreement with Anscombe on this is also a disagreement with what I've said about Wittgenstein on sense and reference as part of his inheritance from Frege (Diamond 2010). See also, on Wittgenstein on sense and reference and the relation to Frege, Kienzler 2011.

there was a significant contrast—one which is important in thinking about the *Tractatus,* and which can be seen when we look at Anscombe's account of the picture theory. When I wrote about this in Essay 3, I explained the contrast in two ways. I first referred to the contrast drawn by Warren Goldfarb and Peter Hylton between an object-based view of propositions and a judgment-based view. I quoted Goldfarb's characterization of Russell's view: the primitive parts of propositions "subsist in and of themselves"; they are put together into propositions, but are recognizable independently of the particular role they may have in this or that proposition (Goldfarb 2002, 190–191). I argued that the Russellian readings of the *Tractatus,* which Anscombe was criticizing, ascribed to Wittgenstein an object-based view of propositions, while Anscombe's own reading of the picture theory involved a judgment-based approach. I then looked at the role of the context principle in Anscombe's account of the picture theory, and contrasted it with (what I took to be) Russellian readings of the picture theory—those of Norman Malcolm and David Pears.

It might be objected to my approach in Essay 3 that it depends on the contrast between a supposedly Fregean judgment-based view of propositions and a supposedly Russellian object-based view, and that that contrast doesn't hold up. Although I think such an objection doesn't work, I won't here lay out the putative objection or defend my formulation of the contrast, but will instead try to get at the contrast in a different way, from within Russell's own thinking. That is, I want to contrast Russell's Russellian approach to propositions and their constituents with an unRussellian approach to which Russell is driven in one sort of case. Focusing on Russell's general Russellianism will bring out how different it is from the unRussellian approach he very reluctantly takes in the case of propositional functions. The contrast as we can see it in Russell's own thought can bring into clearer view what is at stake in Anscombe's insistence on unRussellianism. (Russell's own unRussellianism is in fact picked out by Frege as something he agrees with. I'll get back to this.) My aim is not just to give an alternative explanation of the contrast that Anscombe had introduced between Fregean and Russellian readings of the *Tractatus.* Thinking about unRussellianism, and thinking unRussellianly, lead, I think, into the most fundamental issues with which the *Tractatus* is concerned; and this was what Anscombe saw. I am trying here, not to defend unRussellianism, but to present the significant contrast between the kinds of approach I had set out originally as "object-based" and "judgment-based." It turns out to be more complicated than I had realized.

In chapter 4 of *The Principles of Mathematics*, there is a good statement of Russell's Russellianism. He says there that every object of thought, everything we can think of, everything that can occur in a proposition, counts as what he calls a *term*, an expression that he treats as synonymous with the word "entity." (Here "proposition" is used to mean nonlinguistic propositions.) Every term is a logical subject, and Russell argues that any attempt to treat anything as not a logical subject leads to contradiction. He does allow for a possible exception in the case of some denoted complexes of terms, but he does not make any exception for concepts. Thus, for example, he holds that the concept *human,* when it occurs *as concept* in the (nonlinguistic) proposition "Socrates is human," is intrinsically the same as the concept when it occurs as logical subject—for example, in the proposition "Humanity is a term." The concept as concept is no less self-subsistent in its occurrence-as-concept than in its occurrence-as-logical-subject. Although it can be a part of a proposition, it is an independent self-subsistent entity. It is clear in Russell's discussion of such examples as *human* and *humanity* that he believes that *what it is* that is being thought of can be separated from *how* it occurs in a proposition. He continued to hold versions of this view even while much else in his thought shifted. In 1913, for example, he wrote that the relation *precedes* can occur in the two different ways, in "A precedes B" and in "Preceding is the converse of succeeding" (Russell 1992, 80).

Russell's Russellianism comes under strain when he discusses propositional functions, in chapter 7 of *The Principles of Mathematics*. He had introduced the notion of propositional functions in chapter 2, and had there explained it this way: "$\phi x$ is a propositional function if, for every value of $x$, $\phi x$ is a proposition, determinate when $x$ is given" (Russell 1937, 19). If this or that term occurs in a proposition, we can imagine replacing it by other terms. Thus, in the case of the (nonlinguistic) proposition "Socrates is a man," we can imagine replacing the term Socrates by other terms; and in that way we get such other propositions as "Plato is a man," "Aristotle is a man," and so on. Because Russell was there simply introducing the notion of propositional function, he did not deal with complications. These come up in chapter 7, when he tries to give an account of how we can distinguish in a proposition *the subject* and *what is asserted about the subject.* The background idea, as Russell begins the discussion, comes from the earlier treatment of propositional functions in chapter 2—the idea that the way to get hold of *what is asserted about Socrates* by the proposition "Socrates is a man" is to omit the term Socrates from the proposition. In that way, we get what is also asserted about Plato by "Plato is a man," what is asserted about Aristotle by "Aristotle is a man," and so on. While this appears to work for "Socrates is a man," it emphatically does not work for "Socrates is a man implies Socrates is mortal." We may indeed take that to be asserting of Socrates what "Plato is a man implies Plato is mortal" asserts of Plato, but we cannot get hold of what *that* is by removing Socrates from "Socrates is a man implies Socrates is mortal." For the result of omitting Socrates is *this:* ". . . is a man implies . . . is mortal," which does not include any indication that the same term must be included in both places, if we are to get a proposition asserting about the term in question what "Socrates is a man implies Socrates is mortal" asserts about Socrates. Here we seem to have something that we cannot *pull out of the proposition* in which it occurs, the what-is-asserted-about-the-term. This is what then drives Russell to conclude, reluctantly, that "the $\phi$ in $\phi x$ is not a separate and distinguishable entity: it lives in propositions of the form $\phi x$ and cannot survive analysis." When I say that Russell takes this view reluctantly, I mean that he believes he has no choice, and that the view may indeed lead to contradiction (although he also thinks that the opposite view leads to contradiction). The unRussellianism of the view that Russell has wound up with is plain. In contrast with the Russellian account of how the concept *human* can occur in a proposition as concept or as term, and is an entity independent of its occurrence in this or that way in this or that proposition, Russell is led to a "non-entity" account of what is in common to "Socrates is a man implies Socrates is mortal" and "Plato is a man implies Plato is mortal." Those propositions are values of the propositional function "$x$ is a man implies $x$ is mortal"—but what is in common to the propositions isn't something that can occur independently of the propositional contexts within which it is recognizable, within which it "lives." One might well ask how close Russell has come, in this sort of case, to what Frege speaks of as a function, and Russell himself recognized the Fregean-ness of the view to which he had been driven, when in his exposition of Frege, he said (in appendix A of *Principles*) that, if his conclusion in chapter 7 is right (that is, the conclusion that the $\phi$ in $\phi x$ is not an entity), then what Frege calls a function is not an entity.

When Frege comments on *The Principles of Mathematics*, he singles out the passage in chapter 4, which I used to explain Russell's Russellianism, in explaining his disagreement with Russell. And he then mentions that Russell "appears to incline" toward the Fregean position in the passage cited in my last paragraph, where Russell is explaining Frege's views and says of the unRussellian conclusion that he reached in chapter 7, that if that is right, then a Fregean function is in general not an entity. Frege then summarizes his view:

> It is clear that we cannot present a concept as independent, like an object: rather it can occur only in connection. One may say that it can be distinguished within, but that it cannot be separated from the context within which it occurs. (Frege 1984a, 282)

Frege's way of putting the point there—in terms of what is distinguishable within but not separable from the context—is close to Russell's "the $\phi$ in $\phi x$ is not a separate and distinguishable entity: it lives in propositions of the form $\phi x$ and cannot survive analysis."

In discussing the influence of Frege on Wittgenstein, Warren Goldfarb (2002) has argued that the resemblances between features of Frege's view and ideas that are significant in the *Tractatus* should not be assumed to have come from Wittgenstein's reading of Frege. It may be, as he suggests, that Wittgenstein started off with a Russellian view, and, in thinking it through, arrived at an understanding of propositions and ontology that was close in various ways to Frege's unRussellian understanding. I want to think about the issues here in a somewhat different way: there is Russell's unRussellianism, Frege's unRussellianism, and the quite distinctive unRussellianism of the *Tractatus*. I want to get into view some of the differences between the unRussellianisms. What I came to see, in thinking about these different unRussellianisms, is that one of the starting points for Wittgenstein's unRussellianism may have been Russell's Russellian account (in *The Principles of Mathematics*) of the directionality of asymmetrical relations. Another likely starting point is Wittgenstein's dissatisfaction with the theory of types. This is not to discount influences directly from Frege, some of which are indeed spelled out by Goldfarb.

### i. Russell's UnRussellianism and That of Wittgenstein

Russell's Russellianism, as I have explained it, involves nonlinguistic propositions and what Russell speaks of as terms—that is, whatever can occur in propositions, where Socrates is his most frequent example. (The word "occur" there is meant in a logical sense; so Parkinson, for example, does not occur in most of the nonlinguistic propositions in which Parkinson's disease occurs as term.) Russell's unRussellianism involves what is common to the values of a propositional function, where these values themselves are nonlinguistic propositions. What is common to the values of a propositional function (the $\phi$ in $\phi x$) is some nonseparable feature of propositions. These nonseparable features of propositions, then, do not fit what Russell had said about "everything that can be an object of thought." To see the relation to Wittgenstein, think of two changes from Russell's unRussellianism. First, switch from talking about nonlinguistic propositions to talking about propositions in the *Tractatus* sense, as propositional signs in use. And, secondly, switch from talking about what is in common to the propositions that are values of a particular propositional function (where this is what Russell says "lives in" the proposition) and talk instead about *whatever* is in common to some propositions and is a mark, in them, of a shared form and content; and say of *this* that it lives in the proposition. What meaning this proposition-feature has, it has in its occurrences in propositions. These two changes from Russell's unRussellianism move us closer to the unRussellianism of Wittgenstein's "An expression has meaning only in a proposition."[2] But there is then a question what Wittgenstein's route was to that form of unRussellianism. I have no definitive answer to that question, but I think it involved his ideas about the theory of types, which I discuss at the end of Section 1.

### ii. Russell, Frege and Wittgenstein: What Is and What Isn't "Self-Subsistent" or "Independent": UnRussellianism in Relation to Versions of the Context Principle

Frege's views about the self-subsistence of objects in contrast with concepts come out when he explains the application of the context principle to numbers. Numbers, he holds, are self-subsistent objects; and in this respect they differ from concepts and other functions; but this does not imply that a number-word means anything outside the context of a proposition. The self-subsistence of numbers rules out a number-word's working logically as a predicate, which would alter what it meant (Frege 1974, §60). Frege's view of objects as self-subsistent is structurally close to Wittgenstein on the self-subsistence of objects. (Wittgenstein's word is *selbständig,* and what Frege speaks of in connection with numbers is the *Selbständigkeit* they have as objects.) And Wittgenstein also speaks of simple names as having meaning in a *selbständig* way, which is consistent with the application to these names of the context principle. Both Frege and Wittgenstein, then, have a complex way of speaking of what counts as *selbständig* in connection with the context principle. For both of them, what counts as *selbständig* nevertheless has also a kind of dependence (*Unselbständigkeit*). *Tractatus* objects depend on the possible combinations in which they can occur, and names depend for their being as names on propositional occurrence. Wittgenstein stressed this dependence in the *Prototractatus* (1971, 2.0122): if names had a meaning both when combined into propositions and outside them, there could be no guarantee that the name out on its own and the name in a proposition really had, in the same sense of the word, *the same meaning.* What

---

2. See Wittgenstein 1963, *Tractatus Logico-Philosophicus* [hereafter cited as *TLP*], 3.314. I discuss Russell's unRussellianism and its relation to Wittgenstein's thought in Diamond 2014a. See also Goldfarb 2002.

would appear to be ruled out by that remark is the idea that you could first of all fix the meaning of a name on its own, as the name of a particular object, and *then* put it into a proposition to which it would contribute that meaning. For Frege also the Selbständigkeit of objects goes along with a kind of dependence: so far as we are concerned with logic (as opposed to psychological associations and so on), the meaning of words for objects (proper names) depends on their occurrence in propositions.[3]

The contrast between Russell's Russellianism and Frege's and Wittgenstein's unRussellianism comes out clearly in their views about what is and what isn't self-subsistent, and in the role of the context principle in their thought. Russell's Russellianism involves the idea of everything—everything that can be mentioned—being self-subsistent, including concepts. Kevin Klement (2004, 12) has argued that this does not rule out a Russellian "context principle," but it is interesting to see what sort of context principle fits in with Russell's Russellianism. What Klement sets out as a principle expressing a kind of contextualism to which Russell was committed is this: "The meaning of a word cannot be fully appreciated except in the context of a complete sentence." The principle is based on the Russellian point that a word that means a concept can occur in a sentence in which it means the concept *as concept,* or alternatively in a context in which it means the concept as *term;* so only when the word occurs in a propositional context can you see *which way* the concept in question is meant. It should be obvious that this is a weak kind of context principle. The principle is entirely consistent with holding that the meaning of a word can be secured altogether independently of its occurrence in any proposition, through acquaintance with one or another of the things that, according to Russell, we are capable of being acquainted with (which would then depend on which of Russell's changing views about acquaintance we looked at).

The kind of context principle that is consistent with Russell's Russellianism is sharply different from the context principle as we see it in Frege and in Wittgenstein. For both of them, it is inseparable from the complex view they take of the interplay of Selbständigkeit and

3. On the issues in this paragraph, see Kremer 1997.

Unselbständigkeit in the meaning of words. It expresses the significance they take *propositional occurrence* to have for the meaning of a word—where it is exactly *that* that is not taken seriously in the supposed Russellian context principle. Consider also here the argumentative role of the context principle in Frege's philosophy and in Wittgenstein's. For both philosophers, the principle is involved in the blocking of psychologistic understandings of the meaning of words, which are virtually inevitable (whatever one's official view about psychologism may be) if one allows for words to have meaning in isolation from propositional occurrence.[4] That point is reflected in Wittgenstein's remark "It is impossible for words to appear in two different roles: by themselves, and in propositions" (*TLP* 2.0122). When you think of them as having meaning "by themselves," you may take yourself to have an object of thought and to be meaning *it,* and *thereby* to be in a position to think something *about it,* and to use this or that word to *refer to it.* It is this picture of meaning that is inconsistent with Frege's or Wittgenstein's context principle and that is perfectly consistent with the supposed Russellian context principle.[5]

### iii. Frege's UnRussellianism, Wittgenstein's UnRussellianism

There are two points at which Wittgenstein expresses what we can take to be the context principle: at *TLP* 3.3 and *TLP* 3.314. The numbering system gives prominence to the first, and its wording is striking:

> Only propositions have sense; only in the nexus of a proposition does a name have meaning.

Here there is expressed in a different way the Unselbständigkeit of the meaning of names: their meaning is dependent, not in a general sort of way on something, "propositional occurrence," but on their connection

---

4. On the role of the context principle in Wittgenstein's criticisms of Russell, see Diamond 2014a.

5. For the importance of this contrast between Russell, on the one hand, and Frege and Wittgenstein, on the other, see Hidé Ishiguro 1969.

with what is distinctive about propositions, their having what Wittgenstein speaks of as *sense,* where what he means is different from what Frege meant. What Wittgenstein means by propositions having *sense* comes out in the analogy with pictures, and their representing a possible way things can be. And when Anscombe writes about Wittgenstein and picturing, she says that "the central point of the picture theory" is that only in the context of a proposition has a name reference; only in the context of a proposition has an expression reference (*IWT,* 93). Propositions having sense (as Wittgenstein understands *that*—as something that can be laid out through the analogy with picturing) is linked in *TLP* 3.3 with the context principle—which is exactly the connection on which Anscombe insisted. A picture element, or a word, can mean (*bedeuten*) this or that only in what has sense (as a picture or proposition does).

I said that what Wittgenstein means there by "sense" is not what Frege meant. There is not just the obvious difference—namely, that as Frege came to use the term "sense," sense is not something characteristic of propositions. Every name has sense, including both complete propositions and subsentential names, where the former are treated as themselves proper names. For commentators, these developments in Frege's thinking raise the question what (if anything) can be left of the context principle, once propositions are thought of by Frege as simply one case of proper names. When Frege had put forward his version of the context principle in 1884, he took complete propositions to provide the kind of context within which words genuinely have meaning, because a judgment is expressed, and one can then ask what the logical elements in the judgment are. Frege's view in 1884 was in one central respect close to that of the *Tractatus:* the kind of context in which a word genuinely has meaning is one in which something true or false is expressed. But for Frege after 1892, the kind of context provided by *complete propositions* is that of proper names of one or the other of the two truth values; and *having sense* is understood by Frege in such a wide sense as not to have any special connection with propositional contexts. Hence the particular significance of the first word of Wittgenstein's "*Only* propositions have sense": there is plainly there a contrast with Frege. But the contrast with Frege goes deeper: there is more of a difference between Wittgenstein's unRussellianism and that of Frege than you can see if you focus simply on how they answer the question "In what sort of context do words have meaning?"

Already in 1913, in "Notes on Logic" (1961a), Wittgenstein had developed a conception of sense that is a long way from Frege's. It is expressed in passages that turn up almost unaltered in the *Tractatus*. In 1913 and again in the *Tractatus*, he uses the image of an arrow in explaining what he means: "Names are points, propositions arrows—they have *sense*" (Wittgenstein 1961a, 97; *TLP* 3.144). The resemblance of propositions to arrows is a matter of their going in this direction, not that. They *can* go the other way; there is the opposite direction, they could go *that way*. We could mean by "q" what we now mean by "not-q"; that is, we could mean it with opposite sense. What, if it were the case, would have made "q" true, would instead (if we mean the opposite by "q") make "q" false. This conception of *propositional sense* as essentially directional goes with the idea that the negation sign works by reversing the sense of the proposition, not by representing anything. The heart of Wittgenstein's conception of sense comes out in his reply to the imagined suggestion that we might make ourselves understood by means of false propositions, so long as it is known that they are false. In the form it takes in the *Tractatus* (at 4.062) the reply runs:

> No! For a proposition is true if we use it to say that things stand in a certain way, and they do; and if by "p" we mean ~p and things stand as we mean that they do, then, construed in the new way, "p" is true and not false.

Logical features of the proposition (including its directionality) belong to our saying by means of it that *this* is so (rather than that *that* is), and thus to its being *true* if indeed things are as we say they are. This understanding of sense does not just give us a way of thinking of negation as reversing the sense of a proposition. Consider further: If (for example) the sense of one proposition is that things are like *this*, and the sense of another is that things are like *that*, we can then *use* these propositions (with an indicator of how we are shifting from their senses to the saying of something else) to say that things are *either like this or like that*. My example comes from Peter Hylton's discussion of Wittgenstein's under-standing of *sense* and its difference from any reifying conception of what a *sense* is.[6] What it is for a proposition to have sense, on this account, is thus inseparable from the possibility of its use in truth-functional com-binations. Hylton ends his discussion with a sentence that alludes to one of Wittgenstein's fundamental ideas:

> To reify the notion of sense and then inquire into the composition of the sense of this or that sentence, as if we were chemists en-quiring into the composition of some sentence—that, I take it, is exactly the view that Wittgenstein opposes. (152)

Hylton alludes here to *TLP* 6.111 and Wittgenstein's rejection of any theory that takes a logical feature of language to be a kind of remark-able fact into which there could be a quasi-scientific inquiry. This is a view of Wittgenstein's to which Anscombe also drew attention; and which I discuss in Essay 3. Here (as part of my trying to make clear the differences between Wittgenstein's unRussellianism and that of Frege) I want to connect Wittgenstein's anti-logical-chemistry view with his conception of logical directionality. And here there are significant con-nections with Russell, and with Wittgenstein's complex critical relation to Russell's views.

### iv. More about Wittgenstein's UnRussellianism and His UnFregeanism; But Also about a Kind of Inheritance from Russell in Wittgenstein's UnFregeanism

Thomas Ricketts has described a striking change in Russell's theory of relations in 1913, shortly after a conversation that Russell had with Witt-genstein in May of 1913 (Ricketts 1996, 66–69). Russell's earlier account of relations (as spelled out in *The Principles of Mathematics*) involved two "fundamental logical facts" of exactly the kind Wittgenstein later decried. One fundamental logical fact, according to Russell, is that in the case of any relation $R$ and two terms $a$ and $b$, there are two propositions

6. Hylton 2005b, esp. 150–152.

to be formed from those elements, as would be exemplified by the propositions "*A* is greater than *b*" and "*B* is greater than *a*." If the first of the two propositions does not imply the second, there is another relation that holds between *b* and *a;* Russell means the converse relation. That there is this *other* relation that holds between the two terms in such cases is another fundamental logical fact. The relation between the two relations is *difference of sense.* Russell then asks whether we need to recognize the converse of an asymmetrical relation as something that is distinct from the original relation. Are the propositions "*A* is greater than *B*" and "*B* is less than *A*" (in which the relations have opposite sense) really two different propositions, or are they merely linguistically different? Russell's conclusions about this in 1903, about which he did not apparently change his mind until the conversation with Wittgenstein in 1913, were that an asymmetrical relation and its converse are two different entities;[7] and that the two propositions "*aRb*" and "*bŘa*" are really different propositions, each of which implies the other. (In the second proposition, Russell uses Ernst Schröder's symbol for the converse relation.) I think Ricketts is right to suggest the significance, for Russell's change of mind, of the conversation with Wittgenstein. For Wittgenstein, anyway, there would have been strong reasons to criticize the original Russellian view: it had involved *logical facts,* of exactly the kind which I think he already took to indicate some sort of misunderstanding. I am suggesting that Wittgenstein's rejection of "logical facts" is not something new in the *Tractatus* but ran deep in his thinking.

The further point here is that asymmetrical relations have logical directionality, and Russell's expression for this was *sense.* Wittgenstein uses the word for the logical directionality of propositions; and I believe the source of his use of the word is Russell's use of it for the logical directionality of relations. But Wittgenstein transforms the understanding of *sense,* and completely detaches it from its connections with Russell on logical facts and on relations as entities. My suggestion is that Wittgenstein's understanding of *sense* looks as if it fits the Goldfarb

7. For the use of the word "entity" in spelling out this conception, see Russell 1992 (the 1913 *Theory of Knowledge* manuscript), 87.

story line—that unRussellian features of the *Tractatus* should not be assumed to reflect the influence of Frege's unRussellianism, but may be responses to Wittgenstein's own thinking through of Russellian ideas. Russell's original way of thinking about asymmetrical relations proved to be unstable, once seen through Wittgenstein's eyes. According to my story line, Russell's conception of relations could be seen by Wittgenstein as incoherently combining logical directionality with Russellian entity-hood. But it had in it an idea of enormous fruitfulness, which could be thought through and elaborated, and which could illuminate the logical character of propositions.

This new conception of propositions was spelled out by Wittgenstein in "Notes on Logic" (Wittgenstein 1961a); and Ricketts has explained it in detail (1996, esp. 69–73). It's not relevant to my purposes here to go into those details. What I want to draw attention to instead is the unFregeanness of the conception of propositional sense, right at the beginning of its articulation by Wittgenstein. One important passage is the one where Wittgenstein contrasts names and propositions, and introduces the image of the *arrow* to help explain the contrast:

> A proposition is a standard with reference to which facts behave, but with names it is otherwise. Just as one arrow behaves to another arrow by being in the same sense or the opposite, so a fact behaves to a proposition; it is thus bi-polarity and sense come in. (97)

For the sense of a proposition to be determined is for it to be determined what it is for the facts to be "of like sense" with the proposition—and what it is for them to be "of opposite sense." Wittgenstein speaks of one account, which he takes to be wrong, of what it is for "p" and "not-p" to be opposites, in contrast to his own account. The first takes "opposite" to be an indefinable relation, which would be part of the content of the negating proposition. The other takes the determination of the sense of "p" to allow for the reversibility of that sense. If the determination of the sense of a proposition makes it a standard with reference to which facts behave, then the possibility of the opposite sense is built in: it simply reverses what counts as the facts *agreeing* with the proposition and what counts as their *disagreeing*. The capacity for *being reversed* belongs to sense, and this then goes with (what Wittgenstein came to think of as) the pictoriality of propositions. We can say, by having the elements of a picture arranged *this* way, that thus-and-such is the case. Here there is a "standard with reference to which the facts behave"; but there being such a standard goes with the possibility of the standard's being taken *the other way*, where what counts as agreement in the one case gets counted as disagreement in the other. The possibility of the proposition with opposite sense is built into what sense is. I won't go into this here, but a parallel account can be given of the reversibility of the direction of relational expressions. The parallel between the two cases is discussed by Peter Geach.[8]

There are passages in Frege's writings where he expresses clearly the importance of the *opposition* between a judgment and the opposed judgment. Here, Ricketts (2002, 244) says, Frege "acknowledges sense in something like the way Wittgenstein understands this notion." The problem is that this acknowledgment of something like Wittgenstein's conception of sense is not reflected in Frege's own systematic treatment of *sense*. In the context of Frege's later views, including his understanding of *sense*, the logical opposition of "p" and "not-p" gets flattened down into the "oppositeness" of two names, when it belongs to their sense (in Frege's sense) that one is a name of one of the truth-values when the other is a name of the other truth value; but this is not genuine propositional opposition. The underlying issue here is what Wittgenstein later thinks of as the pictoriality of what has sense, and the connection of pictoriality with the point (the completely unFregean point) that "nothing in reality corresponds to the sign '~'" (*TLP* 4.05–4.0641). This understanding of pictures and its connection with negation is of great importance for Anscombe. My point here is that it is tied

---

8. Geach (1982) spells out consequences of Anscombe's discussion of converse relations in *IWT*. I discuss the reversal of the direction of a relation in Diamond 2012, where I have an example of an ordinary-language expression that reverses the direction of asymmetric relations (163). See also Diamond 2002, on general rules for reversing the directionality of propositions, or reversing the directionality of asymmetrical relations.

to a distinctively Wittgensteinian treatment of *sense* that is radically different from Frege's and not arrived at as any kind of modification of Frege's views about sense. Frege's unRussellianism and that of Wittgenstein are further apart than one can see if one simply looks at the context principle in Frege and then at the context principle in the *Tractatus* (though I don't want to deny significant connections as well). Wittgenstein's unRussellianism makes use of a deeply insightful idea of Russell's, the idea of the logical directionality, or *sense,* of asymmetrical relations. Wittgenstein recognized the logical directionality of propositions, and worked out and thought through what it meant for an understanding of propositions and of logic.—What it meant, or what it seemed to mean? What it seemed absolutely clearly to involve? These are questions we see him rethinking in *Philosophical Investigations*; see, for example, §102. There are sharp questions, then, about what, in the *Tractatus, remains* important. But here my point is simply that the originally Russellian notion of *sense* as a logical feature of asymmetrical relations became in the *Tractatus* something totally different from anything in Frege or Russell. The understanding of *negation* in terms of the reversal of logical directionality is at the heart of Wittgenstein's understanding of *sense.* It draws on the originally Russellian idea of logical directionality, but brings out the tie between logical directionality and logical reversibility (and the iterability of reversals). I would add that my reading here is deeply Anscombe-Geachian on the central significance for Wittgenstein of negation as reversal of sense, and on the significance of this reversibility for the contrast between propositions and names. But where Anscombe takes Wittgenstein to have a Fregean conception of sense, but different theses about it, I take him to have a uniquely Wittgensteinian conception of sense, which is incorporated into an account with some significant Fregean features.

What I have called the unFregeanness and the unRussellianness of Wittgenstein's conception of sense, as it gets articulated in 1913, is inseparable from two other strikingly unFregean and unRussellian features of the 1913 account. Wittgenstein's view of what in reality corresponds to a proposition differs from that of Frege and Russell not only in respect to *what kind of thing* corresponds, but even more significantly in the claim that it is one and the same fact that corresponds to a proposition and to its negation.[9] A further difference lies in the grammatical point about what it is to describe a proposition, a point that turns up unaltered in the *Tractatus*. In "Notes on Logic" (1961a, 105), Wittgenstein wrote, "One must not say 'The complex sign "aRb"' says that a stands in the relation R to b; but *that* 'a' stands in a certain relation to 'b' says *that* aRb."[10] Wittgenstein clearly means to distance himself from both Frege and Russell. The contrast between propositions and names (where only propositions have *sense* in his sense) is tied to the grammatical point about what kind of sign *signs expressive of sense* are. What the "One must not say" formula brings out is that, in a proposition, signs go proxy for things, but the logic of the facts (here, two-term relationality) is exemplified.[11] What I have spoken of as three unRussellian and unFregean features of Wittgenstein's account are what a single radically innovative conception of propositionality looks like from three different points of view: the proposition as standard with reference to which facts behave, the proposition and its negation as corresponding to a fact, and the proposition as the fact that thus and such signs stand so. I should perhaps note that, in describing these unRussellian and unFregean features of Wittgenstein's early thought about propositionality, I have not wanted to suggest that there are not many other significant features of the *Tractatus* and of Wittgenstein's earlier thinking that are both unRussellian and unFregean. But they don't bear directly on my attempt to rethink the questions that come up at the beginning of Essay 3.

### v. More about Wittgenstein's UnRussellianism:
### A Further Part of the Story

In Wittgenstein's letter to Russell, in January of 1913 (Wittgenstein 1995, 25), he says that he is not certain of the correctness of the kind of analysis

---

9. See the Introduction to Part II for some discussion of the significance of this idea for Anscombe's understanding of different sorts of proposition.

10. The first italics are mine; they correspond to the use of italics in the corresponding passage in the *Tractatus*.

11. On the notion of exemplification here, see Narboux 2014.

of propositions that he has sketched, but what he is certain of is a condition that must be met by a theory of symbolism. The condition is that it should do away with any need for a theory of types, by making clear that what a theory of types tries to exclude is something that isn't even a possibility—namely, a symbol being put into the place of some different kind of symbol. What comes out of any satisfactory theory will have to be that symbols *can't* be substituted for each other in the wrong sort of way.[12] Wittgenstein's previous theory of symbolism had failed to meet this condition, in allowing the symbol "mortality" (for example) to enter propositions in the place where "Socrates" could go—a Russellian feature of the theory. The condition that Wittgenstein is here imposing on a theory of symbolism involves a tie between what a symbol is and how, in general, it occurs in propositions. The symbol is given as a symbol of a certain kind; that is, it is given with its kind of propositional occurrences. This way of excluding a theory of types involves a form of the context principle. It may also fit the Goldfarb story line, in which apparently Fregean features of Wittgenstein's thinking in the period leading up to the *Tractatus* are not reflections of the influence of Frege. They may have been arrived at by Wittgenstein, as he became aware of the clash between Russell's general approach and the idea that he formulated later as "Logic must take care of itself." On the other hand, it is also significant that the January letter comes right after Wittgenstein's visit to Frege at Christmas of 1912, and may reflect Frege's criticism of Wittgenstein's (Russellian) theory of symbolism, as it then was. In any case, the idea that a symbol can't be put in the wrong sort of place may have come from the conversation with Frege, or from reading Frege. Thus, for example, Frege does not allow us to identify the word "Vienna," when it occurs in "Trieste is no Vienna," as the proper name

12. Wittgenstein wasn't saying that in a logically correct notation, one can't make substitutions in the wrong sorts of way: he was saying that *there is no such thing as that*. In other words, what we can recognize to be such-and-such symbol *goes with* the propositional places it goes into. In ordinary language, though, it can *look* as if we have got a symbol in the wrong sort of place for it. For some discussion of the kind of view I am ascribing to Wittgenstein, and some of the apparent problems with the view, see Diamond 2005 and Gustafsson 2017.

of the city, rather than as a predicate, which in that context would mean something like *metropolis*. There isn't such a thing as *the proper name "Vienna"* being in the place where a predicate goes. There is certainly a Fregean feel to some of the arguments in the *Tractatus*, and this is something which Anscombe strongly felt. What she felt is *there*. But it is, I think, just part of the unRussellianism of the *Tractatus*.

The other point that should be noted here is that there are close connections between the (early 1913) idea of what it is for a symbol to be of such-and-such logical kind, and Wittgenstein's later working out of the idea of what shows itself in the ways we use the signs of our language.[13] But I should formulate that point in a different way: There are connections between what the symbol *is* and what shows itself in the ways we use the signs of our language. Here we have come back to the starting point of my discussion of unRussellianisms: Russell's unRussellian views emerged in his attempt to explain *what the values of a propositional function have in common*. What they have in common is something that would count as a symbol, in Wittgenstein's later way of thinking. What is common to the propositions that are the values of the function is something that *shows itself* in the propositions.

2.

My idea was that my disagreements with Anscombe in the essays in Part I come out of my difference from her about how to understand the unRussellianism of the *Tractatus*. I will put this more narrowly. The unRussellianism of the *Tractatus* comes out in various ways throughout the book; but the remarks that begin at *TLP* 3.3 form a particularly significant group. Michael Kremer (1997) has sketched the differences between the *Prototractatus* and the *Tractatus*, of which the two most important are the weight given to the context principle and to the idea of logical space. I focus here on *TLP* 3.3 (the context principle) and the remarks that follow it, since questions about the reading of those remarks are the source of my disagreements with Anscombe. Many of

13. See Narboux 2014, esp. 222. On the connection with the theory of types, see Ruffino 1994.

these remarks can be found in the *Prototractatus,* and some of them go back further in Wittgenstein's thought; but what is striking is that, in the shift from the *Prototractatus* to the *Tractatus,* their numbering is changed, and the new numbering makes them into comments on the context principle. I think this shift in the organization of Wittgenstein's work reflects not only a shift in the significance he attached to the context principle but also a change in his understanding of how the structure of the book was connected to his overall aims. He says at the end that the remarks in the book are meant to be thrown away, but they are meant to lead you to see how to engage in an activity. If the activity that you have been led to is helpful, it needs no further justification; it's just as good after you throw away the remarks that led you to engage in it as it was before you threw them away. I believe that the chunk of the *Tractatus* that follows *TLP* 3.3 is meant to be particularly helpful in enabling the reader to see how to engage in the activity of philosophy as Wittgenstein conceived it. The remarks can indeed be thrown away, but the reader can then go on with the activity.

In the *Tractatus,* there is an example of how the activity works, at *TLP* 3.333, where Wittgenstein discusses Russell's paradox. *TLP* 3.333 comments on 3.3, the context principle, and also on 3.33, which says that in the establishing of logical syntax, "only the description of expressions may be presupposed." Let's suppose, he says at *TLP* 3.333, that the function F($fx$) could be its own argument, so that we would get a proposition "F(F($fx$))". The response is to give a *description of the expressions,* in this case the two expressions, the outer function expression "F" and the inner function expression "F". To give a description of these expressions makes clear, in the case of each expression, what the form is of its argument. Such a description makes clear, in both cases, how the expression occurs in propositions; and this belongs to *what* expression it is. Wittgenstein's point is, then, that the two function-expressions have nothing in common but the letter; they don't signify the same function—although in "F(F($fx$))" it *looks* as if the function takes itself as argument. But there is no such thing as an expression for a function doing *that*. This is, then, an important example of how a description of expressions can resolve a philosophical problem; it's also an important example of an argument that reveals an apparent similarity to be logically a mere accident. A further point is that we don't need the context principle itself, or any of the remarks in the sequence beginning *TLP* 3.3, to engage in the philosophical activity of "descriptions of expressions," as Wittgenstein understands it. So far as there is any justification for this activity, it is what it enables us to see—namely, that the resemblance of the outer "F" to the inner "F" has no logical significance. The justification of what we do in philosophical clarification lies in its helpfulness, not in anything in the *Tractatus*.[14]

I said that my disagreements with Anscombe come out of my difference from her on how to understand Wittgenstein's unRussellianism. I can now make that more precise. I believe that we can take the un-Russellian remarks beginning at *TLP* 3.3 as a guide to philosophical activity (and hence to have significant connections with the remarks at *TLP* 4.112 about philosophy as an activity of clarification). The remarks following 3.3 give us ways to avoid philosophical confusion, or to respond to it. They are discussed by Anscombe in two chapters: chapter 6, "Sign and Symbol," and chapter 7 on Wittgenstein in relation to Frege and Ramsey. But she does not discuss at all in those chapters the significance of the remarks in the 3.3's for Wittgenstein's understanding of philosophical method. In chapter 11, when she is discussing the quantifier notation and its significance, Anscombe quotes one of Wittgenstein's main remarks about philosophical method (*TLP* 3.323). She takes the remark to express Wittgenstein's recognition of Frege's genius in inventing the notation, and she goes on to explain his account of what makes for the goodness of the notation for generality, but she does not discuss the ideas Wittgenstein was expressing about how philosophical confusion can be avoided. Perhaps the most striking feature of her

14. There is a general point here. If one throws away remarks in the *Tractatus* that one takes to be nonsensical, it does not follow that one thereby gives up Wittgenstein's criticisms of Frege or Russell, expressed in the arguments of the *Tractatus*. What is important in the arguments may be that they point us to some way of engaging in the activity of clarification. But ways of engaging in clarification, though we may have been led to them by remarks in the *Tractatus*, do not depend for their justification on the propositions of the *Tractatus*. See Diamond 2014a for discussion of the general issue and of a different example.

chapter "Sign and Symbol" is that she does not discuss anywhere in it the point of the *Tractatus* passage about sign and symbol (*TLP* 3.32–3.328): it is concerned with the sources of philosophical confusion. It's about how such confusion can be avoided and how it can be diagnosed. In the chapter "Sign and Symbol," Anscombe raises quite different sorts of question about the 3.3's, as she follows out their connections with the picture theory and their implications for the theory. My difference from Anscombe on *the philosophical interest* of the 3.3's is then reflected in my disagreements with her in the essays in Part I.

A further point should be mentioned here. What I disagree with Anscombe about involves both a Russellian and a Fregean inheritance. As Michael Kremer has argued, it is *Russell* who shows the power of a good logical notation as a tool for revealing philosophical confusions that lurk within ordinary language (Kremer 2012). One can (I think) take Wittgenstein's use of the sign / symbol distinction (as a tool for diagnosing and responding to philosophical confusion) to be part of his inheritance from Frege, who pointed out, for example, that Hilbert uses the word "point" for both a first-level concept and a second-level concept (Frege 1984a, 284). This is exactly the kind of case Wittgenstein speaks of at *TLP* 3.321, where a sign is common to two different symbols, in a way that may lead to philosophical confusion.

### 3.

I'll turn now to my disagreements with Anscombe, taking first my central disagreement with her in Essay 3. Wittgenstein sets out in the *Tractatus,* in completely general terms, a use of signs, which I call the picture-proposition use. It is set out by the variable that he gives at *TLP* 6, though it has been informally explained in the earlier parts of the book. Can laying out a use of signs exclude any *other* kind of use of signs? I see the setting out of the picture-proposition use of words to be a case of what Wittgenstein speaks about in the remarks beginning at *TLP* 3.31: the presenting of something that propositions have in common, where he takes *saying something is so* to be common to all the values of the variable at *TLP* 6. Any time you clarify some expression in such a way, you enable people to see similarities and differences. If you come to see what is shared by all *sayings that something is so,* by all picture-propositions, you can see more clearly what is *not* a picture-proposition, not a saying that something is so. So mathematical propositions (for example) can be seen not to be such sayings that anything is so. The laying out clearly of a use of words can avert philosophical confusion, if (for example) it helps someone to see that her conception of mathematical propositions drew on an ill-thought-through analogy with picture-propositions, which breaks down. Nothing (I'm suggesting) is excluded by laying out any use of words, including the picture-proposition use.

Anscombe takes the picture theory to rule out some uses of signs: would-be propositions that are not bipolar, that is, that do not have the possibility of being true and the possibility of being false. At various points in *IWT*, she makes a distinction that I need to sketch here, since it is important for my disagreement with her about whether the account of picture-propositions set out in the *Tractatus* excludes anything. On page 79, when she is talking about what can and what cannot be fitted into the *Tractatus* theory, she says that even after Wittgenstein had explained how propositions that might not appear to fit in could be fitted in, there would be a residue of what couldn't be fitted in. These would be "dismissed as nonsensical"; and she adds "perhaps simply nonsensical, perhaps attempts to say the inexpressible."[15] On page 68 she speaks about the relations that must hold between the elements of a sentence, if it is to be a sentence at all, and she says that these "must be there also in any nonsensical sentence, if you could make this have a perfectly good sense just by changing the reference that some part of the sentence had." Here again there seems to be a distinction between two sorts of nonsensical sentences. It may be that when she spoke of sentences that are "simply nonsensical," she meant those that could be used to express a perfectly good sense if the reference of some part were changed; and those sentences that were immitigably nonsensical would be those that were attempts to say the inexpressible. I discuss in the appendix to

---

15. In discussing Anscombe's view, I follow her way of speaking of "the inexpressible," by which she usually means *what we can't express* in propositions. As Narboux (2014) emphasizes, this obscures the *Tractatus* understanding of what *expresses itself* in propositions, and is not "inexpressible."

Essay 1 the question whether Anscombe read *TLP* 5.473 as making a distinction between "possible" propositions and proposition-like constructions that are not "possible" propositions. The idea again would be that there are (on the one hand) immitigably nonsensical propositions, which are attempts to say the inexpressible, and (on the other hand) nonsensical propositions that can be made to express something perfectly respectable if the reference of one of the parts is changed. When Anscombe writes about "Red is a color" and "2 is a number," she says that "the point is easily made out that these propositions cannot express anything that might be false." Well, this is not (I think) so easily made out. Anscombe's idea seems to be that "Red is a color" is *stuck* with its nonsensicality because it is *stuck* with its inability to express anything that might be false. But how is it any more stuck with nonsensicality than "Socrates is identical"—which is Wittgenstein's example of a proposition that is nonsensical, but that can be used to express a perfectly good sense, if an appropriate *Bedeutung* were given to "identical"? When Anscombe says that "Red is a color" can't express anything that might be false, she appears to be putting it into a category of nonsense that is different from that of "Socrates is identical." Here again we seem to have the two categories of nonsense, as on page 79: the "simply nonsensical," on the one hand, and, on the other, "attempts to say the inexpressible": the mitigably and the immitigably nonsensical. Anscombe further holds, I think, that propositions that are attempts to say the inexpressible are prohibited by the *Tractatus*. This comes out in her discussion of "'Someone' is not the name of someone" on pages 85–86 of *IWT*, where she says that that formula counts as prohibited, on Wittgenstein's theory; and she also takes it to count, on his view, as an attempt to say something unsayable. (See also page 162, where the example serves the same purpose, as being something that Wittgenstein would count as an attempt to say what is unsayable.)

The point I want to get to here is that my disagreement with Anscombe, which is expressed in Essay 3 as a disagreement about whether the *Tractatus* view of propositions is *exclusionary,* is more fundamentally a disagreement about something else: about what the *Tractatus* is doing, and what we are supposed to be doing as readers. I see the setting out of the picture-proposition use of words as itself an activity of clarification. We are meant to see more clearly resemblances and differences between uses of words; we are meant to be able to consider whether, in some would-be use of words, we are trying to take our words in several different ways at once. This does come up in Essay 3, at the end of Section 4, but I did not in Essay 3 see clearly that my disagreement with Anscombe involves the contrast between reading the *Tractatus* as a guide to philosophical activity and reading it as the setting out of a complex and powerful theory, and the spelling out of some of the implications of the theory. But I would want to add that Anscombe's view has destabilizing elements within it. That is, she takes as "the central point of the picture theory" two statements of the context principle; and she adds a further point: that a symbol is presented, "not by putting it down and saying it is a symbol of such and such a kind, but by representing the whole class of the propositions in which it can occur." This is a summary statement of the remarks that begin at *TLP* 3.311. But those remarks about *presenting* a symbol enable us to recognize the same symbol in different contexts, and to recognize also difference of symbol. Such recognition is of great importance in philosophical activity; this is surely part of the point of the remarks in the 3.3's. Because "Red is a color" isn't one of the propositions that would be included in presenting the adjective "red" that we use in attributions of color, "Red" in "Red is a color" isn't the same symbol as "red" in such uses. There are also uses of "red" in such constructions as "Red is one of the colors that occur in both pictures." This sort of statement, innocent as it is, can be the starting point for a move into philosophical confusion. It is an unproblematically senseful statement, in which we speak of something as one of the things falling under a formal concept, and say that it has some particular property. This sort of case may then encourage us to think that we can drop the specification of the particular property, and simply say of the thing that it falls under the formal concept. In this case, the result would be "Red is a color." But then there is a question whether the apparent similarity of the use of "is a color" in "Red is a color" and "Red is one of the colors that occur in both pictures" is logically superficial. This is exactly the kind of case in which a logical notation of the sort Wittgenstein speaks of at *TLP* 3.324–3.325 would be helpful. If you write "Red is one of the colors that occur in both pictures" using a logical notation, the formal concept is signified by a variable; and so, seeing the proposition rewritten in logical notation can enable you to see that "is a color" isn't used in the same way in "Red is a color" and "Red is one of the colors that occur in both pictures." (Here I am relying on an argument about how words signify formal concepts, spelled out in detail in Essay 3.)[16]

I have been trying to show that Anscombe's reading of the picture theory as *excluding* some propositions is destabilized by her taking seriously the *Tractatus* point that a symbol is presented by representing the whole class of propositions in which it can occur. If the propositions that she takes to be excluded by the picture theory contain words or other expressions which, in the particular context, have not got a determinate meaning, and are not recognizable as the symbols *they look like* which occur in other contexts, then the arguments that the propositions are supposedly excluded break down. Those arguments depend on the supposed contrast between mitigably nonsensical propositions like "Socrates is identical" and nonsensical propositions like "Red is a color." But the contrast depends upon taking "is a color" to have more than an accidental resemblance to uses of "is a color which . . ." or "is one of the colors that . . ." in propositions that can be translated into logical notation using a variable for the formal concept. The predicate in "Red is a color" does not go over to a variable in logical notation; it has no logically significant resemblance to uses of "color" that do go over to a variable, like the use in "Red is one of the colors that occur in both pictures." When Anscombe says that "Red is a color" cannot express anything false, this reflects the idea that the nonsensicality of the proposition can't be rectified in the way in which the nonsensicality of "Socrates is identical" can be rectified. But both propositions contain words that work in a different way in other contexts; and there is no more impediment in the one case than there is in the other to their being assigned some meaning in the nonsensical proposition, the result of which would be that it would then have a "perfectly good sense," which is what Anscombe says about cases like "Socrates is identical" (*IWT*, 68). Here I would also want to express a disagreement with

16. The argument is not in the originally published version of Essay 3.

Anscombe's way of describing *what we are doing* when we say something like "Red is a color." On page 163 she speaks of this sort of thing as our using a formal concept as if it were a proper concept. The problem is with the phrase "using a formal concept." "Red is a color" uses a word that in other contexts can signify a formal concept, but if one speaks of it as "using a formal concept as if it were a proper concept," one blurs the distinction between using a *word* that in some contexts signifies a formal concept (which is all there is in "Red is a color") and saying something that actually involves the formal concept but in a wrong sort of way (which is what is suggested by Anscombe's way of speaking). If we speak of misuses of words that can signify formal concepts as *uses of formal concepts,* we are suggesting a logical resemblance or a logical connection where there is no such thing. (My argument takes as a model the "accidental similarity" argument at *TLP* 3.333, discussed above. One main thing philosophical activity does is reveal the accidental character of the resemblances that may have taken us in. It was reflection on this argument that made me feel how Fregean the approach was.)

The tension I see in Anscombe's writing about this question reflects two things. One is the significance she gives to the context principle, which implies that we can recognize our failure to mean anything definite by a word that may have a quite different use in a range of senseful propositions. If we take ourselves to be speaking about a formal concept, but use language that would work if we were dealing with a proper concept, the result (on her view) is a sentence-like formation the constituents of which have no meaning in that context (*IWT,* 163). The other side of the tension comes from Anscombe's specification of the picture theory and its implications, and in particular its implications concerning *saying* and *showing.* Her understanding of what Wittgenstein says about what can be shown but not said involves treating propositions like "Red is a color" as failing to make sense in a different kind of way from "Socrates is identical," which fails to make sense merely because some propositional constituent lacks a meaning, but does so remediably. The idea that the two cases are significantly different involves thinking that we can see what "Red is a color" would say, if it said anything (see, for example, *IWT,* 162). The proposition is nonsense, but we can recognize a kind of quasi-propositional content. It is because it has this quasi-content that it isn't "simply nonsensical," to use her phrase from page 79. My reading of this is that Anscombe goes a certain distance with what the context principle implies here—namely, that "Red is a color" has a constituent that lacks meaning in that proposition (163). But Anscombe doesn't go further down that road. If one does go down that road, if (that is) one reads the *Tractatus* as a guide to getting us out of confusion, the recognition that there is a constituent of a proposition that lacks meaning can enable us also to recognize the illusion we were under when we took it to have some kind of quasi-propositional content and not to be simply nonsensical. My disagreement with Anscombe, then, arises from what she takes to be one of the implications of the picture theory. It requires there to be two different kinds of failure to make sense. (I discuss my disagreement with her about *saying* and *showing* in the Introduction to Part II. I am drawing also on material I have added to Essay 3, about what it is to for a word to signify a formal concept, and what it is for it to look as if it does although it doesn't. There are significant connections between what Wittgenstein says about formal concepts and the remarks earlier in the *Tractatus* that follow the statement of the context principle. The crucial connection lies in the idea of the "real sign" for something, which comes up in the 3.34's and then again in Wittgenstein's remarks about formal concepts. Here again my disagreement with Anscombe is closely tied to a disagreement in the way we take the context principle.)

People who give a "resolute" reading of the *Tractatus* are sometimes said to wind up completely *junking* what Wittgenstein says about saying and showing. I've argued (with James Conant) that what needs to be junked is *one way of understanding* Wittgenstein's remarks about *showing*. The point of the argument is that you can junk *that* understanding (that is, junk the idea of what can't be said as a kind of quasi-propositional content) without dropping the idea that what Wittgenstein says about showing is helpful—and there are various ways in which this might be done.[17] Essay 2 is about these issues.

17. See Conant and Diamond 2004 and Narboux 2014. Narboux's essay is the best account of Wittgenstein on *showing* and on the kind of helpfulness the remarks about it can have.

## 4.

At the end of chapter 5 of Anscombe's *Introduction to Wittgenstein's Tractatus,* where Anscombe is discussing what Wittgenstein might have said about the statement "'Someone' is not the name of someone," she suggests that he might have said that it "was something which *shewed*— stared you in the face, at any rate once you had taken a good look—but could not be *said*" (86). To speak of what shows as staring you in the face if you take a good look is actually somewhat odd, since Anscombe herself points out both that it is "pretty well impossible to discern logical form in everyday language" (91), and that this indeed is Wittgenstein's view. She points to the system of Roman numeration to illustrate how a notation can lack perspicuity, and uses the example to bring out how Wittgenstein takes a good symbolic notation to differ from ordinary language. But what this means is that "taking a good look" at a chunk of ordinary language is not in general going to enable what *shows in it* to stare you in the face. What shows in it does not do so perspicuously. On the following page, Anscombe says that the fact that the logic of language is not perspicuously displayed in ordinary language is why we study logic and construct logical symbolisms: to understand the "logic of language," "so as to see how language mirrors reality." But again there is something odd in Anscombe's remarking that *that's* why we construct logical symbolisms, given Wittgenstein's remark that we need to construct a logical symbolism in order to avoid the fundamental confusions that fill philosophy—and given also that, later in the book, she quotes the very passage where Wittgenstein says that it's because of those fundamental confusions that we need to make use of a logical symbolism which avoids the linguistic traps of ordinary language. One of Wittgenstein's most significant ideas about this comes up in *TLP* 4.112, which is the central passage on the kind of activity that Wittgenstein took philosophy to be. When he wrote about those remarks in a letter to Ogden (which hadn't been published when Anscombe wrote her book), Wittgenstein said that "it cannot be the RESULT of philosophy 'to make propositions clear': this can only be its task. The *result* must be that the propositions *now have become clear* that they ARE clear" (1973, 49). I discuss this puzzling remark in Essay 2. Here I want to note its significance for my attempt to set out my disagreements with Anscombe. In the context of *TLP* 4.112, the point is that there is philosophical work to be done in order that what shows in our propositions will "stare us in the face." If the work is successful, the kind of use the proposition has is no longer obscured by misleading similarities to other forms of expression; its logical features are now perspicuous. And what counts as success here depends upon the confusion to which the work is responding. The point in *TLP* 4.112 is thus closely connected with the remarks beginning at 3.32, about the difficulties there may be in recognizing a symbol from its sign, in the context of ordinary language.

Essay 2 is about Anscombe's example of a kind of philosophical clarification. She was responding to what Antony Flew had said about "Somebody" and "Nobody": that the latter is unlike the former in not referring to somebody. The reason this comes up in her book on the *Tractatus* is its relevance to Anscombe's overall view of the picture theory. She thought it was a flaw in the theory that it prohibits saying various things which might be both true and illuminating. It would, for example, prohibit saying in response to Flew, "'Somebody' does not refer to somebody" or "'Someone' is not the name of someone." Such a statement, she says, would be "obviously true" and may be illuminating. Its role in Anscombe's book, then, is to illustrate the unreasonableness of the *Tractatus* prohibition on such statements—statements that can only be true and that are not propositions of logic or mathematics. There are two big issues in the background: What use or uses can there be for such statements, and how can philosophers respond to confusion? These big topics come up again in Parts II and III of this volume. Essay 2 is narrowly focused on the sort of confusion to which Anscombe is responding—confusion that takes the form of failure to understand the difference between "someone" and "somebody," on the one hand, and names, on the other.

Toward the beginning of Anscombe's discussion of "'Someone' is not the name of someone," she asks what it is that that statement *denies*. One thing that is not being denied, she says, is that there is someone who is actually named "Someone." As Anscombe sees the situation in which we might try to respond to confusion about the logic of "Someone" by saying, "'Someone' is not the name of someone," we are not merely saying of the *word* "Someone" that it is not anyone's name. That the word actually has that use (if it has) is beside the point. But what is it then that she takes us to be speaking of? She has an argument that is meant to bring out that it isn't a name and that it is not part of its logic to refer to anybody. She says that, if it were, then on being told that everyone hates somebody, we could ask to be introduced to the universally hated person. Implicitly, in this argument, and in the statement "'Someone' is not the name of someone," what she is speaking about is "someone" and "somebody" *taken as having a certain use.* The possibility of saying "Everybody hates somebody" is part of *that use*; and "someone," when it is used *that way,* isn't being used as a name. But if that use were in fact made clear, would that have already got us past the idea that we might want to say of *it,* of "someone" used *that way,* that it wasn't a name? My disagreement with Anscombe concerns what I think is getting *squashed* in her discussion. While she is engaging in the business of making it easier to see what the sign-together-with-its-use is (and *this* is what she takes Flew to have been confused about), she doesn't see her own activity in the light that the *Tractatus* provides for thinking about that activity. Wittgenstein's distinction between sign and symbol is, in an underground way, present in her discussion of "someone." The contrast between sign and symbol (between sign and sign-taken-together-with-the-logical-features-of-its-use) is among the most important tools Wittgenstein gives us for responding to confusion. But, like the other tools he gives us in the 3.3's, the distinction between sign and symbol is not just meant for responding to confusion; it's a tool also for thinking about what we ourselves are doing in such responses, and what we may be accomplishing. If we forgo them, what will be affected, what will suffer, is our own understanding of what we are doing. This is one of the things involved in my disagreement with Anscombe in Essay 2. But there is more to it than that.

In Essay 3, my disagreement with Anscombe was about whether what Wittgenstein says about pictures and propositions *excludes* anything, puts it out beyond what we should even attempt to say. In Essay 2, the focus of the disagreement is on one particular thing that Anscombe took to be excluded by the picture theory, and that she uses to show the unreasonableness of the general exclusion. In the previous section of this introduction, in discussing Essay 3, I focused on the supposed immitigable nonsensicality of sentences that are supposedly attempts to say what is shown. But in Essay 2, my disagreement with Anscombe is about our being able (supposedly) to find helpful and illuminating something that supposedly lies beyond what Wittgenstein counts as sayable. On Anscombe's view, there is *something out there* that it may be quite reasonable to want to say in the kind of circumstances she describes, and it is an unreasonable feature of Wittgenstein's theory (as she understands it) that it prohibits our saying it. Here, then, is my disagreement: If we take the *Tractatus* as a guide to philosophical activity, this can make the idea of *something out there that we might want to say* disappear. Looking closely at clarification, what it might be like, can undo the impression of there being this excluded-but-helpful thing.

## 5.

In chapter 12 of her *Introduction to Wittgenstein's Tractatus,* Anscombe wrote that "criticism of sentences as expressing no real thought, according to the principles of the *Tractatus,* could never be of any simple general form." She went on, "each criticism would be *ad hoc,* and fall within the subject-matter with which the sentence professed to deal." Yet, in her earlier chapter "Consequences of the Picture Theory," she argues for there being a simple general form of criticism, available on the basis of the principles of the *Tractatus,* by which we can criticize all propositions like "Red is a color," "2 is a number," "'The king of France' is a complex," and so on. They all fail to be bipolar; and they are not propositions of logic. (These are among the propositions I discussed above, as supposedly immitigably nonsensical.) In Essay 1, I discuss the apparent incompatibility between Anscombe's two discussions of Tractarian criticism of propositions. Are there no general principles, or is there in fact a fairly simple general principle? But it seems to me now that I don't, in Essay 1, make clear what is at stake in this issue of *Tractatus* criticism of sentences as expressing no real thought. Here I want to look at my disagreement with Anscombe from a different angle. It is connected with the issue of Russellianism and unRussellianism in the *Tractatus* and in readings of the *Tractatus,* and also connected with the important contrast (originally emphasized in discussions of the *Tractatus* by Peter Sullivan and Adrian Moore) between two ways to understand the idea of the "limits of language" (or that of "the limits of thought"), in the *Tractatus*—on the one hand, as *limit,* and on the other as *limitation.* When Sullivan (2011) introduces the contrast, he speaks first of the notion of a limit in his sense. He emphasizes that "the notion of a limit is not a contrastive one," and he goes on: "There is nothing thought-like excluded by the limits of thought for lacking thought's essential nature, just as there are no points excluded from space for being contra-geometrical" (172). In contrast, then, the idea of "the limits of thought" (or the "limits of language") as *limitations* is an idea of them as "boundaries that separate what has a certain nature from what does not" (172). This is an essentially contrastive notion.

One of the most important things Wittgenstein says about limits is that, so far as his book takes as its aim the drawing of the limit to the expression of thoughts, this will be do-able only within language. As I read the *Tractatus,* what Wittgenstein held is that clarifications (in which we concern ourselves with what is within language) help to bring the "limits of language" into view—from within. I take this to apply to all clarifications, ranging from the setting out of the picture-proposition use of words (all sayings and thinkings that something or other is so) to the much more limited kinds of clarification that we may go in for, in connection with one or another particular philosophical problem. When we engage in the activity of philosophy—whether we make more perspicuous things we may have said or wanted to say, or whether instead we are able to recognize that, in some putative proposition, there were signs to which no determinate meaning had been given—we go some way toward bringing the limits of our language more clearly into view. In this understanding of the *Tractatus,* what is brought into view is limits, not limitations: on the far side, there is nothing "thought-like" but simply nonsense. Putting this another way: Tractarian clarification doesn't involve a contrastive understanding of its subject matter.

The issues here come out in two sharply different ways of thinking about the theory of types. On the one hand there is the *Tractatus* passage about the theory of types (*TLP* 3.333); on the other, there is a kind of Russellian view of the theory of types as specifying what it is or isn't *permissible* to do with symbols. Against this, Wittgenstein's view is: Our symbols don't need permissions.[18] This point goes back to Wittgenstein's 1913 remarks on the theory of types (Wittgenstein 1995, 24–25): that what the theory of types tries to prevent isn't something that needs preventing. There isn't such a thing as a symbol going in the wrong sort of place. I think that, as Anscombe reads the *Tractatus,* the remarks about the limits of language and the limits of thought are understood as about *limitations;* but there are elements in her reading that pull in the opposite direction. It's the presence of both of these elements in her reading that underlies the questions I discuss in Essay 1, about Tractarian criticism of sentences as not expressing a thought, and about her apparently having two incompatible accounts of such criticism.

One of Anscombe's two discussions of Tractarian criticism of sentences is about her response to a question Wittgenstein once asked her: "Why do we say that it's natural to think that the sun goes round the earth, and not that the earth turns on its axis?" She had replied that she supposed it was because it looks as if the sun goes round the earth; and Wittgenstein had then asked what it would have looked like if it was the other way. She saw that she had no real reply, and that her use of "It looks as if the sun goes round the earth" rested unthinkingly on a naive picture that had no application to this case. It is part of our talk of *its looking as if p,* that there is a description that could be given of the different *look* that things would have had, if *not-p.* If we talk of its looking as if thus-and-so, when there is (as we can see if we think about it) *no* available description of the different look things would have, if *not*-thus-and-so, then we have merely picked up the *words* from our familiar use of phrases like "It looks as if," but our use of those words is empty (unless we give them some new use, as Anscombe jokily pretended to do once she realized her previous confusion). We have earlier seen this kind of example, in which one comes to recognize that the occurrence of a familiar word or expression marks only an accidental resemblance. "It looks as if p," as Anscombe used it, was not the *symbol* we have in cases in which there is a description of the different look things

18. See Wittgenstein's response (August 19, 1919) to the letter Russell wrote, on first reading the *Tractatus,* in Wittgenstein 1995, 125.

would have had, if not-p. Although Anscombe does not present the example in terms of the sign / symbol distinction as we see it in the 3.3's, her treatment of the example could easily be taken to illustrate that distinction; and Anscombe's discussion of the case fits well with her account of the *presenting of a symbol*. It's in the context of her discussion of "It looks as if the sun goes round the earth" that she says that Tractarian criticism of a sentence as expressing no real thought, will not be of some general form, but will depend upon the particular subject matter. This is what led to my discussion in Essay 1 of her having two apparently incompatible approaches to Tractarian criticism. Here, though, I want to ask how all this is tied in with *limits* and *limitations*.

Anscombe's discussion of "It looks as if the sun goes round the earth" does not explicitly touch on Tractarian ideas about "the limits of language," but it is compatible with a conception of the limits as *limits*. The sentence that she is criticizing is not presented as any kind of attempt to put into words what lies beyond the limits; it is instead simply something that fails to express any thought. (It is "beyond the limits" only in being simply nonsense.) Anscombe treats the criticism as a good example of Tractarian criticism. But her discussions of propositions like "Red is a color" (in *IWT* and later) are quite different. The criticisms are contrastive in character, and involve an account of why these sentence-like constructions are impermissible. It is not just that they *don't* express a thought. The contrastive understanding is indeed essential to Anscombe's argument that the general exclusion of such sentences is unreasonable. What is supposedly excluded is *thought-like* but (as she reads the *Tractatus*) lacks what Wittgenstein takes to be the essential nature of thought. Anscombe's understanding of these cases thus involves the idea of "the limits of language" as *limitations*. What I think is a kind of duality in her view—seeing the limits as *limits,* seeing them as *limitations*—affects also her understanding of what Wittgenstein's book is meant to get us to *not do*. One conception is this: "Don't *try to say* the things that the *Tractatus* teaches us are not sayable—the things that lie beyond the limits of language." But there is a quite different conception in the final chapter of Anscombe's book, where she makes use of the image of the world *thought of as however things are,* as having "a good or evil expression." So far as this image helps us to understand what Wittgenstein took ethics to be, it can help us to see why he wanted an end to ethical "chatter." But this isn't a matter of wanting us to cease trying to put into words what we can recognize to lie beyond the limits of saying.

I have been trying to show that my disagreements with Anscombe are disagreements in how we understand Wittgenstein's unRussellianism, especially as it comes out in the remarks that start with his statement of the context principle. In writing this introduction, I've come to see the significance especially of this, from *IWT,* page 93: "If 'a' is a symbolic sign only in the context of a proposition, then the symbol 'a' will be properly presented, not by putting it down and saying it is a symbol of such-and-such a kind, but by representing the whole class of the propositions in which it can occur." I take this to be important for Wittgenstein's idea of what it is to *recognize* a symbol by its sign, and to recognize also what only accidentally resembles a particular symbol. And I take these ideas to be crucial in Tractarian criticism of a sentence-like construction as not expressing any thought. This is, then, what is at stake in my disagreements with Anscombe in Essay 1. Whether we take the "the limits of language" or "the limits of thought" as *limits* rather than as *limitations* is then also a reflection of how we understand the unRussellian remarks in the 3.3's. In the appendix to Essay 1, which I wrote for this collection, I look at these questions from a slightly different direction, asking whether Anscombe took criticism of a would-be sentence, on Tractarian principles, to involve two stages, one in which the "permissibility" of the construction is judged, and then one in which its sensefulness is investigated. The idea of "permissibility," which is at the heart of the view I investigate as possibly Anscombe's, implicitly involves questions about Wittgenstein's distance not only from Russell but also from Frege. The *Tractatus* remarks that are important for Wittgenstein on "permissibility" (5.473–5.4733) come from a sequence in the manuscript of the *Prototractatus* that was originally continuous with remarks about the sign / symbol distinction and its importance for thinking about how philosophical confusion arises. Wittgenstein later moved these remarks (about logic looking after itself, and about permissibility) to the place they have in the numbered versions of the *Prototractatus* and the *Tractatus*. In the new position, the remarks bring out a kind of *disconnection:* they make it clear that something *doesn't go* with what you might have thought it *would go with.* The specifying of what is essential to propositions *does not go with* notions of *logical permissibility* that would rule out as impermissible some of the propositional signs that we might construct. Drawing the limits of language is not giving a boundary outside of which there lie logically impermissible uses of signs. The limits are not limitations. *Limits as not limitations* runs through the book, but has two specific locations: its original tie to the remarks in the 3.3's, and its final placement as comment on *TLP* 5.47, about how logic is already present in the construction of propositions—already present in all logical compositeness.

## 6.

What I have learned from Anscombe is reflected in everything I've written about Wittgenstein. I believe that the issues that come up in my disagreements with her go to the core of the concerns of the *Tractatus;* and I hope it may be helpful to have gone over them in these various different ways.

# Finding One's Way into the *Tractatus*

~

Elizabeth Anscombe's *Introduction to Wittgenstein's* Tractatus is an enormously stimulating book. Is it successful as an *introduction* to the *Tractatus*? People disagree about this. Some think that it is so difficult and demanding that one could not recommend it to students as an introduction. It *is* difficult; it *is* demanding—more so, I think, than Anscombe realized. But throughout the book Anscombe teaches her readers what it means to get into the *Tractatus*. She quotes Wittgenstein's remark (from the preface to the *Tractatus*) that his book would perhaps only be understood by those who had already thought the thoughts expressed in it; her comment is "certainly he can only be understood by people who have been perplexed by the same problems" (*IWT*, 19). Anscombe brings out— superbly—the depth and interest of those problems. So *that's* the way in which the book is successful as an introduction. And unlike any perhaps easier introduction, it is a book from which one *continues* to learn.

## 1.

Anscombe took the main thesis of the *Tractatus* to be that propositions (spoken, written, or merely thought) are pictures; and one of her three main aims in *IWT* is to explain that thesis and its consequences, and to judge its significance. I have already alluded to one of her other aims— that of making clear the kinds of question with which Wittgenstein was concerned. The third aim was to change the way in which the *Tractatus* was read. She believed that the empiricist tradition in British philosophy, together with the influence of the logical positivists and of their reading of the *Tractatus,* had made it extremely difficult for the *Tractatus* to be understood. That third aim is inseparable from the second, from the aim of making clear the kinds of question which are important for Wittgenstein, since what blocked such understanding was, she thought, the empiricist preconceptions with which the *Tractatus* was being read, preconceptions which led to its being taken to be a kind of proto-verificationist work. And the second and third aims cannot be separated from the first. That is, Anscombe's account of the picture theory is meant to depend on *dis*connecting it from empiricism and connecting it with what she takes to be interests of Wittgenstein's that lie close to Frege's. The rest of this section gives an overview of the aims.[1]

Anscombe's account of the picture theory is meant to show that the picture theory and the theory of truth-functions are "one and the same" (81). The heart of her account is a two-chapter discussion of negation, which begins by presenting some questions of exactly the sort which she wants to make salient for her readers—questions which will ultimately enable her to show how picturing and truth-functionality are connected. Here are two of those questions:

> (a) Logicians frequently introduce a sign for negation by saying that "not p" is "the proposition that is true when p is false and false when p is true." But with what right do they do so? What assurance can they rely on that there is such a proposition, and no more than one? (51)
>
> (b) In explanations of truth-functions which we find in logic books, we are usually told that "propositions are whatever can be either true or false," that they "can be combined in certain ways to

---

1. My discussion prescinds from my disagreement with her approach to Wittgenstein on propositions and pictures. The reversibility of propositional sense, so important for Anscombe's view, seems to me actually to undercut the "picture theory," in enabling us to see how the "theory" dissolves from within. See Diamond 2002, esp. 273. Whether or not one ultimately agrees with Anscombe about the character of Wittgenstein's views, her way of reading the book, as putting forward a theory, is the natural first reading.

form further propositions," and that, in the developing of the truth-functional calculus, the internal structure of the combined propositions is of no interest to us. But "is the property of being true or false, which belongs to the truth-functions, the very same property as the property of being true or false that belongs to the propositions whose internal structure does not interest us?" And is it supposed to be some kind of ultimate logical fact that propositions can be combined to form further propositions? (53)

Anscombe tries to show how thinking about *ordinary pictures* can enable us to work our way through to clarity about those questions. An ordinary picture can be used to say that things are as the picture shows them to be, or that they are *not* as the picture shows them to be; both possibilities belong to such pictures. Wittgenstein's great insight in the picture theory is, then, an insight into the logical character of pictures, and is expressed in his "fundamental idea" that the logical constants don't represent anything. The difference between a proposition and its negation does not lie in anything represented by any sign; we can see this if we note, about the two different possible uses of a picture (to say that things are as they are in the picture, to say that they are not as they are shown to be in the picture), that the difference is exactly in the "reversal" of what the picture is used to say, not in anything represented through an element in the picture. (The two uses are open as soon as we have fixed who or what is represented by the figures in the picture.) Anscombe shows how the analogy between ordinary pictures and propositions can be developed, and how that analogy can be taken to explain the logical features of propositions. That explanation itself makes plain how the truth and falsity of truth-functional propositions can be understood in the same way as the truth and falsity of the propositions from which they are constructed.[2] Her account of Wittgenstein's central ideas is thus distinguished from that of many other commentators

---

2. There is a criticism of Anscombe's whole approach to the picture theory in Rhees 1970, but it rests on the idea that "if the sign is the same, then it says the same" (11)—i.e., that there is no such thing as using a propositional sign to say the opposite of what it had been used to say. Rhees's objection appears to be incompatible with *Tractatus* 4.062.

through her keeping firmly in the center the idea that Wittgenstein's "picture theory" and his understanding of propositional sense as truth-functional are not two separate ideas which Wittgenstein combined in the *Tractatus,* but are one and the same.[3] Her account has a logical depth missing in many expositions of the central ideas of Wittgenstein's early philosophy.

The importance of her account depends in part on the initial stage-setting with the questions. That is, she wanted to show how Wittgenstein could have taken himself to have "penetrated the essential nature of truth, falsehood and negation with his picture theory" (79); and that means that *we* have to see the questions as demonstrating a *need* for clarity, precisely about truth, falsehood, and negation: a need for clarity about something which is in a sense before our eyes. The arguments through which Anscombe leads us to the picture conception are thus meant to convey to *us* something like Wittgenstein's own sense of clarity achieved. Now Anscombe thought that a shift in philosophical precon-ceptions, in particular a shift away from the epistemological concerns common to traditional empiricism and to the positivists and Russell (as she read them) would make the character of Wittgenstein's achievement in the *Tractatus* available. It would enable us to feel both the significance of the questions and the power of Wittgenstein's insights. That hasn't happened. What is interesting here is *what* hasn't happened. For it isn't as if philosophers nowadays take seriously the questions to which Ans-combe drew attention and prefer alternative solutions. Despite the fact that the philosophical landscape has dramatically altered in many ways since the original publication of Anscombe's book, the shift in philo-

---

3. On the relation between truth-functionality and picturing, see also Ricketts 1996 (esp. 80–84) and Ricketts 2002 (esp. 227–228). Ricketts argues for the insepara-bility of Wittgenstein's understanding of propositions as models or pictures and his treatment of truth-functionality; but, unlike Anscombe, he emphasizes not only the relation between picturing and truth-functional construction but also the relation be-tween Wittgenstein's conception of truth-functionality and his conception of logic, utterly at odds with Frege's and Russell's. See also Gustafsson 2014 on the importance of taking representation and inference to be "equally basic and mutually dependent" (93) aspects of the functioning of the logical connectives.

sophical preconceptions has not made salient the sort of question to which she wanted to lead her readers, the sort of question which would make the *Tractatus* readable by us in the way she hoped it would be read. I shall illustrate how the nonsalience of the issues she took to be central can be seen in contemporary discussions of philosophical logic. (It could be said that the shift in preconceptions has not really been very deep, and that my two examples, below, could be developed to suggest that the "empiricist preconceptions" which Anscombe hoped to challenge have not so much disappeared as changed their form. But, if we were to consider exactly in what ways philosophical preconceptions have not changed, we should need also to consider a topic not directly at issue in *IWT,* although it was an important topic for the *Tractatus*— namely, the relation between philosophical clarification and scientific thinking.)[4]

(a) The most important topic in *IWT,* the topic that is meant to provide the key questions, is negation: Anscombe devotes two chapters to it, chapters meant to explain what (on the *Tractatus* view) would enable us to speak of "the" negation of any proposition. Why can we take for granted, about any proposition, that there is exactly one proposition which is true if it is false, and false if it is true? If we don't give that question the depth of attention it deserves, there is no way to make philosophical sense of "true" and "false." Yet virtually all contemporary discussions of truth proceed with no attention to that question.[5] Take, for example, Jennifer Hornsby's reply to Stewart Candlish. He had objected to her "identity" theory of truth that she would have difficulty accounting for falsehood (Candlish 1999, 238), to which she replied (Hornsby 1999, 243) that her sort of identity theorist, who says that a thinkable is true if it is (is identical with) a fact, can say that a thinkable

---

4. For more about Anscombe's ideas about the philosophical preconceptions which can distort readings of the *Tractatus,* see Essay 3.

5. It is also true, and not unrelated, that such discussions, so far as they mention the *Tractatus* view, often get it quite wildly wrong. See, for example, Walker 1997, 320, which runs together Wittgenstein's treatment of truth with his treatment of sense, and thus makes it impossible to see how the treatment of sense was supposed to have yielded an understanding of what it is for a proposition to be true or false.

is false if and only if it is not a fact (and, if the theorist is not committed to bivalence, "if" can be dropped from "if and only if"). Here, it seems to me, the relevance of the Anscombean questions is altogether invisible. If, for any thinkable, there is some other thinkable that is false if it is true, and vice versa, that (on the Hornsby view) doesn't need to be brought into the theorist's story about how being true and being false themselves are to be understood. Its being the case that some thinkable is a fact isn't something that the theorist needs to see as connected to some other thinkable's not being a fact, and certainly not something connected in such a way as to raise questions about the whole theory, as it well might. For, if one took the truth of p and the falsehood of not-p to be tied to one and the same fact, the falsehood of not-p couldn't be simply said to be a matter of a thinkable's not being a fact; it would seem that it might be as much a matter of another thinkable's being a fact. (It may seem also that, if one doesn't allow such a tie, one's use of "is a fact" and "is not a fact" is in danger of being reduced to a variant expression of "is true" and "is false.") What is interesting here is that these issues do not surface in Hornsby's response to Candlish's challenge: that's what illustrates how Anscombe's sort of question, rather than being given answers by contemporary philosophers different from those in the *Tractatus*, is instead not seen as significant.

(b) Anscombe emphasizes Fregean questions and Fregean theories in *IWT*, as part of her attempt to lead philosophers *away* from empiricist preconceptions and *to* the sorts of question important for Wittgenstein in the *Tractatus*. But a very striking example of the way her back-to-Frege approach did not have the results for which she hoped can be found in Michael Dummett's writings. Dummett's conception of what a semantic theory must be able to do leads him away from the questions which Anscombe emphasizes. This comes out in (for example) some of the contrasts between *IWT* and Dummett's *Frege: Philosophy of Language* (1973). Anscombe regards it as a strength of the *Tractatus* that it puts before us a conception of logic and language within which we can see what it is for truth, considered in relation to asserted propositions, to be the very same as truth, considered as something which helps to explain the role of the constituent propositions of truth-functions. Dummett, on the other hand, explains two distinct notions of truth-value for those two different contexts, and simply says that there is no reason why the two notions should coincide (1973, 417). Here there is a great difference between Anscombe and Dummett concerning the kind of question which a philosophical treatment of logic needs to address, with Dummett treating Anscombe's question as one which can be ignored. (Elsewhere it is obvious that the difference between them goes both ways, since he takes various questions generated by semantic theorizing to be significant when she, implicitly at any rate, does not take such questions to be questions.)[6] The original Anscombean ambition of making Wittgenstein's questions salient for contemporary philosophers by emphasizing the Fregean inheritance rather than the Russellian appears to have been disappointed. At any rate, the Fregean inheritance, taken up as Dummett takes it up within his approach to philosophy, does not make the Anscombean questions any more salient than does the Russellian inheritance, or the Hume-Mill inheritance.

Although I think Anscombe was wrong in believing that what blocked a sound appreciation of the *Tractatus* was the empiricist philosophical preconceptions of analytic philosophers of the midcentury (and that a shift away from those preconceptions would make possible an understanding of the kind of perplexity motivating the *Tractatus* and also of Wittgenstein's achievement in it), I should nevertheless want to argue that a great part of the value of *IWT* lies in the kinds of question she emphasizes, and in particular in her treatment of negation and questions about negation. She says that she devotes as much space

6. See his criticism of Anscombe in Dummett 1999 and 2000. In both essays, he uses an argument which takes to be crucial the supposedly problematic character of the inference from "Jones believes that Tokyo is crowded" and "It is true that Tokyo is crowded" to "Jones has a true belief," if the "that"-clause in the second premise forms a logically transparent context. (The supposed problem would not arise if the clause forms an opaque context.) The problem arises for any attempt to give the kind of account of the validity of the inference which certain sorts of theory provide; but, as far as I can see, from the point of view of Anscombe's writings on the *Tractatus* and other topics, the validity of such inferences can be philosophically clarified without special problems being created by the "transparency" of the context. What is really at stake in the difference between Anscombe and Dummett in the questions that they take to be salient is a difference about the aims and character of philosophical clarification.

as she does to negation because "not", "which is so simple to use, is utterly mystifying to think about" (19); "no theory of thought or judgment which does not give an account of it can hope to be adequate" (19–20). This is why *IWT* is so valuable: other introductions to the *Tractatus* may be easier to follow, but none of them conveys so well how thinking about questions like those about "not" can mystify us. Anscombe has been mystified; and writes from having been. Her inwardness with being mystified makes her push hard at the questions about negation; and that explains why *IWT* is a book from which we can go on learning: it is after the sort of clarity sought by Wittgenstein, which is quite different from what is sought in contemporary philosophy (as comes out in the two examples mentioned above). When, in leading up to her exposition of the picture theory, Anscombe asks us to think about whether we should regard it as an ultimate logical fact that propositions combine to form further propositions, she adds the image "much as metals combine to form alloys which still display a good many of the properties of metals" (53). And she goes on to quote Wittgenstein's own remark that we need to be suspicious if it looks as if it is a kind of "remarkable fact" that every proposition possesses one or the other of the properties denoted by "true" and "false." The view of clarification running through the whole of *IWT* is one which demands that we probe further whenever we seem to be confronted with such a remarkable logical fact; and that is not an idea which informs contemporary analytic philosophy. Anscombe's understanding of clarification, then, provides a kind of critical point of view on contemporary philosophy, and *IWT* is valuable in exemplifying philosophy informed by that understanding.[7] Although I said above that her account of the *Tractatus* has a logical depth lacking in many others, I should also add that there are expositions of the book inspired by a sense of exactly the same sort of question as Anscombe took to be central. An excellent example would be Peter Hylton's "Functions, Operations, and Sense in Wittgenstein's *Tractatus*" (2005b), which focuses on a question very close

---

7. See the treatment of relations and their converses, in *IWT,* chap. 8, for a good illustration of how Anscombe's understanding of philosophical clarity informs her discussion of particular topics.

to the second question quoted from *IWT*, and which ends with an insistence that inquiries into the sense of compound propositions which approach the matter as if there were a kind of logical chemistry involved are exactly the sort of view opposed by Wittgenstein. Whatever differences there may be between Hylton and Anscombe on the details of Wittgenstein's understanding of functions and operations, Hylton's essay exemplifies the kind of reading of the *Tractatus* which Anscombe hoped to encourage.

2.

I began by mentioning three aims of Anscombe's in *IWT*. I want now to comment on two aims that *IWT* does not have. In a foreword to the original edition, H. J. Paton (the editor of the series) mentioned Wittgenstein's remark that his later thoughts could be seen in the right light only by contrast with, and against the background of, his earlier thoughts. Paton then said that he hoped that Anscombe's book might therefore serve as an introduction not only to the *Tractatus* but also to Wittgenstein's philosophy as a whole. Much that Anscombe says in *IWT* is relevant to an understanding of Wittgenstein's work as a whole, but her subject really is the author of the *Tractatus* and his concerns and achievements. The continuities and contrasts with Wittgenstein's later concerns and ideas, while occasionally commented on, aren't really in view as a main aim. Again, Wittgenstein's view of philosophical method is touched on by Anscombe, but it is not one of her aims to make clear what he thought about method, or in what way the method of the *Tractatus* is connected with Wittgenstein's more specific philosophical ideas in the book, or what the importance to the reader should be of his apparently methodological remarks. Each of these two non-aims of *IWT* is worth some more discussion, for reasons having to do with my claim above, that Anscombe's understanding of clarification, informing all her arguments, is one important source of the value of the book as a whole.

It is indeed an odd feature of *IWT* that, although, as I said, philosophical method does get touched on, some methodological issues of great importance, which Anscombe gets very close to, get no mention at all, or are merely touched on and then passed by. She says, for example, that Frege's *Begriffsschrift* is not of merely technical importance. Its philosophical significance, she says, includes its capacity to provide clarity about what is wrong with Descartes's ontological argument; and she explains how it does so. The example is meant to bring out the general philosophical significance of Frege's development of the idea of quantification. Wittgenstein says in the *Tractatus* that a good Begriffsschrift is philosophically important because it will enable us to avoid fundamental confusions in philosophy, but when Anscombe quotes that remark, she takes it simply to express Wittgenstein's appreciation of Frege's genius in the invention of quantification. She explains his ideas about a good symbolic notation but does not bring out how significant they are for his understanding of philosophical method, and of what he meant by philosophical clarity.[8] Again, Anscombe devotes an entire chapter to Wittgenstein on signs and symbols, without ever mentioning that the distinction between sign and symbol is used by Wittgenstein in explaining the ways in which philosophical confusion arises. She discusses Wittgenstein's views about the relation between a Begriffsschrift and ordinary language in that chapter, but does not mention that it is one essential feature of a genuinely adequate Begriffsschrift that the kind of sign / symbol confusion which underlies much that is said in philosophy is impossible in a good Begriffsschrift. Her interests in her chapter on sign and symbol seem to lead her away from what is important in Wittgenstein's diagnosis of the sources of philosophical confusion and his treatment of such confusion.

I am not suggesting that Anscombe is wholly uninterested in the methodology suggested by the *Tractatus*. In chapter 12 of *IWT*, she discusses Wittgenstein's understanding of philosophical method briefly, in criticizing the idea that the *Tractatus* makes the same kind of criticism of metaphysical propositions as did the logical positivists. As Anscombe

---

8. The use of a Begriffsschrift in philosophical criticism is in fact relevant to the two examples which Anscombe uses in *IWT*, chap. 5, to illustrate the kind of criticism available on the basis of the *Tractatus*, but the argument in chap. 5 proceeds without making what would have been a highly relevant kind of connection with what can be brought out through a Begriffsschrift.

notes, there is no suggestion in the *Tractatus* that the correct general method for dealing with an apparently metaphysical proposition is to ask what sense observations, if any, would verify it, and what observations would falsify it. On the contrary, so far as Wittgenstein does suggest a general method, it is that of showing that a person has supplied no meaning for one or another of the signs in his sentence. She then explains what this might come to in a particular case by giving an illustration based on Wittgenstein's later approach to philosophy. He asked her once why people say that it was natural to think that the sun goes round the earth, rather than that the earth turns round on its axis; she replied that it was because it looks as if the sun goes round the earth. But he asked in reply what it would be for it to "look as if" the earth turned on its axis. His question made her realize that, although she had come up with the sentence "It looks as if the sun goes round the earth," she had in fact not given any relevant meaning to "it looks as if" as she had used it in that sentence. There was a kind of failure on her part to think through what she meant; but a naive picture of what turning round would look like (a picture which she recognized immediately, when pushed, that she would not want to apply) made her unaware that she really hadn't meant anything determinate in speaking of its looking as if the sun went round the earth. She points out, on the basis of her example, that criticism of this sort, which shows that a sentence expresses "no real thought, according to the principles of the *Tractatus*," won't be of some general form, but will have to be ad hoc, and will depend on the subject matter of the particular sentence (151).[9] This is an extraordinarily interesting passage for a number of reasons. For one thing, it makes a fascinating connection between Wittgenstein's characteristic kind of approach in his later philosophy and the correct way to understand the activity of philosophical criticism as understood in the *Tractatus*. There is an implicit suggestion that clarification, so far as it is an aim of his philosophy early and late, can be seen to involve (at least sometimes, and in at least some kinds of case) similar techniques early and late. Another reason why the passage is particularly interesting is

---

9. Addendum, 2017: For an excellent example of the approach Anscombe describes, see Foot 2002.

that it seems to raise questions about Anscombe's approach, elsewhere in *IWT*, to Wittgenstein's ideas about philosophical criticism. To these I shall now turn.

Chapter 5 of *IWT* is about the consequences of the picture theory. It contains some quite general remarks about the kind of philosophical criticism available in the Tractatus, as well as examination of several examples. Of sentences like "Red is a color," Anscombe says that the point is easily made that such sentences cannot express anything that might be false. This is a quite different kind of philosophical criticism from that which she discusses in chapter 12 in the case of "It looks as if the sun goes round the earth." For in that case what happens is that an investigation (in which we are invited to clarify what we do mean) shows that we did not mean anything. Although we start from what we might have taken ourselves to mean, what happens is that, on thinking about it, we find that we had nothing in view apart from a naive model (of its "looking as if" it's the sun that is going around the earth) which we can see not to be genuinely applicable. In reply to the question why we think it is the sun that goes round the earth, we have nothing that we mean by its looking this way *rather than the other way*. Our recognition that we meant nothing was not dependent on simply plugging in a *Tractatus* principle; it depends on our capacity to think about what is involved in other uses of "it looks as if." In the case of "Red is a color," Anscombe takes it for granted that we begin similarly with what we take the sentence to mean. How then do we get from that to her point that we can easily see that the sentence cannot express something that might be false? We are not here thinking (as in the case of "It looks as if the sun goes round the earth") about a picture which seemed to give us a sense, but which can, on examination, be seen to give us nothing relevant. In contrast, in the case of "Red is a color," the criticism which she takes to be available on the *Tractatus* view depends upon our recognizing that there are not two possibilities, that red is, and that it is not, a color. Since there are not two possibilities (as the picture theory requires there to be), "Red is a color" is not a genuine proposition. We arrive at the idea that the sentence is nonsensical through an application of a general principle about what it is for a sentence to have a sense. In the case of "Red is a color" we have nothing of the relevant sort, nothing that is going to count as the sentence's having a sense, because, as soon as we examine what we took ourselves to have meant by the sentence, we see that the sentence fails a general sort of test dictated by the picture theory. A crucial difference from the discussion of "It looks as if the sun goes round the earth" is that, in the case of "Red is a color," a general test is supposed to dictate what can count as a genuine proposition. The idea (exemplified by "It looks as if the sun goes round the earth") that the *Tractatus* commits us to an ad hoc procedure in which we attempt to clarify what we did mean, but find we meant nothing by some sign or signs we used, seems to be quite different. There is no reference at all in her discussion of "Red is a color" to finding that we meant nothing by some sign or signs we used.[10]

These issues come up again later in the same chapter of *IWT*, where Anscombe discusses "'Someone' is not the name of someone." This, she says, is obviously true; but if its negation is nothing but a piece of philosophical confusion, then it itself cannot count, on the *Tractatus* view, as senseful, let alone true. This, she argues, shows the inadequacy of Wittgenstein's theory, since it is unreasonable to prohibit the formula "'Someone' is not the name of someone," which we should otherwise regard as quite correct. Anscombe's treatment of this case raises questions which I look into in Essay 2 (on saying and showing) and Essays 4 and 6 (on propositions that can only be true); here I want only to note what her discussion of this example has in common with her discussion of "Red is a color." The *Tractatus* view, as she presents it, involves in both cases a move from a general *Tractatus* principle about meaning to a prohibition of certain sentences which (in the actual cases she gives) there is no reason to think we do not understand except for the supposed *Tractatus* argument that they are not senseful sentences if they have no negation capable of being true. The argument from the *Tractatus* principle can leave us, though, with our conviction intact that the sentence made sense; that is the basis for Anscombe's claim that Wittgenstein's principle must be wrong as a general principle. What we find, when we investigate using the general principle, is that certain

---

10. For some further discussion of Anscombe on the *Tractatus* view of propositions like "Red is a color," see Essay 3; for Anscombe's own views, see Essay 4.

sentences do not count as senseful; but that is not what happened in the case of "It looks as if the sun goes round the earth," where we found we really did not mean anything by "It looks as if" in that sentence. We didn't find that the sentence didn't count, by some theory, as senseful, but that we ourselves genuinely didn't mean anything. Another way of putting the point: Anscombe's discussion in chapter 12 emphasizes the role of asking a person who says that something or other is the case what it would be like if that were *not* so, in making clear that the person meant nothing. But what comes out in her discussion of "It looks as if the sun moves round the earth" is that what makes the question what it would be like for it to look as if the earth turned on its axis relevant is precisely the naive picture of its looking as if something is going around us: that picture is in play in the familiar idea about how it "naturally" looks to us in relation to the question about the sun's movement. It is in play through allowing us to take for granted that we are using "It looks as if" in accordance with the kind of use it has in other contexts, in which, if there is such a thing as something's looking as if so-and-so, there is also such a thing as its not looking that way. In contrast, the demand that there should be something that is red's not being a color, if "Red is a color" is to pass as senseful, is generated purely by the picture theory. The argument that, from the *Tractatus* point of view, "Red is a color" cannot express something false, and hence is nonsensical, proceeds directly from the supposed general *Tractatus* principle allowing the "dismissal as nonsensical" of sentences that do not pass the test of having a significant negation. We can note that no mention is made in the discussion of "It looks as if the sun goes round the earth" of anything that the sentence *could not* express; it is not treated as a "prohibited formula" but rather as something we give up when we see the "thoughtlessness" in our original conception.[11]

---

11. There is, in any case, a problem with Anscombe's remark about "Red is a color," that it cannot express anything false. For what is her remark about—the sign "Red is a color" or the sign in some specific use, i.e., the symbol? It is not at all clear what it would be for the sentence-sign to be incapable of expressing a false proposition, since the signs of which it is composed might be given various meanings; but if the sign-in-some-specific-use is said to be incapable of expressing anything false, that too would

The supposed general principle, in a slightly different form, plays a main role in the organization of *IWT*. The first four chapters give us the picture theory, which tells us what genuine propositions, genuine sayings that something is so, must be, and enables us to recognize also tautologies and contradictions, which say nothing. Anything else, anything that cannot be shown to fit in with that theory, can be "dismissed as nonsensical: perhaps simply nonsensical, perhaps attempts to say the inexpressible" (*IWT*, 79). The organization of the chapters of *IWT* after the exposition of the picture theory itself is thus meant first to make clear where the picture theory leaves us, and then to cover some of the items that need either to be fitted into the theory or dismissed as nonsensical.[12] That there are some problems lurking here can be seen from one of the first things discussed by Anscombe—namely, sentences of the form "'p' says that p." These come up in the *Tractatus* when Wittgenstein says, about "A believes that p" and "A says p," that they are of the form "'p' says p." Anscombe takes him to mean that that is the form of the "business part" of such propositions. She provides an account of the content of the whole of such propositions and of the part that is supposedly of the form "'p' says that p." She then argues that we are thereby given "'p' says that p" as a possible form of proposition, by the standards of the picture theory. If such propositions are (as she suggests) descriptions of conventions of representation, they would be capable of being true and capable of being false; they would fit in with the picture theory

---

need explanation. The use would have to be specifiable in some way which did not involve treating the sentence as meaning that red is a color, and being incapable of expressing anything false because it meant *that*. Similar problems arise in connection with "'Someone' is not the name of someone," which Anscombe speaks of as a formula which the *Tractatus* prohibits, implying (it seems) that it is the sign in question that is faulty, not the sign-in-some-specific-use. But it is then unclear how the *Tractatus* can be supposed to countenance an idea of prohibited signs in ordinary language. Here we can see how important the distinction between signs and symbols is, in understanding the ways in which the *Tractatus* can invite us to criticize things that look as if they are meant to be propositions. On these issues, see also Essay 2 and the Introduction to Part I.

12. The rest of this paragraph was rewritten for this volume. I am grateful for some comments from an anonymous reviewer.

and would not be nonsensical.[13] Two things play a role in Anscombe's thought here: one is taking Wittgenstein to have meant that "'p' says that p" is the form of a part of propositions of the form "A believes that p" (and so on), and the other is her view of the very limited range of kinds of case allowed for by the *Tractatus* as she reads it—the limited ways in which sentences of the form "'p' says that p" might turn out not to be nonsense. But here we might note that at 3.24, Wittgenstein mentions definitions, which do not say that anything is so; and he does not at any point suggest that they are tautologies. He says at 3.343 that they are a kind of rule of translation. They don't count as nonsensical; they have a use, it's just that the use is not a use to describe anything, and they don't count as genuine propositions in the sense specified by the picture theory. In Essays 4 and 5, I discuss other examples of propositions that are not treated by Wittgenstein as nonsensical, although they are not bipolar propositions, and not tautologies or contradictions. If we pay attention to what Wittgenstein says about these various cases, we can see that there is no need to try to show, as Anscombe does, that "'p' says that p" is a genuine proposition by the standards of the picture theory. Rules dealing with signs are explicitly treated in the *Tractatus* passages dealing with definitions and equations; and sentences of the form "'p' says that p" might be taken to have a function analogous in some ways to a rule of translation. So far as this can be seen to fit in with the overall picture of language in the *Tractatus*, it would involve the idea that translation is a kind of operation in the *Tractatus* sense. There is an operation connecting a sentence saying that signs stand in a certain way to a sentence saying that p.[14] But one cannot investigate the issues here

13. In fact it is far from clear that Anscombe's treatment actually does make the example fit the theory, since the theory apparently disallows the occurrence of propositions within other propositions except as arguments of truth-functions. If her account of the example is meant to make it fit that part of the theory, there is no indication how it might do so. See also Kenny 1973, 100–101, for an argument that "'p' says that p," occurring as part of a psychological proposition, is not a senseful proposition.

14. Any explanation of how this fits in with the general view of language in the *Tractatus* would need to include an account of how operations that do not appear to be truth-functional can be fitted in. Some such account is also required by Anscombe's

from the point of view of the *Tractatus* if one takes it for granted that, if something which appears to be a proposition is not nonsensical, it must (if it is not tautologous or contradictory) be a description, in the sense in which the *Tractatus* lays out what that involves. A certain picture of how the *Tractatus* is supposed to work has, I think, been superimposed on the book itself by *IWT*. The irony is that Anscombe, despite criticizing the positivists' reading of the *Tractatus*, provides an overall conception of the mode of criticism to which the *Tractatus* is committed which still owes too much to the positivists and the idea of a theory generating a general criterion for dismissal-as-nonsensical. (For more about why I read Anscombe this way, and what I think is problematic in her reading, see Essays 4 and 5.)

I have gone over the question of Anscombe's view of the method implied by the *Tractatus* not only because it is itself interesting but also because it lies behind one of her main criticisms of the *Tractatus*. She takes Wittgenstein's picture theory to be "powerful and beautiful," and says that "there is surely something right about it"; to hold on to what is right, one would have to "draw the limits of its applicability."[15] She has in the center of her mind the fact that one consequence of the picture theory is the disallowing of any necessarily true propositions other than tautologies. "Drawing the limits of the applicability of the theory" would involve making clear that the theory's dismissal as nonsensical of any purported necessary truth which was not a tautology rested on some kind of illegitimate extension of the theory. An important illustration for her of what is at stake is the statement "'Someone' is not the name of someone": it is "obviously true," but is (apparently) disallowed by the picture theory because it does not have a significant negation. The issues that she raises with this example run through all the essays in this

---

reading of the *Tractatus,* since she makes use of the notion of such operations in treating relations and their converses. Hugh Miller III has discussed these issues in unpublished work. For some further discussion of the issues here, see Diamond 2012.

15. See *IWT,* 77. Anscombe says also that one would have to be able to dispense with the "simples" that the theory depends on in the form in which it is put forward in the *Tractatus*.

volume.[16] Here, though, I want simply to note the contrast with her discussion of "It looks as if the sun goes around the earth," which is meant to bring out the ad hoc character that criticism of a sentence as expressing no real thought will have, on the *Tractatus* view (*IWT*, 151). Further, such criticism leaves one convinced that the sentence in question could be put forward only through failure to attend to what one was saying. It's not that it doesn't "count as" senseful, or that it is disallowed by a theory, but that one sees that one had meant nothing. But, so far as the *Tractatus* does indeed suggest a kind of ad hoc criticism of sentences, the point Anscombe wants to make about a general dismissal as nonsensical of all purportedly necessary truths other than tautologies would not apply to it. This isn't to say that the *Tractatus* "allows" necessary truths, but that the issue of the status of purportedly necessary truths has to be framed in some other way.

3.

Much has been written, since the original publication of *IWT*, about the history of analytic philosophy, in particular about Russell and Frege, and about their influence on Wittgenstein. There are two respects in which, it seems to me, *IWT* has dated. The first is its treatment of Russell and of Russell's influence on Wittgenstein during the period before 1914. Anscombe's treatment of Russell is indeed odd.[17] Immediately after recommending that we look to Frege's enquiries in order to understand the *Tractatus*, she mentions that Russell in fact discusses many of the same questions (*IWT*, 14). So it is not by their questions that Frege and Russell are to be distinguished as influences on Wittgenstein, but rather, as she goes on to suggest, by the fact that "Russell was thoroughly imbued with the traditions of British empiricism" (14). But that is at most a half-truth, as has been made clear by Peter Hylton (1990). Russell had at first been thoroughly imbued with the traditions of British idealism, and then moved toward Moore's equally un-

---

16. See also Conant and Diamond 2004.

17. I discuss Anscombe's treatment of Russell and its relation to her treatment of Frege in Essay 3.

empiricist views; and during both of those phases his anti-psychologism was at odds with the tradition of British empiricism. Hylton lays out the character of the subsequent shift in Russell's views toward empiricism, as well as the very limited role that the notion of direct acquaintance had in Russell's thinking prior to the "turn towards the psychological" (245, and chapter 8). Hylton's study covers Russell's thought up until roughly 1913. During this period, he notes, "Russell's views shift, from a view which has nothing at all in common with the tradition of British Empiricism to a view which shared some important elements with that tradition, though still differing from it in important ways" (9). Anscombe's concern to change the reading of the *Tractatus*, taken together with the fact that she was writing at a time when it was easy to treat Russell as simply standing in the line of British Empiricists descending from Hume and Mill, led her to oversimplify the relation between Russell's views (not only his views during Wittgenstein's prewar Cambridge years, but also the views he had taken in earlier writings which Wittgenstein would have read) and earlier and later British empiricism.[18] And indeed she can be quite unfair in her treatment of Russell, as in her discussion of the difference between Russell's conception of propositional functions and Frege's conception of functions the value of which is the true or the false (*IWT*, 104–105). For Frege, all functions, including those the expressions for the values of which are propositions, are to be explained on the model of arithmetical functions, and from that point of view Russell's treatment of propositional functions as having a restricted range of arguments is objectionable. But Anscombe gives the objection without noting that the kind of function which Frege takes to be the primary case is, for Russell, itself to be explained in terms of propositional functions as Russell understands them. The latter are not a special case of arithmetical functions, and Frege's objection to restricting the range of arguments for a function does not constitute an objection to Russell, unless we take for granted Frege's approach. Anscombe's discussion entirely ignores the underlying difference between the two approaches to functionality,

18. For a more detailed account of Anscombe's views about the relative significance of Frege and Russell as influences on Wittgenstein, see Essay 3.

and this is connected with her tendency to play down the significance of Russell's influence on Wittgenstein. How deep that influence goes has been brought out especially by Ricketts's account of the development of Wittgenstein's ideas and the role of Russell's theory of judgment (Ricketts 1996, 2002). Anscombe does have a brief discussion of Russell's theory of judgment and Wittgenstein's criticisms of it, but the account is inaccurate about Russell (in ignoring the shift from the 1912 to the 1913 version of Russell's theory), and misses the character and importance of Wittgenstein's departures, as early as 1913, from Russell's view of language and toward what becomes the picture conception.[19]

The other respect in which *IWT* has dated is in its treatment of Wittgenstein's view of logic. The final chapter of *IWT* has a brief discussion of the *Tractatus* rejection of the idea of logical facts. But Wittgenstein's view is contrasted simply with what it was "at one time natural to think" about the character of logic, not specifically with the views of Frege and Russell about logic (165).[20] There is no attempt to connect, for example, Russell's understanding of the truth-functional connectives with Russell's conception of logic, so that we could see how Wittgenstein's "fundamental idea," which breaks significantly with Russell on the character of the connectives, is tied closely to his break with Russell on the character of logic.[21] Anscombe refers several times to Wittgenstein's pre-*Tractatus* notebooks, but does not try to integrate into her account the idea with which the notebooks start, that logic must take care of itself, and that that is an extremely important and profound point. A weakness, then, in her account of the picture theory as the main thesis of the book is that the *Tractatus* treatment of logic is not seen as part of the picture theory itself, but rather as one of

19. On the kind of importance Russell's views had for Wittgenstein, see also Goldfarb 2002 and Diamond 2014a.

20. This issue is connected also with the absence, in *IWT*, of the aim of serving as an introduction to Wittgenstein's entire philosophy, since the nature of logic (and what might be meant by speaking of the laws of logic as "laws of thought") is a matter of continuing importance for Wittgenstein.

21. On these issues, see especially Ricketts 2002.

the various consequences of the theory, to be dealt with relatively briefly.[22]

4.

There is no book about Wittgenstein to which I go back more often than *IWT*. There are many books with which one disagrees, which can serve as foils in one's attempt to get clear about some issue. But *IWT*, even where I find myself in disagreement with it, is not for me a source of such "foils." The book has a deep intelligence evident in the treatment of every topic; and this means that virtually every passage one reads, if one turns to it anew, has more in it than one had seen. I have in this review (and elsewhere) expressed disagreement with some of the things Anscombe says in *IWT*, and have criticized some of its features. But the book is an extraordinary example of how far an "introduction" can take one.—This review was published on the occasion of the reprint of *IWT* by St. Augustine's Press. *IWT* is now also available as part of *Logic, Truth and Meaning,* a volume of Anscombe's writings published by Imprint Academic. Both presses deserve our gratitude for making this book available as a great resource for thinking with Anscombe about Wittgenstein.[23]

### Appendix (2017): Anscombe and the Two-Stage View

In Section 2 of this essay, I laid out what I took to be a contrast between two quite different ways in which Anscombe treats Tractarian criticism of sentences that appear to express thoughts. In sketching the contrast, I particularly relied on this remark of hers:

> The criticism of sentences as expressing no real thought, according to the principles of the *Tractatus,* could never be of any very simple

22. Here again I am prescinding from the disagreement I have about the character of the supposed "theory."

23. I am very grateful to James Conant, Roger Teichmann, Ejvind Hansen, and an anonymous reviewer for helpful comments and suggestions.

general form; each criticism would be *ad hoc,* and fall within the subject matter with which the sentence purported to deal. (*IWT,* 151)

There seemed to me a sharp contrast between that general picture and the explanation that Anscombe herself gave of the criticism of "Red is a color," according to the principles of the *Tractatus.* The criticism she sets out is of a simple general form: she says that that proposition cannot express anything that might be false; and she notes that this criticism applies across the board to a variety of cases with very different subject matter. In my argument that she provides two very different descriptions of how the *Tractatus* criticizes would-be propositions, I drew on my reading of the remark that I have just quoted. But a different reading might be offered, which would show that the contrast I had laid out was merely apparent. The quoted remark might be read in the light of what I call the "two-stage" story about *Tractatus* criticism of what appear to be senseful propositions.

On a two-stage view, a senseful proposition is one that would pass two tests. The first stage would test the would-be proposition for permissibility, where this is a test of the structure of the proposition, and is of a simple general form. If the would-be proposition passes that test, the next question would be whether there are any signs in the proposition that lack meaning.[24] If Anscombe is read as taking a two-stage view, the contrast I tried to draw can be made to disappear. On that view, she doesn't have to be read as giving one sort of account of how we can see "It looks as if the sun goes round the earth" as expressing no real thought, and a quite different sort of account of what is involved in seeing "Red is a color" as expressing no real thought. If we ascribe to her a two-stage view, we can read her account of the *Tractatus* criticism of "Red is a color" as *not* a criticism of it as "expressing no real thought." That is, she might hold that the question whether it expresses a real thought *arises only for permissible propositions;* hence it does not arise for "Red is a color." On this view, then, she does not have any discussion of whether it ex-

24. I here draw on Anscombe's own formulation of a two-stage view in Anscombe 1995.

presses a real thought, nor, a fortiori, an account different from her account of why "It looks as if the sun goes round the earth" expresses no real thought. So ascribing to her a two-stage view makes possible an objection to my claim that she has two quite different accounts of how Tractarian criticism works. Blocking my claim requires ascribing to her both a two-stage view and the idea that the question whether a proposition expresses a real thought arises only if it has passed the first test—that is, only if it is a permissible proposition. (I call this "the combination view.")

What speaks for such a reading of Anscombe is that it makes her overall account in *IWT* more clearly coherent, and also that she did later take a two-stage view of the *Tractatus,* in her essay "Ludwig Wittgenstein" (Anscombe 1995). She wrote there that "if the structure of a sentence is permissible and the sentence—the proposition—doesn't make sense, this must be because no *meaning* has been given to some sign or signs as they occur in it." She had taken an apparently similar view a few years earlier, when she wrote about what is excluded by the *Tractatus* conception of propositions from being possible propositions (Anscombe 1989). What speaks against taking her to have held the combination view in *IWT* is the remark I quoted above. To make that remark cohere with the combination view, one has to read what she says about the *Tractatus* criticism of such sentences as "Red is a color" as *not* a matter of showing them *not* to express a real thought. One has to read the question whether a would-be proposition expresses a real thought as arising only for permissible proposition-forms. This seems to me to require an unnatural sort of reading of the quoted remark. On a natural reading, any criticism of a sentence as nonsensical is a criticism of it as not expressing any real thought, and on such a reading, *IWT* does involve two contrasting accounts of how Tractarian criticism works. There is also a question about the soundness of any two-stage view as interpretation of Wittgenstein.

Anscombe does not cite anything in support of the two-stage view which she seems to have taken in the later essays. There are, though, various passages in the *Tractatus* that she might have had specifically in mind in support of a two-stage view. The most likely, I think, is *TLP* 5.473, where Wittgenstein says that if a sign is *possible,* then it is also capable of signifying; and this might be taken to support the idea that illegitimately constructed propositions don't count as "possible." Such a reading is hard to square with 5.4733, though, which says that any possible proposition is legitimately constructed. That form of words would be very odd if the *Tractatus* view was that one infers from illegitimacy of propositional construction to the proposition's not counting as a possible proposition. In the context, it looks as if, in seeing possibility, one is seeing legitimacy of construction.

Here I want briefly to comment on what is going on in *TLP* 5.473 and 5.4733, in the references in both those passages to possibility—to the possibility of the sign and to the possibility of the proposition. It is very natural to read the reference to "possible propositions" as suggesting that Wittgenstein took there to be both "possible propositions" and "impossible" ones; and it is then also a natural step to take the "impossible" ones to be ones that violate some supposed Tractarian principle about propositions. This then provides support for a two-stage view. I think that there is a different understanding of those two passages and the idea of possibility that one finds in them, which fits the general approach of the *Tractatus* much better, and makes good sense of the passages themselves.

The basic idea of the alternative reading is that what makes clear the possibility of a proposition is a description of the proposition. Such a description is essential if we are to have anything to talk about. The "it" that is supposedly senseful or that might be nonsensical has to be described; it is not a mere string of words. If you simply write down "Red is a color" and say that, according to the *Tractatus, that* isn't a possible proposition, or *that* is impermissible, or anything like that, you have not genuinely got a "that" to talk about, unless you have made clear what the propositional sign is that you are talking about. Propositional signs are facts, and you haven't specified anything about which you might say that it has or doesn't have a sense, unless it is clear what its articulation is, what fact it is. When Wittgenstein writes about whether "Socrates is identical" is nonsense, in the background of that remark is that what he is talking about can be set out as the fact that "identical" stands to the right of the name "Socrates," with the copula "is" between them.[25] That description has, internal to it, the possibility of the propo-

---

25. Compare Wittgenstein 1961b, 115, on the significance of how we describe a sign-fact—in this case, the fact that "Plato" is to the left of a name.

sition "Socrates is identical." The description, though it presents clearly the possibility of the proposition, leaves it unsettled whether it has sense or not. Anything you can describe as propositional construction *can* express a sense; it is legitimately constructed. It is part of this reading that, when people speak about this or that proposition as "illegitimate" or "impermissible," according to the *Tractatus,* they are usually speaking about what they have presented as a quoted proposition, while the presentation does not make clear what the sign-fact is, or how it is not a mere string of words. This kind of presentation, which is of a sort apparently excluded by Wittgenstein at *TLP* 3.1432, goes with taking it to be clear what the quoted item is supposed to be "trying to say"—which is then the basis for an argument that the quoted item is illegitimate according to the *Tractatus.* But if people arguing in this way tried to describe what they are talking about, if they tried to describe the symbol, they would find that there was nothing that would be describing what they wanted to describe. I write this here as a kind of promissory note. I have not laid out (a range of examples would be necessary) how this reading deals with supposed illegitimate formulae. But I do want to claim for the reading that it brings out the significance of *TLP* 3.14–3.144 and 3.32–3.333. Wittgenstein's discussion of Russell's paradox illustrates the point that an attempt to *describe* the supposedly paradoxical proposition can make the paradox disappear. I discuss this case in the introduction to Part I of this volume. It brings out the significance of the notion of *description of symbols* for Wittgenstein's philosophical method. A proposition that violated the theory of types might appear to be a paradigm case of an illegitimately constructed proposition. But the attempt to describe the symbols in something one takes to be a violation of logical rules fails to show the supposed illegitimacy.[26]

My argument here is that there is a reading of 5.473 and 5.4733 that does not provide support for the idea that, if Wittgenstein spoke of possible propositions, he must have thought that there were also impossible ones. On this reading, then, those passages do not support the two-stage view. Anscombe may indeed have read 5.473 and 5.4733 as supporting a two-stage view when she wrote the 1989 and 1995 essays,

---

26. On Wittgenstein's response to the theory of types, see Ruffino 1994.

and possibly even also at the time of writing *IWT*. (A two-stage view suggests that there are two different kinds of nonsense: nonsense discovered by the first test, and nonsense that does not fail that test but is discovered in some other way; and Anscombe does appear to hold a two-different-kinds-of-nonsense view—for example, on page 79 of *IWT*, possibly also on page 68. I discuss the two-different-kinds-of-nonsense view in the Introduction to Part I, but I don't there consider the connection with a two-stage view.) If the two-stage view is indeed present already in *IWT*, that means Anscombe might well not have been putting forward two quite different accounts of Tractarian criticism of sentences as expressing no real thought. But if *IWT* does not have two quite different and indeed incompatible stories about Tractarian criticism, what there is in it instead would be a version of a two-stage view, which would most likely, I think, depend on a problematic reading of *TLP* 5.473 and 5.4733.

# Saying and Showing: An Example from Anscombe

~

### 1. Anscombe's Example and Some Questions

This essay was written shortly after the death of Elizabeth Anscombe, and was dedicated to her memory. The criticisms which I make of her treatment of saying and showing rest on ideas which she made clear in her discussions of Wittgenstein's later philosophy.[1] I believe that a problem with her treatment of the *Tractatus* is that she did not see how those same ideas were helpful, indeed essential, in considering his earlier thought.

In her *Introduction to Wittgenstein's Tractatus*, Anscombe has an interesting example which she uses to criticize what Wittgenstein says about saying and showing (*IWT*, 85–86). Speaking of the proposition "'Someone' is not the name of someone," she says that it is obviously true, and that it is an "admittedly rather trivial" example of a proposition which lacks true-false poles. She believes that Wittgenstein would have said that the proposition is an attempt to say something that shows—something that cannot be said. But she thinks that the example suggests instead that what "shows" in his sense *can* (at least in some cases) illuminatingly be said, contrary to what he holds in the *Tractatus* about propositions which lack true-false poles. Although she considers

1. See Anscombe 1981f, esp. 112–116; Anscombe 1963b, esp. §18.

the example to be rather trivial, it is, I should suggest, a good example to think about for a number of reasons, including the fact that it does not directly involve any of the more difficult notions of the *Tractatus*, like pictorial or logical form. It is sometimes useful to move forward an inch at a time; and Anscombe's example, precisely because it is relatively trivial, provides an opportunity to try to move forward a short distance without taking on the topic of "saying and showing" as a whole.

Since I shall be examining her discussion of the example, I shall need to quote the passage in question first. It comes immediately after her discussion of a somewhat different example, intended to bring out that there are cases in which what shows, in Wittgenstein's sense, cannot be *informatively* said. It is at this point that she remarks that what shows in that sense can nevertheless be *illuminatingly* said, and she goes on to give the example of "'Someone' is not the name of someone." She continues:

> This is obviously true. But it does not have the bipolarity of Wittgenstein's "significant propositions." For what is it that it denies to be the case? Evidently, that "someone" is the name of someone. But what would it be for "someone" to be the name of someone? Someone might christen his child "Someone." But when we say that "'Someone' is not the name of someone," we are not intending to deny that anyone in the world has the odd name "Someone."
>
> What then are we intending to deny? Only a piece of confusion. But this *sort* of denial may well need emphasizing. Students, for example, may believe what Professor Flew tells us . . . : namely that "somebody" refers to a person, that it is part of the "logic" of "somebody," unlike "nobody," to refer to somebody. If this were so, then on being told that everybody hates somebody, we could ask to be introduced to this universally hated person. When we say "'Somebody' does not refer to somebody," what we are intending to deny is what Professor Flew meant. But he did not really mean anything (even if he felt as if he did).
>
> Here a statement which appears quite correct is not a statement with true-false poles. Its contradictory, when examined, peters out into nothingness. We may infer from this that Wittgenstein's ac-

count of propositions is inadequate, correct only within a restricted area. For it hardly seems reasonable to prohibit the formula: "'Somebody' does not refer to somebody" or "'Someone' is
not the name of someone"; nor of course, is this logical truth in
any sharp sense of "logical truth." It is, rather, an insight; the
opposite of it is only confusion and muddle (not contradiction).

The example of "'Someone' is not the name of someone" is
particularly clear, because the true proposition is negative. According to Wittgenstein, however, since what our proposition
denies does not turn out to be anything, it itself is *not* a truth; for
there isn't anything which it says is not the case, as opposed to the
equally possible situation of its being the case. Therefore Wittgenstein would either have looked for a more acceptable formulation
(which I think is impossible) or have said it was something which
*shewed*—stared you in the face, at any rate once you had taken
a good look—but could not be *said*. This partly accounts for the
comical frequency with which, in expounding the *Tractatus,* one
is tempted to say things and then say that they cannot be said.
(*IWT,* 85–86)

The case is less clear than Anscombe suggests. We can, to start with,
note the ambiguity on which Anscombe herself comments in the first
paragraph, after she asks what the utterer of "'Someone' is not the name
of someone" intends to deny. Not, she says, that there is a person who
has the odd name "Someone."

Now if the utterer's remark *could* have been used as a denial that there
is a person with the odd name "Someone," it should be possible to re-
cast the remark itself to remove the ambiguity. But, before we consider
that sort of ambiguity, we should note that the original remark is not
ambiguous merely in the way Anscombe herself enables us to recognize.
There is a further sort of ambiguity about which she does not comment.
For the remark might be intended, as Anscombe indeed intends it, to
have a general application, but its intended application might instead
be much more limited. That is, someone might say "'Someone' is not
the name of someone" in response to confusion about the role of
"Someone" in some particular utterance. A child, perhaps, has heard at

school that someone has measles, and thinks that what has been said concerns a person called "Someone": that person has measles. The remark "'Someone' is not the name of someone," spoken to the child, may then be about the word "Someone" as it occurs in "Someone has measles." This is different in significant respects from the case in which the speaker of "'Someone' is not the name of someone" is responding to confusion of the sort that might be induced by Professor Flew. The response to Flew is not directly about any specific occurrence of the word "Someone." The speaker means to speak about all its uses.—But is that right? Surely not, for, as Anscombe notes, the remark isn't meant to cover cases in which we are concerned about whether anyone has the odd name "Someone." So what sort of generality does the remark about "Someone" not being a name have, when it is meant to have general applicability? Is the point that "Someone," whenever it hasn't got the logical role of a name, isn't a name? That won't do; for, understood in that way, the remark no longer appears to be something *illuminating*—something that might be called an *insight*. And Anscombe insists that the point she takes herself to be expressing is not a logical truth in any sharp sense of the term. Whatever exactly she means to include in "logical truth in a sharp sense," it would presumably encompass the kind of truth that might belong to "'Someone,' when it isn't used as a name, isn't used as a name."[2]

I hope to have shown that Anscombe's example needs some clarification. But before attempting to provide it, I should comment that the

2. Addendum, 2017: Anscombe examines related issues in "The First Person" (1981a). She was concerned there to deny, of "I", that it is used to stand for an object in something like the way a proper name does, and she lays out the logical features of names and namelike uses of words. Within *IWT* she could not have gone into such detail, but there is, in any case, an underlying problem that comes out if we suppose, for example, that the statement about "Someone" ran this way: "'Someone' (when we exclude the odd case in which some person, or dog, or whatever is called 'Someone') is not a name, in the sense in which, if it were a name, one could respond to every statement '. . . someone . . .' by asking to be introduced to the person meant." This would enable Anscombe to argue straightforwardly that "Someone" was not a name; but the problem would then be that there is no evidence that Flew was committed to the idea that "Someone" was a name in that sense. See Section 3 below.

issues here are directly connected with questions about how to read the *Tractatus*. Anscombe evidently believes that at least some of the propositions that Wittgenstein does not recognize to be significant propositions are significant; they cannot, though, be recognized as significant if one accepts the *Tractatus* account. She would not take these propositions to be logical truths in a sharp sense, any more than she takes "'Someone' is not the name of someone" to be logical truth in a sharp sense. What I shall be trying to show is that, when we are clearer about the kind of clarification that would be helpful in the case of the confusion that she has described, we shall see that the activity of clarification can, in some cases, be thought of as adding tautologies to the propositions that need clarification, and contrasting them with propositions to which somewhat different tautologies have been added. While this process can make clearer how we are using a sentence, it does not have the character which Anscombe takes clarification to have. What I intend to demonstrate in this essay is that we need to clarify philosophical clarification if we are to think clearly about the question how the *Tractatus* is to be read, the question whether it should be read as containing propositions which are genuinely significant but which could not have been recognized as significant by its author because of the doctrines which he accepted when he wrote it. One case cannot show us how to read the book; it can show us some of the things we need to think about.

I should add that this essay is directed also against an idea of John Koethe's, that it is an objection to a reading of the *Tractatus* as not genuinely intended to convey doctrines through its propositions, that that reading leaves us dealing with the differences between sense and non-sense piecemeal.[3] My point against that is: Right! That is, the only thing wrong with the idea is that Koethe takes it to be an objection. It is, indeed, by working through what is involved in a piecemeal approach to philosophical clarification that we can see how Wittgenstein thought of the activity of philosophy. That is, I want to suggest that it is no accident that Anscombe goes wrong in her discussion of "'Someone' is not the name of someone." She moves directly from the proposition's supposedly saying something true and its lacking true-false poles to its

3. Koethe 2003, 200.

failing to count as a significant proposition on the *Tractatus* view. (Indeed, she describes the proposition as counting, from the point of view of the *Tractatus*, as a "prohibited formula," a description at odds, at least apparently, with Wittgenstein's claim that no possible sign is logically impermissible, which seems to mean that there is no such thing as a "prohibited formula.")[4] Her own view is that the proposition does connect with what the confused person, in this case Professor Flew, took himself to have in mind. So she does not look at the details of how it might be supposed to connect. My argument is that only if we do go into the details can we see the status of the proposition. We have to look at its use from close to.

In *Philosophical Investigations* Wittgenstein speaks of our reluctance to look at the use of words "from close to"—our reluctance to consider the details (1958, §§51–52). This is certainly meant as a criticism of his own former approach. But our recognition that it is meant as such a criticism may make it hard for us to see the complexity of the case, and may make it difficult for us to see what exactly was involved in his earlier method. It may make us think that the earlier method was meant to enable us to show that some proposition or other was nonsensical with a mere wave of the hand. So Anscombe thinks that her own proposition simply turns out to be nonsensical by the application of a general *Tractatus* principle, and the issue of what its use *is*—of what she really wants to do with it—is not examined. She knows in her bones that she means something—something illuminating, though lacking true-false poles. So, although she also knows that the sense one may have of meaning something when one speaks is capable of misleading one (she says that Flew is misled in just that way), she does not turn a careful analytical eye onto the details of what she wants to say. Here, I am trying to point to a kind of parallel between Wittgenstein's earlier and his later philosophy, a parallel in the role that he gives to *our reluctance to look at details of use*. Wittgenstein's understanding of clarification, early and late, goes with conceptions (somewhat different, early and late) of what, in philosophy, we may be reluctant to do.

---

4. Addendum, 2017: I was referring to *Tractatus* 5.473. For a discussion of 5.473 and 5.4733, and of how Anscombe may have read them, see the appendix to Essay 1.

## 2. An Easier Case

It will be useful to consider, first, the kind of case in which the remark "'Someone' is not the name of someone" is intended to apply to a particular utterance. Although this is not the kind of case Anscombe herself has in mind, our discussion of her case will be made easier if we approach it after considering this other case.

We are imagining, then, that what has been said is "Someone has measles," and a child is confused about what that means. The confusion may have been shown in her attempt to treat "Someone" as a name; perhaps she shows by something she says that she takes it that the proposition's falsity would be inferable from the falsity of a proposition about some one individual. If *that* child has not got measles, then "Someone has measles' "would have to be false, or so she thinks.

Now we can make clear her mistake by making it explicit that the role in inferences of "Someone has measles" is different. If we are talking about some specific group of possible measles-havers and measles-not-havers, we can make it explicit that only from the premise that each and every one of them has not got measles could we infer the falsity of "Someone has measles."

Anscombe herself imagines explaining to the confused person that "Someone" does not figure in multiple quantification as a name of someone. In the kind of case I am imagining, in which the confusion concerns the role of "Someone" in a particular utterance, the point about multiple quantification is, as it stands, not directly helpful (even if it could be put in language plain enough for the confused person to follow). For, if someone thinks that "Someone" in "Someone has measles" is the name of some particular person, she won't be helped by being shown that "Someone" in "Everyone hates someone" is *not* a name, unless she is given some explanation how that is relevant to its use in "Someone has measles." Perhaps the confused person would be helped by the discussion of "Everyone hates someone" if it helped her to drop an assumption that "Someone" in *every* context had to be a name. Anscombe would, I think, hold that "Someone" has a single characterizable use such that both "Someone has measles" and "Everyone hates someone" contain

"Someone" used in that way. This, too, is fine; but what it means is that the bearing of the use of "Someone" in "Everyone hates someone" on the use of "Someone" in "Someone has measles" cannot be explained without bringing in what it is for these sentences to contain "Someone" used in the same way.

Consider a particular kind of case, one of the kinds of case that lie behind Flew's remark.[5] If one says "James loves somebody," one might then be asked other questions about the person. If what one said was true, there must be such a person about whom such questions might be asked. Or, again, someone might ask to be introduced to the person. Flew (who was, after all, concerned to contrast "Somebody" and "Nobody") may have wished to emphasize such possibilities, which don't exist with "Nobody" in its usual use. If this kind of case is behind the confusion which Anscombe wants to address, the problem mentioned in the last paragraph plainly arises when we try to help the person suffering from the confusion by noting that there is, in the case of "Everybody hates somebody," no appropriate request that one be introduced to the person universally hated. The difficulty can be explained in terms of the ways in which we may think about the differences from each other, and similarities to each other, of the three propositions: "James loves Alice," "James loves somebody," and "Everybody hates somebody." A would-be helper of someone in the confusion induced by Flew can show us, by explaining the behavior of the third proposition, that we cannot treat the middle proposition as logically like both the first and third propositions. But, unless we are helped to see that "Somebody" in the third proposition exemplifies the *same* use as "Somebody" in the second, we may remain overly impressed by just those similarities between the first and second propositions which lead into the original confusion.[6]

One of the problems with Anscombe's clarification is that she takes it to be useful to point out that "Somebody" doesn't refer to some-

5. For Flew's discussion, see Flew 1951, 7–8.

6. This paragraph and the following one have been revised for this volume. I am grateful to a reviewer for Harvard University Press for bringing out problems in the original version of these paragraphs.

body, taking the word "refer" not itself to be in need of clarification. But its use is complicated. Take, for example, the point that I don't tell you who stole the pie by saying "Somebody stole the pie" (unless, say, "Somebody" is the name of the dog). That point can be used to bring out the contrast with expressions which do refer to the culprit by name, or which pick out the culprit by a description. But that kind of point makes salient only part of the complex use of "refer." There are respectable uses of "refer" in connection with remarks that contain "Someone" and the ways in which we may continue to speak of the person in question.[7] (I shall return to this point in Section 3.) We can also see that Anscombe's point, that Flew did not really mean anything, although he may have felt that he did, is too strong. For he sees plainly enough that Lewis Carroll's jokes about "Nobody" in *Through the Looking Glass* would not be jokes about "Somebody." (See the quotation from Flew in Section 3 below.) Flew uses "refer" to explain the difference, without seeing any need to explain any contrast between a use of "refer" which can be connected with some occurrences of "Somebody" working as a variable and other ways of using "refer." Anscombe's claim that Flew has nothing in mind depends on her sharing with Flew the idea that the word "refer" can easily bear the kind of weight we may want to put on it in our clarifications. That it cannot do so is shown by the way in which Flew fails to make clear what he means and instead says something which easily leads into confusion, and by the way in which Anscombe fails to see that he *does* mean something.

On Wittgenstein's view, we cannot make fully clear the use of a word in one proposition if we are not clear what *further* uses of the word would be uses of it in the same way. So the issues raised by Anscombe's imagined use of "Everybody hates somebody" cannot be set aside.

---

7. Addendum, 2017: See Geach 1964, on speaking about "the man I meant a little while ago," where my talk of *meaning that person* draws on a previous use of "There's a man on the quarry-edge." That earlier *thought* enables me a little while later to speak of the man I had meant, about whom I can now ask whether *he* has fallen in. Here I *refer to the same man again*. See ibid., 73–74, where Geach also discusses the connection between such cases and his account of proper names.

However, we can temporarily set them aside and focus simply on what might be involved in removing a confusion about the occurrence of "Someone" in a particular utterance.

In fact, it is useful to consider the way in which the clarification of the particular utterance can involve a point related to that made by Anscombe when she brings in multiple quantification, without actually bringing in multiple quantification. For we should consider the way in which the child's confusion about "Someone has measles" might show itself in inferences from "Someone has measles and someone has mumps" to "Someone has measles and mumps." (I simplify my discussion of the example by leaving out qualifications for odd cases such as those in which someone takes "measles" and "mumps" to be two names for the same disease.) To infer in that way is to take "Someone" to be a name; but it is possible to take "Someone" to be a name, and nevertheless not to regard the inference as available. One might, for example, take "Someone" in "Someone has measles" to be a name of one person, and "Someone" in "Someone has mumps" to be the name of someone else. So the point about the unavailability of the inference to "Someone has measles and mumps" might help the child but it might not; for it leaves it open that "Someone" is a name—a name of more than one person. If it does not help, one might pursue the point, assuming a child with a rather unnaturally good uptake for logic, with "Each of measles and mumps is had by someone" and its not allowing (if it is understood as one wants it to be understood) the inference to "Someone has measles and mumps." But what we need to see here is that the process of clarification involves making clear as much of the inferential behavior of the utterance with which we are concerned as is necessary.

I have been describing how an explanation of the inferential connections of "Someone has measles" may enable a child to grasp the role of "Someone" in it. Here we can note a couple of *Tractatus* points. First, if you add a tautology as a conjunct to a senseful proposition, the result will be identical with *the original senseful proposition:* you have what counts, from the point of view of the *Tractatus,* as the same proposition (see *TLP* 4.465). Secondly, in the *Tractatus,* inference is fundamentally tied to tautologies. To any valid inference, there corresponds a tautology.[8] Logical propositions are tautologies and they are forms of proof: "they shew that one or more propositions *follow* from one (or more)."[9] If you can infer some conclusion from some set of premises, you can construct a proposition which has truth-functional "implies" as its main connective, using the conjunction of the premises of the inference as the antecedent, and the conclusion of the inference as the consequent; you will have a proposition that can be seen to be a tautology. That it is a tautology can be mechanically determined, although making it clear that it is a tautology involves something which cannot be carried out mechanically—namely, the working out of the analysis of the component propositions far enough for the tautological character of the combination to become evident. Further, the mechanical demonstration that a combination is tautological depends on taking signs that recur as recurring with the same meaning. In *TLP* 4.1211, Wittgenstein says that two propositions "*fa*" and "*ga*" show that they are both about the same object; but they show this only in that "*a*" is being used in the same way in both. But, for *that* to be something that shows, we must be using "*fa*" and "*ga*" so that we can infer that there is something that is both *f* and *g* from the two propositions together. For a combination to be a tautology and for us to be using the component symbols in inferences in certain ways are the same thing. Nevertheless, we can clarify a proposition, help make clear to someone what proposition it is, what its use is, by writing it with a particular helpful tautology added to it.[10]

I have just claimed that, on the *Tractatus* view, there is a tautology that corresponds to a valid inference, and hence that the use of a proposition in inferences can be clarified by adding a helpful tautology, corresponding to the valid inference, to the proposition. That one proposition does not follow from some set of propositions is also reflected in a tautology. One can write out the truth-functional implication cor-

---

8. This is clear in the *Tractatus* in the 5.ls and 6.12s; see also "Notes Dictated to G. E. Moore in Norway" (Wittgenstein 1961b).

9. Wittgenstein 1961b, 108.

10. For further discussion of the issues in this paragraph, and more generally of the issues in this essay, see Kremer 2002.

responding to the non-allowable inference, and all the non-tautological combinations of all the propositions which are components of the premises of the non-allowable inference and of the proposition giving what cannot be inferred from them, carrying through the analysis of the various propositions as far as is necessary. There will be a tautological equivalence between the truth-functional implication corresponding to the inference and one of the non-tautological combinations. That tautological equivalence of the implication with the non-tautology reflects the invalidity of the inference. Wittgenstein made a closely related point later on, when he said that we do logic by proving that certain propositions are tautologies, but we could do it as well by proving that certain propositions are not tautologies.[11] (That a combination is non-tautological depends on the use of the symbols, just as does the fact that some particular combination is a tautology.)

The two *Tractatus* points—namely, (1) that if you add a tautology to a proposition, the result is the original proposition, and (2) that both the availability of some inference and the unavailability of some inference can be made clear by writing tautologies—mean that any clarification of a proposition which works by clarifying its inferential behavior can be thought of as adding a tautology to the original proposition; and this is to say that any such clarification could be described as adding nothing to the original proposition. It simply rewrites it, giving us the same proposition, expressing the same thought, with fundamentally the same mode of use of signs; it rewrites it, though, in a way that may remove unclarity.[12]

Let us apply this point about the character of clarification to the case of the confusion about "Someone has measles." Write down the sentence "Someone has measles" twice. Add to the first a specification of one kind of inferential behavior; add to the second a specification of a different pattern of inferential behavior. By this I mean the two patterns of inferential behavior discussed above—that is, the use of "Someone has mea-

11. Wittgenstein 1989, 278.

12. For a related view, see Wittgenstein 1967, §321: "When a rule concerning a word in a proposition is added to the proposition, the sense of the proposition does not change."

sles" so that its negation can be inferred from a single proposition about one person not having measles, and the use of "Someone has measles" so that its negation cannot be inferred from any premise short of one denying of every member of the group in question that she has measles. The second use also disallows the inference from the two premises "Someone has measles" and "'Someone has mumps" to "Someone has measles and mumps" and so on. To specify the two patterns of inferential behavior is to do something that could also be done by adding one group of tautologies to the original sentence, to clarify one use, and another group of tautologies to the sentence, to clarify a distinct use. It is worth emphasizing here that no tautologous addition does the work of clarification except by being picked up, and the "picking up" in question involves the very matters being clarified—that is, the uses of "someone." From the point of view of logic, any tautology is equivalent to any other. So how can one tautological addition help to clarify one proposition, and another clarify a different proposition? The answer is: by being taken as a helpful guide to use; in other words, a proposition rewritten with the tautology in question as part of it may be seen in a certain way. It may be seen with its use more clearly in focus.[13]

Wittgenstein held not only that there is a sense in which we cannot go wrong in logic, but also that we cannot specify the sense of propositions in some wrong way. This means that neither of our specifications of inferential behavior for "Someone has measles" contains any logical error, but we might well find that, if we in fact used the sentence in these two different ways, people would run into practical problems; having both the uses would be inconvenient. We might be well advised not to opt for a use which allows the inference from the negation of a proposition saying of some particular person that he has measles to the negation of "Someone has measles"—that is, not to use "Someone" as a name. ("Someone" and "Somebody" may sometimes be used as nonce-names, as "Nobody" occasionally is—for example, by Chesterton's Father Brown, who speaks of "Nobody's glass" in drawing attention to the presence of

---

13. See Kremer 2002, 299n22, on the matter of how different tautologies may show different things.

a glass of whisky drunk by someone not yet considered by the investigators of a murder. "Nobody's glass" does not here mean a glass that isn't anybody's; rather, the word "Nobody" is a nonce-name for the man otherwise identified as "The Quick One." "Somebody" and "nobody" are also used as predicates meaning someone of some consequence and someone of no consequence.)

Suppose, then, that you have specified the two patterns of inferential behavior, and that you explain them to the person who was confused about "Someone has measles." If she sees that there are these two different uses, her confusion may disappear. You may, if you like, say: "When there is *this* type of inferential behavior, I call 'Someone,' used this way, a name, and if there is *that* type of inferential behavior, I say that 'Someone,' used that way, is not a name." But, then, if that is your explanation of "is a name" and "is not a name," all you would be doing if you later described a use of "Someone" as not a use as a name is adding a specification of the inferential behavior of the propositions you are speaking about to those propositions; and on the *Tractatus* view that is doing the same as adding tautologies to the propositions in question. What is more important is that the use of the label "name" is not what is significant in the clarification, since the removal of confusion is entirely a matter of seeing the differences in the inferential patterns, and not a matter of applying any label to one use rather than the other.

So, in connection with the kind of case we are considering—namely, a confusion about the role of "Someone" in a particular utterance—one thing you can illuminatingly *do* is clarify the inferential behavior of the proposition. This activity can be regarded, on the *Tractatus* view, as in effect the addition of tautologies to the proposition being clarified, perhaps with contrasts to other propositions with tautologies added to them. Clarity about clarification in this kind of case thus raises the question whether there is room in such cases for the sort of point in which Anscombe is interested—a point expressed in a proposition which is illuminating but which lacks true-false poles and is not a mere tautology.

Although we are not yet dealing with the kind of case Anscombe has centrally in mind, we should turn back here to the final paragraph of the quoted passage from Anscombe. She says there that she does not believe that there is a more acceptable formulation (from the point of view of the *Tractatus)* of the point made by saying that "'Someone' is not the name of someone," and she contrasts that with what Wittgenstein seems to be inviting us to do—namely, look hard at something which supposedly stares us in the face. I have not argued that there is some more "acceptable" formulation of Anscombe's kind of point, available to us in the case of the confusion about "Someone has measles," but rather that the sort of proposition which she takes to be illuminating is not what does the work of clarification. To clarify in the relevant way, in this kind of case, is to make plain the use of our expressions; this is not done by saying of such-and-such a sign that it is or is not being used in such-and-such context as a name, unless we are already able to connect "is being used as name" with a pattern of use. It is the capacity to make the connection with the pattern of use that is essential. But the signs in question, in this case the sentence "Someone has measles," can be used in various ways; we cannot say that "Someone" in the mere sentence isn't a name. It might in some use be a name. What we want to speak of is "Someone has measles" used in a particular way. But if we succeed in making clear what use of the sentence we are talking about, we have already made clear how the word "Someone" is being used in it; to say that it is not a name would not add anything to the clarification we had achieved of what use of the sentence we had in view. (My own earlier reference to someone who thinks that "Someone" is being used as a name of two different individuals has to be taken in the way I have just specified. If my description can be followed, it is because the person who can follow it knows how to discriminate between two different patterns of inferential behavior, which might be labeled "use as name of one individual" and "use as name of two individuals.")

Anscombe speaks of Wittgenstein's supposed view that all we need to do is look hard at what stares us in the face in order to see that "Someone" is not a name. Well, suppose that Wittgenstein would indeed have said that the proposition "Someone has measles" shows that "Someone" in it is not a name. This is hardly to say that we have only to look hard at the sentence to see that "Someone" is not a name. What would "looking hard" be? We need to look at signs with their use, and, while it might in some sense be true to say that this "stares us in the face," it isn't obvious in what sense it is supposed to do so. But Wittgenstein did think that there was an activity through which a proposition can be turned into a new version of itself; the activity helps us grasp what we might then realize had shown all along (had shown in that the proposition had such-and-such determinate use). The activity of clarification turns propositions into versions of themselves that enable us to see clearly what the propositions had in a sense shown all along. I believe that some such account of clarificatory rewriting can be seen to be involved in Wittgenstein's conception of analysis—analysis being a form of clarificatory rewriting tied to the principle that, if $p$ follows from $q$ and $q$ from $p$, they are the same proposition. But I cannot here attempt to give an account of Wittgenstein's view of analysis.

Philosophy, the *Tractatus* says, aims at the logical clarification of thoughts. It is an activity which results in propositions getting clear, not in philosophical propositions. By giving us new versions of our propositions, it takes thoughts that were not in focus, and makes it possible for us to avoid the confusions that came from that lack of focus. I hope that this section has demonstrated how it is (in some cases) possible to get that shift from lack of focus to focus by doing something that we can, from within the point of view of the *Tractatus,* regard as adding tautologies to our propositions.

I said that the activity of clarification turns propositions into versions of themselves that enable us to see clearly what the proposition had shown all along. This description of the activity is meant to connect with a problem about the translation of *TLP* 4.112. In a letter to Ogden about this passage, Wittgenstein wrote that he thought "it cannot be the RESULT of philosophy 'to make propositions clear': this can only be its task. The *result* must be that the propositions *now have become clear* that they ARE clear."[14] This remark is almost bound to be misleading if we do not bear in mind that very different ways of writing a proposition will give us what still counts as the same proposition; and what proposition the proposition is, what symbol it is, may be far easier to take in

---

14. Wittgenstein 1973, 49. I have spelled out abbreviated words and followed the editor's indicated corrections of punctuation.

in some modes of writing than in others. A Russellian analysis, for example, rewrites propositions in a way that might be said to make it clear that they "were" clear. That is, the sense in which they "were" clear is that they were all along the same proposition as the proposition now written in a way which eliminates certain possibilities of confusion. To say, as I did, that philosophy results in propositions getting clear may seem to contradict Wittgenstein's point in his letter to Ogden. That is, it looks as if I am saying, against Wittgenstein, that the propositions in question were not already clear. And the response (if someone made that objection to me) would be to say that, on his view, in one sense they were already clear and in another sense they weren't. The sense in which they weren't is that we have work to do before their clarity (in the sense in which they have it all along) is available to us. This leaves open the question how far we need to push the work of clarification.

### 3. Back to Anscombe

In a footnote in Section 2, I mentioned Peter Geach's discussion of how we may continue to refer to someone as the same man over a period of time.[15] In the sort of case imagined by Geach, I might initially look up and see someone on the quarry-edge, and say "There's a man on the quarry-edge," or "There's someone on the quarry-edge," and I might then refer to him again a few minutes later, saying "He's gone now!" Here I speak again of the man I had meant. The initial judgment can be taken to refer to the particular man through its occurrence in a particular sensory context (Geach 1964, 64). On Geach's view, a series of statements about the same man can be regarded from the logical point of view as one long existentially quantified statement, given the use of the original statement in the sort of context in which a particular person is picked out, and given the various sorts of connections between that original statement and subsequent statements, through which it can be clear that the later statements refer to *the same man*. On this account,

---

15. Addendum, 2017: In revising Essay 2 for this volume, I have made a number of changes in the first half of Section 3. I am indebted here to a reviewer for Harvard University Press for pointing out problems with the earlier version.

the presence in my statement of such expressions as "a man" or "someone" does not in general indicate that the judgment I make has any reference to a particular person. Whether there is a reference to a particular person depends not only on the context but also on the form of the statement. Thus, for example, I may say, "If someone took the jewels, there should be fingerprints on the jewel-box," but my statement does not refer to the person who took the jewels, whether or not I was actually thinking when I said it that it was So-and-so who took the jewels. That a thought about a particular person was going through my mind does not make it the case that my statement is *about him*. My statement in this case doesn't refer to any particular person. What Geach gives us, then, is a way of using "refer" of some statements containing "someone" or "a man" (and so on); whether a particular statement or judgment refers to a particular person depends in complex ways on its logical features and on its context, including its relation to previous judgments.

I can now turn to Flew's example and his remarks about it—the remarks that led Anscombe to say that Flew meant nothing, even if he thought he meant something. My argument will be that what Flew is concerned with is Geachian reference, which he nevertheless discusses in a somewhat misleading way. Flew quotes Lewis Carroll:

> "I see nobody on the road," said Alice.
> "I only wish *I* had such eyes," the King remarked. . . . "To be able to see Nobody! And at that distance too! Why, it's as much as *I* can do to see real people by this light!"

Flew says that the King's mistake is to treat "Nobody" as if it had the logic of "Somebody," as if "Nobody" referred to somebody, albeit a rather insubstantial somebody.[16] Flew's confusion, if he is indeed confused, does not lie in the first part of his claim, about the King having treated "Nobody" as if it had the logic of "Somebody." What he means by its having the logic of "Somebody" is clear in the quotation from Carroll: you treat "Nobody" as having the logic of "Somebody" if you

16. Flew 1951, 8.

take it to be possible to infer from Alice's "I see nobody on the road" that you also would be able to see whoever it is Alice sees, if you had Alice's capacity to see. If Alice sees someone, you ought to be able to see that person if you had eyes as good as hers. (And, since you can, although perhaps just barely, see all real people in the available light, the person whom Alice sees and whom you can't see can't be a real person.) To think in that way is to treat "Nobody" as having the logic of "Somebody." When Anscombe argues that Flew was confused, she says that, if he were correct that "Somebody" refers to somebody, we could, if told that everybody hates somebody, ask to be introduced to the universally hated person.

But what stands behind the use of "refer" in Flew's remark about the Carroll example is the possibility of a Geachian use of "refer" about such sequences as

"I see somebody on the road," said Alice.
"I can only just manage to see him," the King remarked.

On a Geachian account, the King may be referring to the person Alice had spoken of. What makes it possible for the King to be referring to him is that Alice has just drawn attention to him; the King also needs to have identified the man Alice spoke of. He may get the identification wrong, and then not be referring to the person Alice had spoken of. The King could indeed ask to be introduced to the person she had spoken of. On the Geachian view, as I understand it, it would be an invitation to confusion to speak of *the word* "somebody" as referring, in Alice's remark, to somebody. But suppose that what Flew had meant (in speaking of "Somebody" as referring to a person, and of "Nobody" as not doing so) was that the difference between the presence of "somebody" in "I see somebody on the road" (supposing Alice to have said *that*) and the presence of "nobody" in what she did say *makes* the difference between Alice's referring to the person on the road in the former case and not referring to anybody in the latter case. If that were all that he had meant, the appropriate criticism would be that his way of speaking was infelicitous and could lead into confusion. Anscombe, who quotes only a part of Flew's discussion, takes him to intend also to be speaking about a range of other cases in which "Somebody" is used, including such statements as "Everybody hates somebody" (but not including cases in which "Somebody" is actually used as somebody's name), and to intend the word "refer" in a particular sense, in which to say of a word that it refers to someone is to say that it functions as a name of that person. But it is not clear what range of cases he meant to be talking about. He does not at any point say that "Somebody" is a name; and it is questionable whether his remarks suggest that it is.

If my arguments in Section 2 are correct, it would follow that the work of clarification of use is not in general done merely by description of a use of a word as a referring use, or as the use of the word as a name, or as a variable: behind such a description there has to be a grasp of different patterns of inferential behavior. This is particularly clear in the case of "refer."

There is, here, a methodological point about demonstrating that what someone has said is nonsense, as Anscombe wants to do in Flew's case. For, if an utterance appears to be nonsensical at first, there may very well be some not-nonsensical way of taking it. In the case of Flew's remark, it is plain that there is a way of taking his quoted example, together with his remarks about the contrast between the logic of "Nobody" and the logic of "Somebody," so that he is understood as using "refer" merely to mark the contrast between the role of "Somebody" in statements that, in appropriate contexts, refer in the Geachian sense to someone, and the absence of any such role for "Nobody." If Anscombe takes what Flew says to be nonsensical, it is (I think) because she is convinced that she sees what he is trying to mean, and she takes *that* to be mere confusion. Taking his use of "referred" as she thinks the word should be taken, she reads Flew as saying what could also be put as "'Somebody' is a name of somebody," and, while that could (on the view she takes in the passage quoted) mean something true if there were indeed someone called "Somebody," what Flew intends is, she thinks, something else—something that is mere confusion. I believe that the idea of a nonsensical sense plays a role in her reading (or what I take to be her misreading) of Flew. If one believes that one has grasped what a person is trying to say and that *that* is nonsense, is no meaning at all, there is almost a guarantee that one will not attend to possibilities of sense of the sort that can be obscured if there is some unsuspected difference in the way a word is being used. If one wanted to show that what someone had said was indeed nonsense, one would need to go about it differently: one would need to think through how his words could perhaps be taken this way or that way, and so on, and one would need, then, to bring out why one took it that none of the possibilities would answer to his intentions. Obviously here there can be no conclusive demonstration, for the person might well be able to show that the words had been intended in some other way.[17]

I have argued that there are problems with Anscombe's attempt to show that Flew was confused. I want now to turn to another matter: her claim that we can illuminatingly say "'Someone' is not the name of someone," and that this indicates that we can indeed say the kind of thing that Wittgenstein took to be showable but not sayable. We have seen, though, that it is not clear what (if anything) is said by "'Someone' is not a name of someone" unless, at the least, it is clear what use or uses of "Someone" the person making the remark means to be speaking about. Anscombe herself recognizes this, but does not, I think, follow through on the consequences. We can lay out this or that use of "Somebody," which would involve the same kind of activity that Anscombe herself engages in in connection with the use she has in mind of "Everybody hates somebody." Her intention is to criticize Flew's description of "Somebody" as referring to someone; and her talk of whether it is or isn't a name is meant to make clearer what she is objecting to. She gives us part of a specification of what it is to use a word so that it could be said to refer; but suppose she were to lay this out more clearly. And suppose she were also to lay out the use of "Somebody" that she has in mind. Could it illuminatingly be said that that use was not the sort of use that she took to be properly describable as a referring use? If so, in what way is it illuminating? For to say it is not a referring use will be to distinguish it from the use she has laid out as what she wished to call a referring

17. See Gustafsson 2006, 11–34, for a discussion of these issues in relation to Wittgenstein's later thought. See also Anscombe 1981f and 1963b for Anscombe's own treatment of the idea of a "sense that is nonsense" in connection with Wittgenstein's later thought.

use. But the difference between the use she had laid out as "referring use" and the use she had laid out as the relevant use of "Someone" (the use about which she wants to say something) will be as evident as it can be quite independently of any label for the uses. It may be illuminating to point to one thing, and to point to another, and to say, "Look!"—or, in this case, to give a specification of one sort of use, and of another, and to say "Look!"—but Anscombe's conception of what she is engaged in is meant to be contrasted with any such directive; it is meant to be a saying of something which is true and which is not a logical truth in any sharp sense of logical truth. But that a mode of use that allows such-and-such inferences (and so on) is not a mode of use that disallows those inferences (and so on), if it is any sort of content, would not be the kind of content she takes her remark to have. Here I want to emphasize that I am not disputing that a remark of the sort she makes may, in some contexts, be illuminating; the question is whether, when it is illuminating, it does anything different from specifying, to the extent that it is helpful, some use or uses and saying "Look!"

If I am right, then, Anscombe takes herself to be conveying something with a genuine content, although there is no content of the sort she takes herself to be conveying. Attempts at spelling out what is meant by her remark would involve laying out uses in such a way that their differences from other uses were plain. If, as I think, her own account is beset by problems, these arise in part through a blurring of Wittgenstein's distinction between sign and symbol, and in part through the use of formal concepts as if they were ordinary concepts. When Anscombe says that "'Someone' is not the name of someone," she immediately makes the move to eliminate an irrelevant use of the *sign* "Someone"—its use as an honest-to-goodness name. But her remark nevertheless retains its appearance of content largely because she does not specify the use of "Someone" about which she *does* want to speak. She does not enable us to have the symbol in question, the symbol about which she wants to speak, clearly in view. But if the symbol were made clear, were put clearly before us, the appearance of there being something that she wants to say about it—something to be said which is not logically true in any sharp sense—would be harder to achieve. It may be helpful in understanding the issues here to note that "Somebody" and

"Nobody" are frequently used in ordinary language as predicates. When Anscombe says "'Somebody' is not the name of somebody," she does not mean "Somebody" as used in "He really thinks he's somebody," just as Flew does not mean to talk about "Nobody" as used in "His people are nobodies." Each of them intends to speak about a different symbol; and, if it is necessary to clarify their remarks, clarification will involve making plain what symbol they mean. One doesn't have to think of cases in which "Somebody" or "Nobody" might actually be used as a name to make it clear that the purported subject matter of their remarks is not a sign. Again, "is a name of someone" is, on the *Tractatus* view, a characterization of a mode of use of signs; the expression for it, in a logically perspicuous symbolism, is a variable, the values of which are propositions containing signs used in the relevant way. There need be nothing the matter with talk of something's being or not being a name, or of some sign's being or not being a name of two distinct items, or whatever; but the appearance that such remarks may have, of saying something that goes beyond what Wittgenstein allows to be sayable, is created in part by not looking behind the label "name" or "name of two things" to the pattern of use. At *TLP* 4.1211, Wittgenstein says that the proposition "*fa*" shows that the object *a* occurs in its sense. This obviously makes it look as if what is shown is something that can be put into a "that" clause. And since what follows the word "that" does not count as sayable, it looks as if we have the comical case Anscombe refers to, of remarks that say what it is that cannot be said. The crucial thing we need to attend to here is not what comes after the "that" clause but what comes before it. For what is it that supposedly does the showing? Signs used in a certain way. But what way? To lay out the use in question, including the inferential behavior of the proposition, would let us see the proposition itself more adequately. In this case, it would include being able to see clearly the use of the sign "*a*". If we see the proposition itself clearly, there is then nothing at all *further* to be had, nothing further that might be said or thought or conveyed in some wordless way or even left unsaid.[18] That a proposition shows its sense means only that to see

18. On these issues, see Kremer 1997, 98. Kremer lays out the kind of inferential behavior of propositions in virtue of which the sign "*a*" as used in those propositions is

its use is to see what it says to be so. The seeing here isn't a grasping of an inexpressible something that can "only be shown," but a logical capacity, a capacity for intelligent use, for use in accordance with the rules of logical syntax.[19]

## 4. Conclusions

I have not argued that Anscombe's remarks about "Somebody" and "Someone" are nonsense. I would argue that, if her claim is that there is something she means that is not tautologous, not logical truth in a sharp sense, it is not at all clear what this might be. The difficulty is that of finding something that is what she wants to say, given that any clarification that turns it into a tautology or anything like a tautology will not be what she wants. She does not want to speak merely about the signs "Someone" and "Somebody," divorced from their use as ordinary-language variables. For, if we talk about the mere signs, what would be meant by denying that they were names of anybody would be merely that they had not been given a particular kind of use: no one has been given the name "Someone" or the name "Somebody." And that is not her point. (I would think it likely, in fact, that the name "Somebody" had been borne by some cat or dog.)[20] On the other hand, she cannot be said to have wanted to talk about this or that particular symbol, or at any rate not clearly to have wanted to do so. For if she had wanted to say something about a symbol, she would have had to lay out what use of the sign she had in mind—that is, what symbol she was talking about. And then the question would be what she wanted to say about the symbol that had not already been made clear in giving what symbol it

---

the name of a simple object. Here "name of a simple object" is a label for the kind of symbol, the revealing sign for which is a variable.

19. See, on these issues, Kremer 2001. Addendum, 2017: James Conant and I discussed Wittgenstein on saying and showing in Conant and Diamond 2004, esp. 65–67. See also Narboux 2014.

20. Addendum, 2017: Apparently the poet and suffragette Lila Ripley Barnwell had a dog called "Somebody"; and there is a song with the lines "I have a dog named Somebody, I named him after you."

was. I have argued that the impression she had of there being something illuminating to be said about "Someone" something distinct from "Look at these uses!" or "Here is one sort of use of signs, and here is another"— is misleading. And so is the idea we may have, in reading Wittgenstein, that it is easy to come up with examples of propositions that are perfectly intelligible although they lack true-false poles—propositions which are not logically true in a sharp sense, propositions which are not mere tautologies.[21] We may think that Wittgenstein's own book provides us with many such examples: when he speaks of what shows itself, we may think that we grasp the kind of content or quasi-content in question. But what does the showing, if anything does, is not a sign, but a sign in use; and to lay out what does the showing by clarifying propositions would destroy the impression we have of "what is shown" as something to be said or something to be grasped, a kind of content which we naturally represent to ourselves using a "that" clause. Only by clarifying propositions—that is, making plain what our symbols are—can we come to recognize that the impression we get of reaching beyond what supposedly can be said is itself a misleading impression. I mean the discussion of Anscombe's example to illustrate that point: she thinks that Wittgenstein held that something she takes herself to grasp (and indeed to be able to communicate) is beyond the reach of saying. My claim is that that impression is created by failure to carry through the task of clarifying what she herself is saying; and that, more generally, the impression of having made sense can be created by failure to clarify what we take ourselves to be talking about and what we take ourselves to be saying about it. This is meant to apply also to the impression we may have that the propositions of the *Tractatus* are intelligible propositions. There is no once-for-all demonstration in the *Tractatus* that propositions of such-and such sorts are nonsensical: the

21. Addendum, 2017: Some time after I wrote this essay, I recognized the significance for the *Tractatus* of propositions that are not bipolar, not tautologies or contradictions, and not nonsensical. These propositions can have various kinds of role, and are spoken of, at *TLP* 4.242, as *Behelfe der Darstellung.* I touch on the significance of these propositions in Essay 1, and discuss their various roles at greater length in Essays 3, 4, 5, and 6.

task of clarifying propositions is a one-by-one task. Only the activity of philosophical clarification, or of attempting philosophical clarification, can reveal whether, in a particular case, there is or isn't something that we mean.[22]

22. Addendum, 2017: I would no longer want to express the conclusion in the way it is put in that last sentence. It misses the significance of the different kinds of use that propositions can have, even as seen from the point of view on language of the *Tractatus*. See the discussion of mathematical equations in Essays 4 and 5, and of the contrast between "preparatory" propositions and the propositions of the *Tractatus* in Essay 4.

# THREE

# Reading the *Tractatus* with
# G. E. M. Anscombe

～

Wittgenstein wrote in the preface to the *Tractatus* that he believed the book to show that the reason philosophical problems are posed is that "the logic of our language is misunderstood." At the end of the preface, he said that he took himself to have in essence arrived at a definitive solution of such problems. The book was meant to revolutionize philosophical thinking. In *An Introduction to Wittgenstein's Tractatus*, Elizabeth Anscombe wrote that almost everything that had been published about the *Tractatus* "has been wildly irrelevant." She meant to inaugurate a rethinking of what sort of book the *Tractatus* was and how it should be understood. In this essay, I want to look at these two intentions together: Wittgenstein's intention of bringing about a revolution in philosophical thinking and Anscombe's of inaugurating a radical change in how the *Tractatus* was read. Looking at Anscombe's intention and at what she does in carrying it out will help us to see what Wittgenstein was hoping to achieve.

In the introduction to her book, Anscombe explains why virtually all that has been said about the *Tractatus* has been fraught with misunderstanding. But the story she tells has problems, and they are the subject of Section 1 of this essay. If, however, we look at Anscombe's account of the picture theory, we can take it to demonstrate how she thought the *Tractatus* should be read; and there are lessons to be drawn about what was wrong with the kinds of reading she rejected. The transformation which Anscombe hoped to bring about in how the book was read helped to transform also the study of both Frege and Russell. This latter transformation can help us to see what underlies her claim in the introduction that it was neglect of Frege and overdependence on Russell that led to the irrelevance of so much of what had been written about the *Tractatus*. An approach to the *Tractatus* can be Russellian in two different senses. It can depend upon reading Russell himself as a Humean thinker, as "imbued" with empiricism; or it can take from Russell, or at any rate share with Russell, a form of thinking which goes deeper and is not dependent on his empiricism, however nicely it fits with empiricism. I mean the kind of thinking which is described (by Warren Goldfarb and Peter Hylton) as Russell's "object-based" approach to metaphysics and meaning, and which can be contrasted with Frege's "judgment-based" approach.[1] Anscombe's reading of the *Tractatus* is un-Russellian, in both senses. Section 2 is meant to lay out the issues here, first by summarizing Anscombe's account of the picture theory, and then by showing the importance of the contrast between "object-based" and "judgment-based" accounts of meaning—its importance for understanding what Anscombe was trying to achieve, and how she differs not just from the readers of Wittgenstein whom she plainly did have in her sights, but also from such later readers as David Pears and Norman Malcolm. Her account of the contrast between Russell and Frege, in her argument for the importance of not neglecting Frege, does not reach to the largely implicit understanding of the contrast that is evident in her treatment of the picture theory. I shall not argue for this, but it seems to me that the character of the contrast begins to come out explicitly in Hidé Ishiguro's "Use and Reference of Names" (1969). Much of the criticism of that essay (for example, in Malcolm 1986, chap. 2) can be seen to be directed at a view which is already present in Anscombe's book. Section 3 of my essay is about how to understand Anscombe's achievement, not just as a reader of Wittgenstein but as someone engaged in the practice of philosophy as Wittgenstein conceived it. The larger aim of this section of the essay is to show how Anscombe's philosophical practice can lead us into further questions

---

1. Goldfarb 2002, esp. 190–191; Hylton 2005a, esp. 177–178.

about Wittgenstein's understanding of philosophical activity. Sections 4 and 5 are about how we can be helped thereby to see the aims and achievements of the *Tractatus*. One of my aims in this essay is to suggest a revision in the history laid out by Warren Goldfarb in "Das Überwinden: Anti-metaphysical Readings of the *Tractatus*" (2011). I shall have some brief words about that in Section 6.

## 1. Anscombe, Russell, Frege

*An Introduction to Wittgenstein's Tractatus* was published in 1959, and drew on material that Anscombe had developed in lectures over successive years up to 1957–1958. In his 1956 study of the history of philosophical analysis, J. O. Urmson presents an interpretation of the *Tractatus* of exactly the sort Anscombe criticizes.[2] He mentions that some philosophers (unnamed, but presumably including Anscombe) have called into question the kind of interpretation of the *Tractatus* which he presents. He goes on to say that, whatever the accuracy of that interpretation, it is the "received" view, the view generally accepted in the period going up to the Second World War (Urmson 1956, ix–x). A central feature of the interpretation he presents is that the *Tractatus* is read with Russell's *Lectures on Logical Atomism;* both works are seen as fundamentally Humean in character. Both Russell and Wittgenstein are seen as empiricists, updating empiricism with the aid of recent developments in logic.

That reading of the *Tractatus* is the main target of Anscombe's remark about the irrelevance of most of what had been written about the book. If this irrelevance has any one cause, she says, the cause is neglect of Frege "and of the new direction he gave to philosophy" (*IWT,* 12). She adds that "empiricist and idealist preconceptions, such as have been most common in philosophy for a long time, are a thorough impediment to the understanding of either Frege or the *Tractatus*" (12–13). She makes a contrast between Frege and Russell, the point of which is that readers of Wittgenstein have tended to see him as resembling Russell in respects in which he is much closer to Frege. Frege, she notes,

2. On the "old" interpretation of the *Tractatus,* see Griffin 1964, 4–5, 15.

is engaged in inquiries that are "in no way psychological"; he had no interest in "private mental contents," while Russell, unlike Frege, is concerned with immediate experience and with private mental contents, and introduces those notions into his account of language and his theory of judgment (14). He is "thoroughly imbued with the traditions of British empiricism"; many readers of Wittgenstein share that background with Russell, and it leads them to misunderstandings of Wittgenstein's concerns in the *Tractatus* (14). In the following chapter, Anscombe develops further her account of the usual, and (as she sees it) deeply mistaken, reading of the *Tractatus*. She quotes Karl Popper's summary of the *Tractatus*, which ascribes to Wittgenstein a version of the verifiability criterion of meaning. Popper treats Wittgenstein's *Elementarsätze* as statements describing directly observable states of affairs; and he adds that, for Wittgenstein, "every genuine proposition must be a truth-function of and therefore deducible from, observation statements" (quoted at *IWT*, 25). Anscombe mentions that Popper's account fits with a further feature of the usual reading of the *Tractatus*, which sees it as combining two independent theories: a "picture theory" of elementary propositions and a truth-functional account of nonelementary propositions. Before she turns to her own positive discussion of Wittgenstein on elementary propositions, Anscombe argues briefly against Popper's view of them as observation statements like, for example, "Red patch here," and mentions another respect in which the empiricist tradition may lead to misreadings of the *Tractatus*. Unlike Russell, and unlike the logical positivists and contemporary British readers of Wittgenstein, Wittgenstein was not concerned with epistemological issues, which he took to be irrelevant to "the foundations of logic and the theory of meaning" (25–28).[3] Anscombe's account of Wittgenstein's view of epistemology is meant to connect with her earlier remark about the cause of the misreading of the *Tractatus* being neglect of Frege and "the new direction he gave to philosophy." That is, for the "old direction" in philosophy, epistemology is central; but the questions with which Frege is concerned, and which we should see as significant for Wittgenstein, are not epistemological.

3. For discussion of Anscombe's argument, see Ishiguro 1969.

In explaining the sorts of question with which Wittgenstein was concerned, Anscombe gives as an example the question of the relation to reality of what I say, as, for example, if I say that Russell is a clever philosopher. The relation cannot be explained in terms of the truth of what I say, since even if my statement had been false, it would still have said something. As Anscombe notes, Wittgenstein was concerned with this problem throughout his life. She mentions that Russell discusses many of the problems that Frege discusses, and indeed, this last question, which is meant to exemplify Wittgenstein's sort of concern, is a central question for Russell. What, then, of her contrast between a reading of the *Tractatus* which sees it as Russellian in its approach to philosophical questions and one which sees it as Fregean? The contrast (if it cannot rest on a difference between Russell's sort of question and Frege's) has to rest on the difference between Russell's psychologism and Frege's anti-psychologism, and between the direction of philosophy as understood in the light of Russell's empiricism and the new direction given to philosophy by Frege. But it is far from clear that the contrast can be made out in that way. Peter Hylton (1990) has argued in detail that the conception of Russell generally accepted by British philosophers involved a misleading assimilation of his views in the period before the First World War to those of traditional empiricism, and Anscombe herself takes the view of Russell criticized by Hylton. She passes by Russell's anti-psychologism and the complicated character of his move away from it. Here I want to quote part of a paragraph of Hylton's about Platonic Atomism, the view developed by Moore and Russell when they gave up the idealist views which they had earlier accepted. The period about which Hylton is writing includes the period during which Russell wrote *The Principles of Mathematics:*

The anti-psychologism of Platonic Atomism . . . is complete and thoroughgoing. Platonic Atomism does . . . imply or suggest a picture of the mind and its capacities, but this picture is very much a by-product of the view. There is no overt concern at all with the nature of thought or the mind or experience, in any sense. It is not that Moore and Russell are concerned to advance a view of these notions which is different from that of the Idealists, it is rather that

these notions almost cease to be the subject of explicit philosophical concern. This seems to be because the notions are looked on
as psychological, and for this reason of no interest to philosophy.
(Hylton 1990, 108)

Hylton's remarks suggest that, if we look for a source of Wittgenstein's anti-psychologism in the *Tractatus*, Frege's views are no more
obviously the source than are Russell's, though Russell begins what
Hylton calls a "turn towards the psychological" in the years after the
publication of *Principles*. If Russell is the source, it would be Russell in
his Platonic Atomist or idealist periods. Kant's anti-psychologism is itself in the background of Frege's and in that of idealists like Bradley.[4] It
is not obvious that Wittgenstein's anti-psychologism in the *Tractatus*
should be thought of as belonging to a new direction given to philosophy by Frege. Among idealist "preconceptions," one might be said
to be that a main thing wrong with empiricism was its psychologizing
tendencies.

Anscombe's brief account of the importance of Frege for an understanding of the *Tractatus* involves also a problematic contrast between
"empiricist and idealist preconceptions" and the "new direction" given
to philosophy by Frege. We can see one of the problems if we consider
Anscombe's discussion of the question whether, when I say that Russell
is a clever philosopher, I mention both Russell and what I say about him,
that he is clever. If I do mention it, what is the connection between the
two mentioned things? And, if I do not mention it, what account should
be given of the words expressing what I say about Russell? This is one of
Anscombe's examples of the sorts of question which contrast with those
which are central for us if we start off with empiricist or idealist preconceptions. But here we can note that the questions mentioned by Anscombe are important for Bradley, and indeed his discussion of them is
famous; further, his account of judgment stresses questions about how
judgment is related to reality, questions again of exactly the sort which
Anscombe is suggesting we need to be struck by if we want to under-

4. See also Griffin 1964, 120–123, on the "descent" of anti-psychologistic critique of
philosophy from Bradley through Moore to Wittgenstein.

stand the *Tractatus*. Idealist preconceptions would not stop us from seeing the force of such questions. The other part of the contrast between "empiricist and idealist preconceptions" and the "new direction" given to philosophy by Frege does not work much better. Epistemological concerns are supposed to belong to the "empiricist and idealist preconceptions," but epistemological questions are not ignored by Frege. This point is perhaps clearer in the light of material in Frege's *Nachlass* that was not available to Anscombe when she wrote the *Introduction,* but *The Foundations of Arithmetic* would in any case suggest that Frege was deeply interested in the question of the source of our knowledge of arithmetic. The contrast with Russell on the matter of interest in epistemology is indeed complicated.[5]

Nothing that I have said would cast doubt on Anscombe's argument that Popper and the logical positivists had misread the *Tractatus,* and that they were in part responsible for the prevalent misreadings of the book. But I have tried to show problems for her argument that it is neglect of Frege, more than anything, that underlies the irrelevance of most of what had been written about the *Tractatus*. The features of Frege's views which she emphasizes can't bear the weight of the argument. The sorts of question which she suggests we need to think about when we read the *Tractatus,* questions like that of how a proposition hangs together, and that of how thought and reality are related, are of concern to Bradley and (as Anscombe herself notes) also to Russell; they are not more especially problems that should be associated with Frege; they are in no way out of place in the thinking of those with "empiricist or idealist preconceptions," if that is meant to cover Bradley and

---

5. For the significance of epistemology for Frege, see, e.g., Weiner 1999, chap. 2. On the development of Russell's interest in epistemology, see Hylton 2005a; for Russell's pre-1905 view, see Hylton 1990, 197n33. Hylton argues that Kant and the logical positivists "share an interest in knowledge, and a conception of what it is to account for it, which is not to be found in Russell's work" in the period during which he wrote *Principles.* See also 361–362, where Hylton, writing about Russell's interest in knowledge after 1910, says of Russell's earlier works that they "show no sign at all of any such interest"; also 235, where Hylton explains the changing role given to acquaintance as Russell's views change after 1905.

Russell. While anti-psychologism is profoundly characteristic of Frege, it can be found within the idealist tradition and in Russell's idealist and post-idealist views; and the turn away from epistemology is by no means as marked in Frege as Anscombe's discussion of the period suggests. Russell wasn't the empiricist Anscombe paints him as being, though his views were becoming more like those of the empiricists during the period in which he was working with Wittgenstein. There are all sorts of problems with the picture Anscombe gives us, of idealists and empiricists on one side, with their preconceptions and their familiar sorts of question, and Frege on the other side, giving a new direction to philosophy, and asking questions much more like those of ancient philosophy than like those that had been taken to be central for a long time. What I want to argue is that, despite the fact that practically everything Anscombe says in sketching why neglect of Frege will lead us astray needs qualification, her intention of following out what she takes to be Fregean in Wittgenstein's thought leads her right to the heart of the book. But how does she turn out to be right, if her account of the history is, as it stands, unconvincing?

## 2. Anscombe's Reading of the *Tractatus*

The heart of Anscombe's reading of the *Tractatus* is her account of the "picture theory" of the proposition in the first six chapters of her book.[6] The view that she rejects is that the "whole theory of propositions" in the *Tractatus* is "a merely external combination of two theories: a 'picture theory' of elementary propositions . . . and the theory of truth-functions as an account of non-elementary propositions" (25–26). She had argued in her introductory chapter that, in order to understand Frege or Wittgenstein, it is best not to start with philosophical preconceptions, but rather to be capable of "being naively struck" by questions like the one, mentioned above, of what the relation to reality is of the statement that Russell is a clever philosopher. The two central chapters of Anscombe's presentation of the picture theory begin with questions of just the sort she had claimed we need to be naively struck by. They

6. The scare quotes around "picture theory" are Anscombe's (*IWT*, 19, also 25, 41).

are questions that arise from the usual explanations, in logic books, of truth-functional composition. "It is usual for us to be told [ . . . that] propositions are whatever can be true or false"; that "propositions can be combined in certain ways to form further propositions"; and that "in developing the truth-functional calculus, we are not interested in the internal structure" of the component propositions. One question which may then strike us is whether "the property of being true or false, which belongs to the truth-functions, [is] the very same property as the property of being true or false that belongs to the propositions whose internal structure does not interest us." And, further, if that is so, "is it to be regarded as an ultimate fact that propositions combine to form further propositions, much as metals combine to form alloys which still display a good many of the properties of metals?" I shall quote her comment:

> In short, is there not an impression as it were of logical chemistry about these explanations? It is this conception that Wittgenstein opposes in the *Tractatus* at 6.111: "Theories that make a proposition of logic appear substantial are always wrong. It might be thought, for example, that the words 'true' and 'false' denote two properties among other properties, and then it would look like a remarkable fact that every proposition possesses one of these properties. This now looks no more a matter of course than the proposition 'all roses are either red or yellow' would sound, even if it were true." (53)

Here, interestingly, in the opposition to "logical chemistry," we can see Anscombe picking out a feature of Wittgenstein's philosophizing that is highly distinctive, and not apparently derived from Russell or Frege or any of the other thinkers whose influence on Wittgenstein can be discerned. (She quite explicitly argues that Frege, for example, in discussing whether every well-formed sentence the names in which are not empty has a truth-value, takes for granted a kind of logical-chemistry view of the nature of concepts.) Anscombe's own reading of the *Tractatus* reflects a sense, not just of what sort of questions one needs to be struck by, but also of what constitutes a genuinely satisfying resolution of the puzzlement expressed in the questions. Hence the importance of her treatment of negation. It is not just a pivotal topic for Wittgenstein's early thought but one through which she can demonstrate what is involved in reaching the kind of clarity at which he aimed. If we think about ordinary pictures, she says, we shall be able to see how the possibility of using a picture to represent that things are so goes with the possibility of using the very same picture to represent that that is how things are not. We can, that is, see in ordinary pictures the possibility of being used in two opposite ways, to say two opposite things. What is central in her account of what a picture is, is that "the way the elements are connected in the picture is the same as the way [the picture] sets forth the things as being connected." Hence, the possibility of things being connected that way is in the picture itself. It is then, as occurring in such a picture-context, that the elements can have the use of representing this or that thing. We can move from that initial insight to an understanding of negation which does not appeal to some kind of ultimate logical fact. The basic idea is that the possibility of using a picture in two opposite ways, to say this is how things are, and alternatively to say that that is how they aren't, depends upon correlating elements of the picture with things; and such correlating is something we can do so far as we take some way in which the marks or figures are related to each other to be significant. Only so far as they stand in such significant connections are these items elements of a picture; only in such connections can the picture-elements stand for this or that person or object or whatever it may be. Here is her summary: "Only in the connections that make up the picture can the elements of the picture stand for objects" (67). The picture-character of an ordinary picture is then what makes it possible, once correlations have been made, for there to be a *this*, such that there are two opposed ways of representing how things are: "*This* is how things are"; "*this* is how things aren't"; where the *this* in question is the same. And Anscombe's account of the picture theory is then that that picture-character that is in ordinary pictures is also in propositions. Only in the connection that makes up the proposition do the expressions in it stand for anything. It is through the significant connection of its parts that it can say that anything is the case; and so far as those significant connections make it possible to represent that *this* is how things stand, those same connections make it possible to represent that *this* is not how things stand. If what a picture represents as being so is its sense (*TLP* 2.221), we can say that a picture's sense is reversible: it can represent the opposite as being the case. We can see what propositional sense is, if we see propositions to have the reversibility that belongs to pictures, if (that is) we see in propositions the possibility that belongs to pictures of representing that *this* is how things are, or (the *this* being the same) that *this* is how they aren't. (See *TLP* 4.05–4.0621, where the point that reality can be compared with propositions is tied to the reversibility of sense of propositions.)

Two chapters after her account of the picture theory, Anscombe summarizes that account, and connects it with Wittgenstein's remarks about how a symbol can be presented:

> We have to remember the central point of the picture theory which we have already explained: "Only in the context of a proposition has a name reference"; "Only in the context of a proposition has an expression reference." This prohibits us from thinking that we can *first* somehow characterize "a", "R" and "b" as symbolic signs, and *then* lay it down how we can build propositions out of them. If "a" is a symbolic sign only in the context of a proposition, then the symbol "a" will be properly presented, not by putting it down and saying it is a symbol of such and such a kind, but by representing the whole class of the propositions in which it can occur. (93)

There Anscombe quotes *Tractatus* 3.3 and *Tractatus* 3.314, two statements of the "context principle," to give the heart of the picture theory as she had earlier explained it. Here we should pause and ask some questions. The context principle, as it occurs in the *Tractatus*, certainly appears to mark a connection with Frege's appeals to the context principle in *The Foundations of Arithmetic*. But what, then, is the connection? Warren Goldfarb has argued that it is not clear how far some apparently Fregean features of the *Tractatus* reflect the influence of Frege's thought on Wittgenstein.[7] It may be that Wittgenstein started with views which were profoundly influenced by Russell, but, in working through the

---

7. Goldfarb 2002, *passim* but see esp. 187, 197.

difficulties of those views, came to a position which is close to Frege's in significant respects. I shall leave open the question whether these "Fregean" features of his thought reflect the direct influence of Frege.[8] I want instead to ask what these features are, and how they are important for Anscombe's reading of the *Tractatus*. Goldfarb is very helpful here in laying out differences between Frege's thought and Russell's. Goldfarb connects Frege's commitment to the context principle with what he calls the "judgment-based nature" of Frege's view. Frege does not think of judgments as put together from parts which have some prior independent logical character. In a remark that has become well known (but that was not available in any of Frege's published writings when Anscombe wrote her *Introduction to Wittgenstein's Tractatus*), Frege said, "I do not begin with concepts and put them together to form a thought or a judgment; I come by the parts of a thought by analyzing the thought" (1979c, 253). While that remark concerns the parts of a thought, a parallel point holds, on Frege's view, for propositions: the parts of a proposition which have reference are identifiable only through the logical relations of the proposition to other propositions. Goldfarb notes the sharp contrast with Russell's approach: For Russell, the primitive parts of propositions "subsist in and of themselves." They are put together into propositions, but are recognizable on their own, independently of their role in propositions. Russell's account of propositions and their constituents is described by Goldfarb as "object-based," in contrast to Frege's "judgment-based" view. As a feature of Russell's thought, it can be found as early as *The Principles of Mathematics*. Its presence doesn't indicate that Russell was an empiricist, though such a view of propositions and their parts is indeed found in the writings of empiricists.[9]

In Section 1, I argued that, although Anscombe had claimed that neglect of Frege was the main explanation why what had been written about the *Tractatus* had been for the most part wildly irrelevant, her account of the differences between Frege and Russell left it unclear why neglect of Frege should have so distorted understanding of Wittgenstein. But her presentation of the picture theory and the connection that she

8. On this topic, see the Introduction to this volume, and also Diamond 2014a.
9. A classic statement of the view can be found in chap. 1 of Mill 1843.

makes there with Wittgenstein's version of the context principle show (I think) why she sees Frege as leading us in the right direction. My suggestion is that Goldfarb's contrast between Frege's judgment-based view and Russell's object-based approach, although it doesn't correspond to anything Anscombe explicitly says in laying out the contrast between Frege and Russell, lets us see why Anscombe insists on the importance of Frege for an understanding of the *Tractatus*. Consider the remarks of Anscombe's that I discussed in Section 1, that Russell differs from Frege "by introducing the notion of immediate experience, and hence that of private mental contents, into his explanations of meaning and his theory of judgment"; for he is, she says, "thoroughly imbued with the traditions of British empiricism." (14) We should, I think, read those remarks as containing three distinct points—about immediate experience, private contents, and empiricism. If we use "experience" to include what Russell means by "acquaintance," we could then say that Russell introduces into his account of meaning and judgment a notion of immediate experience, but we cannot then go on: "hence of private mental contents." There is no "hence," since one can have a notion of immediate acquaintance (even: of immediate acquaintance conceived on the model of acquaintance with the taste of a pineapple) in which the objects with which one is immediately acquainted need not be private mental entities, but may be such things as the indefinables of logic and universals. Indeed, even sense-data need not be conceived as "private mental contents" on a Russellian view of acquaintance. A notion of immediate acquaintance can play a central role in a philosophical account of meaning and judgment, which may be quite far from empiricism in various ways, or indeed opposed to it.[10] So one needs to separate from each other Anscombe's point that Russell worked with a notion of immediate acquaintance and her characterization of his views as

10. On these issues, see Hylton 1990, esp. 328–333. As Hylton notes, even as late as 1913 the point of acquaintance, for Russell, is that it is to be "an unproblematic meeting ground between the mind and what is outside it" (331). That the notion of acquaintance is not tied to empiricism is also evident in the writings of Gareth Evans and those who are influenced by him, who use the idea of the direct availability of something for thought, an idea developed from Russellian acquaintance.

thoroughly empiricist. Anscombe is certainly right that the *Tractatus* was misunderstood by her contemporaries in large part because they saw it as a working out of a radically empiricist view; they saw Russell as arguing for a very similar kind of empiricism. But we need to focus here on the notion of acquaintance, and in particular on Russell's principle that one can understand a proposition only if one is acquainted with its constituents. The principle is stated in "On Denoting" and repeated in *The Problems of Philosophy* and "Knowledge by Acquaintance and Knowledge by Description."[11] The idea that understanding a proposition depends on acquaintance with its constituents goes with the point mentioned by Goldfarb in characterizing Russell's views: the primitive parts of propositions subsist on their own, and are recognizable independently of the propositions of which they are parts.

Although I am in the middle of a line of argument here, I shall introduce a digression to indicate where the argument is going. Some years after the publication of Anscombe's book, Hidé Ishiguro, B. F. McGuinness, and Peter Winch developed readings of the *Tractatus* which explicitly reject the idea that the connections between names and objects are supposed to be established prior to the use of the names in propositions; on the reading that they reject, Wittgenstein held that the logical form of the object with which a name was correlated determines how the name can be correctly combined with other names in propositions. Their readings depended on taking seriously Wittgenstein's expression of the context principle at *TLP* 3.3.[12] It thus became incumbent on anyone who wanted to read the *Tractatus* as committed to the idea that objects have their own independent nature, and that it is first of all through the connection between names and such objects that language has its connection with reality, to explain what sort of force the context principle has, since it at least appears to imply that there is no such thing as a name having meaning prior to its use in propositions. It will be helpful if I summarize here, very briefly, one such line of response, that of David Pears (1987). He argues that it is possible to interpret the con-

11. Russell 1956, 56; 1967, 32; 1932, 219. See also Hylton 1990, 246: the principle of acquaintance is, he writes, implicit in *The Principles of Mathematics*.

12. Ishiguro 1969, e.g., 22; McGuinness 1981, esp. 65–66; Winch, 1987, esp. 8–10.

text principle so that it is consistent with the idea that contact between names and things is prior to the occurrence of names in propositions; the principle implies merely that the association between a name and the object it names is "annulled" if the name occurs in a context that doesn't correspond to a genuine possibility for the object.[13] Pears's treatment of the context principle is developed in the course of his criticism of Ishiguro and McGuinness, and is meant as a basis for rejecting their understanding of the context principle and of the relation between names and objects. Anscombe does not share that understanding, but Pears's account, if correct, would equally constitute an objection to Anscombe's view.

Anscombe's account of the picture theory is incompatible with any idea that setting up the connections between names and things is prior to putting the names into significant combinations. As she says, only if significant relations hold among the elements of a picture can we correlate the elements with things, so that the picture-elements stand for the things, and so that their arrangement shows a way in which the things can stand. When she wrote that the Russellian connection leads to misunderstandings of the *Tractatus,* one of the main things she had in mind was this: that if you read into the *Tractatus* Russell's view that the intelligibility of propositions depends upon acquaintance with their constituents, you cannot understand the picture theory. But what would block understanding of the picture theory is not merely Russell's doctrines about acquaintance and meaning. If Anscombe is right about the picture theory, it is incompatible not just with Russell's own views and his version of logical atomism but also with any object-based account

13. Pears 1987, 1:75–76, 102–103. See also Malcolm 1986, 28–31; Malcolm appears to hold both that there is no such thing as a "preliminary preparation" for language in which signs are correlated with objects outside of propositions and that, if I am to construct a proposition using a name for an object, I must know its possible combinations with other objects. The correlations settle for me the propositional contexts in which that name can occur. This latter point appears to involve granting to correlation-making a kind of logical priority close to the kind of "preparation" for language which he had explicitly ruled out three pages earlier. The idea is certainly that the correlations between names and objects allow certain sign-combinations and disallow others.

of meaning. Thus, for example, Pears (1987) takes himself to be dis-agreeing with any strongly Russellian reading of the *Tractatus,* because he does not think that the objects of the *Tractatus* can be identified with sense-data and their properties, but whether an account is object-based has nothing to do with the question what sorts of thing the objects are; and Pears's account is a paradigmatically object-based account of meaning.[14] For Pears, as for Russell, the primitive parts of propositions subsist on their own; and the initial correlation between names and things is prior to the use of the name in propositions.

Consider also Anscombe's point, quoted above, that a symbolic sign "a" is properly presented, "not by putting it down and saying it is a symbol of such and such a kind, but by representing the whole class of propositions in which it can occur." Here the recognition of some oc-currence of the sign "a" as an occurrence of that symbol is dependent on its occurrence in a proposition of the class in question, and there is no question of setting up which propositions it can occur in by consid-ering its correlation with an object, taken to impose restrictions on its use, allowing some combinations of signs and disallowing others. The logical characteristics of what "a" means are plain from its role in the propositions in which it can occur.[15] It is a consequence of this view that there is no logical error in using the sign "a" in other sorts of proposi-tion; for in those contexts it would not be the same symbol. There is here a substantial difference from the approach taken later by Pears, who speaks of the occurrence of a name in a context which doesn't corre-spond to a genuine possibility for the object named as "annulling" the connection between name and object (1987, 1:75). It is hard to see how this way of speaking can be connected either to Wittgenstein's (and An-scombe's) talk of signs or to Wittgenstein's (and Anscombe's) talk of

14. See also McGinn 2006, 271–272, n. 6.

15. Anscombe's view, that logical characteristics of what a symbol means are plain from its role in propositions, is weaker than the views of Winch, Ishiguro, and Mc-Guinness. Anscombe's view leaves room for a distinction between presenting what kind of thing a symbol means and settling which thing of that kind it means; but Winch, Ishiguro, and McGuinness give accounts of the *Tractatus* which don't leave room for that distinction, at any rate in the case of simple names.

symbols. The name-with-its-connection-annulled isn't a mere sign, in their sense: for the supposed name, if it is thought of as a name at all, is being thought of as if it had at any rate a shadow of an attachment to an object of a particular kind. Otherwise one could not speak of *its* connection with some object being annulled. But a mere sign has no logical connection to any particular kind of object. But isn't that the status of the name after the connection is "annulled," on Pears's view? The trouble with that reply is that the connection can't be "annulled" unless it is there to be annulled; and if the connection is there, then what has the connection is a symbol, not a sign; and if it is indeed a symbol, then it is in use in the sort of context of which such symbols are features, and there would then be no question of the connection being "annulled" by the name's being in the wrong sort of context.

The difficulty in an attempt to explain Pears's view is that the context principle in the *Tractatus,* as Anscombe points out, appears to rule out the idea that we can identify a sign as a name of some particular object, and *then* go on to note that the combinatorial possibilities of that object permit such-and-such propositional occurrences of the name, and rule out others. The context principle is closely tied to the distinction between a mere sign and a symbol; but Pears's account of what is involved in putting a name into a propositional combination of the "wrong" sort cannot coherently be explained in terms either of the name as a mere sign or of the name as a symbol. The word "resolute" has been given a use in discussions of the *Tractatus,* in connection with the interpretation of Wittgenstein on sense and nonsense, but I want to suggest that, in the contrast between Anscombe's treatment of the context principle and that of Pears, we can see another sort of issue of resolution and irresolution. Pears's interpretation of the *Tractatus* allows the context principle to rule out the idea that "a" can occur genuinely as a name anywhere except in senseful propositional combinations; but the idea of the name as occurring in the "wrong" sort of context, and thereby having its connection with the object "annulled," employs the idea of a name-object connection that is *there,* independently of the occurrence of the name in propositions. *This* connection requires that the name itself not be thought of either as a sign or as a symbol, if a symbol is a symbol only in the context of a proposition. The sign/symbol contrast helps us to be clear about what we want to say and about when we are dithering and not saying anything. There is (I am suggesting) a wiggle or dither in Pears's account, that operates in what is only apparently a space of possible philosophical conceptions.[16] The fundamental difficulty is the attempt to combine an object-based understanding of language, shared with Russell, and the context principle. But a weakened version of the context principle is quite different from the version of the context principle that underpins the distinction between sign and symbol. Putting this point another way: there is no room for the *Tractatus* understanding of what a symbol is if one tries to read into the book an object-based understanding of names. Pears supports his reading of the context principle (as consistent with an object-based understanding of names) by reference to passages in Wittgenstein's *Notebooks* from November 1914. These passages are hardly unambiguous, but more important, they were written well before Wittgenstein began to take the context principle seriously. If one takes Wittgenstein's views to have been evolving during the years before the final version of the *Tractatus* was written, and in particular, if one takes his treatment of the context principle (and of the relation between the meaning of a name and its occurrence in propositional contexts) to be among the things that changed, it becomes questionable how far remarks from November 1914, or from elsewhere in the *Notebooks,* can be taken to impose on the context principle in the *Tractatus* an interpretation weak enough to make it consistent with object-based readings of the *Tractatus*.[17]

A strong version of the context principle, like that which Anscombe ascribes to Wittgenstein, has been held by some philosophers of language and some commentators on Wittgenstein to be incompatible with the compositionality of language. So (on this view) if Wittgenstein did hold such a version of the context principle, his account of language is in trouble. It is far from obvious, though, that there is such an in-

16. A corresponding problem emerges in Malcolm 1986, if one works through Malcolm's treatment of the context principle and tries to connect it with Wittgenstein's distinction between signs and symbols.

17. On the development of Wittgenstein's treatment of the context principle and of his understanding of its consequences, see Kremer 1997.

compatibility, and there are good arguments against it (Bronzo 2011). I shall not, however, examine the issues here.

I have argued that there is indeed a fundamentally Russellian way of reading the *Tractatus,* and that it is common to the interpretations Anscombe criticized and to later readings like that of David Pears. Part of my argument has been that what being "Russellian" in this context amounts to becomes clear only later, in a line of discussion which develops from Anscombe herself, and which includes the writings of (among others) Hidé Ishiguro, Warren Goldfarb, Thomas Ricketts, and Peter Hylton. Anscombe's interpretation of the *Tractatus* can be described as Fregean, not in that she claims that Wittgenstein's approach was in relevant respects derived from Frege (which it might or might not have been) but in that Wittgenstein, as she reads him, came to share with Frege an approach later described as "judgment-based." I have also argued that there is an important feature of Anscombe's understanding of the central ideas of the *Tractatus,* a feature which is neither Russellian nor Fregean. I mean her treatment of the idea of "logical chemistry." I quoted her discussion of *Tractatus* 6.111, where Wittgenstein says that theories that make a proposition of logic appear substantial are always wrong, and where he criticizes any account of logic that makes it look like a queer sort of fact that every proposition is either true or false. Anscombe's account of the picture theory is meant to make the truth or falsity of propositions fall out of what it is for propositions to be pictures. There is to be no "logical chemistry"; and her argument is that, if we think through the analogy with pictures, and take as central the way ordinary pictures can be used to say that something is so, or used to say the opposite, we can see how the logical character of propositions is thereby made "extremely intelligible." What she speaks of as the "grounds for being struck even to the point of conviction" by the account is that it opens up the logical character of propositions, without appeal to ultimate logical facts of any sort. If, at the end of her two chapters on negation, she says that there is surely something right about the picture theory even if it is not correct as it stands, her conviction that there is something right about it comes from being "struck even to the point of conviction" by the "extreme intelligibility" given to the logical character of propositions. The idea is not, I think, that we have antecedently available a conception of philosophical clarity, and that the *Tractatus* account of propositions provides that sort of clarity. Rather, the making intelligible of the logical character of propositions provides a way of understanding what philosophical clarity can be. My account of Anscombe's reading of the "picture theory" is not intended to be complete. The most important thing that I have omitted is her discussion of elementary propositions—a discussion which is essential to her claim that the *Tractatus* makes "extremely intelligible" the logical character of propositions.[18] Without going over all that matters in her account, I have tried to show the kind of change she hoped to make in how the *Tractatus* was understood. In the next three sections, I shall be following out a line of thought that starts from what Anscombe actually does in presenting the picture theory. That will put me in a position to discuss, in Section 6, how Anscombe's approach fits into the history laid out by Warren Goldfarb of anti-metaphysical readings of the *Tractatus*.

### 3. Anscombe and Philosophical Method

Here is something I said in Essay 1:

> Wittgenstein's view of philosophical method is touched on by Anscombe, but it is not one of her aims [in *An Introduction to Wittgenstein's Tractatus*] to make clear what he thought about method, or in what way the method of the *Tractatus* is connected with Wittgenstein's more specific philosophical ideas in the book, or what the importance to the reader should be of his apparently methodological remarks.

That now seems to me a stupid and misleading thing to have said. I was too impressed by a very partial truth, and failed altogether to see the kind of attention to methodology in Anscombe's own approach. What, after all, does she *do* in the book—in that part of it that I have been considering? She lays out, makes open to view, a way of using words, the picture-proposition use. She is not simply expounding a

18. See also Ricketts 1996, esp. pt. 4, on logical interconnectedness.

theory held by Wittgenstein; she is attempting to put before the reader—with the "extreme intelligibility" with which the account can (she thinks) be presented—what it is to say that something is so, on analogy with using a picture to say that *this* is so, a picture capable of being used also to say that *this* isn't so. I mentioned her having quoted Wittgenstein's criticism of any account of logic that makes it look like a queer sort of fact that every proposition is either true or false. She herself is presenting a use of language, the picture-proposition use, which will *not* make it look like a queer sort of fact that every proposition is either true or false, but will instead make obvious, open to view, the connection between picturing and the possibility of truth and falsehood, and which will also make it clear, open to view, how such picture-propositions can be combined to form others, which will also be true or false.

In Section 2, I quoted Anscombe's statement that, if "a" is a symbolic sign only in the context of a proposition, then the symbol "a" will be properly presented not by putting it down and saying that it is a symbol of such-and-such a kind, but by representing the whole class of the propositions in which it can occur. There are various ways in which we might represent such a class of propositions; but what such a presentation of the class will do is make evident what the entire class has in common. Wherever a class of propositions has a feature in common, it can be presented in some such way; and although the point as Anscombe makes it concerns sub-sentential expressions, it is also applicable to the entire class of picture-propositions. What they have in common can be laid out. They have in common *saying that something is so.* Anscombe's account of the picture theory, I am suggesting, can be taken to be a specification of a use of signs. Presenting the use of signs to *say that something is so* is a case, indeed a quite special case, of presenting a class of propositions with something in common, of presenting a class so that what the members have in common is open to view. In any such case, the propositions in question are all values of some variable; and making plain what the values of the variable are is the way in which the variable itself is given.

I am suggesting that Anscombe's presentation of the picture theory can be taken to be a case of making plain what the values of a variable are, where the values of the variable are propositions. This is a case of making plain a use of signs, and is not (in that respect) different in principle from the case Anscombe mentions, of presenting the symbol "a" by representing the whole class of propositions in which it can occur—the class of propositions which have in common the presence in them of that symbol. If (as the *Tractatus* has it) anything essential to their sense that propositions can have in common with one another is an expression or symbol, then picture-propositionhood is itself a symbol common to picture-propositions, a common formal feature (propositional form), and the class of propositions with that feature (all propositions) can be presented; and this is what Anscombe has done. In fact, Anscombe presents this class of propositions twice over in her book, as does Wittgenstein in the *Tractatus*. In the *Tractatus,* the presentation of picturing and of truth-functional construction leads up to *TLP* 4.5: Symbols constructed in the way described are sayings that *this is how things stand.* And Wittgenstein also claims that that class of symbols can be given by specifying a formal series, the members of which are the symbols in question. Anscombe's account of the picture theory in the first part of her book gives the class of symbols and what they have in common informally; her chapter on formal concepts and formal series indicates how the symbols can be given as members of a formal series. There are questions about whether Wittgenstein actually succeeds in giving such a variable, and whether, if he does, what its use would be (Sullivan 2004). I have discussed these questions elsewhere (Diamond 2012), and here I take for granted that the word "proposition" can be used in ordinary talk without philosophical confusion, and that, in such cases, it would (on Wittgenstein's view) go over in a conceptual notation to a variable.

In the rest of Section 3, I draw out two consequences of this way of looking at Anscombe's philosophical method in her account of the picture theory—as a matter of presenting a use of signs, the picture-proposition use. I shall also adduce another example of the method, before turning in Sections 4 and 5 to some questions about it.

1. *Connection between this method and the context principle.* The idea that any symbolic feature that signs can have in common, essential to their sense, can be given by representing the entire class of propositions that have the feature is based on the context principle. (See *TLP* 3.3–3.317; and *IWT,* 93.) So, if we view *giving the picture-proposition use of signs—the*

use of signs to say that something is so—as a case of presenting a class of propositions with something in common, and thereby presenting the common feature, we can see the philosophical method in use in such a laying out of a class of propositions as an application of the context principle.

2. *Connection with Wittgenstein's remarks on philosophy.* Wittgenstein says, at *TLP* 4.112, that philosophy is an activity that results in the clarification of propositions. One way in which philosophy can do this is by making plain what expressions have in common, and also by making plain their differences from each other. Later in the *Tractatus,* Wittgenstein suggests that the activity of philosophy is, properly speaking, appropriate only in response to philosophical confusion, when the activity involves showing the confused person that he hasn't given meaning to some signs in his propositions. Taking this suggestion seriously would mean that one might, for example, present the symbol "a" to a person who was using the sign "a" without a meaning in his propositions, to show that person the emptiness of his employment of "a". Presenting to that person the class of propositions of which the symbol "a" is the common feature might help him to see that he was not using that symbol at all, since his proposition was not in the class in question. This picture of philosophical activity doesn't have the implication that there would be no other sort of occasion for presenting the symbol "a" (for example, to someone learning a language), but the implication would be that such occasions were not cases of philosophical activity. If this is the way to understand what constitutes a philosophically appropriate sort of case of presenting the use of an expression, it would follow that Wittgenstein's own presentation of the picture-proposition use, and similarly Anscombe's presentation of the picture-proposition use, are appropriate if the activity helps to show that we are using some words with no meaning. The "picture theory" then can be taken to be a case (indeed a rather special case, but a case nevertheless) of presenting to people a class of propositions with a common feature, unclarity about which is reflected in their (or, rather, our) use of words with no determinate meaning.

I am suggesting that the *Tractatus* can be read as a manual for philosophical activity, for philosophical clarification. You clarify by making plain commonalities and differences. I shall not here go into details about making differences plain, but one way of doing so is by making commonalities plain: if you make plain, for example, what is shared by all uses of "is" as an expression for existence, and what is shared by all uses of "is" as the copula, you may thereby make plain the difference between the uses. A shareable feature of propositions is represented by a variable, which can be presented by specifying its values in such a way as to make plain what they all have in common. I am also suggesting, then, that the relevance of Anscombe's book to the question of the *Tractatus* understanding of philosophical method is in part that the book provides an example of philosophical activity in presenting the picture-proposition use of signs.

It will be helpful here to look briefly at Peter Sullivan's account of the picture theory (2001). His approach is in some respects unlike Anscombe's, but there are interesting similarities which I want to bring out. Like Anscombe, Sullivan takes questions about the relation between thought, the meaningfulness of propositions, and truth to be important in his account of the aims of the picture theory. He uses the metaphor of logical space to explain how a proposition's meaning something is independent of its truth: its "coordinates" determine a place in logical space. But his examination of the metaphor leads him to the question why we can count on it that *what we can think to be so* is genuinely a possibility for reality. Why should the possible combinations in which we use the names in our language enable us to represent genuine possibilities of existence for the objects named? It looks, Sullivan notes, as if it would be a kind of leap of faith, or superstition, to think that this was so. That is, it looks as if our capacity genuinely to represent possibilities for reality in our language depends on a kind of magical getting right of the logical character of the names, getting their possibilities to match those of the objects.[19] Sullivan responds by explaining the *Tractatus* conception of pictorial form, using the idea of a kind of transparency in representation. Transparency is exemplified by the use of color in a naturalistic painting, in contrast with the use of color to represent

19. Sullivan 2001, 100. Compare Goldfarb, unpublished, on the question what assurance we have that the sentences we put together express genuine possibilities.

which nation (say) has sovereignty over some part of the world, as with maps in which the British Empire was colored red. In the first or "transparent" case, color "represents nothing other than itself"; "a feature of reality has simply been taken up into the system of representation" (107–108). It is that notion of transparency, in its most abstract form, which is at the heart of the picture theory. In a transparent representation, the arrangement of the proxies for objects is the arrangement the objects are represented as having. A name, then, is a name—is a proxy for an object—in the context of a representation with such transparency. This account of the picture theory leads Sullivan to remark that Wittgenstein might well have taken the context principle to be his fundamental thought, since it underlies the idea of pictorial form as common to picture and what is pictured (109). Although Anscombe and Sullivan give somewhat different accounts of the picture theory, both of them take the context principle to be absolutely central to it.[20] What I want to emphasize is the role the context principle thus has, for both of them, in their account of how the picture theory makes propositionhood "extremely intelligible." The logical characteristics of propositions, their capacity for truth and falsehood, their relation to reality, can be made clear without appeal to substantial metaphysical facts, which would have to turn out right if our thought is genuinely to be in contact with reality. In somewhat different ways, Sullivan and Anscombe lay out the picture-proposition use of signs. We can take both of them to be engaged in laying out a use of signs in such a way as to achieve philosophical/logical clarity, and thereby to reshape our understanding of what we need in order to solve our philosophical problems. They each start with questions that may seem to demand answers in terms of

---

20. Anscombe (1989) gives an account of the central ideas of the *Tractatus* which makes rather more explicit (than does *IWT*) some points of resemblance between her reading and that of Sullivan. Some of the features of her reading had indeed changed, but the claim that she makes—that Wittgenstein had in the picture theory solved the ancient problem of the relation between thought and reality "by the thesis of the *identity* of the possibility of the structure of a proposition and the possibility of the structure of a fact"—does not seem to me to mark a change, except in explicitness, from her earlier account.

logical and metaphysical facts; but in response they provide what we might call a perspicuous presentation of a way of using words, and for both of them, the context principle is at the heart of this perspicuous presentation. Obviously, I am pushing a certain way of reading what they are up to. And I'll push it further: they are responding to the *Tractatus* by doing what the *Tractatus* does, and doing philosophy in the sense in which the activity of philosophy is described in the *Tractatus*.[21]

### 4. Problems about Philosophy

There is an important contrast between two ways of taking talk of presenting a use of signs. If I lay out a use of signs, I might claim that what I have laid out is the use of *propositions*. Or I can simply lay out a way of using signs, say, the picture-proposition use, and make no such claims. In the first case, it looks as if I will have achieved what I claim to have achieved if the use that I have laid out is indeed the use words have in *propositions*. It looks, that is, as if something out there, *propositions* and the use words have in them, makes my account right or wrong. But what items are we to take to be the ones the use of which makes my account right or wrong? If *proposition* is what Wittgenstein calls a formal concept, then what falls under it are the values of a variable, a variable which can be given by specifying its values. But that is what the account itself purports to do. Underlying the idea that the laying out of the use (say, the picture-proposition use) might be compared with the way we genuinely do use words in *propositions* there is an unclarity about what philosophy can accomplish. The problem can be put as a dilemma. If what I have done is simply lay out a use of signs, what is its interest? Unless I make a claim about what sort of symbol it is, the use of which I am laying out, how is what I have done relevant to any philosophical problem? But if I do make such a claim—for example, that what I have laid out is the *propositional* use of words—I use a term, in this case "propositional," to pick out, or try to pick out, a class of symbols, but

---

21. On whether one can throw away the context principle, and nevertheless continue to engage in the clarificatory activities to which one had originally been led by the principle, see Diamond 2014a.

how can I take myself to have done *that*? Do I take myself to have, independently of specifying a kind of use of symbols, some way of understanding "propositions"? But if my best specification of the symbols is just precisely what I have given, I don't have some other specification up my sleeve by which to give content to my claim that I have specified *that* class of symbols. Nor can the difficulty be avoided by saying that the symbols, the use of which I have laid out, are those we would call "propositions." For that certainly isn't correct, since all sorts of sentences and sentence-constructions, used in a variety of ways, may be called "propositions," and what I have attempted to lay out is a class which can be distinguished from the rest by the logical characteristics of its members, which of course are what I have attempted to lay out. The dilemma then, is this: How can a philosophical presentation of a use be illuminating, if it is not accompanied by such claims? But how can such claims be understood? In Sections 4 and 5 I shall be discussing this problem; Section 6 contains a brief discussion of a corresponding problem for Frege's treatment of *concepts*. In this second half of the essay, I shall be making problematic my own way of talking in the first half, in which I have unselfconsciously spoken of the *Tractatus* view of *propositions,* and of Anscombe as giving an account of the logical features of *propositions.*[22]

It has been suggested that we can view (at least some) *Tractatus* propositions as having a function akin to what Wittgenstein later spoke of as grammatical propositions, and that they are nonsense only in a technical sense. On this view, one use of "nonsense" is simply as a label for propositions that give the characteristics of senseful propositions.[23] It might seem that such an approach could resolve the difficulty I have sketched, by leaving room to say that the use that has been laid out is that of *propositions,* and that saying so is nonsense, but nonsense only in a technical sense. But such an approach cannot actually resolve the difficulty; for its source is a genuine unclarity about what one wants to

22. On the issues raised in this paragraph, see Floyd 2007, 184.

23. Moyal-Sharrock 2007. In discussing her view I look only at reasons why it does not provide a solution to the difficulty with which I am concerned. There are other problems with Moyal-Sharrock's account connected with the topics of Section 4, but I cannot examine these problems here.

say if one characterizes a use as that of *propositions.* In any case, what from the *Tractatus* point of view corresponds to what Wittgenstein later spoke of as making clear the grammar of some term is *specifying the values of a propositional variable.* That is how a way of using signs is presented. It is then about that kind of presentation that the question arises whether we can say that the use presented is that of *propositions.* The suggestion that *Tractatus* propositions themselves should be taken to have a function analogous to that of grammatical clarifications in Wittgenstein's later writings seems to depend on not noticing that there already is something else that genuinely does have a comparable function from the point of view of the *Tractatus:* the specification of the values of a propositional variable. In any case, the supposed parallel between *Tractatus* propositions and grammatical remarks would hardly resolve the difficulty, since questions parallel to those which arise about presentations of use in the *Tractatus* can arise about grammatical remarks. There is indeed a further objection to the idea that *Tractatus* propositions are nonsense only in a technical sense, and are actually in the same business as are Wittgenstein's grammatical remarks in the later writings. The objection is that saying that a remark is only technically nonsensical hardly makes clear how it is to be understood, if it is not clear that there is any way to arrive at what it means through familiarity with the meaning of its parts. If we are to understand it, surely we must have some way of understanding the words in it, in their context. But do we have any such way of understanding the words in the case of the sort of *Tractatus* remarks that are in question? A good example is *TLP* 5, "Propositions are truth-functions of elementary propositions." If that is only "technically" nonsense, the first word must mean something, in its occurrence *in that context.* It looks as if it is meant to be a word for the formal concept *proposition,* but it also appears not to have the use, in that context, of a word signifying that formal concept. (See *TLP* 4.1272: words that can signify a formal concept, when they are used unconfusedly to do so in ordinary language, will go over into variables if the proposition is put into conceptual notation. For more on both unconfused and confused uses of words like "proposition," "object," and so on, in ordinary language, see Section 5.) If the remark is supposed to give part of the grammar of "propositions," the problem is that it plainly isn't meant to give even part of the grammar of all that we might call "propositions," since obviously many sentence-constructions which might get called "propositions" don't have the use that Wittgenstein is aiming to present, and he certainly didn't think they did. If he meant to characterize any linguistic items, it was linguistic items used in a certain way. What way? Well, as truth-functions of elementary propositions. But it is not going to be a grammatical remark to point out that truth-functions of elementary propositions are truth-functions of elementary propositions. The trouble with the idea that the *Tractatus* remarks are merely "technical" non-sense is that, at the very least, when a sentence is called nonsensical, this should make one worry about whether one might be mistaking a conceptual blur for a meaningful remark. To characterize a sentence like "Propositions are truth-functions of elementary propositions" as "grammatical clarification" may make it appear that the only problem with such a remark is the label "nonsensical," which (as being merely a label) is not a genuine problem. Hence, the real problem what it means, where there is indeed such a problem, disappears from view.

Two remarks in the *Tractatus* can help us with the difficulty I have sketched: *TLP* 3.317 and 4.126. At 4.126, Wittgenstein says that the sign for the characteristics of a formal concept is a distinctive feature of all symbols whose meanings (*Bedeutungen*) fall under the concept. I take this remark to imply that the formal concept *proposition* has, falling under it, symbols with a characteristic kind of *Bedeutung*. In this context, the word "*Bedeutung*" is used so that, not just names, but also symbols other than names, can be spoken of as having *Bedeutung*.[24] At 3.317, Wittgenstein says that when one gives the values of a propositional variable, and in that way gives the variable, one gives a description of the propositions whose common characteristic the variable is, and such a stipulation of the values of the variable will be concerned only with symbols, not with their meaning (*Bedeutung*). I am interested in the implication of these remarks for the case in which we are laying out what I have called the picture-proposition use of signs. I take the remarks to imply that we should not add that signs with the picture-proposition use

24. On Wittgenstein's use of "*Bedeutung*," see Kremer 2002, 283–284.

that has been laid out are *propositions,* for that appears to be a specification of the *Bedeutung* of the symbols.

Even if what I have said is correct as a bit of *Tractatus* exposition, it hardly resolves the dilemma about what the philosophical relevance can be of laying out the use of an expression. If Wittgenstein indeed implies that we should not characterize the use which has been laid out as that of *propositions,* some alternative story has to be told of what the value can be of such an activity. But we should note anyway that the view which I have ascribed to Wittgenstein has an important consequence. If there is no saying that such-and-such use is that of *propositions,* then there is also no saying that, so far as you use words in some other way, what you are uttering is not *genuinely a proposition.* So far as laying out a use is nothing but laying out a use, it can exclude nothing. And yet, of course, the *Tractatus* is usually thought of as excluding something, or some things. How does it exclude anything, if it is in the business of laying out a use, and if laying out a use excludes no other use?

Suppose, then, that I lay out the picture-proposition use of words. For a sentence to have this use is for it to have "logical form," where that means that the connection of its elements sets forth that things are connected in the same way as the elements; hence the connection itself shows the possibility both of things being as they are represented as being and of their not being as they are represented as being. The two possibilities for the things represented are thus internal to this way of using signs. The laying out of such a use doesn't exclude any other use of signs, but it does help to bring out a certain kind of confusion, in which one is at one and the same time using, or apparently attempting to use, signs in such a way, and also not using them in that way. The laying out of the picture-proposition use of signs makes clear how the two possibilities—things being as represented, or their not being as represented—are part of that use of signs, part of the proposition's being a representation in logical space. If you want to give to words the use of expressing a *substantial necessary truth* (let us say), what you need to do is make clear what it is for what you say to be how things are, how they *necessarily* are. You need to do that without letting yourself slide into relying on what it is to use words in the picture-proposition way. *That* use does provide a way of saying how things are, but you are not going to be able to appeal to it. What is excluded by laying out the picture-proposition use is a kind of unconscious slipperiness, in which you take for granted the picture-proposition use and its abrogation at the same time, in which you take yourself to be saying something that really is *so,* necessarily so, and slippery-slide into a conception of a space in which this is said to be so, a space in which there is an opposite way things might be said to be, but they *cannot* be that way. This is a space in which there lie certain cases that are *excluded,* a space in which what is impossible can be thought of as impossible. But, as Wittgenstein points out at *TLP* 5.61, only confusion lies in this direction. It can unmisleadingly be said that the *Tractatus* excludes substantial necessary truth only if it doesn't mean that some way of using words is excluded. Again: no use of words is excluded by laying out a use of words; but laying out a use of words can be meant to sharpen our eyes to the fact that a supposed way of using words is not anything at all. Let me briefly specify more clearly what I mean and what I don't mean by saying that laying out a use of words does not exclude any way of using words. I don't mean that, once you have laid out the use of picture-propositions, you cannot *say* that certain other ways of using words are excluded because they are not genuine propositions, although indeed they are excluded. I mean simply that, if you lay out a use of words, you have not thereby excluded anything. If you lay out the picture-proposition use, put it clearly before us, the only thing that is thereby made clear about other uses is that they are not that use. If there is to be any "exclusion" going on, it is at any rate not done by laying out a use. It is important, in reading the *Tractatus,* whether one takes it to exclude certain uses of words as not genuine propositions. Such readings, among which would be Anscombe's, might be labeled "exclusionary." I shall have more to say about such readings in Sections 5 and 6, but shall first turn back to the problem of describing what the *Tractatus* does.

## 5. More about the Problem of Section 4

Before trying a different approach, I shall restate the problem. One can say that Wittgenstein in the *Tractatus* was giving *the essence of propositions,* but what he was giving the essence *of* can only be made clear by giving that essence itself—that is, by giving a variable the values of which have "propositional form" in common. To think that one might helpfully convey something by saying "What he is giving the essence of is *propositions*" is nonsense; not nonsense because it doesn't count as a proper proposition, but nonsense because of the incoherent demands that we make on what the word "proposition" can be thought to do. But that point leads right back to the question how it can be philosophically illuminating to lay out the picture-proposition use, if there is no claim that what is laid out is *propositionhood*. After discussing this problem again, I shall end this section by showing how philosophical activity, as I have been describing it, is connected with questions about nonsense. Although in this section I shall be wrestling with Anscombe, my aim is to think about what she herself does in presenting the picture theory. I see her philosophical *doing* as in tension with what she says about what the picture theory was supposed to accomplish, and in tension, in particular, with her exclusionary reading of the theory.

Consider again the philosophical activity of laying out the picture-proposition use. We are invited to have before our minds an ordinary picture: perhaps a realistic picture of a tree, perhaps a schematic diagram of people fencing. We are then led to *take* that picture differently. The ordinary picture that is used as an example will be one in which it is easy to see that the connection of the picture-elements that represent things is the connection that those things are represented as having. It will be easy to see that the possibility of such a connection of the things is there in the picture itself, in the connection of its picture-elements. By being led to note these features of the ordinary picture, we can be led to *take it in as a logical picture,* to take it in as having logico-pictorial form. I want to suggest that this transformation to *logical taking-in* is central in the way the ordinary picture is used in the philosophical activity. This transformation is not a matter of taking in the picture as having a property of which we had been unaware. When we come to see something as having a property of which we had been unaware, we can grasp that other things can also have the property; the grasp of such generality is part of what is involved in recognition of a property. But the generality involved in the transformation of our understanding of an ordinary picture is different. To take in an ordinary picture as a logical picture is to see something generalizable in it, but the generality of "logical picture-hood" is not that of a property. When Wittgenstein says, in the *Tractatus,* that every picture is also a logical picture (2.182), this doesn't mean that, for all $x$, if $x$ is a such-and-such, it is also a thus-and-so.

[Added in 2017: It might be useful here to add something about how Wittgenstein understood the contrast between two kinds of generality—the generality of a property and the generality that is expressed through a variable. This is at the heart of the contrast between what it is to fall under a concept, in the ordinary sense, and what it is to fall under a formal concept. Ideas about the apparent similarity and the difference are important for Wittgenstein not only in the *Tractatus,* but after his return to philosophy as well; and in 1933, in *The Blue Book,* there is a helpful account of what is at stake here. Wittgenstein notes that there are two different senses in which the word "kind" is used: "We talk of kinds of number, kinds of propositions, kinds of proofs; and, also, of kinds of apples, kinds of paper, etc." When "kind" is used as in the second sort of case, the kind is defined by properties; but in the first sort of case, the different kinds are "different grammatical structures" (Wittgenstein 1964, 19). In the *Tractatus* and in *The Blue Book,* Wittgenstein emphasizes that we are liable, in philosophy, to get these cases confused. We may find ourselves thinking of grammatical kinds as if they were kinds-defined-by-properties; we may think of *formal concepts* as a case of *concepts,* and of *falling under a formal concept* as a case of *falling under a concept.* "Something which different things share" covers logically distinct kinds of case; what we are speaking of, when we speak of something shared, should not be thought of as always a matter of *a property,* and as always reflected in functional generality. This point is central in the *Tractatus,* and is at the heart of Wittgenstein's understanding of the general form of a proposition (what it is that propositions share), which is given by a variable. Just as there are shareables that are properties of things and room also for logical shareables, which are not properties, there is room for generality which is not that of "for all $x$, if $x$ is a such-and-such, it is also a thus-and-so." Wittgenstein's conception can be seen in the passages which comment on *TLP* 3.3. The idea is that propositions have features that are essential to their expressive capacities—features that are shared by a class of propositions that can be taken to be the values of a "propositional variable." The generality of a variable is thus a matter of logically essential features of the class of propositions that are values of a propositional variable, the most important of which in the structure of the *Tractatus* is that specified at TLP 6. What this means is, for example, that the generality of propositionhood is not given in propositions that say "All propositions are thus-and-such," but is "presented" through the variable whose values are all propositions.[25]]

In being led to take in the ordinary picture as a logical picture, we see the logical kind in the particular case; we see in it a logical shareable. To take in the picture as having logico-pictorial form is to take it in as having a logical characteristic that can be present in cases which do not share the particular pictorial form of the simple example from which we started, but which share only the most general logical feature of the example—namely, that the way things are represented as being is the way the picture-elements are themselves connected, and the possibility of the things being that way is present in the connection of picture-elements. This identity may be present in only the most abstract sense, in contrast with the ordinary kinds of case used as examples, in which the identity of form is identity in the role of color or spatial relations in the representation and in what is represented. Consider now what Wittgenstein does in introducing the idea of propositions as themselves pictures. He invites the reader to consider a case in which *taking in* a proposition as a logical picture will be easy: the case in which the propositional sign is composed of spatial objects rather than written signs (*TLP* 3.1431). Just as we can be led to *take in* an ordinary picture as a logical picture, the core of which is its logico-pictorial form, we can be led to *take in* the spatial-object proposition as a logical picture, led (that is) to *take it in* as having logico-pictorial form. In

25. For more about the generality of the variable given by Wittgenstein at *TLP* 6, see Diamond 2012. See also Narboux 2014 for a discussion of the connection between the generality of a variable and what shows itself in our symbols. I am grateful to an anonymous reviewer for pointing out the need for some discussion of the contrast between the generality of a property or of a function and the generality of a variable.

both cases we are led to recognize a kind of generality (that of a logical kind) through a transformed taking-in of a simple case. In both cases, what we are supposedly able to see clearly after the philosophical activity is not something of which we can be thought to have been totally unaware beforehand. We could hardly operate with pictures without any awareness of their logical character; we could hardly say what was the case without being able to take in, to some degree, what Wittgenstein means when he says that in a proposition a situation is in a sense constructed by way of experiment. But the point is that such takings-in of the logical features of propositions and pictures are inchoate. What is essentially in common to all such cases is not seen.[26] The philosophical activity, focusing at first on simple cases, is meant to open our eyes to what I have called a logical shareable. It can be represented by means of a variable, the values of which are all the symbols that share the logical characteristic in question.

In Section 3, I suggested that Anscombe's account of the picture theory lays out a way of using language, the picture-proposition use, and that what she does can also be described as making plain the values of a variable. I've been arguing here that, when the picture-proposition use is laid out, the starting point is a transformation of our way of taking in ordinary pictures; we are led to take them in as logical pictures, led to see them as characterized by a logically shareable feature. That's the starting point, but it is also the point that lets us see the significance of laying out the picture-proposition use. When I take in the ordinary picture as a logical picture, I take it in as exemplifying a logical characteristic. I take in, in this case, *picturing.* The laying out of the picture-proposition use gives the reach (as it were), the logical generality, of the feature which I originally take in when I conceive an ordinary picture as having an identity of form with what it represents. The significance

---

26. See *TLP* 4.012, where Wittgenstein says that it is obvious that we take in a proposition of the form "aRb" as a picture. We take in the two names, and that they are combined in such-and-such relation in the proposition, and that is indeed why we take the proposition to signify the holding of a relation between a and b. But no more is implied; to see such a proposition as a picture in this minimal sense does not involve awareness of any logical characteristics shared with other symbols.

of "laying out the picture-proposition use" should be tied particularly to *TLP* 2.1, the first *Tractatus* remark about picturing. "We make to ourselves pictures of facts." We are meant to take in what we thus do in simple cases; we are meant ultimately to see *that* in its full generality. Suppose I come to see it so: I take that feature, in its logical generality, to reach through my thought, through my language, through my world. What I have called "laying out the use of picture-propositions" is meant to connect with my self-understanding; it is meant to let me see an essence in my own thought, what it has "within" it, "what we see when we look *into* the thing" (*Philosophical Investigations* §92). It is this reconception of the ordinary, as having within it something hidden, special, and with a unique total generality, that is indeed the target of Wittgenstein's later thinking.[27] In one of the early drafts of the *Investigations,* Wittgenstein spoke of how we take a "clearly intuitive" case, and treat it as an exemplar of *all* cases; we take in a single proposition as a picture, and think that we have thereby grasped an all-comprehending essence, lying *beneath* the surface.[28]

All kinds of expressions are called propositions in ordinary talk; and Wittgenstein's remarks about propositions being pictures plainly don't imply that mathematical propositions, or logical propositions (and so on) are pictures. But note now that it cannot be said that the reason his remarks don't apply to such cases is that he is making clear what is a

27. Marie McGinn (1999) also emphasizes the role of a reconception of the ordinary in Wittgenstein's method. Her account differs from mine in drawing a distinction between elucidations which make possible the disappearance of philosophical problems through the kind of reconception of the ordinary to which they lead us and remarks which reflect Wittgenstein's theoretical preconceptions, including centrally the idea of logical form as expressed in a variable. I think that Wittgenstein's understanding of logical generality (the generality of a variable) is not separable from the kind of reconception of the ordinary at which he aimed in the *Tractatus* and which he took to be capable of resolving philosophical problems, but I cannot here go into my reasons for disagreeing with McGinn.

28. Wittgenstein 2000, Ts220 §93 / Ms142 §§105–106; cf. also Wittgenstein 1967, §444. Wittgenstein also in these remarks says that it is a characteristic of the sort of theory that he accepted that it doesn't present itself as a theory; one takes oneself merely to have seen what is there *in* the clear intuitive case.

*genuine proposition,* as opposed to those other things. What constantly guides our thought here, and constantly leads us in a wrong direction, is the idea that we have a concept of *propositions* and Wittgenstein is clarifying it, or trying to show what is involved in it. We constantly think in terms of a *concept* here, and what *genuinely falls under it;* but what we have to do with is a *formal concept*—that is to say, *not* a concept. As long as we think of the *Tractatus* as doing something or other with *the concept of a proposition,* we set ourselves up to miss what he is doing. An essential contrast for the book is that between a property and a logical shareable; and what lacks a particular logical shareable is not thereby shown in any way to be "rejected" or "excluded."

That last point is important when we think about Wittgenstein's later criticism of the *Tractatus.* For it is sometimes said, as Anscombe herself says, that what was wrong with the picture theory is that "it is correct only within a restricted area"; the idea is that there are various sorts of expressions that are genuine propositions, but that are excluded from the realm of propositions because they are not in the "restricted area" to which the picture theory applies. But this criticism depends upon taking the picture theory to be at one and the same time a presentation of a logical shareable (which it is) and a general account of propositionhood or sense (understood in some other way). For the idea is of a "larger area," including both the "restricted area" and what has been left out of it; and if the "restricted area" is that of picture-propositions— that is, the region characterized by the logical shareable—the larger area must be understood differently. Wittgenstein's own criticism is quite different; it is that the supposed "logical shareable" was actually part of the form of description of a multitude of very different cases; it was read into them, not discovered in them. And he rejected also the idea that a logical kind was presented by a variable, the values of which shared a logical characteristic.

It might be objected to my claim that laying out a use doesn't exclude anything that it misses the point, since the *Tractatus* is engaged, not just in laying out the picture-proposition use, but in characterizing all other kinds of cases of proposition-like constructions, apart from tautologies and contradictions, as nonsensical. What is this if not some kind of exclusion? And, indeed, doesn't the image that I used in explaining

Wittgenstein's aim—that the reader should come to think of logico-pictorial form as reaching, in its generality, right through "my thought, my language, my world"—suggest that everything that lacks logico-pictorial form is pushed out into outer darkness? Consider here Anscombe's way of thinking, as it emerges at the end of chapter 4 of *IWT* and the beginning of chapter 5. She speaks of how, in the light of the picture theory, Wittgenstein had the task of showing how propositions which don't appear to fit in with the picture theory do in fact fit in with it, in virtue of being bipolar propositions or logical truths of a sort allowed for by the theory, while the residue that do not fit in would count in one way or another as nonsensical (78–79). But I think we should follow Michael Kremer (2002) in reading the *Tractatus* to allow for various kinds of sentences which, like tautologies and contradictions, guide us in inferring nonlogical propositions from nonlogical propositions. These auxiliaries to inference are without sense, but not nonsensical; far from it. They have an important kind of use, but it is not the use of saying how things are. I believe that there are quite a number of different types of auxiliaries to ordinary talk (*Behelfe der Darstellung*) recognized in the *Tractatus,* and there is no reason to think that other sorts of auxiliaries would not also be capable of "fitting in" to the overall picture. Thus, for example, the sentence "*Aus, bei, mit, nach, seit, von* and *zu* take the dative," if it is taken to express a rule (rather than a generalization about German-speakers) can be regarded as an auxiliary to description, in the sense that it guides the construction of propositions. Indeed, one could read *TLP* 3.343, which says that definitions are rules for translating from one language into another, as introducing a quite broad category of rules of translation, which would include the rule about German prepositions. It would, I think, be wrong to take the *Tractatus* to imply that such rules are nonsensical. Kremer discusses in detail the *Tractatus* account of identities and of mathematical equations. He argues that such expressions fit in to the overall *Tractatus* view in roughly the same kind of way as do tautologies and contradictions, and should be taken to be senseless, rather than nonsensical.[29]

---

29. See *TLP* 5.5303, where Wittgenstein contrasts two sorts of cases of sentences that are not senseful, one sort being nonsense and the other "saying nothing," i.e.,

Other cases, discussed in the *Tractatus,* of auxiliaries to description include the presentation of an expression by means of a variable whose values are the propositions containing the expression, and again also the stipulation of the values of a variable. Besides those cases, there are the laws of mechanics, which are not logical pictures of the world, but give forms in which descriptions can be cast.[30] Wittgenstein's later discussions of "hypotheses" suggest a similar sort of use of sentences which may look like descriptions but which function as a kind of auxiliary to description. My point here, in opposition to Anscombe, is only that there is much more room in the *Tractatus* for miscellaneous uses of language than we might think. It follows that, when a kind of sentence can be seen not to have the use of a picture-proposition, nor to be tautologous or contradictory, it is not thereby cast into outer darkness. It is indeed excluded from the realm of picture-propositions, of sentences that are used as such sentences are, sentences that represent a situation in logical space. But the question what use it has, if any, is open.[31]

Anscombe's discussions of what is allegedly excluded by the *Tractatus* account of propositions are somewhat puzzling, in any case. For consider what she says about "Red is a color" (82). She says that, for such a case as this, the point is easily made that the sentence cannot express anything that might be false, since there are not two possibilities: that red is and that it isn't a color, of which the first happens to be the case. Here she sees the sentence as being excluded from sensefulness because it is not bipolar; but she herself has given, as Wittgenstein's view, that we present a symbol, not by putting it down and saying that it is a symbol

---

being senseless. Here he apparently allows for sentences that do not have sense but are not nonsense, though not tautologies or contradictions. The passage seems inconsistent with readings that ascribe to Wittgenstein the view that the only sorts of sentences that lack sense but are not nonsensical are tautologies and contradictions. See Kremer 2002 for further discussion of *TLP* 5.5303.

30. Cf. Griffin 1964, chap. 8, §5, esp. 102–103.

31. The relevance of Kremer 2002 and Griffin 1964 to Anscombe's reading of the *Tractatus* is discussed in Essay 4, and the issues are discussed in more general terms, in relation also to White 2006, in Essay 5.

of such-and-such a kind, but by representing the class of propositions in which that symbol occurs. What, then, if we take the symbol "red" that is used in color-attributions, and think of presenting it through the class of propositions in which it occurs as that symbol? The symbol is a mark of a form and content that propositions can have in common, but "Red is a color" isn't one of the propositions with that shareable form and content. It has only the sign in common with those propositions, and the practice of using "red" as a color-word in those propositions (that is, in describing things) doesn't settle what meaning, if any, it has in "Red is a color" (in which nothing is being described as red).[32] There is a further question about the formal concept *color.* Anscombe's view appears to be that the reason why formal concepts can't be presented by a function is that the attempt to do so (as in the attempt to treat being a color as a property of *red*) leads us to construct propositions that cannot express anything that might be false. But that is not the problem. That is, the problem isn't that falling under a formal concept is a matter of having a property that *can't be said* to hold of the things in question. It is rather that it honestly and truly isn't a matter of a property *at all,* but is seen in a shared feature of a class of senseful propositions. A logical kind isn't a kind that things necessarily belong to; it's not a kind that you can't say things fall into; its difference from nonlogical *kinds*—kinds as we usually think of them—goes deeper than that. The word "color," in Anscombe's example, does not in that context have the kind of use that it has when it signifies a formal concept. It is not clear what other meaning, if any, it has in that context. (An example of a sentence in

---

32. The sign "Red" in any case has a variety of uses: it is a nickname, and people also may say that Red is what it is worse to be than to be dead, or that Red is what Virginia ceased to be in 2008. One might try to rule out such uses of "Red" by saying "The *color* Red is a color," but that spoils the example by making the sentence appear to be totally empty. The example is meant to be a sentence that appears not to be empty, but that also appears not to be capable of being false. See also Wittgenstein (1956, I, §105) on the use of color-words as names of colors in contexts like "Black is darker than white." Although Wittgenstein does not there use the contrast between sign and symbol, the point he makes is that there is a question what the use, if any, is of "Black is darker than white," since the words "Black," "white," and "darker than" are plainly not being used as they are in ordinary useful statements.

which "color" is in use to signify a formal concept is "There is a color which occurs in both of these pictures." I discuss below how one can recognize when a word that can be used to signify a formal concept is actually doing so.) Anscombe discussed "Red is a color" to illustrate the kind of sentence that is excluded from sensefulness on the *Tractatus* view. She wanted to show that the *Tractatus* account covers only some of the territory of what we take ourselves to be able to say; but the *Tractatus* does not imply that "Red is a color" is not capable of being false, and that it is, for that reason, excluded from sense. An argument based on the *Tractatus* would investigate what use, if any, had been given to the words in "Red is a color" which were taken over from a context in which they had a different sort of use.[33]

Most of Wittgenstein's propositions in the *Tractatus* use words like "object" and "proposition" which have an unproblematic use in everyday talk to signify formal concepts. In conceptual notation, he says, the use of these terms would go over to variables. But in the *Tractatus*, these words are not used as they are in ordinary talk, and the *Tractatus* remarks would not go over in a conceptual notation to formulae with variables. The contrast is clear in Wittgenstein's own pair of examples (*TLP* 4.1272): "There are two objects which . . ." and "There are objects." The trouble with the latter proposition is not that it is not capable of being false; it is that "objects," in that context, seems not to have any meaning. In "There are objects," "objects" hasn't got the use it has in "There are two objects which . . ," which goes over, in conceptual notation, to a formula with quantifiers and variables. The sentence "There are objects" appears to give to "objects" a logical role of the same sort as that of "books" in "There are books." If "objects" in "There are objects" were given an appropriate sort of meaning, as a word for a kind of thing, the sentence would be meaningful. The fact that in other contexts the

---

33. For more about "Red is a color" and my disagreement with Anscombe about this case, see the Introduction to Part I of this volume. Anscombe has another example, "'Someone' is not the name of someone" (85), which I discuss in Essay 2. I consider the *Tractatus* treatment of necessary truths in Diamond 2011. See also Essays 4, 5 and 6, which discuss from a number of different angles Wittgenstein and Anscombe on what can only be true.

word signifies a formal concept doesn't carry over to its use in "There are objects," which has only the sign, not the symbol, in common with such other sentential contexts. The difficulty is, of course, that we don't want to give the word "objects" some other meaning; we want it to carry with it the role it has in other contexts in which it signifies a formal concept, and to mean, in "There are objects," the logical kind *objects*. And similarly with *Tractatus* remarks containing the word "propositions." We read the word as meaning *propositions,* regardless of the fact that the word does not there have the kind of use it has when it signifies a formal concept. We don't read those remarks with any doubt or suspicion about what the word means *in them*. But the *Tractatus* view is that the word "propositions" occurs with the meaning that we unthinkingly suppose it to have in those remarks when it is used in a certain way: when it occurs in a sentence which would go over in conceptual notation to a formula containing the variable given in *TLP* 6, "the general form of proposition." I think it can be shown, for example, that "Every proposition uttered by Cheney is false" is, on the *Tractatus* view, translatable into a sentence with that variable.[34] Because it has that use, the word "proposition" in that sentence signifies a formal concept, just as, in "There are two objects which . . . ," the word "object" is used so that it signifies a formal concept. But the *Tractatus* remarks containing the word "proposition" do not give the word the kind of use it has when it signifies a formal concept. It is used, one might say, as a word pretending to be a formal concept word, and it is not given any other determinate use.

[Added in 2017: I have been relying on *TLP* 4.1272, not one of Wittgenstein's most lucid passages. It has, I think, been badly misunderstood. I am adding here a summary of what I take to be its implications. There are words which, in some contexts in ordinary language, are used unproblematically to signify one or another formal concept. There are three different ways in which these words may occur within ordinary language, which should be carefully distinguished. First, any of

---

34. The sentence does not involve quantifying over propositions, although it looks as if it would do so. It involves the use of operations to construct a new proposition. See Diamond 2012.

these words—for example, "number"—can occur in a context in which it does not signify a formal concept, and is not being used confusedly, but has some quite different sort of use. Thus, "In the April number of *English Life*, there is an article by Lady Grey of Fallodon" contains a use of the word "number," and in this use it does not signify the formal concept *number*. The sentence is perfectly respectable and not nonsense. The word "thing" can be used to signify at least two different formal concepts, but in "I have a thing about spiders," it is used to mean some kind of psychological state. The sentence is not made to be nonsense by the occurrence in it of a word that can signify a formal concept in other contexts. "*Satz*," "proposition," and "sentence" can be used to signify this or that class of written or spoken signs, which are not taken to have anything logically in common—as, for example, in considering typographical uses of upper and lower case. The second sort of case we need to distinguish is that in which a word that can signify a formal concept in ordinary language is unconfusedly used to do so. In "There are two things I want to tell you," the word "thing" is used in a way that would go over in conceptual notation to the variable specified in *TLP* 6. "There are two things in the fridge that have gone way beyond their expiry date" contains a use of "thing" to signify a formal concept, but in this case the translation into conceptual notation would use "$(\exists x,y)$. . . ." The two sentences in ordinary language are not nonsensical. Wittgenstein did not hold that the *only* way to signify a formal concept and not talk nonsense involves the use of the appropriate variable in conceptual notation. What he held is that when words that can be used in ordinary language to signify formal concepts are used unconfusedly to do so, the propositions in question will be translatable into propositions in conceptual notation in which what is doing the work of expressing the formal concept is a variable of the appropriate sort. What comes out in this way is that the word in ordinary language which can be said to "signify a formal concept" is *in that context working as a variable*. The *eigentliche Zeichen* for this or that formal concept is the appropriate variable, but this does not mean that the variable has to appear explicitly as a variable and not as a word or expression of ordinary language that is *doing the work of the appropriate variable in the particular context*. Wittgenstein's ideas about what the *eigentliche Zeichen* for something is can be understood in the light of *TLP* 3.34–3.3411, where we have the idea that the *eigentliche Name* for an object is whatever is common to all the ways in which it can be symbolized. This point applies to ways of signifying a formal concept.[35] The unconfused use of an ordinary-language word that in context signifies a formal concept is just as good as the expression in conceptual notation, because their essential features are the same, the *eigentliche Zeichen* is the same. The conceptual notation is not required in order to signify a formal concept. It doesn't *fix* anything that wasn't already logically in order in the ordinary language formulation. It simply makes perspicuous the kind of role that the ordinary language word has when it is used unconfusedly to signify a formal concept. This is a general point about paraphrasal or translation into conceptual notation. If a version of a proposition done over into conceptual notation makes sense, so does the ordinary language version; they are simply alternative modes of writing, one of which is more perspicuous and avoids terms with more than one kind of use. (The contrast that comes up in *TLP* 4.1272 between "There are two objects which . . . ," and "There are 100 objects" is thus important. Only the latter is held by Wittgenstein to be nonsensical. "There are 100 objects which . . ." would be fine; and it would go over into conceptual notation in the same way as "There are two objects which . . ." except that the quantifier-variable notation would use more variables. "There are 100 objects which . . ." is not an attempt to say something that can

35. Unfortunately, in the English translations of the *Tractatus* the connection of ideas between the remark about the *eigentliche Name* for an object and the remark about the *eigentliche Zeichen* for a formal concept is made harder to see by the fact that neither of the English translations uses the same word in the two contexts in translating the two occurrences of "*eigentliche.*" (The same is true of the Granger translation into French.) The notion of the *eigentliche Zeichen*, in 4.1272, needs to be seen with the idea of *all signs capable of serving a particular purpose* and what they therefore have in common, enabling them to do so. A better translation of 4.1272 would use "real sign," since that makes clearer the idea of what is really doing the sign's essential work when it is serving that purpose. That translation would bring out the connection with the contrast *essential/accidental* at 3.34. Failure to see the relevance of what Wittgenstein had said about the *eigentliche Name* underlies some misunderstandings of 4.1272.

properly be said only in conceptual notation, any more than is "There are two objects which. . . .") The third sort of case we need to consider is that in which a word that can be used unconfusedly in ordinary language to signify a formal concept is used confusedly. There will be nothing that is translating what is said into conceptual notation in such a way that the word in question goes over to the appropriate sort of variable. A good way to bring out what is involved here is to consider the translation into conceptual notation of an unconfused proposition like "There is some proposition believed by A and B." Looking at the translation in the unconfused case will make clear what there is *no such thing as doing* in the confused cases. In this case, you can start by considering an operation that can be carried out on any number of propositions. Call it the "at-least-one-of-the-base-propositions-is-believed-by-both-A-and-B operation," and abbreviate it as "C". If C is carried out on one proposition, *p*, as its base, the result is "A believes that p and B believes that p." If C is carried out on *p* and *q*, the result is "(A believes that p and B believes that p) or (A believes that q and B believes that q)"; and so on. If C is carried out on all propositions, the result is a proposition that says that there is some proposition believed by A and B; and the variable that is given in proposition 6 of the *Tractatus* is used in specifying the bases for the operation. They are not enumerated, as they can be in the cases I gave in explaining the operation. What comes out when we consider "There is some proposition that is believed by A and B," and how the variable given at *TLP* 6 figures in that proposition, is that there is no quantifying over *propositions*; rather, the variable the values of which are *all propositions* gives the bases of an operation. You have got a proposition that unconfusedly uses the word "proposition" to signify a formal concept, if the proposition goes over into conceptual notation in a way that uses the variable given at *TLP* 6 to give the bases of an operation. In contrast, if you want to make some kind of generalization about propositions, and you have a proposition that goes (for example) "Propositions are truth-functions of elementary propositions," the *structure* of that sentence goes with saying something about whatever falls under the concept meant by the first word, as in "Mammals are descendants of reptiles," which says something about whatever falls under the concept of a mammal; but if you want to use "propositions" so that it signifies a formal concept, you have to be using the word "propositions" in such a way that your sentence will go over, in conceptual notation, to a formulation that uses the general form of proposition to give the bases for some operation. But this isn't what you have with "Propositions are truth-functions of elementary propositions." Wanting to give what propositions have in common, you have put together a sentence-construction of a sort that enables you to say something about whatever falls under the subject concept. But that sort of construction does not in this case go over into conceptual notation in a way that uses the general form of proposition to give the bases of an operation. (There are sentence-constructions that are only superficially of the form exemplified by "Mammals are descendants of reptiles" and that have some quite different logical form, but that is not what is at stake with "Propositions are truth-functions of elementary propositions.") Your word "propositions" in "Propositions are truth-functions of elementary propositions" does not use the first word so that it signifies the formal concept which *is* signified by "proposition" in "There is some proposition believed by both A and B." This is a matter of there not being anything that would be a translation of "Propositions are truth-functions of elementary propositions" in which you are using the general form of proposition to give the bases of some operation used to construct propositions. If you call the word "propositions," in the context of "Propositions are truth-functions of elementary propositions," a "formal concept word," all that is meant by its being a formal concept word is that in other sorts of context, the *sign* can be so used that it does signify a formal concept. The basic idea here is that *no* word that has thus-and-such signification in some contexts simply carries that signification with it into other contexts. When it is put into a context in which it *does not have* the use that it has elsewhere, it may, *there,* be empty, and the sentence itself be nonsense, in that it contains a word with no meaning in that context. The account I've given of how to recognize whether a word that can be used to signify the formal concept *proposition* is being used unconfusedly to do so can be applied to the case of other formal concepts. The basic idea is to work with an unconfused case to see what sort of going-over to a variable is involved in that kind of case. If you have a philosophical proposition in which there is a word that can be used to signify a formal concept, but there is no translation that you would accept of the philosophical proposition in which that variable plays a corresponding role, what has come out is that the word does not in that context signify the formal concept, and may not mean anything there. The method I have described is that of using translation into conceptual notation as a tool for learning how to recognize the presence in a proposition of the *eigentliche Zeichen* for the formal concept in question, and hence also of learning how to recognize its absence. The absence of the *eigentliche Zeichen* for the formal concept *proposition* in "Propositions are truth-functions of elementary propositions" brings out that the first word there does not signify the formal concept *proposition*. There is no translation of that proposition into conceptual notation in which there would appear the *eigentliche Zeichen* for the formal concept *proposition*.

In the original version of this essay and elsewhere, I have used the expression "formal concept word" for words like "proposition," "number," "object," and so on, but I think the expression can lead to misunderstanding, since what it comes to is nothing more than "word that in some contexts can be used to signify a formal concept." If one thinks of *formal concept words* as words "for" formal concepts, it is a very short step to thinking that, since *proposition* is a formal concept, the first word of "Propositions are truth-functions of elementary propositions" is a formal concept word; and this understanding then leads to the idea that that proposition is *about propositions in the logical sense* and is an attempt to say something about them that supposedly then cannot be said. If one substitutes for "formal concept word" the expression "word that in some contexts signifies a formal concept," one has much more obviously left it open what work, if any, is being done by the first word of "Propositions are truth-functions of elementary propositions." In their occurrences in philosophical contexts, words that may in some contexts signify formal concepts can be taken to call for interrogation: What is it that one wants this word to do? Does one want it to work as a term that signifies a formal concept (for which the *eigentliche Zeichen* is the appropriate variable) *or* as a word for a concept that, in the particular context, operates like such general terms as "mammal," or is one somehow confusedly trying to have it both ways?

Am I saying that "propositions" doesn't mean propositions? That sounds crazy! The point is rather that "propositions" can be used in various sorts of ways: in some contexts it will signify a formal concept, in some contexts it may signify a concept proper, and in some contexts it may reflect nothing more than a blur of different significations, just as a use of the word "concept" can, as Frege suggests, reflect a confused mishmash of the logical and the psychological (1984b, 182). The word "proposition," in its occurrence in what appears to be a straightforward sentence about propositions, may have no meaning there. The importance of getting straight what Wittgenstein thought about what was and what wasn't an expression for the formal concept *proposition* is in part that this is one of the central points about which he later changed his mind. If you don't see the sharp distinction Wittgenstein wanted to make between the formal concept and concepts proper, and thus also between the formal concept *proposition* and cases like the typographic concept of a sentence (which is not a formal concept), you won't then be able to see the importance for him, later on, of the notion of family resemblance—in the transformation of his ideas about what is essential and what is accidental, and about how what is essential shows itself.[36]]

I have been arguing that *Tractatus* remarks containing the word "proposition" do not in general convey a content of a special sort which cannot be put into senseful language; they contain words with no meaning and are nonsense. They have a function within the context of the book, a book meant not only to present a use but to lead its readers to *take* their own thought and language to have in it the logical shareable that the book presents. Their function within the context of the book is described by the metaphor of the ladder that is thrown away. They are helps on the way to recognition of the contrast between logical shareables and kinds of things, a contrast the recognition of which undoes the impression they initially make of conveying a content. The recognition of that contrast is not a matter of taking *being a proposition* to be something we can't speak of; it is a matter of getting the point of

36. For more on the issues in this paragraph and the last, see the Introduction to Part II and Essay 4.

philosophy as a kind of practice, in which logical shareables are displayed, as in the case of the laying out of the picture-proposition use of words.[37]

A full discussion of exclusionary readings of the *Tractatus* would have to look at Wittgenstein's treatment of the limits of language. Exclusionary readings take Wittgenstein's talk of limits to involve a conception of what lies outside, what cannot be said, and what sorts of attempted sayings fail because they are attempts to speak of what lies outside. Such readings involve what Peter Sullivan has called a *contrastive* understanding of the notion of a limit. There are then questions how far, and in what ways, such an understanding might be taken to be undercut by the *Tractatus*. Peter Sullivan (2011), A. W. Moore (2007), Juliet Floyd (2007), and I (Diamond 2011) have discussed these questions, but to have gone into them here would have doubled the length of this essay.

## 6. Conclusions

The technique, of sharpening the reader's eyes to a logical shareable through attention to linguistic patterns and their ties to inference, is Fregean, as is the connection between the recognition of a logical shareable and the use of the context principle. Frege also (in "On Concept and Object") confronts the problem that I have been discussing. He presents a logical shareable, call it "Fregean concepthood," and makes it clear that he is not attempting to capture what is usually meant by the term "concept," which, as he notes, is used in various ways (1984b, 182). He is not suggesting, that is, that all and only Fregean concepts are *concepts*. At the end of his reply to Benno Kerry, he says that Kerry can use the words "concept" and "object" however he likes, but Frege, too, has a right to use "concept" and "object" in the way he has laid out (193). But then the question arises, if what he has laid out is his way of using the terms, and if he is not giving an account of *concepthood*, what is the significance of what he has done? We have, he thinks, only a "vague notion"

37. See note 43 below on my use of the contrasting pair of predicates "logical shareable" and "property."

of what is involved in our own thinking and inferring (1979c, 253). We can take his logical distinctions up into our understanding, and thereby bring the logical characteristics of our thinking into focus, at the same time separating off what is inessential, and what is the result of psychologistic accretions.

Wittgenstein takes over from Frege, or simply gets on his own, the connection between the idea of a logical shareable and the context principle.[38] He takes over from Frege, or simply gets on his own, the idea that laying out features of our use of words can make "extremely intelligible" what we might otherwise have taken to be a kind of ultimate logical fact, as, for example, that every proposition has exactly one negation. There is already in Frege a conception of a technique by which thought itself can be clarified, the technique of making plain logical having-in-common, a technique we can see already in the *Begriffsschrift,* in the suggestion that we think of "subtracting" from a proposition a part or parts that can be thought to vary, leaving a part that is *logically in common* with other propositions. Wittgenstein's distinction between signs and symbols (where symbols are logical shareables) is an application of the context principle, and a corresponding distinction is clearly at work in Frege, in "On Concept and Object" and elsewhere. But Wittgenstein gives the sign / symbol distinction a particular twist, by applying it to the question what it is for us to be using a word for a logical kind. In Section 5, I argued that what is shared by words used for a logical kind, when they are used for a logical kind, is clear if the propositions in which they occur are thought of as they would appear in a conceptual notation, in which sameness of sign invariably does indicate sameness of symbol, unlike the situation in ordinary language. In such a notation, words that in ordinary language are genuinely in use as words for a logical kind go over to an appropriate variable. In this notational point there is reflected the profound difference between words for logical kinds and words for ordinary kinds. Now put together the Fregean point and the Wittgenstein

38. See Diamond 2014a for an account of the possible role of Russell's treatment of propositional functions in the development of Wittgenstein's contextualism.

twist.[39] We can clarify logical features of our thought by making plain logical having-in-common, as in laying out the picture-proposition use of words. If, on the other hand, we think of ourselves as trying to give a theory of *propositionhood* (say), we can come to see that, in doing so, we will use the word "proposition," which we want to use as a word for a logical kind, in a way which defeats our purpose. When theorizing about propositionhood, we use the word "proposition" so that it is not the equivalent of a variable, but a word with the grammar of a word for an ordinary kind. Because we want to investigate a logical kind, we are not going to give "proposition," in these investigations, a use as a word for something else; but since it is (in the context of these investigations) not a word for a logical kind, and not a word for anything else, what we say is nonsense. It is noteworthy that in criticizing Wittgenstein's account of language, we may find ourselves doing exactly the same thing, and thereby missing a fundamental point of the book. We think of the *Tractatus* as an attempt to convey that thus-and-such is *what propositions are,* but the point is rather this: If you talk about *propositions* as you want to, you will not be saying anything at all. You misunderstand what you are after: you want to speak of a logical kind, and you also want to theorize about it in the language of ordinary kinds; and these two aims together will lead you to talk *real rubbish.*[40] The same point can be made about other topics of philosophical investigation. Philosophical investigation is self-defeating when it aims at an understanding of logical kinds, but investigates them in language which is not logical-kind language. You can show understanding of the aim of the book in turning from philosophical theorizing to a form of philosophical activity that can illuminate logical shareables by laying out the ways in which we use language. This is a very different kind of procedure, as

---

39. The "Wittgensteinian twist" is still very Fregean. See Ricketts 2010, pt. 5, esp. the discussion of the "self-stultifying" character of the attempt to use the predicates "concept" and "object" to make clear the distinction between concepts and objects.

40. The expression "real rubbish" comes from Anscombe's discussion (1989, 10–11) of the contrast between ethical nonsense of the sort for which Wittgenstein had great respect and ethical nonsense which he would have liked to see disappear. But I am not using the term in exactly the way she does.

comes out especially in the fact that laying out a use does not exclude anything, but can lead us to a different way of conceiving what had appeared problematic. Juliet Floyd (2007, pt. 2) makes a related point about Wittgenstein's understanding of how philosophical problems are posed. Philosophical problems are those "whose very formulation contains terms that require interrogation, or reconception, in order to be solved" (189–190), and she connects Wittgenstein's conception in the *Tractatus* of philosophical problems with his lifelong interest in the contrast between searching when you have a framework for finding an answer and searching when you do not know in advance what will count as a solution.[41]

Philosophical activity, as Wittgenstein understands it, reshapes desire. We start off wanting to know *the essence of propositions,* or how *thought* is connected with *reality.* So long as we use the language in which the problems present themselves, we will get nowhere; the questions are not the sorts of questions we take them for. The activity of presenting a logical shareable, of putting it into a sharp focus, can put the logic of our thinking before us, and we can recognize in what we thus come to see (although it wasn't the sort of answer we had been in search of) what we had wanted. If we let the philosophical activity shape our self-understanding in this way, we may give the logical shareable a label. What I have in mind is illustrated by labeling Fregean concepts "concepts" and by labeling picture-propositions "propositions." The word "proposition" can be taken over from its use in our attempts to discover *what propositions are.* It can be turned into a label for the picture-proposition use, where the choice of such a label reflects seeing our own thought through the logical-organizing lens of the logical shareable, and seeing the importance (the reach through our thought) of that logical shareable. This (I'm suggesting) is not a matter of our taking ourselves to have discovered what propositions are; and speaking of Fregean concepts as concepts isn't taking ourselves to have discovered what concepts are; we are sharpening our focus on a logical form, and seeing it in, or seeing it "into," our thought. The label itself is no more than a reminder; it points us toward a previous clarification of a logical shareable. Wittgenstein

41. See also Floyd 1995 and 2000.

can say, "Here is the general form of the proposition," but this is not the discovery of *what propositions are,* and a fortiori not the discovery of *what is excluded from being a proposition.* Sentences which are not picture-propositions are not picture-propositions. That's what they aren't. It won't be all that they aren't (they may also not be heroic couplets, quotations from Hume, or whatever), but there's nothing that, in not being picture-propositions, they thereby aren't. I want to pick up a Fregean way of putting these issues from Thomas Ricketts. Frege's elucidations make use of "concept" and "object" as a contrasting pair of predicates. Once his intended audience has mastered his conceptual notation, the confusion latent in the elucidations becomes manifest, as they try to paraphrase the remarks into the notation; but they find no thought to which "No object is a concept" (for example) corresponds. A master of the notation is free to discard the contrasting use, in Frege's elucidations, of the predicates "concept" and "object," free to take the elucidations to be so much hand-waving. There isn't, then, something left over that is not expressed in the notation.[42] What corresponds in the case we have been considering is the contrasting pair, "proposition" "not a senseful proposition," as predicates in the *Tractatus.* When we have mastered what Wittgenstein is presenting through elucidatory propositions that use such predicates, we are free to drop the predicates, and to take the elucidations to be so much hand-waving, There isn't then something left over that we haven't been able to put into words.[43]

Anscombe wanted her book to change how people read the *Tractatus.* In Section 1 of this essay, I brought out problems in her story about what was wrong with earlier readings. I tried to show that her account of the

---

42. Ricketts 2010, 191–193. I have stayed very close to Ricketts's wording in this summary of his account of how we are meant to take Frege's elucidations of "concept" and "object," but I have departed too far from his exact words to use quotation marks.

43. The case is similar with my use of the contrasting pair of predicates "logical shareable" and "property." Like the use of "concept" and "object" as a contrasting pair of predicates, such talk can serve a purpose, despite the confusion latent in it. It can help point us to philosophical activity in which differences can be perspicuously presented; and (as with "concept" and "object"), there isn't then an unexpressed something that is left over.

picture theory points us to fundamental connections between Frege's approach and Wittgenstein's. While the sorts of reading she attacked are less popular than they once were, her critique can be taken to be directed also against many later readings—readings which resemble those of her contemporaries in their dependence on an object-based understanding of language and thought, which they read into Wittgenstein. I have also argued that the *Tractatus* is meant to lead its readers to a different kind of practice of philosophy, and that, although Anscombe doesn't say much about philosophical activity, what she actually does in her account of the picture theory can be thought of as exemplifying the kind of philosophical activity to which the *Tractatus* was meant to lead. In Sections 5 and 6, I have tried to set against each other some of Anscombe's own remarks about the *Tractatus* and ideas to which one can be led by following out what I think is implicit in her philosophical practice. I tried to show the tension between her remarks about what Wittgenstein's conception of propositions *excludes* and her own insistence on the central importance of Frege and the context principle for a reading of the book. For it is just such an approach that helps us to see problems with the word "proposition," as it is used in claims about what Wittgenstein's theory excludes from propositionhood, helps us to see how the word can cover over a blur in our thought. I should want to claim that, if we follow out ideas implicit in Anscombe's practice, together with points she makes about "logical chemistry" and about how symbols can be presented, we can get a good idea of how Wittgenstein hoped his book would revolutionize philosophy.

In his study of anti-metaphysical readings of the *Tractatus,* Warren Goldfarb (2011) includes Anscombe among metaphysical readers, along with Peter Geach, David Pears, Norman Malcolm, and Peter Hacker. He traces the development of anti-metaphysical readings of the book, beginning in 1969 with Hidé Ishiguro's "Use and Reference of Names." As he mentions, it is the realism of readings like those of Malcolm, Pears, and Hacker that was at first the focus of criticism. Anscombe's position is very interesting and in some ways anomalous, since her account of the *Tractatus* has features in common with both the metaphysical and the anti-metaphysical readings. She would have found unexceptionable the statement of Hacker's that Goldfarb uses to set out the metaphysical reading. Hacker says, and Anscombe would agree, that Wittgenstein was committed in the *Tractatus* "to a host of claims about logic, language, thought and the logical structure of the world, which cannot be stated in well-formed sentences of language" (2000, 383). But it is not clear how much further Anscombe's agreement goes—not clear whether she takes the Hacker-Pears-Malcolm view that Wittgenstein's "objects" are independent of us and prior to language, and impose on language the structure it must have in order for what we say to express genuine possibilities.[44] But besides the question how close Anscombe really is to the metaphysical readers, there is the question how close she is to the anti-metaphysical interpreters.[45] The starting point of Ishiguro's essay is the ascription to Wittgenstein of a view that the meaning of a name cannot "be secured independently of its use in propositions by some method which links it to an object, as many, including Russell, have thought" (20); but that contrast between Wittgenstein and Russell is already present in Anscombe's interpretation, and is central in her exposition of the picture theory. I should want to take Anscombe out of the group with which Goldfarb puts her, and treat her as in important ways an inaugurator of the anti-metaphysical readings. I'm suggesting that metaphysical readings like those of Hacker, Pears, and Malcolm combine the ascription to Wittgenstein of a Russellian object-based view of language and thought with the idea, sometimes labeled the "ineffabilist view," that the *Tractatus* is committed to substantial claims about propositions, objects, facts, and so on, claims which Wittgenstein is supposed to have taken to be correct although not statable in significant language. Although Anscombe accepts such a view, it is (I think) under far greater pressure within the overall context of her interpretation than it is in the writings of Hacker, Pears, and Malcolm. We do not need to appeal to any specifically *Tractarian* views to see the kind of

44. There is a sentence of Anscombe's in which she refers to objects as the "original seat" of form (*IWT,* 110). This might be taken to imply something like the realist reading of the *Tractatus,* but her sentence is meant simply to summarize *TLP* 2.0121. I don't think it should be taken to indicate agreement with the kind of object-based readings given by Hacker, Pears, and Malcolm.

45. See McManus 2006, 68n5, for comments on a related issue.

pressure, for we can simply look to Frege. Frege is, quite explicitly, not telling us about *concepts;* he is constructing for us an understanding of "concept" as a logical shareable, to be thought of as "arising from the decomposition of a judgeable content" (1980, 101). He isn't getting *concepts* right; and Wittgenstein isn't getting *propositions* wrong (say) by excluding too much; he isn't getting *propositions* right by getting just the right things in. In that sense he is not making substantial claims "about propositions," but constructing for us an understanding of "proposition" as a logical shareable. If an expression has the use of a picture-proposition, it doesn't "show" *that it is a proposition.* What shows in its use as a picture-proposition is simply *that.*[46]

Exclusionary readings and ineffabilist readings are closely linked. The ineffabilist reading ascribes to Wittgenstein a view of *what propositions are,* a view that cannot be stated but can be communicated despite its unsayability. And the idea that the *Tractatus* excludes from propositionhood sentences that are not bipolar (or whatever the excluding criterion is supposed to be) depends upon the idea that Wittgenstein held in the *Tractatus,* but took to be unsayable, the claim that thus-and-such is what genuine propositions are, and that all other putative propositions are excluded from genuine propositionhood.[47] Against this, I have argued that Wittgenstein, like Frege, presents logical shareables, and that to do so is to invite a kind of reconceptualization of one's own practice-of-thinking-and-inferring; one sees the logical shareable reaching through that practice. As a result, features of thought that had appeared philosophically puzzling can come to be seen as unproblematic; this, at any rate, is the hope. Peter Geach (1976, 70) had argued that there is a test whether someone has *got* the differences in logical kind that Frege was trying to convey through his elucidations. The test (which could be carried out by university examiners, say) would be whether she can work properly with a logical notation like Frege's. A test for whether someone has got the point of Wittgenstein's elucidations would be what she went on to do when she took herself to be engaging in philosophy.

46. See Kremer 2007, esp. the discussion of "features," 159–162; and Narboux 2014.

47. For a good illustration of how ineffabilist and exclusionary readings may be linked, see Hacker 2000, esp. 353–356.

In our thinking, speaking, and inferring—in such doings—logical shareables are displayed. Learning to see these shareables clearly is a kind of philosophical achievement—on a remarkable and interesting and highly original conception of philosophy. An appreciation of the dangers of this conception of philosophy came later for Wittgenstein. When Wittgenstein said that the way we pose philosophical problems reflects misunderstanding of the logic of our language, he did not mean that we go around saying things that are excluded from the realm of sense; he meant that the misrepresentation of logical kinds is deep in our understanding of our problems.[48]

48. I am grateful to James Conant, Michael Beaney, Alice Crary, and an anonymous reviewer for their comments and suggestions.

# Wittgenstein, Anscombe, and What Can Only Be True

## INTRODUCTION

In 2011 Mary Geach and Luke Gormally published the collection *From Plato to Wittgenstein: Essays by G. E. M. Anscombe* (Anscombe 2011a). Three of the essays in that volume quite changed my understanding of both Wittgenstein and Anscombe by making me see questions that I hadn't thought about.[1] I begin here with a brief account of what particularly struck me in those three papers. Then I'll explain how the Anscombe essays opened up questions for me—questions that are not visible at all in Part I of this book, and that shape the rest of it. I'll then summarize the main themes of Part II, and explain how the two essays in it hang together. Finally, there is a brief discussion of Frege, meant to clear up some points that come up in Parts II and III.

---

1. The three essays are "Truth: Anselm and Wittgenstein" (Anscombe 2011d), which I refer to here as "Truth"; "The Simplicity of the *Tractatus*" (Anscombe 2011c), which I refer to here as "Simplicity"; and "Wittgenstein's 'Two Cuts' in the History of Philosophy" (Anscombe 2011f), which I refer to here as "Two Cuts." "Truth" was the text of a lecture that Anscombe gave in 1983; "Simplicity" was originally published in 1989; "Two Cuts" was a lecture given in 1981 and published in 1982.

## 1. Three Striking Passages from Anscombe's
## Essays in *from Plato to Wittgenstein*

In "Truth: Anselm and Wittgenstein," Anscombe writes:

> I have been arguing that there *is* an equality, a parity [of two rela-
> tions that a proposition stands in to what it signifies], and that what
> Wittgenstein says *supports* this; that is, what he says about a prop-
> osition and its negation, and about one and the same reality cor-
> responding to both. And this parity is essential to the meaning, the
> sense or *significatio,* of the sort of proposition that can be true or
> false. (2011d, 74)

What interested me there was the idea that the sort of proposition that
*can be true or false* is one sort of proposition. Anscombe is (apparently
quite carefully) indicating that there is at least one other sort of proposition. There are two similar passages in this essay: another one in which
she speaks of "the sort of proposition which can be true or false" (73),
and one where she says, giving Anselm's view, that "the false is only
possible because the true (in this sort of proposition) cannot be the sole
possibility" (76).

Toward the end of "The Simplicity of the *Tractatus*," Anscombe
writes about Wittgenstein's later view of the *Tractatus,* the central ideas
of which she has been explaining. She mentions the well-known story
of his having said of the book, "It isn't like a bag of junk—rather it is
like a clock that doesn't tell the time right" (2011c, 177; compare *IWT,* 78).
She then says:

> It would be accurate to say that the book offers a strange and
> powerful account of meaningfulness, truth and falsehood. It
> would, I think, also be correct to say that the more Wittgenstein
> worked—and he worked immensely hard—when he resumed phil-
> osophical investigation, the more he came to see: *It's not as simple
> as all that.* One of the powerful attractions of the *Tractatus* is a sort
> of simplicity. (178)

On the next page, she says:

> It would be a worthy task to explore what of that first great work
> was not, and what was, rejected, gradually or suddenly, and to fill
> out my sketch of Wittgenstein as in effect coming to say "It's all
> *more complicated* than that." (179)

What struck me there was not just Anscombe's conception of the task of
exploration of what remained and what was rejected, as Wittgenstein's
thought developed, but also the role of the notion of *complicatedness* in
the change, and implicitly also in Anscombe's own view of what was
inadequate in the *Tractatus*.

The third of the passages that led me into new questions was in
"Wittgenstein's 'Two Cuts' in the History of Philosophy," where Anscombe discusses "the desire for necessary explanations, necessary
connections" (2011f, 184). She considers a reaction we may have to
the fact that what we take to be a picture of an old man climbing a hill
with a stick might in other circumstances be taken to be a picture of
someone sliding downhill. Thinking about this, we might ask, "How
do we *know* what we see?" I will quote here her comment on this:

> Asked in that fashion, the question reveals a demand that we ought
> to scrutinize. And one thing that is implicit in the demand is the
> demand for something that gives us necessities. Professional phi-
> losophy is to a great extent a huge factory for the manufacture of
> necessities—only necessities give us mental peace. It is no wonder
> that Wittgenstein arouses a certain hatred among us. He's out to
> deprive us of our factory jobs. (184)

She had earlier discussed Wittgenstein's remark "that a vast number of
philosophical and metaphysical statements are disguised statements of
grammar," and had commented that any particular claim about some
metaphysical statement being a disguised statement of grammar would
have to be examined on its own.[2] There is exactly such a treatment of

---

2. Anscombe 2011a, 203. This is in the essay "A Theory of Language?" (2011a, 193–203),
originally published in 1981 but given as a lecture in 1976.

a particular case in "The Reality of the Past" (Anscombe 1981f). "The past cannot change" might certainly appear to be a statement of a metaphysical necessity, but she had argued there that this is a misunderstanding and rests on a kind of grammatical illusion. And, in particular, she had argued that the impression one may have—that in saying "The past cannot change," "one is saying of something *intelligible* that it is an impossibility"—rests on grammatical illusion.

## 2. How Those Passages Opened Up Questions

When we read Anscombe's discussion of Wittgenstein on necessary statements and her remarks about our desire for necessary explanations and necessary connections, it may seem unclear what she herself thinks about such statements. Her talk of our "factory jobs," and of our manufacturing necessities to give ourselves mental peace, does not sound very friendly to necessities! And this impression may be strengthened if we recall also her treatment in "The Reality of the Past" (1981f) of "The past cannot change"—although we should note that that essay comes originally from 1950, long before any of the other work of Anscombe's that I am discussing, and her views may well have changed during the intervening years. But if, after reading "Two Cuts," we do indeed wonder what Anscombe's own view of necessary statements is, we can see how something of that view comes out in her references, in "Truth," to "the sort of proposition that can be true or false," allowing for a further sort or further sorts of proposition that do not have both possibilities. What sorts of necessary proposition, or propositions that can only be true, should she be read as leaving room for? This line of thinking puts into a new light her treatment in *IWT* of the statement "'Someone' is not the name of someone." Anscombe had used the example in showing what she took to be wrong with the picture theory. On her reading of the picture theory, the only propositions that do not have the possibility of truth and the possibility of falsehood, and that are *not* excluded by the picture theory, are tautologies, contradictions, and mathematical propositions. One of her objections to the theory was then that it excludes such statements as "'Someone' is not the name of someone," which, she says, is "obviously true," and which can be illuminating. We can now see her argument in *IWT* as a claim that Wittgenstein understands *too narrowly* what may be included in *the sort or sorts of proposition that do not have the possibility of truth and the possibility of falsity.* But then we may ask about her example and what it shows: If there is some sort of proposition of which "'Someone' is the name of someone" stands as a representative, *what sort* of proposition is that? And what does her treatment of the particular case show, more generally, about Anscombe's interest in propositions that do not have the possibility of truth and that of falsehood?

In Essay 2, when I discussed "'Someone' is not the name of someone," I quoted the whole passage in which Anscombe sets out her example and says of that statement that it is "obviously true," but I did not focus at all on her saying that what the statement denies is nothing but a piece of confusion, and that its contradictory, "when examined, peters out into nothingness." Anscombe's description of her example takes on new importance if we connect it with her remarks in the essay "Truth" and the allusion there to a sort or sorts of proposition that do not have the possibility of truth and of falsehood. The "sort" exemplified by "'Someone' is not the name of someone" may be taken to be *propositions that do not have a significant negation* and that can nevertheless, on Anscombe's view, be true. This, then, is one sort of proposition that can only be true. And here we can see a number of questions. What other sorts of propositions did Anscombe think there were for which truth is the only possibility? She mentions tautologies and mathematical propositions, but did she think that there are also propositions which are true and which have contradictories that state to be a fact something that cannot be the case, *in addition to* there being some propositions which are true and the contradictories of which peter out into nothingness? Are there, besides the tautologies, contradictions and equations that Wittgenstein allows for, two types of can-only-be-true propositions, on her view, or is there only the latter sort, the ones whose contradictories peter out?

Anscombe had said, in the passage I quoted above, that it would be a worthy task to fill out her sketch of Wittgenstein as having come to recognize that things were *more complicated* than he had allowed for in the *Tractatus,* and at the same time to explore what he had held onto and what he had rejected of that "first great work." But when I read this, there was a question in my mind whether Anscombe herself had underestimated the complicatedness of the *Tractatus*. Did it allow for more sorts of things than she saw? She took it to be a flaw in the picture theory that, besides propositions that have the possibility of truth and that of falsity, it allowed only for logical and mathematical propositions. But did that objection depend on her having taken the *Tractatus too simply*? How much of what she wanted might Wittgenstein have allowed for?

In Essay 2, when I discussed Anscombe's treatment of "'Someone' is not the name of someone," I did not think at all of the wider class that it represented, of propositions that can only be true and that lack an intelligible negation; nor did I think about how propositions that lack an intelligible negation may figure in responses to confusion. I focused closely on the particular case and the particular confusion with which Anscombe was concerned; but when I was reading "Truth," "Two Cuts," and "Simplicity," these further questions about *propositions that can only be true* took shape. In thinking about the questions, I set aside the difficulties that arise from Anscombe's account of her particular case (the difficulties discussed in Essay 2), and began to see that case instead as leading us into much wider issues about Anscombe's thought in relation to Wittgenstein's. And—further—I was also becoming aware that Anscombe's interest in a particular case of a *response to confusion* could be seen along with her interest in other sorts of case in which our thinking seems to have gone deeply wrong—as, for example, in ethics.

### 3. How Essays 4 and 5 Came into Being

Not realizing that I was biting off more than I could chew, I tried to set all this out in a paper, for the Kirchberg Wittgenstein Symposium in 2013, called "Wittgenstein, Anscombe, and What Can Only Be True"—not surprisingly, an extremely long paper. Not long afterward, though, a question from Warren Goldfarb led me to see something that *wasn't* in the paper. What I was saying about Anscombe on "'Someone' is not the name of someone" seemed to be parallel to what one might say about Frege on "The concept *horse* is not a concept." Anscombe had said that what "'Someone' is not the name of someone" denied was nothing but a piece of confusion; might one not argue also that what Frege's statement "The concept *horse* is not a concept" denies is nothing but a piece of confusion? Was my general argument about statements that do not have an intelligible negation, and their role in responses to confusion, applicable to Frege? It was plain that the connection Gold-farb made to Frege was enormously interesting and deeply relevant; but it was also plain that I could no longer hope to discuss all of these issues in a single paper, and that even making clear how Frege's thought re-sembled but also differed from that of Wittgenstein on these issues was itself a large topic. The two essays in Part II were the result of my at-tempt to pull apart and explore separately some of these issues. "Wittgenstein and What Can Only Be True" is the first of the two essays. It has an account of the overall project at the beginning, and a sum-mary at the end of what is and what isn't covered in that essay. Although both the essays range widely, the focus of Essay 4 is on propositions that do not have an intelligible negation, as seen by both Wittgenstein and Anscombe, and on responses to confusion. I also introduce a fur-ther way of thinking about "sorts" of proposition: some come in pairs, some don't. Thus, the kind of proposition that can be true and can be false comes along with a contradictory proposition that also has both possibilities; and tautologies and contradictions come in pairs. It is at least arguable that there is another sort of "paired" proposition: a nec-essary but non-tautologous truth and its contradictory, an intelligible but necessarily false proposition. These sorts of proposition can then be contrasted with sorts of proposition that do not come in pairs. Ans-combe's example of "'Someone' is not the name of someone" leads, in Essay 4, into a discussion of "unpaired" propositions. Although one can formulate the negation of one of these propositions, there is a kind of asymmetry between the proposition and its negation. Here is how I explained it: "the proposition itself might be said to have a use, or to be intelligible, or to be thinkable, or to be illuminating, or indeed (as in Anscombe's example) to be true, while its negation falls apart, is not something thinkable, has nothing to it but confusion—or something of the kind." (In Essay 6, I come back to this topic of "unpaired" proposi-tions.) The focus of Essay 5 is on what is involved in taking to be true a proposition that has no intelligible negation—a topic that bears on disagreements between Anscombe and Geach, and between Anscombe and Wittgenstein. I also touch on an apparent disagreement between Anscombe and much contemporary philosophical work on truth—a disagreement that emerges in her willingness to speak of propositions that lack an intelligible negation as *true*. A further theme of Essay 5 is Wittgenstein's recognition of the ways in which the tools of our thinking can be responsive to the realities of the world and of our nature. (The germ of Wittgenstein's ideas here can be seen in Hertz's conception of how different representations of the principles of mechanics can be more or less appropriate, given different purposes of ours.)[3]

Warren Goldfarb's question to me about possible connections with Frege on the concept *horse* led me to think also about both Frege and Wittgenstein on propositions that are in some sense *preparatory* for what we go on to do with other propositions. This is a main subject of the second half of Essay 4; and it suggests a way of thinking about a whole range of cases of propositions with no intelligible negation. Some of them may be thought of as *setting up or indicating paths our thinking can take,* whereas others may be thought of as *blocking paths down which our thought might go astray.* I came to think of both groups of propositions as *path-indicators,* or more generally as *guides to thinking.* In writing Essay 5, where my concern was especially with *truth* in connection with such propositions, I realized that there was a connection with a long-lasting interest of Anscombe's in Aristotle on practical truth, about which she wrote two essays. In both of them, she draws on ideas of Aristotle's about "the business of thinking," its job, as one might say. In the later essay, she refers to Aristotle's saying that for theoretical thinking, the "well and badly" are truth and falsehood, and that that does not apply solely to theoretical thinking, but is "the business of *any* thinking" (Anscombe 2005, 152). What is worth asking at this point is whether we can take *the guiding of thinking* to be part of the business of thinking. We could think of it then as being done well or badly; and the "well and badly" would be truth and falsehood. So here there is a way of thinking about *responses to thought that has gone astray*—about responses that help to put it back on track, or that help to block paths into

3. Hertz 1899, 3; compare Griffin 1964, 99–108.

confusion—that draws on elements in Aristotle that are important for Anscombe in writing about practical truth, and that helps to draw together *responsive* elements in her philosophy. We can see such *responsiveness* in her treatment of what Flew said about "Somebody"; and we can see it too in her discussion of the use of fantastic apparent dilemmas in moral philosophy, along with her responses to confusion in Hume, and to confusion about action and intention. Much of her philosophizing comes out of her acute sense of how thinking has gone astray. There is no one *kind* of response, and her greatness as a philosopher lies partly in the variety and insight and sharpness of the responses. My Anscombean-Aristotelian treatment of *the guiding of thinking* comes up again in Part III, in Essays 6 and 7.

There is one topic included in both essays in Part II, the "everything else is nonsense" reading of the *Tractatus,* and what is the matter with it. In the form in which Anscombe held it, this is the view that the *Tractatus* allows only senseful propositions (that is, propositions that have the possibility of truth and of falsity) and logical and mathematical propositions. Everything else is nonsense. There is a clear expression of this view in *IWT* on page 78, but it can be seen also in various other places in Anscombe's writings, including her discussion of Antony Flew in *IWT*.[4] Other readers of Wittgenstein have held other versions of the "everything else is nonsense" view. The *Tractatus* has, for example, been read as holding that the only things-that-look-like-propositions that are not nonsensical are either senseful propositions by the standards of the *Tractatus* or tautologies or contradictions; on this view, even mathematical propositions count as nonsensical. The "everything else is nonsense" view can be seen at work whenever someone argues that the *Tractatus* supposedly excludes thus-and-such, just because the thus-and-such is not x and is not y. When I said that Anscombe's reading of the *Tractatus* does not fully take into account its complicatedness, I had particularly in mind the way the "everything else is nonsense" view

4. There are other contexts where the "everything else is nonsense" reading of the *Tractatus* is playing a role in Anscombe's exposition, but this could be shown only by spelling out her arguments in detail. I include here *IWT,* 82 and 87–90, and Anscombe 2011a, 175.

blocks out Wittgenstein's treatment of a variety of kinds of indicative sentence that have "helpful" roles in language. What Wittgenstein thought about these cases is important in both of the essays in Part II. In Essay 4, my argument about their role in the *Tractatus* draws on James Griffin, who wrote about Wittgenstein on natural laws in 1964, and on Michael Kremer, who discussed mathematics in the *Prototractatus* and the *Tractatus* in 2002. When I was writing Essay 5, I realized that there was a more complex and far-reaching argument that could be constructed about the main issues here, which started from Roger White's discussion of mathematics in the *Tractatus,* and the important connection he drew between Wittgenstein on equations and on definitions. White's argument, I saw, was generalizable in a way that brought out some underlying problems with Anscombe's approach. It's worth noting here also another recent argument against the "everything else is nonsense" view, in Chon Tejedor's account (2015) of the *Tractatus* on principles of the natural sciences. What Griffin, Kremer, White, and Tejedor bring out in different ways is that questions about how the *Tractatus* deals with equations and natural laws are of great importance in seeing how the work hangs together, and what its relation is to many of the later developments in Wittgenstein's thought. Thus, for example, Wittgenstein's conception in the *Tractatus* of mechanics as a kind of ground-plan for description is connected not only with his remarks about skepticism at *TLP* 6.51, but also with his ideas about "hypotheses" in the 1930s. An overly simple picture of the *Tractatus,* on the general lines of the "everything else is nonsense" view, also makes it impossible to see clearly the relation between Wittgenstein's thought and that of such other thinkers as Ramsey.[5]

My disagreement with Anscombe about the "everything else is nonsense" reading of the *Tractatus* reaches beyond the matter of "helpful"

---

5. See especially Griffin 1964, 102–108. Griffin's account of the *Tractatus* on natural science makes it clear that ideas that are sometimes taken to show Ramsey's influence on Wittgenstein's writings in the 1930s are present already in the *Tractatus,* and that the influence goes from Wittgenstein to Ramsey, not the other way round. On the connections between Wittgenstein's ideas about physics in his early thought and his ideas about skepticism, see Diamond 2014b.

propositions. It is tied closely to another disagreement with her—about Wittgenstein on saying and showing. In *IWT* and in Anscombe's later discussions of the *Tractatus,* she takes Wittgenstein's references to *what is shown* in a quasi-propositional way; and I would argue against any such reading of those remarks.[6] The picture with which Anscombe works is of *what can be shown* as a kind of quasi-propositional content that we can recognize in (what we take to be) attempts to express that content. What we thus take ourselves to grasp then plays a role in the argument that such sentences are supposedly nonsensical. That is, we recognize that the sentence produced in the attempt to say what is shown does not have both the possibility of truth and that of falsehood, nor is it a tautology or contradiction, and so (on the "everything else is nonsense" reading) the sentence is taken to be nonsensical. The recognition of the sentence as not having the possibility of truth and of falsehood, and of its not being tautology or contradiction, depends upon the idea that *we can see in the sentence what it is after,* where that is something understandable well enough for us to see that the sentence cannot pass the supposed *Tractatus* test for allowability. It is close *enough* to propositionality for us to judge what sort of proposition it would be if it were a proposition at all. Take, for example, Anscombe's saying of "Red is a color" that it "cannot express anything that might be false" (*IWT,* 82). The idea there is that we can see what it is aimed at saying, and we see that that precludes falsity as a possibility for what the sentence would express, if it actually managed to express anything, which, we then conclude, it doesn't.

There is a connection here with the ways we may understand what Wittgenstein says about *the limits of sense.*[7] I had argued, in "The *Tractatus* and the Limits of Sense" (2011), that we should not take Wittgenstein to have construed the limits as *limitations*—as restrictions that call for a kind of resignation. In the Introduction to Part I of this volume, I explain the contrast drawn by Peter Sullivan between two ways of understanding the notion of *limits* (as limits, and as

6. See the Introduction to Part I of this book; also Narboux 2014, and Conant and Diamond 2004.

7. I am very grateful to Jean-Philippe Narboux for pointing out the connection.

limitations), and I discuss its relation to my disagreements with Anscombe.

## 4. Frege and Confusion

My reading of Frege on confusion is central to Essay 4, and it is not easy to see what exactly Frege holds. In "Concept and Object" he says, "The word 'concept' is used in various ways; its sense is sometimes psychological, sometimes logical, and sometimes perhaps a confused mixture of both" (1984b, 182). He does not specify what its use in a psychological sense might be, and in fact there might be all sorts of psychological uses. Concepts may be taken to be mental representations; or the word "concept" might be used to mean a kind of psychological capacity, and so on. If someone is speaking about a mental image of something, and says of it that it is a concept, the word "concept" in that use may indeed be logically unproblematic. It may, that is, have the use in that context of a first-level concept-word under which fall some, but not all, mental images. The word "concept" in this use does not mean a Fregean concept—not at all. This kind of use Frege clearly allows for; what he cares about is that such uses be sharply distinguished from his own. But he does also speak of there being "perhaps" cases in which the word "concept" has a sense that is a confused mishmash of the logical and the psychological, and it seems likely that he meant this to apply to Benno Kerry. When Kerry says that the concept *horse* is "*ein leicht gewinnbarer Begriff*" (1887, 274), he appears to be thinking of the ease with which one can come to have some kind of purportedly general representation of horsehood. Such a mental representation would count, from Frege's point of view, as an object, and, if it is called a concept, this would be a paradigmatic example of a psychological use of the term "concept." The trouble is that Kerry also wanted to use his statement "The concept 'horse' is an easily attained concept" in disputing what Frege had said about concepts and objects; and in order to do so, he has to be using the word "concept" to mean what Frege had meant. In discussing Frege's criticism of Kerry, Kelly Jolley says, "Frege . . . does not just treat 'concept' as psychologically / logically ambiguous, but he also registers the possibility that the word can be used in a way that cannot be disambiguated to one or the other, but hovers confusedly between them" (2015, 116). But Frege at least appears to be making a claim that goes further than merely a criticism of Kerry's particular sort of confusion. That is, there is indeed a critical point that Frege can make that is specific to Kerry's "The concept 'horse' is a concept easily attained," since the first three words there are apparently meant to refer to a concept in the psychological sense, and Frege can point out that they don't refer to a concept in the sense in which he uses the word. But Frege in the same essay also speaks about the statement "The concept *man* is not empty," and in this example the first three words do not refer to a concept in the psychological sense. If someone says "The concept *man* is a concept," Frege would still object, and would still take the remark to show confusion, although there is not, in this case, the kind of confusion there was in Kerry's running together of the logical and the psychological uses of "concept." The first three words of "The concept *man* is a concept" would be regarded, on Frege's principles, as a proper name—that is, as denoting an object, not a concept. But then why should saying "The concept *man* is a concept" be taken to be any kind of confusion, as opposed to something simply false? Frege explicitly allows for there being things we can say about concepts in informal discussion, using a form of words in which the concept in question is "represented" by an object, as when we say "The concept *man* is not empty." Why not then say "The concept *man* is a concept," using the predicate to apply to the object doing the representing, if what it represents is indeed a concept, just as we can predicate "is not empty" of the representing object when the concept is realized? But here one is taking the first steps into what Frege would indeed take to be confusion. What you would be saying *is not empty,* if you say "The concept *man* is not empty," is the representing object (which might be taken to be a set)—that is, it is something that you can perfectly straightforwardly say is empty. (On Frege's principles, you can—without making a grammatical mess—use that predicate of anything that you refer to by a proper name.) But now take saying, or purportedly saying, of the concept *man* that it is, or that it isn't, a concept in Frege's sense. In Frege's formal language, you can say that every value of this or that function is a truth-value; and this is easy to symbolize if you are able to use "$2 + 2 = 4$," for example, as a name of the True, and

"$2+2=5$" as a name of the False. You say that every value of the function is equal either to $2+2=4$ or to $2+2=5$, and you will thereby have said that the function in question is a concept. Or you can say of a function that it is not a concept, by saying that it is not the case that for every argument its value is either $2+2=4$ or $2+2=5$. That is, you say of something that it is or isn't a concept in Frege's sense by saying something about its values. But in "The concept *man* is a concept," the subject about which you are speaking is *the concept man,* which doesn't have values: it's not grammatically the sort of thing that has values. You can *certainly* have a predicate that you could use of this representing object, if what it represents is indeed a Fregean concept, but if you say of it, using this predicate, that it *is a concept,* you won't be saying of that object that it is a concept as Frege uses the term. Nor would you be denying of it that it is a Fregean concept, if you say of the object that it is not a concept, using this predicate. It's grammatically a first-level predicate, and means something that objects can fall under, including any object that represents a Fregean concept. When Frege speaks of the awkwardness of saying, as he does, that the concept *horse* is not a concept, he is thinking of saying this as a kind of puncturing of confusion— the confusion of taking yourself to be saying of something that it is a concept *as Frege uses the term,* though in your way of speaking of it, it is not grammatically a concept, but an object. The confusion here is not the confusion of the psychological with the logical (as it was in the Benno Kerry case). If you say "The concept *man* is a concept," and take yourself to mean that *it is a concept as Frege uses the term,* the confusion could also be described as that of taking yourself to mean a second-level concept by your predicate, while you are operating with what is plainly an expression for a first-level one. One can say that Frege is denying what you take yourself to mean; but my argument is that what he is denying, when he says "The concept *horse* is not a concept," is not something false, but a piece of confusion. I should note that, throughout this paragraph, I have used the way of speaking that is described by Frege as needing to be taken with a "pinch of salt." Questions about what it is to use such a way of speaking, in response to what one takes to be confusion, are central in Essays 4 and 5.

The issues here are of great importance for early and late Wittgenstein. They are the same issues that came up in Part I and in the new material in Essay 3 about formal concepts and about what Wittgenstein takes to be the *eigentliche Zeichen* for this or that formal concept. A way of putting the confusion against which Frege's "The concept *horse* is not a concept" is directed is that someone who says "The concept *horse* is a concept," taking herself to mean that it is a concept as Frege understands the term, thinks of "meaning" the formal concept in question as something that somehow manages to get attached to a sentence independently of its grammar. This is like the idea that one can mean the formal concept *proposition,* although one is using the word "proposition" with the grammar that "mammals" has in "Mammals are descendants of reptiles," and not with the grammar it has in contexts in which it signifies the formal concept *proposition.* The same issues are important in Wittgenstein's later writing, and are expressed in the slogan "Grammar tells what kind of object anything is" (Wittgenstein 1958, §373). Grammar tells what we are talking about, where that may not be what we think of ourselves as *meaning.* Here I want simply to note that Anscombe's insistence in *IWT* on the need to read the *Tractatus* along with reading Frege should be connected with the strand in both Wittgenstein's thought and Frege's of seeing *what kind of thing you are talking about* in the grammar of what you say.[8] And this strand itself is interwoven with another: Both Wittgenstein and Frege are concerned with the possibility of our thought getting into a mess by our having an "idea" of what we mean to be talking about, while what we say has the grammar of talk of something of a quite different kind. This is, then, one important way in which what we say may fail to mean anything. A final point about "grammatical" views like Frege's and Wittgenstein's

---

8. For a relatively early discussion of this strand in Frege's thought, see Dummett 1973, 56–57. See also Thomas Ricketts (1986 and 2010) on the connection between this strand in Frege's thought and his conception of judgment; and see Essay 3 in this volume on the relation of Frege on judgment to Anscombe's claims about the importance of Frege for understanding the *Tractatus.* In Diamond 1991, I argued for a "grammatical" reading of Frege, but my treatment of the concept *horse* problem was different from what I have argued for here.

is that they do not in general involve a commitment to any kind of linguistic idealism or anti-realism (although some holders of such views may indeed accept a form of idealism or anti-realism). This is a main subject of Anscombe's "The Question of Linguistic Idealism" (1981e); the same issue is examined from a Fregean perspective by Agustin Rayo (2015).[9]

9. I have been greatly helped, in writing this introduction, by comments and suggestions from Jean-Philippe Narboux and from an anonymous reviewer for Harvard University Press.

# FOUR

# Wittgenstein and What Can Only Be True

~

I want to explore here an issue that comes up in thinking about Wittgenstein. My approach is shaped by a question that Warren Goldfarb asked. To explain the problem, I first set out how things seemed to me *before* the Goldfarb question, and then I show how his question led me to rethink the issue.

I start from something that Anscombe took to be a major flaw in the *Tractatus*—that it excludes propositions that can only be true, apart from tautologies and mathematical propositions (*IWT*, 78, 85). One might ask how much of what Anscombe wanted Wittgenstein could allow for; and that leads to two questions: what Wittgenstein could allow for, and what Anscombe wanted. Let me add something about what the interest is of the overall question. When Anscombe wrote her book about the *Tractatus,* she argued against interpretations that took Wittgenstein to be putting forward two separable theories: a picture theory of elementary propositions and a truth-functional account of composite propositions (*IWT*, 25). That idea is incompatible, she thought, with the fundamental insights about truth and meaning that there were in the book. So what I am asking is how far one can hold on to a more or less Wittgensteinian account of propositions that can only be true, that allows for (at least some of) the propositions Anscombe took to have been wrongly excluded, while not dropping the features of Wittgenstein's thought that are tied to his fundamental insights as she saw them. Anscombe herself at one point did ask a related question (2011c, 179–180): What important thoughts from Wittgenstein's first great work remain, if we explore what was not and what was rejected by Wittgenstein later on?

Here is another way of putting the issues. What Anscombe took to be right in the *Tractatus* was inseparable from its not being a mere combination of a theory of the picture-character of elementary propositions and a truth-functional account of composite propositions. Rather, the essential thing is its account of propositions which have the possibility of truth and of falsity, and of how one and the same reality corresponds to both such a proposition and its negation (see, for example, 2011d, 74). What is built into this understanding is the connection between the possibility of truth and falsity for such propositions and there being one proposition which is true if the proposition is false and false if it is true; what is also built into it is a profound distinction between such propositions and those which do not have the possibility of truth and of falsity. That distinction, as Anscombe understands what becomes of it in the *Tractatus,* is the basis of her complaint about what the book excludes. I believe that the distinction as it works itself out in the *Tractatus* is not exactly what Anscombe thought, and also that (as she herself insists) things become a lot more complicated later (2011c, 179). The distinction itself belongs to the things that are insightful on her view; but the question is how to understand it, and this involves seeing both what it was to start with, as well as how it all gets more complicated. Sections 1 and 2 of this essay are about the distinction as it can be seen in the *Tractatus;* Section 3 is about a class of propositions that Anscombe thought were wrongly excluded by the *Tractatus.* In Section 4, I turn to Goldfarb's question, and there and in Section 5, I show how it reshapes the question about what Wittgenstein might allow for. In a larger project of which this is part, I consider both how the issue gets more complicated in Wittgenstein's later work, and also how far apart, in the end, Wittgenstein and Anscombe were.

## 1.

I begin with what I call the everything-else-is-nonsense assumption, which structures many readings of the *Tractatus.* According to that assumption, Wittgenstein held in the *Tractatus* that anything that appears proposition-like but is not a contingent description of how things are, and is not a tautology or contradiction, is nonsense. The assumption also appears in the form of the idea that, according to the *Tractatus,* everything that looks proposition-like, but is not a truth-function of elementary propositions, is nonsense. Sometimes the assumption is expressed in a way that explicitly allows for mathematical propositions not to count as nonsensical. But in whatever way the assumption is expressed, the basic idea is that, according to the *Tractatus,* there are sayings how things are, and also logical propositions and possibly also mathematical propositions; and then beyond that, there are propositions which, in virtue of not being of those types, are nonsensical. Anscombe accepted a version of the assumption, and it is important in what she takes the *Tractatus* to *exclude*.[1] So I need to consider what might be wrong with the assumption. My argument will depend upon Wittgenstein's treatment of mathematical and scientific propositions, which Anscombe does not discuss. Her overall presentation of the picture theory and what it supposedly excludes depends upon there being available a story about Wittgenstein on mathematics and science that does not undercut the everything-else-is-nonsense assumption (*IWT,* 78–80), and it is at least questionable whether there is any such story.

Here I need to mention that there is a question about the use of "proposition" in discussing Wittgenstein's thought, since the word "*Satz*" can be translated either as "proposition" or as "sentence," depending on context. Moore, in his notes to Wittgenstein's lectures, said that Wittgenstein often used the English words interchangeably (1959, 268). I shall look in more detail at the use of "*Satz*" in discussing his thought in Section 2. My view is that the reader needs to see what is

---

1. Anscombe's commitment to the assumption comes out in various ways in *IWT*—for example, on p. 78. On p. 85, it plays a role in her argument that "'Someone' is not the name of someone" is prohibited by the picture theory, in that it lacks true-false poles and is not logical truth in any "sharp" sense. It also plays a role in her treatment of Wittgenstein's account of "A believes p," etc. (*IWT,* 88). Anscombe works, I think, with a limited conception of what alternatives there may be for understanding his account, and in particular for understanding his remark about such propositions being of the same form as "'p' says p."

involved in Wittgenstein's use of any of these words at any particular point, and that questions of this or that translation are not usually significant. I stick to "proposition" for "*Satz.*"

There are two philosophers who have brought out, in different but related ways, what is the matter with the everything-else-is-nonsense assumption. One is James Griffin, in his explanation of the *Tractatus* treatment of scientific propositions (1964, 102–108). Griffin points out that "many general statements in science need not be treated as truth-functions of elementary propositions" (102–103). They are not empirical propositions, and are not tautologies or contradictions; they are not propositions in the logical sense specified through the general form of proposition. But these propositions do have an important function: they supply "representational techniques." These techniques may be very useful for a time but then may be superseded when more useful ones are found. There is no suggestion that scientific propositions that are not truth-functions of elementary propositions would count as nonsensical on the *Tractatus* view. Rather, they have a function which is quite different from that of propositions in the logical sense, and which can be spelled out. What is significant in Griffin's treatment of Wittgenstein on scientific laws is how his thought moves. He takes the fact that many general statements in science are not truth-functions of elementary propositions to set the question what exactly their use is. His discussion makes clear an important possible response to the fact that some kind of proposition is neither a contingent proposition nor a tautology nor a contradiction. Griffin's approach relies implicitly on a way of taking the *Tractatus* on *meaningfulness.* Something that looks proposition-like may not be a senseful proposition, in the sense specified in the *Tractatus.*[2] But it is not nonsensical, it is not meaning*less,* if it has a function tied in with our use of senseful language. That idea, which is implicit in Griffin's treatment of scientific laws, is made explicit and defended in detail by Michael Kremer (2002). He argues that the most general notion of meaningfulness in the *Tractatus* is *having a linguistic function,*

2. My further uses of the expression "senseful proposition" in discussing the *Tractatus* should be taken to be abbreviations for "senseful propositions in the sense specified in the *Tractatus.*"

and he shows the bearing of that general point on the specific case of mathematical equations—which have a distinct function, but are not empirical propositions and not tautologies. To see the status of both mathematical propositions and tautologies in the *Tractatus,* we need to attend to their role in facilitating inferences with senseful propositions. It's because they have such a role that mathematical propositions, like tautologies, are not nonsensical, not meaning*less* (2002, esp. 300). And, like tautologies, mathematical propositions can be described as *senseless,* where this indicates their lack of sense but does not imply nonsensicality. (As I read the *Tractatus,* nonsensical propositions count as senseless, but the inverse doesn't hold.)

There is a label available in the *Tractatus* for things that look like propositions and that have a role in what we do with senseful propositions but are not themselves senseful propositions. An expression constructed by putting an equal sign between two signs means that either of the flanking signs can be substituted for the other; and Wittgenstein speaks of such expressions as *Behelfe der Darstellung:* aids to representation (*TLP* 4.242). There are two other labels we can use, which come from Wittgenstein's later philosophy. In 1939 Wittgenstein spoke of the contrast between propositions that belong to the apparatus of language and those that belong to its application; and this suggests one label we might use for things which look like propositions saying that something or other is the case, but which function as part of the apparatus of language. We could speak of "apparatus propositions" (Wittgenstein 1976, 250). We could also speak of propositions as "preparatory" if what they do is, in a sense, prepare language for what we go on to do with it, as definitions, for example, do.[3] My claim right now is that the *Tractatus* allows for various apparatus propositions, sentences that

3. The idea of mathematical propositions or grammatical propositions as belonging to the "preparation" of language comes up in various ways in Wittgenstein's lectures during the 1930s. See, for example, the statement in 1931 that "mathematics can be learned beforehand" (1980b, 62). Here we have the idea of a kind of logical "before," where what belongs to grammar comes "before" the application of language. See also Moore's notes from Wittgenstein's lectures in 1932–1933 (Moore 1959, 279). I return to the topic of Wittgenstein on "preparatory" uses of language in Section 4 of this essay.

have a function tied in with making inferences, or tied in in other ways with the use of senseful propositions. These, I am arguing, are not non-sensical. This means that there is no general inference from some sentence's not being a contingent description of things, nor a tautology nor a contradiction, to its counting as nonsense on the *Tractatus* view. It's part of my claim that you'd have to look at the use of a type of proposition to see whether propositions of that sort were apparatus propositions. So, for example, linguistic rules of various sorts in propositional form, including translation rules, would count as apparatus propositions, and hence would not be meaningless according to the *Tractatus*. I don't think that Wittgenstein, at the time of writing the *Tractatus,* had any interest in the variety of kinds of case there might be of such propositions apart from the cases actually mentioned, but his absence of interest should not be read as an implicit denial of their existence. The basic idea is: if some type of apparent propositions (*Scheinsätze*) have a use in aiding what we do with senseful propositions, those propositions are not nonsense. Uses are not specified in advance. One way of putting what is common to Griffin's reading and Kremer's is that they reject a reading of the *Tractatus* which models it on the sort of everything-else-is-nonsense structure that genuinely can be found in Ayer's *Language, Truth and Logic.* The everything-else-is-nonsense assumption may be a remnant of a logical positivist reading of the *Tractatus.*

In Section 2, I will consider some objections to the account so far, but first there are two important general points about apparatus propositions. First, they fit in with an important remark in the *Tractatus,* that everyday language depends upon all sorts of conventions and other arrangements that we don't usually think about, and that help to conceal the underlying logical structures. Secondly, everyday language, because it has all these arrangements, is responsive to the particular realities of our lives, again in ways we don't usually have any reason to think about. Thus, for example, definitions are or aren't useful because of what sorts of things we happen to need to speak about in particular ways. So there is room in the *Tractatus* for the idea that language-structures can be responsive to particular realities, but the kind of way it actually works is not taken to have any significance for the philosophical project of the *Tractatus.* But the fact that there is room for such responsiveness suggests another label we might use for propositions that function to make language responsive to particular realities, as definitions, for example, do, or the representational techniques provided by scientific laws. We can call these "accommodatory" propositions. The basic ideas here come out in a striking way in the passage that begins at *TLP* 3.34, where Wittgenstein emphasizes the contrast between what is essential and what is "arbitrary" in our notations, where it is the essential with which philosophy is concerned. In the same passage, we have a reference to all notations for truth-functions and what they have in common (*TLP* 3.3441). What they most emphatically do not have in common, though, is *ease of use*. Now, it has no *logical* significance that most human beings cannot do logic using only the stroke notation. But it is in this passage that Wittgenstein also refers to the way definitions allow us to translate from one language to another; and it is such definitions that enable us to set up a logical notation that human beings find readily comprehensible. Wittgenstein refers to an obviously similar sort of case at *TLP* 6.341, where he mentions that we can write down any number we wish in the number system, where this applies to the binary number system, the decimal one, and so on: no such system is *logically* preferable to any other, but they differ greatly in convenience, given what we human beings are like, and what we might be trying to do. That different forms of representation may be more or less convenient or useful is also true of different representations of the principles of mechanics. This general point fits with the metaphor of language as having an "outward form," as it were its "clothing," and as having, underneath that clothing, its genuine "bodily form" (*TLP* 4.002). The clothing is designed for various purposes, and "accommodatory propositions" are a part of the way language serves those purposes—they shape the clothing to particular needs, but in doing so, may obscure the underlying bodily form, as comes out in the way our usual logical notation is shaped by what we find convenient, but doesn't make at all obvious what all such notations have essentially in common. The general point here is entirely compatible with the logical irrelevancy (as Wittgenstein sees it) of which notations actually do suit our needs.[4]

4. This paragraph has been rewritten for this volume. I am grateful to a reviewer for the Press for comments on the earlier version.

## 2.

It may be argued that there is an obvious tension between suggesting that Wittgenstein allowed for the existence of apparatus propositions in the *Tractatus*, and his recurrent emphasis on propositions' being representations of how things stand. It looks (that is) as if there is a pretty strong presumption in favor of the everything-else-is-nonsense reading of the *Tractatus*. (I am very grateful to Lars Hertzberg for putting this point forcefully to me.)

To reply to the objection, I need to consider the complicated use of the word "*Satz*" in the *Tractatus*. I want to put it into perspective by considering it along with a passage from Frege and one from Russell.

In "Concept and Object" (1984b), Frege pointed out that the word "concept" was used in various ways. At no point did he claim that the use he set out in his great essay was *correct.* He said that he did not dispute Benno Kerry's right to use the word in his own way, and asked of Kerry only that his own equal right be respected, and that Kerry admit that Frege had got hold of a distinction of the highest importance. *That,* indeed, is the aim of the essay: to make that distinction and its importance clear. To understand Frege, to get the point of the essay, is to see what it is he calls a concept, *what counts as that.* It would be misleading to say that he is explaining *what concepts are,* as if Kerry had got that wrong. The word "concept" is not what is at stake, but is essentially secondary. I don't want to suggest that Frege should have used the word "pumpkin" (say) instead of "concept," but it would not have affected the philosophical point. When Frege said that there were various uses of "concept," he added that its sense was sometimes psychological, sometimes logical, and sometimes "a confused mixture of both" (1984b, 182). The logical use needed to be put clearly before us, in the face of the various and to some degree confused existing uses of "concept"; and if Frege can achieve the "meeting of minds" at which he aims (a shared understanding of the logical use), the appropriation of this or that particular word rather than some other for what is thus understood, is not important.

The idea of a philosophical task of getting something indefinable and of logical importance clearly into view is understood in a somewhat different way by Russell, who appeals in this connection to the notion of *acquaintance with an entity:* the idea is that philosophy should present the entity in question to the mind in such a way that it may have the same sort of acquaintance with it as it has with the taste of a pineapple (1996, xv). Prior to the success of such an endeavor, there would not be a way of *fixing on* what it is you are trying to put before the mind. The clear putting-before-the-mind itself is the only kind of focused specification there can be of *what* is being put before the mind.

Wittgenstein's idea of philosophy as an activity of clarification is similarly tied to the idea that what it is that is being clarified comes out in the clarification. What he wants to clarify in the *Tractatus* is *propositionhood,* but what actually is being clarified you can see only in the clarification, the setting out of a use of words, which you can call the proposition-use. But he does this in two different ways, and so there are two central uses of the word "proposition": (1) the word is used for representations of situations (and what that means is spelled out through the discussion of pictures and of construction from elementary propositions), and (2) the word is used for whatever can be constructed by truth-functions from all elementary propositions (thus including, in addition to everything counted as a proposition according to the first use, tautologies and contradictions, taken as a kind of limiting case of propositions). Philosophy as an activity of clarification can get both of these uses clear; and indeed, if you prefer "pumpkin" for one use in order to distinguish it from the other, that would not interfere with the achieving of the kind of clarity Wittgenstein was after. So long as you are clear what is going on, there is also nothing wrong with using the word "proposition" in connection with both of the logical uses. The question is *what is getting counted as that;* and in each case, if you are clear about *that,* then call it what you like.

In discussing Wittgenstein's use of "*Satz*," Michael Kremer has argued that, so far as we take the paradigm case of *Satz* to be *sinnvolle Satz,* "tautologies and contradictions are *Sätze* in some more parasitic and secondary sense" (2002, 275); but one could also argue that the recursive specification of *propositions* as constructed by truth-functions from elementary propositions gives *propositionhood* a logical generality tied to the generality of propositional construction by operations, and that it was in that sense logically deeper. I do not think that the *Tractatus* suggests that readers should fix on one aspect-seeing of *propositionhood* rather than the other; the point would rather be to demand of readers that they are aware of the different ways of using "proposition." It should be noted that the *Prototractatus* contains a fairly clear expression of preference for the first way of looking at the use of "proposition" (the second sentence of 4.4303), which is not in the *Tractatus;* and the *Tractatus* reverses the order of the discussion (under proposition 4) of tautologies and contradictions, on the one hand, and the generality of propositionhood, on the other. There is also a very significant shift from *Prototractatus* to *Tractatus* in the treatment of propositions at the beginning of the 6's. The *Prototractatus* does not identify the general form of truth-function with the general form of proposition (as the *Tractatus* does); and it has no propositions corresponding to the *Tractatus* on the general form of transition between propositions.

While Frege did say that Kerry had a right to use the word "concept" in his own way, he might well have thought that it wasn't a great idea to use the word "concept" to mean something psychological: some kind of mental representation, or the psychological capacity to think about such-and-such kind of things (so that one could say that the concept *horse* was easily attained, and mean that the mental representation in question, or the relevant capacity, was easily attained). Any such use, which Frege was clearly committed to allowing, might nevertheless have seemed all too likely to be run together confusedly with the logical use. The situation is somewhat different, though, if we consider the *Tractatus,* and uses of "proposition" other than the two central logical uses.

We can note first the use (*TLP* 6.34) of "proposition" for various *a priori* insights; these are neither tautologies nor senseful propositions. In discussing probability, Wittgenstein again uses the word "proposition" (*TLP* 5.154–5.155) for the result of a kind of calculation. Such propositions are not senseful propositions and they are not tautologies. They could as well, I think, have been described by him as *Scheinsätze,* which would draw to attention that they *resemble* senseful propositions. And Wittgenstein does speak of the propositions of mathematics as equations and "therefore" as *Scheinsätze.* The "therefore" harks back to *TLP* 4.241–4.242, where Wittgenstein says that expressions in which an equal sign is flanked by two expressions are merely *Behelfe der Darstellung,* and that they don't say anything about the things meant by the expressions that flank the equal sign. That is, they don't represent a situation involving those things. They aren't, that is, senseful propositions.

The point at *TLP* 4.241–4.242 has an important implication for the argument here. It implies that you cannot, in general, tell from what a proposition looks like what it is about, if indeed it is about anything. (This is in fact also implied, though in more general terms, by Wittgenstein's remark about Russell's having made it clear that you can't discern a proposition's logical form from its apparent logical form, *TLP* 4.0031.)[5] If one does not attend to the point, it may seem that there is an easy line of argument that will show that the sorts of proposition at issue here are nonsensical. Here is an example of the argument, as applied to probability propositions.

> According to Wittgenstein, a probability proposition is a proposition of the form "Proposition B gives to proposition A the probability m / n $(0 \leq m/n \leq 1)$." These are overtly propositions about other propositions. Such propositions are excluded by the *Tractatus.* What probability propositions are supposed to affirm thus lies outside the domain of what can be expressed by meaningful propositions. The propositions are therefore nonsensical.[6]

If, in speaking of what a proposition is about, you are going by its sheer look, then you cannot infer anything at all from what a proposition is about (in this sense), concerning whether the proposition attempts to assert something that lies "outside the domain of the sayable." In contrast, if you restrict yourself to a logical use of "about" (as in *TLP* 4.242), then telling what a proposition is about in this sense will depend on

---

5. But see also Kremer 2012. *TLP* 4.242 has an important connection with Kremer's argument, in that a misreading of the form of identity propositions is tied to the misunderstanding of "identical" that Kremer discusses.

6. The argument here is based on Pasquale Frascolla's discussion (2007, 182, 200).

considering its use, not its look. But the *Tractatus* view would then be that, if you consider the use of probability propositions (they give the results of a kind of calculation, and are useful in judging the assumptions that we may be making about a situation), you will see that probability propositions are no more *about propositions* (in the restricted sense of "about") than equations or identity propositions are *about* the things meant by the signs that flank the equal sign. Putting the point another way: the argument that I imagined depends on assuming that, for Wittgenstein, "Proposition B gives to proposition A the probability m/n" is *either* a senseful contingent proposition about propositions (and that possibility can be ruled out) *or* a nonsensical pseudo-proposition that attempts to say something a priori about the two propositions.— What is the matter with that assumption can be spelled out in various ways; here I briefly note two. (1) The two possibilities, the "either"-"or", will appear to exhaust the possibilities only if one does not take into account that the superficial form of probability propositions may be misleading. (2) The "either"-"or" assumption has built into it the idea that one can set aside the question how a proposition is used in considering what the form is of a proposition and what it is about. And this further has built into it the idea that one could first establish that the proposition is nonsensical and then go on to investigate what uses it might have.

What is important about the flawed argument above is that it illustrates how a useful kind of proposition, which indeed *lacks sense,* can be misunderstood as making, or trying to make, an assertion of something that supposedly cannot be said, according to the *Tractatus.* The stage at which the misunderstanding occurs is the stage at which, without considering at all the use of the proposition, one imagines that one can discern in its superficial form, the form of a kind of would-be assertion.[7]

---

7. Frascolla does discuss the use of probability propositions, but puts consideration of use after the setting out of the logical character of these propositions. His argument reflects very clearly the idea that the use is not relevant to the form of the propositions in question. That the propositions are supposedly nonsensical can be established prior to and independently of considering their use. For an account of the *Tractatus* understanding of probability propositions and their use which does not read their form

Although I am here focusing on the *Tractatus*, we should note that in his lectures in the early 1930s Wittgenstein speaks explicitly of the possibility of using the word "proposition" in a strict sense and also in a sense in which it includes mathematical propositions and what he speaks of as "hypotheses," which are rules that provide forms of description. He notes that the wider use of "proposition" goes with significant logical analogies between propositions in the strict sense and propositions in this wider sense.

In the *Tractatus*, Wittgenstein speaks of nonsensical *Scheinsätze* at various points, but he also uses the plain word "*Satz*" in talking about other cases of nonsense, including (for example) "Socrates is identical" and "1 is a number," as well as the propositions of the *Tractatus* itself. When they are called *Sätze*, though, nothing is meant by this beyond their mere appearance: they more or less resemble senseful propositions.

One important point should be added to this account of how the *Tractatus* uses the word "proposition." Wittgenstein introduces a way of speaking of "same proposition" at 4.465 and 5.141. These ways of speaking of the identity of propositions are not applicable to senseless propositions other than tautologies and contradictions, although there is no reason why one could not (for example) treat mathematical propositions written in different notations as "the same mathematical proposition." Again, one could also introduce a way of treating the identity of propositions, which allowed *TLP* 5 (for example) to count as the same proposition whatever language it was written in, and which at the same time recognized the proposition as nonsensical.

I have three conclusions about the way the *Tractatus* speaks of *Sätze*:

1. The reader of the *Tractatus* is expected to distinguish the various cases here. The important thing is not the word "*Satz*" itself. There are four groupings of cases that might be labeled with the word "*Satz*":

---

from what they look like, see Juliet Floyd 2010. See also the Introduction to Part II of this volume, where I discuss some views of Anscombe's that resemble Frascolla's. Both of them ascribe to Wittgenstein the idea that recognition of what a sentence is supposedly an attempt to say can enable us to judge that it is not an allowable sentence according to the picture theory.

(a) senseful propositions; (b) senseful propositions and logical propositions; (c) senseful propositions, logical propositions, and other propositions which lack sense but which are useful in connection with the uses of senseful propositions and which have some logical analogies with senseful propositions; (d) anything looking like a proposition. With these different cases in view, the reader will also be able to consider whether some particular use of the word "*Satz*" (or "proposition") might involve equivocating (in the sense of taking for granted a wider and narrower use of the word at the same time), or might involve simply failing to make any definite determination.

2. The *theme* (as one might put it) of *propositions being representations of situations* is central in the *Tractatus,* but the presence and significance of that theme leaves unsettled the question what the status is of anything which appears to be a proposition but which does not represent a situation. There is no inference from something's not being a senseful proposition to its being a bit of nonsense; nor is there an inference from its not being a senseful proposition and not being a tautology or contradiction to its being a bit of nonsense.

3. The superficial form of a propositional construction tells us nothing about what its use is, if indeed it has any use. It does not enable us to see in the propositional sign a tie to a would-be assertion of some sort. There is no route from the superficial form of a propositional construction to a diagnosis of nonsensicality. If we imagine that we see "what the proposition is trying to say," we are taking its superficial form as a guide to the form of something that (as we think) would have to be outside the limits of sense; but the confusion here lies in a misunderstanding of what it is for something that looks like a proposition to have this or that "form." When Wittgenstein says of a bit of language: "That can't be said," that implies that it has nothing but its superficial form—that is, that there is nothing to it; it dissolves.

I am not in this essay arguing that the *Tractatus* excludes no sort of proposition, although I take that to be so. I will comment here only that the idea that the book excludes "synthetic necessary truths" depends upon the idea that we can recognize some propositional constructions as would-be synthetic necessary truths, and as therefore lying outside the limits of language. But what is the matter in the case of such propositions is something that is the matter with *us,* with our taking the superficial form of a propositional construction as an indication of a kind of would-be assertion.[8]

I have been arguing against the "everything-else-is-nonsense" reading of the *Tractatus.* But it might be objected that my account clearly goes too far. If I am suggesting that something that looks like a proposition, but has a use, does not count as nonsensical on the *Tractatus* view, am I not (the objection goes) committing myself to the idea that the propositions of the *Tractatus* itself don't count as nonsense, since plainly they are intended to have a use? And wouldn't that run against Wittgenstein's calling them nonsensical? But the objection rests on misunderstanding: I am not suggesting that everything that looks like a proposition but has a use is therefore meaningful. We need to distinguish cases like that of equations, which are Scheinsätze, which may look as if they are about things named in them, and which have a usefulness which is not dependent on taking them to be about those things, from cases of Scheinsätze which look as if they are about things named in them (and are such that, taken in that way, they are nonsensical because they contain some sign or signs with no meaning), and which have a usefulness dependent upon both their capacity to mislead us (through their apparent aboutness) and our ultimate capacity to see through the deception. Propositions of mathematics and logic, definitions, scientific laws, probability propositions, and so on have a usefulness tied in, in various ways, with the functioning of senseful propositions, a usefulness which is in no way dependent upon taking them to be a kind of failed senseful proposition, whereas there are other propositions which are useful in particular contexts precisely through the recognition of such failure.

*Summary of Sections 1 and 2.* According to the *Tractatus,* the apparatus of language includes a variety of proposition-like structures which in various ways aid in the application of language. These are not senseful propositions, but there is no indication in the *Tractatus* that Wittgenstein took such propositions to be nonsensical. Such propositions may, however, be mis-seen as would-be assertions of something supposedly

8. For more on the topics of this paragraph, see Essay 3.

outside the limits of language. This kind of mis-seeing can be avoided if you take it seriously that you cannot tell from the superficial appearance of a proposition-like structure what its form is, or what, if anything, it is about, and if you take it seriously that you cannot judge a proposition-like structure to be nonsensical without considering what kind of use in the language such propositions may have.

### 3.

This section starts from Anscombe's claim that one thing wrong with the picture theory was that it excludes too much. My aim in this section is to get into view a class of propositions in which she was particularly interested, and which she took to be excluded by the *Tractatus*.

A lecture of Anscombe's on truth, from 1983, is relevant here.[9] In the lecture, she explains Wittgenstein's idea that one and the same reality corresponds to a proposition and its negation, and she adds that this is indeed essential to the meaning, the sense or *significatio,* of the sort of proposition that can be true *or* false. And later in that lecture, she speaks of the sort of propositions that are such that *truth* cannot be the sole possibility for them. So her idea there is that the sort of propositions that the *Tractatus* theory fits constitute one sort of proposition, the ones such that truth cannot be the sole possibility for them. Her words imply that there is at least one other sort of proposition. One such "other sort" would then be propositions that do not have two possibilities, the sole possibility for propositions of this sort being truth. In 1959, in her *Introduction to Wittgenstein's Tractatus,* she had discussed a proposition about which she says both that it is true, and that it is prohibited by the *Tractatus* because there is nothing that it says is not the case (as opposed to the equally possible situation of its being the case), and it is not a logical truth in the strict sense. This is the proposition "'Someone' is not the name of someone." She argues that this can be illuminatingly said, though what it denies is nothing but confusion; its contradictory, she adds, "peters out into nothingness." For the proposition itself, the sole possibility is truth, which means, she says, that it

---

9. Anscombe 2011d. Anscombe's title for the lecture was "Truth."

is not allowed by the *Tractatus* (*IWT*, 85–86). And she also says that this is a reason why Wittgenstein's theory is inadequate, because it excludes such propositions—where these would be among the ones that she pointed out also as possibilities in the 1983 lecture. I shall speak of propositions for which the only possibility is truth as can-only-be-true propositions. Her point, that the *Tractatus* treatment of these propositions was inadequate, needs to be put carefully. The *Tractatus*, as she reads it, does not exclude tautologies and mathematical equations; and these are indeed propositions that do not have the possibility of truth and that of falsity. So Anscombe's objection to the *Tractatus* is that it excludes all can-only-be-true propositions except for tautologies and equations.

I think that there are problems in Anscombe's discussion of "'Someone' is not the name of someone." (See Essay 2.) But I am interested here in a general claim that is not dependent on the particular example. The claim is that, in excluding all can-only-be-true propositions apart from tautologies and equations, the *Tractatus* is excluding a significant group of propositions, the contradictories of which peter out into nothingness. It is part of this claim that such propositions may have a use; they may be illuminating. It may be that, in her objection to the *Tractatus*, Anscombe was concerned also with other types of can-only-be-true propositions, in addition to those whose contradictories peter out. But I shall be concerned only with those propositions that do not have anything intelligible opposed to them.

I want to consider some other possible cases, but how exactly should these cases be described? At this point, in as noncommittal a way as possible. They will be cases where there is a kind of asymmetry between a proposition and its negation: the proposition itself might be said to have a use, or to be intelligible, or to be thinkable, or to be illuminating, or indeed (as in Anscombe's example) to be true, while its negation falls apart, is not something thinkable, has nothing to it but confusion—or something of the kind. This asymmetry then can be contrasted with the symmetry of two different kinds of case. There is first the symmetry of senseful propositions in the *Tractatus* sense, each of which is a member of a pair, both members of which have the possibility of truth and the possibility of falsehood. My cases will also involve a contrast with necessary truths the negations of which do not peter out into nothing but supposedly express *something that cannot be the case*—"substantial impossibilities," as they might be called. The negations of the propositions with which I am concerned are not expressive of anything but confusion. Tautologies and contradictions constitute a special case. Examining the reasons for putting them either with symmetric pairs or with asymmetric propositions would take me too far out of the way. (See Essay 6 for some discussion of how they can be fitted in.)

The first set of cases comes from the *Tractatus* and the *Prototractatus,* and is discussed by Michael Kremer (2002). Kremer argues that we should read the *Tractatus* on mathematical equations as involving an asymmetry of the general sort specified above. Correct equations have a use, and on the *Tractatus* view, they count as meaningful though not senseful; incorrect equations (and presumably this would apply also to incorrect inequations) have no use in the language and are meaningless nonsense. Kremer also discusses the related case of the *Prototractatus* description of correct mathematical propositions as self-evident, and of incorrect ones as nonsense; and again there is an asymmetry of the sort with which I'm concerned. (Kremer argues that the changes we see later, in the 1922 version of the *Tractatus,* reflect the idea that incorrect equations do not even count as "mathematical propositions," which is a view that maintains the asymmetry but expresses it differently.) Although I want to focus here on the *Tractatus,* we should note that in the lectures reported by Moore, Wittgenstein said that there were a large number of different sorts of propositions that have no intelligible negation, including mathematical propositions, logical propositions, and some propositions about color (Moore 1959, 267). Kremer's account of Wittgenstein on equations has an important consequence. We can see that behind the usefulness of the equation there lies the calculation of which it is the record. The corresponding point is somewhat obscured in Anscombe's treatment of "'Someone' is not the name of someone," of which she says that it may be illuminating. But it is not so much the statement itself which is illuminating, but rather the clarification (which she gives) which underpins the statement by explaining how different the use of "someone" is from that of a name. Her proposition has the clarificatory activity behind it in something like the way the equation has behind it the carrying out of the calculation.

Cases of the sort which interest me can come up in the context of philosophical controversy, as is illustrated by two examples. The first is from Sophie Grace Chappell's account of Bernard Williams on internal and external reasons. She formulates the "wider" version of Williams's claim this way: "Nothing can be a reason for me to do such-and-such, unless doing so furthers some motivation I have or would come to if I deliberated fully rationally." The structure of Williams's view (as Chappell describes it) is the same as the structure of Anscombe's account of her example. In both cases, the true proposition is negative, and what it denies is, as Chappell puts it, "only a piece of confusion."[10] A second case comes from Peter Geach's description of the statement "A proposition can occur now asserted, now unasserted, without losing its identity or truth-value." He describes the point there ("the Frege point") as "not a thesis, or a conclusion derivable from premises, but an attainable insight," and says that what is opposed to it is "not a contrary arguable thesis" but mere muddle (1979, 223). Geach also wrote about this sort of case in his autobiographical memoir, where he said that he learned from Wittgenstein "that philosophical mistakes are often not refutable falsehoods but confusions," and that the contrary insights "cannot be conveyed in proper propositions with a truth-value" (1991, 13).

## 4.

In this section and in Section 5, I consider the relevance of Frege's ideas to the questions I have been discussing, beginning with what he says about "The concept *horse* is not a concept," which I shall refer to as "the concept-horse proposition." (I am grateful to Warren Goldfarb for asking how this case would fit into my discussion of Wittgenstein, Anscombe, and what can only be true.)

We should note that the concept-horse proposition, as Frege uses it, resembles several of the cases we have seen so far in being negative in surface form, and intended to correct a confusion. Frege's specific target was Benno Kerry's use of the proposition "The concept *horse* is a concept

---

10. Chappell 2010. The version I quote has been replaced. The later version is not so neatly quotable but makes the same point: what is opposed to Williams's view is not something intelligible.

easily attained," but the target would include any similarly constructed proposition purporting to ascribe a property to the concept *horse,* where that is purportedly a concept in Frege's sense; and the target also includes "The concept *horse* is a concept."

It is not entirely clear how to see the relation between the concept-horse proposition and Anscombe's problems about the *Tractatus.* A different region of Frege's thought provides us with a tool that we might try to use here. He allowed for there being a phase in the working out of a systematic science prior to the system's actual use, a phase in which the expressions that will be used in the system are prepared for use. In what Frege speaks of as the propaedeutic, both complex notions and logically primitive elements can be clarified. The clarification of complex notions makes it possible to stipulate the sense of some signs to be used in the system, through definitions which will form part of the system. Frege treated the propositions that are used to give definitions as having two different roles, one role when they are used to stipulate a meaning for a sign which does not as yet have a meaning, and a different role afterward. Speaking of the context in which the stipulation is given, one can say that the definition "is concerned only with signs"; but it then "goes over into a sentence asserting an identity" (Frege 1979b, 208). Definition-propositions, then, are striking in initially having a non-assertoric role and in being capable of functioning as assertions afterward. Thus, for example, if the definition-proposition defines what logically has the role of a proper name, the proposition can afterward be used to say of the thing named that it stands in the relation of identity to itself; and the two names that flank the identity sign will have the same sense. In this use, the proposition asserts something about the thing named, but did not do so in its initial use. In general, if a proposition is used in the preparatory phase or propaedeutic, or if it is used as a definition within the system, it may look as if it is expressing an assertion about things that are named in it, but it may have, at that stage, a quite different sort of use.[11]

---

11. Added in 2017: I have corrected some errors in the originally published version of this paragraph.

When Frege explains what he means by "concept," "function," and "object," these explanations belong to the preparatory phase; and I think we can take what Frege says, when he is trying to clear up misunderstandings of his remarks about concepts, as also belonging to the preparatory use of language. If the proposition "The concept *horse* is not a concept" can be taken to belong to the preparatory stage (that is, to the stage of sharpening of linguistic tools, prior to the use of these tools), might this affect its characterization? My idea here is that Frege's allowing for the different role a proposition may have in different contexts suggests that in general there may be a question whether a proposition occurring within the "preparatory" stage might have a use that is different from what one might assume (if one takes it to be straightforwardly an assertion about the things meant by the words in it). I am not here suggesting that the general issue is one on which Frege had a view, but only that the view that he did indeed have—that definition-propositions have two distinct roles, one when they are used to stipulate a sense for a sign and another afterward—can be used to frame a question: How far do any other types of proposition work in different ways, depending on whether they are actually in use within a system after the initial clarifications and stipulations, or instead belong to those initial phases?

I want to explore this idea, and also to connect it with themes in Wittgenstein's thought. In fact I want to make a wild speculative claim: We should think of there being parallels between Frege on preparation of language for use in a systematic science, and Wittgenstein on the kinds of propositions I discussed in Sections 1 and 2, which I said could be labeled as *Behelfe der Darstellung,* or as apparatus propositions, or as preparatory propositions. I think that Wittgenstein's treatment of this class of propositions has some resemblances to Frege on propositions used in the preparation of expressions for use in a systematic science; but Wittgenstein's treatment of this category of uses makes it much more extensive than the corresponding category as we see it in Frege (as comes out especially in Wittgenstein's willingness in the 1930s to think of mathematical propositions as belonging to the preparation of language for its use). What I take to be important for both Wittgenstein and Frege is the idea that a particular proposition may occur with a "preparatory" role and, in a different context, with a non-preparatory role, in which the signs may now function differently. A further point (that comes up in different ways for the two philosophers) is that in many cases it may be easy to misunderstand a proposition which has a preparatory-type use, if you try to read it as if it were straightforwardly an assertion about the things meant by the words in it.[12] An important difference between Frege and Wittgenstein on "preparatory" propositions is that, for Wittgenstein, many propositions that have this character *keep it.* Their use may *continue to be* that of enabling other types of uses of propositions. I think that this idea, which marks a significant difference from Frege, can be seen in the *Tractatus;* but it is explicit later on—for example, when Wittgenstein in 1939 invited his students to think of mathematical and logical propositions as *"preparations* for a use of language," and he added "almost as definitions are" (1976, 249). In the *Tractatus,* Wittgenstein said that a definition was a rule dealing with signs, and had the form "a = b", but he then went on to make the point, quoted in Section 2, that expressions of that form state nothing about whatever it is that is meant by the signs that flank the identity sign: they are not used referentially. This is not far from what Frege says about definition-propositions *when they are in use to introduce a new sign,* but it is very far from what Frege held about the use of definition-propositions afterward. They go on afterward to have an assertoric use, in which the signs flanking the identity sign and the identity sign itself are used referentially; and this is, then, very different from the *Tractatus.* My plan now is to use Frege's treatment of "preparatory" propositions to deepen the questions about Wittgenstein's approach, and to use Wittgenstein's treatment of the asymmetric propositions that I have been concerned with to help us understand Frege on the concept *horse.* Section 5 starts from Frege and then moves back to Wittgenstein.

## 5.

What Frege says in making clear what he means by "concept," "function," and "object" was held by him to belong to the phase in the develop-

---

12. But see Weiner 2008 on the variety of kinds of uses of language that can occur within the propaedeutic of a systematic science, as Frege understands it.

ment of a systematic science in which the signs that are going to be used in the science (in this case, signs belonging to Frege's notation) are prepared for their use. Frege's attempts to clear up misunderstandings of what he had said as part of this propaedeutic also belong to the propaedeutic. That is, "On Concept and Object" (1984b) should be taken to belong to this kind of use of language. (We should note here the connection also with Anscombe's example "'Someone' is not the name of someone," which is meant to correct a misunderstanding about the use in ordinary language of "someone" as existential quantifier.) I mentioned that the concept-horse proposition is directed specifically against Benno Kerry's "The concept 'horse' is a concept easily attained"; and Frege believed that the underlying confusion in Kerry's writings, including in particular his use of that example, was the running together of the logical sense of "concept" (as Frege had attempted to present it) and uses of "concept" to mean something psychological (as it does in Kerry's account of concept formation). This muddling together leads Kerry to take for granted that the words "The concept 'horse'" in "The concept 'horse' is a concept easily attained" refer to something that is both a concept as Frege understands it and an object falling under the concept *easily attainable concept.* Frege wanted to make plain how this muddle operates; he wanted to block the route to the muddle—a route that it is all too easy to take, through exactly the blur between the logical and the psychological exemplified by Kerry's treatment of the concept *horse.* The point of the concept-horse proposition is, in large part, what it is *against,* and what Frege shows about how not to get *there.* The concept-horse proposition is a kind of roadblock, blocking a road to confusion. Frege himself, reflecting on the problematic character of the proposition, said that "by a necessity of language, my expressions, taken literally, sometimes miss my thought" (1984b, 193). But we cannot infer straightforwardly from that remark that Frege took there to be a thought, in his sense of that word, that his proposition was unable properly to express. The problem in ascribing to him such an understanding is that, for him, a thought is something that can be grasped as the sense of an interrogative question, before one answers the question. If there is nothing but muddle in "The concept 'horse' is a concept easily attained" or in "The concept 'horse' is a concept"—if there is no intelligible thought that the utterer of such things is struggling to express—it is not clear that what Frege finds himself unable properly to express, when he uses a proposition formed by negating the confused utterance, counts on his own terms as a thought. A thought has an opposite thought; a muddle isn't a false thought.

[Added in 2017: While I still think that the point of the concept-horse proposition is, in large part, what it is against, and what Frege shows about how not to get *there*, I now think that the originally published version of this essay identified Frege's target too narrowly. Frege's target includes cases that do not involve the kind of confusion of the psychological and the logical that characterizes Kerry's approach. Here is how to get into confusion without muddling the psychological and the logical, by starting from Frege's own discussion of such statements as "The concept *man* is not empty." Frege takes that to be a legitimate way of speaking within informal logical discussion. But this then may lead one to ask why one should not, in a parallel way, legitimately say "The concept *man* is a concept." And one may mean by this, or take oneself to mean by it, that it is a concept in Frege's sense. If so, one has moved into the kind of confusion against which Frege had directed the concept-horse proposition, but one will not have confused the logical with the psychological. I would now also want to bring out something that is not explicit in my original discussion: that the confusion to which Frege is responding involves not seeing that one may be trying to use an expression for a first-level concept as if it could somehow *mean* a second-level concept. That is, it is important here to consider what one may be taking oneself to be doing with "is a concept." I discuss the issues here in the last section of the Introduction to Part II of this book. Although I now understand differently what the confusion is to which Frege was responding, this difference doesn't affect the way I see Frege's response itself.]

Here I think we can be helped to move forward by going back to Wittgenstein.

First, there are a couple of points to note about the idea that a proposition used in the "preparatory" phase of language can also have a different sort of use. This idea comes out in Wittgenstein's discussion in 1939 of "putting a proposition in the archives" (1976, 107, 112–114), where the image of "the archives" indicates something that will have a future application, just as the depositing of a platinum rod in the archives might be preparation for its future use as a standard of measurement. Wittgenstein says that a particular proposition like "20 apples plus 30 apples is 50 apples" might be an experiential proposition about what happens with apples, or it might be used as a mathematical proposition, might (that is) be put into the archives, might have a "preparatory" use (1976, 113–114). But we should also note that a proposition that has a "preparatory" use may be misread, if we take it, or try to take it, as asserting something about the things that appear to be referred to by the signs in it. On this point, we can consider Moore's report of Wittgenstein's "astounding" claim that Russell was wrong in distinguishing as he did between the meaning of " = Df" and " = " (Moore 1959, 290). Russell took definitional propositions to be concerned solely with the signs, not the things meant, while identity propositions are, he thought, about the things meant by the signs flanking the equal sign: identity is (according to Russell) a reflexive property and a symmetric relation (Whitehead and Russell, 1962, 22). A criticism of Russell's reading of identity propositions (as leading into confusion) is suggested by *TLP* 5.473, and the confusion in question is blocked by *TLP* 4.241–242: *Don't read identity propositions as being about the things named by the signs flanking the " = ".* The important idea, there, is that trying to read a proposition the use of which is "preparatory" as if it were straightforwardly about the things meant by the signs in it can lead into confusion.[13] That idea was at the heart also of the discussion of probability propositions in Section 2 of this essay. If one tries to read probability propositions as expressive of a relation between two propositions, they appear to affirm something that lies outside the domain of the sayable.

We need to consider more fully Kremer's account of the use of mathematical propositions, as understood in the *Tractatus*. The important background fact for his account is that we may use calculations in carrying out an inference from one experiential proposition to another.

---

13. To say that the proposition is not about the things meant does not imply that it must be about the signs. Contrast Moore's discussion of Wittgenstein on Russell and identity (1959, 289–290); and see also Wittgenstein 1975, 143.

But once we have done a particular calculation, we may keep a record of it for future use: and that is what equations should be taken to be—records of calculations, useful in making inferences from one proposition to another, in cases in which we could not make the inference without a calculation. Similarly, if a proposition is shown by a logical calculation to be a truth-functional tautology, the tautology may be kept, as being the record of the calculation, and can then also come in handy in making inferences.[14] Equations and tautologies show us roads that are open for us, roads by which we can go from one proposition to another. But in some cases it might be useful to have "Road closed: dangerous" signs. Suppose, for example, we found ourselves frequently multiplying 2 times 24 and getting 46 (perhaps because we tended to slip from multiplying 2 times 4 to adding instead). So in these cases an inequation might come in handy: "$2 \times 24 \neq 46$." As I mentioned earlier, it would be a consequence of Kremer's reading of Wittgenstein on equations that such an inequation has the same asymmetry (of not being opposed to anything meaningful) that correct equations have. There is no reason we might not write down inequations and put them in the archives as indications of common inferential dangers. Wittgenstein himself, shortly after his return to philosophy in 1929, did indeed suggest that, just as equations can be construed as rules for signs rather than as propositions (using the term "proposition," there, in a narrow sense), inequations could be treated in the same way (1975, 249); he added that there may also be cases when it would be useful to recognize that such-and-such proposition does not follow from some other. Alongside the suggestion that inequations might be put into the archives as warnings, we should put a suggestion of Wittgenstein's. He wrote (2005, 312):

> Language has the same traps ready for everyone; the immense network of easily trodden false paths. And thus we see one person after another walking down the same paths and we already know where he will make a turn, where he will keep going straight ahead without noticing the turn, etc., etc. Therefore, wherever false paths branch off I ought to put up signs to help in getting past the dangerous spots.

14. Kremer 2002, 299–300.

My suggestion here is that the role of false-path markers is not very different from that of equations, as Kremer discusses them: equations indicate useful paths. Path-indicators—indicators of useful paths, on the one hand, and of paths leading into confusion, on the other—belong in the general and varied group of "preparatory" propositions. But this point should then be seen with the preceding one: that propositions with a preparatory use may be misunderstood if one tries to read them as straightforwardly assertoric, straightforwardly about the things named by the signs in them, or straightforwardly about the signs themselves. The path-blockers, the indicators of confusion, most frequently take the form of negative propositions, of denials of something that peters out into nothing. But the negation in them can be taken to be like the negation we see in "Don't": "Don't go that way"; that is, they can be thought of as like rules about where not to go in using signs, just as identity propositions were taken by Wittgenstein to indicate something we could do with signs: we can substitute the sign on this side of " = " for the one on the other side. The "Don't" of a path-blocking proposition properly follows a process of making plain what the danger is, what the confusion is, that lies on the blocked path; and this is, of course, what Frege does in "On Concept and Object." My suggestion, then, is that, just as we may carry out a calculation, and make a memorandum of it for future use, so we may make plain a kind of confusion, and make a memorandum in the form of a negative proposition, a path-blocker. If we recognize a path-blocking proposition as having a kind of preparatory use not altogether far from that of such path-opening propositions as equations and identities, and not far from simple path-blocking propositions like inequations, this has two consequences. First, following Kremer on mathematical propositions: Propositions that are not themselves senseful propositions, but that are useful to us in operating with senseful propositions, are not nonsensical. Secondly, if we try to read them as straightforward assertions, we may be flummoxed: that is clear already in the case of Wittgenstein on taking identity as a property.[15]

15. Added in 2017: In writing about inequations, I had in mind those written with the not-equal-to sign, not those written with any of these: $<, >, \leq, \geq$. I think that Wittgenstein's remarks about inequalities in *Philosophical Remarks* (1975, 248–249)

I have suggested that "The concept *horse* is not a concept" can be thought of as a path-blocker, and as having a use like that of a warning about how not to use words in order to avoid confusion. I've suggested too that path-blockers have the asymmetric character of mathematical equations, as described by Kremer. I am not suggesting that that is how Frege himself thought of the concept-horse proposition. It's rather that I want to do something analogous to what Wittgenstein does: he invites us to consider mathematical propositions as having a role like that of setting up a unit of measurement before we actually start measuring things. The philosophical suggestion is: *Try thinking of it like this.* So I'm suggesting that we try thinking of the concept-horse proposition as an asymmetric proposition used as a path-blocker. I also would want to emphasize the importance of not treating the concept-horse proposition as if the alternatives we confront in thinking about it are that it is either nonsensical or a significant bit of referential language, in which case the problem arises of how it is about what it is apparently meant to be about.

In Section 2 of this essay, I discussed the difference between the non-sensical propositions of the *Tractatus,* which are indeed meant to be useful, and senseless but not nonsensical propositions like mathematical equations and probability propositions. I made the distinction this way: that although probability propositions and other apparatus propositions may resemble senseful propositions, the fact that we may be taken in by that appearance has nothing to do with their usefulness, whereas the usefulness of the *Tractatus* propositions depends on our first being taken in by them, and our then recognizing that they are not what we took them for. But there is a further distinction that we can make now. While responses to confusion, and other sorts of asymmetric propositions, may have a merely nonce-use, it is significant that many of them—mathematical equations, definitions, probability propositions

---

are also about those with the not-equal-to sign. My treatment of inequations as path-blockers needs to be supplemented by the point that inequations can indicate useful inferential paths. So, for example, if there are seven of us, the drinks cost $6 each, and I have $50, I can use "$7 \times 6 < 50$" in inferring that I can pay for all the drinks and even have something left over. I am grateful to Steven Methven for pointing out this kind of use of inequalities.

(and so on)—may be *kept*. Indeed, the image Wittgenstein uses for propositions used in these kinds of ways is that of their being put *into the archives*. In contrast, the nonsensical propositions of the *Tractatus* are meant to be *thrown away*. A proposition like "The configuration of objects produces states of affairs" is meant to *lead us on*, in an activity the outcome of which is meant to be a reconception of what doing philosophy is, and of what we can achieve by it. The justification that there will be for doing philosophy that way is that it will be helpful; problems will disappear (supposedly). There is (that is) no need to keep hold of the *Tractatus* propositions as if they were needed to provide a justification for anything that the book teaches us to do. Unlike "7 + 5 = 12," the propositions of the *Tractatus* have no ongoing role; nothing depends on keeping them around. But there is a "but." Propositions may have different uses. There is no reason why a proposition in the *Tractatus*, the role of which there is to lead us on, and which indeed (in order to play that role) needs to appear misleadingly to be an a priori assertion of some sort, should not also come to have a use as a path-blocker (for example).

Philosophers *try* to read propositions referentially; and this tendency is one of the things at the heart of Wittgenstein's treatment of mathematical propositions. There is a sense of "about" which is at work in the *Tractatus*, and in that sense, propositions with some or other asymmetric sort of use are not *about* what the signs in them might stand for in other contexts; nor are they about the signs themselves. One can speak of what an asymmetric proposition is about, but "about," there, is not used in the same way it is used when we speak of propositions that come in intelligible pairs.[16] We don't have to first read an asymmetric proposition referentially and then take it to be nonsense, in order to be clear about its use; and this point applies to all sorts of asymmetric propositions, including path-blockers. You don't have to take "The concept *horse* is not a concept" to be "about the concept *horse*" first, in order to move to a clearer view of its use: it is not like *Tractatus* nonsense. Its use does not depend on its taking you in. The model of *Tractatus* nonsense is not a great model for path-blockers like "The concept *horse* is

16. See Wittgenstein 1979, 155; Wittgenstein 1976, 33, 112–114, 250–251, 254, 279.

not a horse"; and it seems to me that one reason it has been taken to be a good model is that we may tend to consider just two models: the would-be-expression-of-a-thought model, in which the concept-horse proposition is taken as aiming to express a thought about the concept *horse* but not quite managing to do so properly, and the Tractarian-nonsense model. Try instead the "2 times 24 is not 46"–model, where that is understood as an asymmetric path-blocker.[17]

**6.**

"'Someone' is not the name of someone," understood as a response to confusion, was Anscombe's example of a proposition which is prohibited by the *Tractatus*. She took this to be unreasonable and to illustrate one important inadequacy of the *Tractatus* account of propositions. In this essay, I've tried to show that the *Tractatus* is not as unwelcoming to *responses to confusion* as she thought. The heart of my argument is that their status can be conceived on the model of inequations, and that we can see the use of inequations by seeing how it resembles and how it differs from that of equations: correct inequations and correct equations have a function in language, though they do not have, opposed to them, propositions which also have a function in the language. I have made a start, but only a start, on the questions from which I began. I have not discussed what might be involved in calling *true* a proposition that responds to confusion, as Anscombe does. I have not discussed how Wittgenstein's treatment of apparatus propositions changed and developed in his later philosophy; nor have I spelled out the views of Wittgenstein on modality that are implicit in my procedure.[18] But the main thing I

17. For a quite different sort of approach, see Anscombe 1981b, and the discussion of Anscombe's remarks about the concept-horse proposition in Jolley 2007.

18. In the essay, I use a contrast between asymmetric propositions (some or all of which one might want to think of as *propositions that can only be true*) and two types of symmetric propositions: contingent propositions, on the one hand, and, on the other, necessary truths taken to have, opposed to them, propositions which do not dissolve into nothing but which express something that cannot be the case. What underlies this mode of treatment is the idea that it is useful to think of the *Tractatus*,

haven't discussed is *the range* of Anscombe's objection. It may be that propositions that function as responses to confusion can (as I've argued) be accommodated within Wittgenstein's approach. But that sort of case figured only as an example for Anscombe. Her general point was that, apart from tautologies and equations, propositions that can only be true were excluded by the *Tractatus*. The question then remains how far her objection would still be that there are kinds of proposition that can only be true, that are excluded by the *Tractatus,* and that would not be excluded by an adequate philosophical understanding of language. So there is much that remains to be done.[19]

---

not so much as having a stance on "modality," as *disrupting* the idea of modality as a topic. The *Tractatus* is concerned (on the one hand) with tautologies, contradictions, and such asymmetric propositions as equations and (on the other hand) with various kinds of confusion that are involved in taking some or other proposition to express, or to be trying to express, or intended to express, something that is necessarily the case. For a different account of modality in the *Tractatus,* see Shieh 2014.

19. An earlier version of parts of this paper were part of a paper presented at the Kirchberg Wittgenstein Symposium and at the Wittgenstein Workshop at the University of Chicago. I am very grateful to the members of the audience on both occasions, and to Adrian Moore, Silver Bronzo, Jean-Philippe Narboux, Lars Hertzberg, and Anselm Mueller for helpful comments and suggestions.

# FIVE

# Disagreements: Anscombe, Geach, Wittgenstein

## 1. Anscombe and Geach on Responding to Confusion

In his autobiographical memoir, Peter Geach says that he learned from Wittgenstein, partly from the *Tractatus,* but more from personal contact, "that philosophical mistakes are often not refutable falsehoods but confusions," and that the contrary insights "cannot be conveyed in proper propositions with a truth-value" (1991, 13). In the memoir and elsewhere, he gives as an example of an insight that has opposed to it nothing but confusion, the statement "A proposition can occur now asserted, now unasserted, without losing its identity or truth-value."

In *An Introduction to Wittgenstein's Tractatus,* Elizabeth Anscombe discussed a case of such a response to confusion, but what she says about it is strikingly different from what Geach says about such cases (*IWT,* 85–86). The confusion with which she was concerned was that of Antony Flew, who had said that it was part of the logic of the word "somebody," unlike "nobody," to refer to somebody. "If this were so," Anscombe said, "then, on being told that everybody hates somebody, we could ask to be introduced to this universally hated person." In criticism of Flew, one might then say, "'Somebody' does not refer to somebody." Anscombe says about that statement and about "'Someone' is not the name of someone," that they express an insight. What is opposed to them "is only confusion and muddle." So far, this is parallel to what Geach said. But Anscombe says of the statement "'Someone' is not the name of someone" that it is "obviously true." This comes up in her argument that Wittgenstein's account of propositions is inadequate, since it results in prohibiting such statements as "'Someone' is not the name of someone." It lacks the bipolarity of senseful propositions: there is no possibility of its being false, since what is opposed to it is mere muddle. Anscombe thinks that there is no alternative formulation of the insight that would not run up against the *Tractatus* prohibition, and that Wittgenstein would have said about the insight itself that it was something that *showed*, but could not be said. Later in her book, she discusses in general terms the things that "would be true if they could be said," where these are things that are supposedly "shown"; and again she uses "'Someone' is *not* the name of someone" as an example (162). On the *Tractatus* view, as she explains it, what that sentence "intends to say" could be described as quite correct, and it would be true if it could be said. That view can then be contrasted with hers—namely, that one should be able to grant the obvious truth of "'Someone' is not the name of someone."

There is apparently disagreement between Geach and Anscombe about responses to confusion, responses that express an insight opposed to which there is nothing but muddle. What, if anything, is at stake in the question whether a statement expressing such an insight may be "obviously true" (as Anscombe says), or whether instead it is not, properly speaking, a proposition with a truth-value (as Geach held)? A second sort of disagreement is that between Anscombe and Wittgenstein about the picture theory. As she sees the issue here, it is about the theory's excluding types of proposition that should not be excluded. The notion of truth is at the heart of both disagreements. I focus first, in Section 2, on the relation between Anscombe's views about truth and her ideas about the inadequacies of the picture theory. I try to show in Section 3 that Anscombe's criticism of the picture theory is not as straightforward as she takes it to be. Where that leaves her disagreement with Wittgenstein is the topic of Section 4. Sections 5 through 8 explore further the disagreement between Anscombe and Wittgenstein, and in Section 8, I return to the disagreement between Anscombe and Geach. A third disagreement—this one between Anscombe and contemporary theories of truth—appears at the end of Section 2, and again in the final section.

## 2. Anscombe, Truth, and What the Picture
## Theory Excludes

An essential part of the *Tractatus* account of senseful propositions, as Anscombe explains it, is that one and the same reality corresponds to *the proposition and its negation.* Propositions of this sort can be true *or* false; truth is not the only possibility for them. But this is not the only sort of proposition; there are also propositions that do not have both possibilities (2011d, 74). What was the matter with the *Tractatus* was that it excluded all such propositions except for tautologies, contradictions, and equations. Anscombe's discussion of "'Someone' is not the name of someone" was meant to bring out the unreasonableness of that exclusion. She says of that statement that its contradictory, "when examined, peters out into nothingness"; and her argument about "'Someone' is not the name of someone" would apply also to other statements expressing an insight in response to confusion, if their contradictories peter out into nothingness. Such statements, then, are among those that she takes to be wrongly excluded by the *Tractatus* (*IWT*, 85).

In the *Introduction to the Tractatus,* Anscombe also discusses propositions like "Red is a color" and "Two is a number." I am not sure she would say of these cases something parallel to what she says of "'Someone' is not the name of someone." About "Red is a color" and "Two is a number," she says that these propositions cannot express anything that might be false, and that there are not two possibilities, that 2 is and that it is not a number, and that red is and that it is not a color, of which only the first happens to be actual in each case (*IWT*, 82). Her wording leaves two readings open. (1) She might say about these propositions that, in each case, the contradictory of the proposition peters out into nothingness. (2) The second possibility is that there is opposed to each of these propositions a proposition that says that something is the case, but it is something that cannot be the case. In other words, the contradictory of each of the propositions does not peter out into nothingness; it does express something, but something that we can see to be impossible. It is necessarily not true, but not a mere piece of confusion. The difference between the two ways of reading Anscombe might also be put like this. On the first reading, the contradictory of "Red is a color" does not have truth-conditions; on the second reading, "Red is not a color" has truth-conditions which are necessarily not fulfilled.

A question arises at this point. Anscombe plainly thought that the *Tractatus* theory was faulty through excluding all propositions that can only be true, except for tautologies and mathematical propositions. But the passages I have discussed do not settle whether she thought there were propositions that can only be true and that have contradictories that state to be a fact something that cannot be the case, *in addition to* there being some true propositions the contradictories of which peter out into nothingness. Besides tautologies and mathematical propositions, are there, on Anscombe's view, two types of propositions that can only be true, or is there only the latter sort, the ones whose contradictories peter out?[1] I shall focus on the latter kind of case. It is not included in many contemporary discussions of truth, which take the notion of truth to be applicable to a proposition (or to whatever they take to be the kind of thing that can be true or false) only if it has a significant negation. So something the opposite of which is muddle would not (on such accounts) be "truth-apt." There is a slogan derived from Wittgenstein, "The negation of nonsense is nonsense,"[2] and one might come up with a related slogan "The negation of muddle is muddle," or "Negating a muddle doesn't give you a truth," which looks as if it ought to count against Anscombe. But slogans aren't going to be helpful. There is here, though, a further disagreement concerning truth. Anscombe's willingness to describe as true a statement that has no intelligible negation expresses some kind of disagreement with ideas that shape contemporary theories of truth. I shall say more about this disagreement in Section 9.

---

1. For Anscombe on whether what is impossible can be thought, see her 1981c.

2. Wittgenstein 1995, 216; see also Frege 1984a, 379.

### 3. What Does the Picture Theory Exclude?

On Anscombe's understanding of the picture theory, it excludes every-thing but propositions that happen to be the true or the false member of a pair of possibilities, and logical and mathematical propositions (*IWT*, 78). Whatever cannot be fitted into one of those categories is treated as nonsense (79). The *Tractatus* is thus taken to have a structure parallel to that of *Language, Truth and Logic,* in which there is a speci-fication of some kinds of proposition, which are all that are allowed to count as meaningful, and *everything else is nonsense* (Ayer 1962, 41). I questioned this understanding of the *Tractatus* in Essay 4; and here I want to give a different argument. It starts from Roger White's discus-sion of mathematical propositions in the *Tractatus* (White 2006). He ar-gues against the idea that, when Wittgenstein describes mathematical equations as "pseudo-propositions," he means that they are nonsensical. What Wittgenstein holds, about such propositions, White says, is that "despite having the apparent form of propositions (being expressed in the indicative mood), they are not true or false, but have a completely different function in our language" (110). White connects Wittgenstein's view of mathematical equations with a *Tractatus* passage (4.241) about definitions. Definitions are also expressed in the indicative mood, and so they also have "the apparent form" of propositions, but they are not true or false; they are rules for the use of signs. The general point White makes is that the expression of a rule (for example, "Bishops only move diagonally") is not a proposition. Mathematical equations can be re-garded as "rules for the manipulation of signs"; and White links this account to Wittgenstein's idea that the application of mathematical equations in operating with senseful (contingent) propositions is essen-tial to the kind of meaning that mathematical equations have. There are three points we should note about White's account.

1. White's treatment of equations is implicitly open-ended. In ex-plaining how we can view equations as expressions of rules, and can thus fit them into the *Tractatus* account of language (as expressions that may have the apparent form of propositions but an entirely different function), he implicitly allows for a question to arise about other sorts of things-that-look-like-propositions, besides equations. Thus, for ex-

ample, White himself treats the laws of mechanics as alternative expressions of vast truth-functions (2006, 112); but, given his own account
of the kinds of significance that rules can have, a treatment of the laws
of mechanics as rules for construction of senseful propositions is an alternative kind of way in which they might be fitted into the *Tractatus*.[3]
His account might also be applied to probability propositions (which,
on the *Tractatus* view, are a priori but not tautologies).[4] Given any kind
of apparent proposition which one might be inclined to think was excluded by the *Tractatus*, the question can arise whether it has the function
of a rule in connection with the uses we make of senseful language, and
it would then not be nonsensical. Further, the notion of *rule* is not doing
the work here; it is the notion of *having a function in language different
from what is suggested by the expression's having the apparent form of a
proposition*. White's discussion of equations, that is, suggests that in general one cannot establish that some (non-tautologous) apparent proposition is nonsensical by an inference from its being in the indicative
mood and being apparently a priori; one has to consider whether it has
some function in language, tied in with the uses of senseful propositions, different from what one might at first take it to have.

2. White's account of equations as rules for manipulation of signs
makes use of the analogy with rules of chess; and his treatment resembles Wittgenstein's own use of an analogy with grammatical rules in his
later discussions of mathematical propositions. But the notion of a rule
is not given for us in a narrowly delimited way; and once the notion of
a rule is taken over and used within the context of an explication of

3. See Griffin 1964, 102–103; compare also Tejedor 2015.

4. On the *Tractatus* on probability propositions, see Essay 4. The applicability of
White's account isn't limited to kinds of proposition mentioned in the *Tractatus*. It
might, for example, also be applied to the kind of natural history propositions discussed by Michael Thompson (2008), like "The tiger has four legs." Here, it may look as
if this is not an empirical proposition (as are propositions about particular tigers and
how many legs they have, or about the distribution of four-leggedness in a population
of tigers), and it is not a tautology. It may look as if, on the *Tractatus* view, the proposition would be nonsensical. But there may well be an account that can be given of the
use of such propositions, as a kind of helpful tool in descriptions of the natural world
and the animals in it.

Wittgenstein's views on mathematical propositions, that use may contribute to shaping for us what we count as a rule, what we take to belong to *being a rule,* and so on. Thus, for example, White says that the rule "Bishops only move diagonally" is not made true or false by the movements of bishops, but we might ask whether it could be described as *true* on some other basis. If we say that the expression of a rule (of language, or of chess, or whatever) is not *true or false,* this gives one way of characterizing rules. I shall get back to the question of truth in relation to things we understand as rules or rule-like in Section 5.

3. Michael Kremer's account of the *Tractatus* on equations (2002) and Roger White's agree in taking as central the function of equations in our dealings with senseful propositions. Kremer argues that equations are senseless but not nonsensical, White that they are rules and not nonsensical; and both Kremer and White make connections with the treatment, earlier in the *Tractatus,* of rules for substitution of signs (4.241– 4.242). I should argue that there is no other convincing kind of way to read the *Tractatus* on equations. This is not just a matter of the specific passages that they discuss, but of responsiveness to what White speaks of as "the spirit of Wittgenstein's remarks on mathematics." Anscombe held that Wittgenstein had to have some way of fitting mathematical propositions into the picture theory (*IWT,* 79); but she did not herself discuss how he fitted them in, and later said that she did not understand it (2011b, 165). Her account of the picture theory leaves out the general issue that surfaces in both Kremer's account and White's (and would, I think, surface in any adequate account of the *Tractatus* on equations), of the misleadingness of the apparent form of some propositional constructions that have a function tied in with our uses of senseful propositions. There is a problem, then, for Anscombe's argument about "'Someone' is not the name of someone." Her argument cannot work as it stands, since her claim that the statement is unreasonably prohibited by the *Tractatus* relies on its not being bipolar and not being "logical truth in any sharp sense of 'logical truth.'" If "logical truth" in a supposed sharp sense is identified with *being a tautology,* her argument won't work because equations are not tautologies; but her argument also won't work if "logical truth" in a supposed sharp sense is explained in

a way that allows for the role of equations and does not take them to be tautologies. The principles that allow for equations do not involve a sharp line cutting off everything beyond tautologies and equations, since what they allow for is the existence (and non-nonsensicality) of apparent propositions that may appear to be a priori truths but that have a function tied in with our uses of senseful propositions.

What I have shown in Section 3 is that, if indeed the *Tractatus* does exclude "'Someone' is not the name of someone," this is by no means obvious, and cannot be inferred from its not being bipolar and not being a tautology or equation. But how far does this affect Anscombe's disagreement with Wittgenstein? That is the topic of Section 4.

### 4. Anscombe's Disagreement with Wittgenstein Again

Any suggestion that the argument of Section 3 has any real effect on Anscombe's criticism of the picture theory might be met by two objections.

*The first objection.* Anscombe would still have wanted to argue that the theory excludes things that should not be excluded. Even if there were a question whether "'Someone' is not the name of someone" might be taken to have the function of a *rule for handling senseful propositions*, or a function analogous to that of such a rule, there is no doubt that *other* propositions that Anscombe took to be wrongly excluded would still be excluded. She said that the picture theory would be "death to natural theology," because its propositions are not supposed to be logical or mathematical propositions, nor propositions "that happen to be true out of pairs of possibilities." But the propositions of natural theology can hardly be sneaked into the somewhat fuzzy-edged category into which equations, and perhaps the laws of mechanics and probability propositions may go, of propositions that do not count as nonsense on the *Tractatus* view because they have a function tied in with our uses of senseful propositions.—The objection is important, and will reappear in a different form in Section 7. But, as it stands, the objection is as fuzzy as the category. The fuzziness is not just a matter of *which* propositions are or aren't included, but of how far our understanding of the category might get stretched or developed, if we try to put into it some of the propositions that Anscombe took to be wrongly excluded by the picture theory.

*The second objection.* Anscombe was concerned with the exclusion of necessary truths from the *Tractatus,* apart from tautologies and equations. And even if it can be argued that the *Tractatus* does not exclude various kinds of proposition that we may at first take to be necessary truths, their non-exclusion goes with their not being *true or false,* as comes out in White's account of the *Tractatus* view of equations as rules. Any account of miscellaneous non-excluded propositions as rules must still recognize that there is no room in the *Tractatus* for necessary truths apart from tautologies.—But this objection, too, is less clear-cut than it may at first seem. There is no easy route from what the *Tractatus* does say about logical truth to any conclusions about what it might be to speak of any of these miscellaneous non-excluded propositions as true. The complexity of the issue comes out in Wittgenstein's allowing, when he returns to philosophy, that some but not all of what can be said about propositions in a narrow sense is applicable as well to hypotheses and mathematical equations, which are not propositions in that sense; and what is thus applicable includes some elements of the usage of "true" and "false." And it is not clear, either, what is at stake on the Anscombe side. What it is for one of the propositions with which she was concerned to be true is evidently not a matter of its being the true member of a pair of propositions, both of which have the capacity to be true and to be false. She had an account of what it is for that sort of proposition to be true (2011d). But so far as she was concerned with propositions the truth of which cannot be construed in such a way, her account does not cover what it is for them to be true, and it is unclear how it might be related to the logical characteristics of such non-excluded propositions as equations.

Sections 5 and 6 use Wittgenstein's 1939 lectures to provide a vantage point for thinking about the disagreement between Anscombe and Wittgenstein.

### 5. Wittgenstein on the "Correspondence to Reality" of Mathematical Propositions

In his 1939 lectures on the foundations of mathematics, Wittgenstein came back again and again to Hardy's conception of mathematics. Two of the lectures take off from the idea (ascribed by Wittgenstein to Hardy) that mathematical propositions in some sense *correspond to reality* (Wittgenstein 1976, 239–254). Wittgenstein got into this topic because of the apparent clash between what he had been saying about mathematics and the belief that mathematical propositions correspond to reality. The worry he wanted to address is this: "Aren't you, Wittgenstein, really denying that mathematics has to be responsible to reality?" In both lectures, he said in response that we can indeed speak of mathematical propositions as responsible to reality, but what this is, is very different from what we may be taking for granted it has to be.

In the second of these lectures, Wittgenstein made a contrast between the correspondence to reality of experiential propositions and the correspondence to reality that we might say that *a word* has. There are some words such that, if you were asked what reality corresponds to them, you might point to something—say, if you were asked what reality corresponds to the word "sofa." But in the case of other words, there is nothing obvious that one would point to—say, the word "perhaps," or the word "and." But here too we can nevertheless speak about a reality corresponding: the reality that corresponds is the great number and variety of things, things about us—things in our lives and our surroundings—that make it extremely useful to us, important to us, to have the word. And then the further point that Wittgenstein makes is that the correspondence to reality of mathematical propositions is much more like the correspondence to reality of a word, say the word "and," than it is like the correspondence to reality of an experiential proposition. Just as you have the word "and," and then you can go on and do all sorts of things with it as you use language, so too, you have "$12 \times 12 = 144$"; and this is an important and enormously useful tool that we have available in language. It corresponds to reality, in this sense, then, that there are all sorts of things about us and our world, because of which "$12 \times 12 = 144$" has an enormously important range of uses within our lives.

Although Wittgenstein speaks in these lectures of there being a sense in which we can say of mathematical propositions that they correspond to reality, he does not speak of there being a sense in which we could say that they are true. But, within the context of these lectures, there is nothing to indicate that he would want to block such a way of talking. Here there is a relevant comment made by Stuart Shanker, that "what matters . . . is not whether it is 'legitimate' to describe mathematical propositions [as Wittgenstein understood them] as 'true', but . . . in what sense this 'truth' should be understood; i.e., how this differs from empirical contexts" (1987, 69)

What you have in these lectures, then, is the idea that there are *words* that, reality being what it is, are enormously useful; there are *propositions of mathematics* that, reality being what it is, are enormously useful, and that we could not do without—and that we can speak of these words, or of these propositions, as "corresponding to reality." Here I would suggest that what Wittgenstein says about such words and propositions is applicable to tools of thought and language more widely than he explicitly suggests. There are concepts, there are samples and paradigms and measures; there are metaphors, stories, and other things, through which we think, through which we understand ourselves and our world, and what we can and cannot do, and what we are doing; and some of these concepts, metaphors, stories, and other things are (reality being what it is) enormously useful, while others we could well do without, others may be disastrous, as elements in our lives, others may be somewhat useful and somewhat baneful. Which, in any case, any of these things is, is something we can consider. Here I will just give one example, drawing on Strawson's wonderful essay "Freedom and Resentment" (1962). When he wrote the essay, a set of concepts was under attack: the related concepts of *desert, responsibility, guilt, condemnation, justice,* as these concepts were and are in use in our lives. Strawson argued against a certain philosophical picture of there being metaphysical conditions that would have to be satisfied, if these concepts and our ways of using them were to be genuinely justified; he argued instead that we should look for the human appropriateness—reality being what it is, including the reality of the kinds of being we are—of these concepts and their widespread complex modes of application in our lives. If we cannot do without "$12 \times 12 = 144$," so too, we, being the kinds of being we are, cannot do without some version of these profoundly significant concepts. We can read Strawson as bringing out the correspondence to reality, in Wittgenstein's 1939 sense, of these concepts. I'm not suggesting that we have to agree with Strawson; I am trying to look at what he is doing in that essay in terms of Wittgenstein's talk of correspondence to reality of words and mathematical propositions. The general philosophical point that Wittgenstein makes about correspondence to reality leaves open what counts as *things in reality* which make some concept or word or proposition or whatnot so useful that we cannot do without it. Think, for example, of what is involved if we include *our nature, what we are like,* in *things in reality that make a word or proposition or concept or whatnot useful.* Consider, for example, Iris Murdoch, who thought that what sort of beings we are is *beings who turn away from reality;* and such a characterization of reality makes centrally important the concepts of patient attention and just discernment. The importance of those concepts depends on how one understands the realities of human nature; and that structure of argument resembles that of Strawson's essay, in which an argument for the indispensability of certain conceptual structures rests on a story about the realities of our lives and our nature. We should note here too that words, concepts, and other tools of thought may be significant in human lives for a very long time and in many different cultural contexts, or perhaps for just a short time, perhaps only in very limited sorts of context.

The story I have given, based on Wittgenstein, about the correspondence to reality of words, mathematical propositions, concepts, and other things that are for us tools of thought and language—this story does not imply that the realities that determine the indispensability or dispensability or harmfulness of these tools of thought might be considered *bare* of various tools of thought that belong to understanding the world and ourselves. There is no suggestion, that is, that the issue of correspondence to reality, in the sense in which Wittgenstein speaks of it in the lectures, can be thought about and examined from some kind of Archimedean point. As comes out very clearly in the Strawson essay that I mentioned, our capacity to judge the value or perniciousness or dispensability of any tool for thinking-with develops from our own experience and that of others, and from our familiarity with the ways in which experiences like our own or unlike our own have been presented and worked over in literature and the arts; it depends also on our ability to reflect on experience.[5]

An objection might be made to Wittgenstein on correspondence to reality, that his account results in there being two entirely distinct senses of "correspondence to reality." The same objection might be made to the idea that we might use the word "true" so it has two uses parallel to the two uses of "correspondence to reality": the objection would be that we then have two entirely distinct senses of "true." But are there not cases in which we may say that a word or an expression that is used in more than one way nevertheless has a single meaning? Wittgenstein discusses this in *Philosophical Investigations*, §§551–570: a word's having two different *uses* doesn't settle whether it has two different *meanings*.[6] There is also an Anscombean reply to the objection. Anscombe's reading of Aristotle on practical truth (and of Anselm on "true") suggests that she allowed for the univocity of "true" in its application, not only to bipolar propositions and other propositions, but also to actions.[7] Neither Wittgenstein nor Anscombe has a simple "use" theory of meaning, which would imply that a word with multiple sorts of use had multiple meanings.

How far from the *Tractatus* is the 1939 view? There are two issues here. (1) How far is it a departure from the *Tractatus* in allowing that the realities of ourselves and our world shape the resources of thought (including as "resources of thought" such things as mathematical propositions and the words of our language)? (2) How far is it a departure

---

5. This paragraph and the previous one draw on my "Murdoch Off the Map, or Taking Empiricism Back from the Empiricists" (unpublished).

6. Wittgenstein had earlier described the application of the word "true" to mathematical propositions as a use "in a different sense" from its use of experiential propositions (Moore 1959, 268); but this talk of different senses is implicitly called into question by the discussion in *Philosophical Investigations,* and in any case leaves open the question what relation there is between the supposed different senses.

7. See Anscombe 1981g and 2005, also Section 8 below. For a discussion of the univocity issue in Aristotle, see Broadie 1991, 221–223. Anscombe's reading of Aristotle on practical truth has been controversial.

from the *Tractatus* in allowing that things other than bipolar propositions can be called "true" or said to "correspond to reality"?

First, then, the matter of how far it's a new thing for Wittgenstein to
allow that realities of ourselves and our world shape the resources of
thought. It may seem tempting to suggest that this is entirely a new development. But in fact the *Tractatus* leaves room for accommodation of
thought and language to realities, although Wittgenstein did not take it
to matter to his philosophical project what the details of such accommodation might be. (See the discussion in Essay 4 on "accommodatory
propositions" and on relevant passages in the *Tractatus*.) There is, nevertheless, an important difference from the *Tractatus*, which one could
put by saying that such accommodation as the *Tractatus* allows for does
not go all the way down. This comes out in the status of propositional
logic. In the *Tractatus*, the possibility of the application of propositional logic belongs to the possibility of senseful talk. It does not depend upon what the world is like—that is, on how things are.[8] But in
the context of Wittgenstein's later thought, one can lay out the ways in
which the usefulness, the significance, of propositional logic does depend upon central features of the kinds of beings we are, and the way
things go in the world—as has been done, in enormously illuminating
detail, by Peter Railton (2000).

There is the other part of the issue: How far is it a departure from the
*Tractatus* to allow that things other than bipolar propositions may count
as true? Well, obviously tautologies count as true in the *Tractatus*, and
they are not bipolar; they are propositions that can only be true, and
that have no truth-conditions. So in this case Wittgenstein allowed for
a use of the word "true" different from that of its application to bipolar
propositions.[9] The situation with equations is not so clear. Wittgenstein

---

8. See Marie McGinn on the *Tractatus* view: "Le fondement de l'universalité de la
logique ne repose pas dans la nature des choses mais dans les conditions préalables de
possibilité du jugement" (2002, 30).

9. It might be thought that Wittgenstein's classification of tautologies as "senseless"
should have ruled out any treatment of them as true. But Wittgenstein's account
of what is involved in the use of "true" for senseful propositions is not in any kind of
tension with allowing a use of "true" in which it is not tied to the fulfillment of
truth-conditions.

says in the *Tractatus* that a (correct) equation must be self-evident; in the *Prototractatus* (and the first edition of the *Tractatus*), he had said that an equation must be self-evident or nonsensical (allowing there for incorrect equations).[10] He discussed different applications of "true" in *Philosophical Remarks* (1975, 282–285) and in subsequent material from before the 1939 lectures. In lectures in 1931–1932, he allowed for a number of different uses of "true," including its application to hypotheses that are useful, but at other times he objected to some uses of "true"—for example, its application to *the series of natural numbers.* But once Wittgenstein began to draw attention to the various ways in which tools of thought are made useful by the realities of the world and of our own nature, and began at the same time to criticize the forms of logical sublimation in his earlier thought, it was not a hugely different sort of move to suggest a use of "corresponds to reality" in connection with the profound usefulness of some of those tools of thought. Certainly this is a departure from the *Tractatus,* but it is a move that is consonant with retaining the central significance of the use of "true" for propositions that have the possibility of truth and of falsity. The *difference* between such propositions and mathematical propositions is exactly what Wittgenstein in fact emphasizes in the passage in the lectures that I have been discussing. One could indeed say that what is central in that passage is that the distinction is not a matter of the one group of propositions "corresponding to reality" while the other does not, and that Wittgenstein's view of mathematical propositions should not be characterized as a denial that they "correspond to reality."

### 6. Wittgenstein in 1939: A Vantage Point for Thinking about the Disagreement between Anscombe and Wittgenstein

I want to use here a different sort of example of a statement that apparently lacks the possibility of being false. The example builds on another Anscombe case, that of a person who says, apparently seriously, "I am dead"; perhaps he has just been in an accident, and is suffering from confusion. She says that one might tell the person that he was alive,

10. See Kremer 2002.

which might get him out of the confused state of mind. The statement she imagines addressing to the confused person, "You are not dead," might miss its mark if he has just that moment died, and one might in those circumstances call the statement false. My example is of someone who suffers from Cotard's delusion, one form of which is taking oneself to be dead. The person, in combatting the delusion, might find it helpful to tell himself "I am not dead"—where the uttering of that sentence is not so much a move in any language-game as a help toward getting himself back to engaging in ordinary life. Certainly there is nothing the matter with saying that his statement is true; but it does not function as an expression of a first-person version of "NN is not dead"; it involves an essentially reflexive use of "I". His "I am not dead" is not one of a pair of propositions both of which have the possibility of truth and of falsity. What the person with Cotard's delusion is denying is a "piece of confusion," a reflection of a mental disturbance. (It would be a quite different sort of case if someone says of him, in his hearing, that he is dead, and he replies, "No, I'm not." That is, it matters *what* is being denied, and what is being denied cannot be specified by *identifying the person who is said to be dead.* The Cotard person is denying the statement that he is inclined to make about *himself,* "I am dead." What is being denied cannot, that is, be specified without its confusion being brought out at the same time. My example draws on my reading of Anscombe 1981d, and the relevance of her account would need more discussion than I can give it here. So too would the point that whether a remark is or isn't an expression of confusion depends on the context, not on the verbal form alone.)

[Added in 2017: My treatment of the example depends on my following Anscombe on uses of "I", and, in particular, on there being non-referring uses of "I". There is a further point that plays a role in my understanding of the Cotard case. Anscombe held that "[we] must accept the rule 'If $X$ asserts something with "I" as subject, his assertion will be true if and only if what he asserts is true of $X$'" (1981a, 32). This rule holds of cases where $X$ has asserted something; but if there is a question whether $X$ has asserted something, or whether instead what $X$ has said dissolves into confusion, the rule can't be applied to settle the issue. The application of the rule doesn't come first, and thereby determine what would have to be the case for what $X$ said to be true. If there is a question whether $X$ has or hasn't *said anything,* that comes first. A corresponding point could be made about unspoken "I"-thoughts. We can give a rule for when such thoughts are true in terms of what is true of the thinker of the thoughts, but it would be a rule that specified conditions for the truth of coherent "I"-thoughts. In general, one cannot argue from the fact that both "NN is dead" and "NN isn't dead" have the possibility of truth and that of falsity to the corresponding point about "I am not dead" and "I am dead," as said or thought by NN. Anscombe's discussion of "I" has been very controversial, and I cannot here discuss the many questions which can be raised about it, and which would have implications for my understanding of the Cotard case. I also cannot discuss the connections with Descartes and the deceiver who tries to make him take himself to be *nothing.*[11]]

On my understanding of it, the Cotard person's statement resembles Anscombe's example, "'Someone' is not the name of someone," in that it does not have the possibility of being false, and is not a proposition of logic or mathematics. It is meant also to be describable in the same way she described that statement—namely, that its contradictory is nothing but a piece of confusion. Does it fit into the expanded category of words, mathematical propositions, and other tools of thought and language which might be said to correspond to reality so far as they may be of great usefulness, given the realities of us and our world? What I want to emphasize is the kind of use the statement has, as not so much a move in a language-game as a help in a return to engagement in life, to talking and thinking in a way not prevented by mental disturbance. The use of "I am not dead" is meant to fit things that Wittgenstein says in the 1939 lectures about propositions that are "preparatory" to engagement in language. A use of language that is meant to effect a kind of return to such engagement might be said to be, in a broad sense, preparatory. A definition is a piece of language the use of which is preparatory; so too the use of mathematical propositions, Wittgenstein says, might be said to be preparatory (1976, 249). The idea of a contrast between preparations

11. I am grateful to a reviewer for Harvard University Press, who brought out some of the issues that were elided in the earlier version of this essay.

for the use of language, and the use that the preparations were preparations for—this is one way of getting at the idea that is in play in Wittgenstein's speaking of mathematical propositions as belonging to
the "apparatus" of language rather than its application (1976, 250); and
these ideas go back to the *Tractatus*. Here I am suggesting that we can
see the use of a sentence to bring someone out of confusion and back into
engaged life with language as a preparatory use, alongside other preparatory uses. The Cotard man's statement is useful within the context of
his confusion. Its usefulness does not *continue,* and his statement is in
that regard utterly unlike the propositions of mathematics; but this
case can be seen as one of the miscellaneous kinds of case in which a
proposition's usefulness depends on various sorts of reality of ourselves
and our world, which indeed include our capacity to become unhinged
in various ways. Anscombe's example of "'Someone' is not the name of
someone" was meant to fit a case in which someone, Antony Flew, had
in a sense got *logically unhinged,* and had come out with something that
was only confusion (as she saw it). So far as there are forms of logical
unhingedness which may affect many people, there may be responses
that have a general usefulness, unlike remarks addressed to particular
and relatively idiosyncratic forms of unhingedness.[12]

There is an objection to what I have been doing. I have looked at a
not very huge development of ideas that are present in the *Tractatus*—
in that the *Tractatus* allows for propositions that, as it were, work alongside contingent propositions; it allows also for a use of the word "true"
which is not a matter of the fulfillment of truth-conditions, and which
applies to propositions that do not have truth-conditions. These ideas
can be developed to allow for some propositions that can only be true,
the contradictories of which are nothing but confusion; and this covers,
then, one sort of case with which Anscombe was concerned, the kind
meant to be illustrated by "'Someone' is not the name of someone." The
objection to what I am doing is that it doesn't begin to go far enough to
allow for Anscombe's concerns. What she was concerned about, the objector says, includes natural theology, and natural theology isn't even
nearly going to be fitted into an expanded sort of *Tractatus* view that

---

12. I discuss various "preparatory" uses of language in Essays 4 and 6.

allows for mathematical propositions to count as true, or as corresponding to reality, merely on account of their usefulness, or merely on account of there being no alternative to them for us. That wouldn't be to count them as *true* because *what they say is the case is indeed the case, indeed necessarily the case.* And it is therefore not going to include any reasonable understanding of the propositions of natural theology, to the exclusion of which from the *Tractatus* theory Anscombe had objected. Another way of putting the objection would be to say that what Anscombe was objecting to was the exclusion of necessary truths in a robust sense, and all that I have allowed for is necessary truth in an extremely attenuated sense.

Section 7 is about the objection, which I'll call "The Big Objection." It reformulates and combines the two objections that came up (in Section 4) to my account of how Anscombe disagreed with the picture theory.

### 7. The Big Objection: The Exclusion of Necessary Truths in a Robust Sense

The Objection can be approached from the Wittgenstein direction and from the Anscombe direction. I shall indicate how both approaches work, but won't follow them out in detail. But first I will give my own view of what is wrong with the Objection. It confuses the idea of a proposition's being robustly situated within our lives, doing real and important work, with its being construed as logically robust in a way that Anscombe herself, I think, might have regarded as problematic.[13]

### 1. From the Wittgenstein Direction

The Objection appeals to the idea of a proposition "saying that something or other *is the case.*" It runs up against something important in Wittgenstein's philosophy, early and late. In philosophy we put weight onto notions which can be taken in various different ways. (Here, the notion on which we want to put weight is that of *saying that something*

13. See Anscombe 1981c and 1981f.

*is the case.*) Wittgenstein responds to this philosophical tendency of ours differently in his early philosophy from the way he responds later; but early and late, Wittgenstein teaches us to ask, for any of these notions, the question *what counts as that,* where that question can be answered only by considering the kind of use or the kinds of use that count as the application of that notion. The Big Objection rests on the idea that, although Wittgenstein allows talk of mathematical propositions as "corresponding to reality," he is nevertheless denying that such propositions are *genuine sayings that something is the case;* and hence any kind of treatment of other propositions on the same lines would also be a denial that those propositions *say that something is the case.* I don't want to develop this objection and how Wittgenstein might respond to it; I simply want to note that it is parallel to the objection to Wittgenstein on "mental processes," which he discusses in §§305–308 of *Philosophical Investigations.* As in that case, there is an analogy that plays a significant role in the objector's initial understanding of the situation, but an analogy that "falls to pieces." What is at work in the insistence that mathematical propositions, understood as Wittgenstein understood them, do not really *say that something is the case,* and are not being taken by Wittgenstein to be *true because they do so,* is the analogy with ordinary experiential propositions saying that something is the case. The objector holds that what Wittgenstein is denying is that what mathematical propositions do in relation to the mathematical realm is analogous to what ordinary bipolar experiential propositions do in relation to their realm. He thinks that there is such a thing, and that that is what is at stake; but it is obscure how the analogy might be thought to work—that is, what it is that Wittgenstein is supposedly denying. With experiential propositions, their saying that something is the case is a matter of the kind of way they function; any such proposition is one of a pair, both members of which have the possibility of being true and of being false. If we consider *their* saying that something is the case, it is a matter of the functioning of one proposition of such a pair; and plainly *that* cannot be transferred to the case of mathematical propositions, so long as they are not taken to be bipolar. In what way, then, do ordinary experiential propositions and their *saying that something is the case* make available an analogous understanding of *saying that something is the case* that is applicable to mathematical propositions, which Wittgenstein is then denying? This isn't seen to be a question; we take it that the notion of *saying that something is the case* can bear the weight we want to put on it. The place in our thought of *one* sort of case makes it seem unnecessary to consider what counts as, or what we might count as, saying that something is the case when we are concerned with mathematical propositions or the propositions of natural theology.

Another important kind of reply "from the Wittgenstein direction" would emphasize a point touched on earlier, the *variety* of kinds of cases in which a proposition may be extremely useful because of what these or those realities are like, and in which there is taken not to be some alternative to the proposition's truth. Here my point could be put by saying that Wittgenstein doesn't have a general theory of "grammatical propositions." There are different things that different propositions that can get called "grammatical" do. Wittgenstein often wanted to emphasize a contrast between "grammatical" and "experiential" propositions; and, in many philosophical contexts, that contrast was more important than the variety among propositions contrasted with "experiential" propositions. But, if we are concerned with a different sort of question, about how far and in what ways the propositions about which Anscombe was concerned can be accommodated within the kind of view I have been developing, that question requires that we not take there to be some general logical category of "grammatical propositions," given in advance. That is the essential point of the methodology of *On Certainty* (Wittgenstein 1969), in which an examination of cases expands what we might take to belong to grammar, at the same time as ideas about "grammar" may make possible ways of thinking about the logical character of *certainty*.

Another important point that emerges from *On Certainty* is that the idea of "bipolar propositions" can be understood in two quite different ways. A practice, like that of investigating and establishing historical claims, involves not taking certain judgments to be open to doubt. There are, that is, propositions that are not members of pairs of propositions, such that both members of the pair have the possibility of being true *and the possibility of being false*. In the case of these propositions, the possibility of their being false is ruled out. And in this sense, one could say, such propositions are not bipolar. On the other hand, these propositions may in other respects be ones that we might want to categorize as empirical propositions. That a particular planet existed for more than a few centuries and was not destroyed by an asteroid in its first thousand years is an empirical matter. But a "mistake" about whether the Earth has lasted more than a thousand years is ruled out. Is "The Earth has existed for more than a thousand years" a "bipolar proposition"?— or is it rather that the character of the cases discussed in *On Certainty* shows the limited usefulness of the notion of bipolarity, and hence the complicatedness of any kind of contrast one might want to draw between propositions that "can only be true" and "propositions that have the possibility of being true and the possibility of being false"?

## 2. From the Anscombe Direction

Anscombe had said that the *Tractatus* theory would be death to natural theology, because the propositions of natural theology are not "supposed to be the ones that happen to be true out of pairs of possibilities" and are not logical or mathematical propositions (*IWT*, 78). She says nothing further about what sort of propositions they are; and apart from their being propositions that can only be true, it is not clear how she understands them. It is not clear whether she took any or all of them to have contradictories that "peter out into nothingness," to be expressions not so much of mistakes as of confusion. What is plain is that there are various ways of understanding the theology of natural theology, and indeed also of understanding what such-and-such theologian was doing in doing what gets called natural theology. This is perhaps especially true in regard to the question what Aquinas was doing in those parts of his work taken to be natural theology. Although many discussions of that issue postdate Anscombe's reference (in *IWT*) to natural theology, what they bring out is that there is no single obvious understanding of the theology of natural theology that could simply be ascribed to Anscombe, and one certainly could not argue that she would have accepted whatever conventional account might have been available when she wrote, since she was not a philosopher who accepted widespread conventional views.

The Big Objection was essentially that my Wittgensteinian account of propositions that can only be true was not robust enough to capture the sense in which the propositions of natural theology are at any rate supposed to be necessarily true. But, continuing to look at the issue from what I am calling the Anscombe direction, I think we should ask whether the robustness of the necessary truths of natural theology would be compromised by the sort of account I sketched. Recall the importance for Anscombe of there being truths the contradictories of which peter out into nothingness. Why should not the propositions of natural theology be thought of like that? This would mean that they had, opposed to them, forms of confusion. Would that imply that they were, qua truths, less than adequately robust? What is a truth that has opposed to it nothing but confusion?

Here is a statement about natural theology; I don't know what Anscombe might have made of it, but it is relevant to the question how one might think of the propositions of natural theology in relation to their contradictories. It is by Helmut Gollwitzer, a Lutheran theologian influenced strongly by Barth. Writing about the relation between Christian affirmation of the existence of God and the "old proofs" (including in particular the Five Ways), he says that one thing they were concerned to show was that without God, all thinking about the world ultimately goes astray (Gollwitzer 1965, 213). That is a form of the idea that the propositions of natural theology may be taken by those who put them forward to have, opposed to them, profound confusion, a profound "going astray" of thought about the world. This seems to me an exceedingly robust claim; it would be hard to get more robust. An account of the propositions of natural theology which took them to be such propositions could not be assumed to be not robust enough for Anscombe's understanding of natural theology. It is another matter, though, whether the Wittgensteinian account I have given of propositions that can only be true is "robust" enough. In Section 8, I shall consider again the question of "robustness," but I shall move the focus away from natural theology. (In Essay 6, I consider an example of apophatic natural theology, from a Roman Catholic theologian, directed against one of the ways in which thought about God may be taken to have gone wrong.)

### 8. Anscombe and What Can Only Be True, and the
### Disagreement between Anscombe and Geach

I said in Section 2 that it was not clear whether Anscombe's objection to the *Tractatus* concerns propositions that can only be true *and* that are such that their contradictories "peter out into nothingness." Her concerns are, I think, of great interest—here I am taking those concerns to be about propositions that can only be true, and the negations of which are not statements that something obtains that necessarily does not obtain. Many of them are, rather, indications of thought that has *gone astray;* and thought can indeed *go astray* in various ways. Think even of an example going back as far as the *Tractatus:* if someone's thought has got into a mess by her failure to recognize a logical consequence of things she has said, a tautology may help to show her the possibility of inference from the things she says to the conclusion she is inclined not to recognize. The tautology, although it may be called "true," does not (on the *Tractatus* view) say that anything is the case; but it is plainly capable (on the *Tractatus* view) of being illuminating, in relation to a kind of going-astray of thought.

Consider here a different sort of example, of great importance to Anscombe. In "Mr Truman's Degree" she said, "For men to choose to kill the innocent as a means to their ends is always murder" (1981d, 64). This is part of the grammar of *murder;* and she takes us to be losing the conception of murder. This is a corruption of thought, a going astray of thought. The point, in her essay, of coming out with the statement that to choose to kill the innocent as a means to one's ends is murder, is that it may reshape people's understanding of their situation, in which they are going to vote on whether to give Truman an honorary degree: they may come to see that voting for the degree is *voting to honor a murderer.* If indeed that statement ("To choose to kill the innocent as a means is always murder") does not have the possibility of falsehood, that is entirely consistent with its being used to throw light on the situation. I spoke about the possibility of taking Wittgenstein's remarks about correspondence to reality to be applicable to concepts; and Anscombe took the understanding of *murder*—an understanding that she thought we were in danger of losing—to answer to our real needs. So I am suggesting that the concept, given its significance as she sees it, could well be said to correspond to reality. And equally the grammatical remark that *it is murder to choose to kill the innocent as a means* could be taken to correspond to reality in the sense discussed by Wittgenstein. "Modern Moral Philosophy" (1958), "Mr Truman's Degree," "War and Murder" (1965), and *Intention* are (among other things) responsive to what Anscombe took to be widespread corruptions of thought, goings astray of thought. They are works of conceptual recuperation; they aim at making truths operative. The truths with which these essays deal are, as she sees them, truths which are not the true member of pairs of propositions, each member of which has the possibility of truth and the possibility of falsity.

I am inviting you to see a similarity of structure linking these cases to Anscombe on "'Someone' is not the name of someone." The fundamental structure of her thought in both cases is that there may be illumination for us in a particular situation—a situation of thought's having gone astray—if this or that statement (or statements) that can only be true can be put before us, and if the things that we may tell ourselves (or the things that we may be told, or take for granted), and that lead us astray or confirm us in those paths, are also brought into clear view. The robust significance of the statements that can only be true does not depend upon their having negations that are not one or another kind of miscarriage of thought. Certainly there is in this Anscombean structure an understanding of what thought is, what it is for us to be thinking beings, that allows for the characterization of various cases, apparently of thinkings, as apparent thinkings, miscarryings, peterings out, goings astray, confusions, and corruptions, and corruptions that feed on confusions. The conception or image here of *thought* is an image also of the relation between thought and truth, one that is present in Anscombe's essays on Aristotle and practical truth (1981g, 2005). She draws in the earlier essay on a passage in the *Ethics* beginning at 1139a 21, and doesn't explicitly mention the part of the passage where Aristotle says that "truth is the business of everything intellectual," but that idea is important in Aristotle's, and hence Anscombe's, willingness to speak of things other than statements as "true." In the later essay she summarizes Aristotle on "the business of *any* thinking," and that idea (that connects *thinking truly* with *the business of thinking being done well*) comes up also in her discussion of Anselm and Thomas on truth. If she describes as "obviously true" the insight that enables the *getting right* of thought that has gone astray, that use of "true" is related to her understanding of how "true" may be used of actions: in both cases, thinking would be *getting its business done well*. Her approach would allow for its being part of the business of thinking to guide, or help put back on track, the business of thinking—and this can be done well or badly. What it will be to do this well cannot in general be laid out in advance of *miscarryings of thinking*; and when it is done well, what it provides is *true*.

We can now return to the apparent disagreement between Geach and Anscombe—about whether the insights that respond to confusion *have no truth-value*. In Geach's denial that they do, there is in play a different image of the relation between thought and truth, the image of thinking and speaking as capable of pointing toward or away from Truth. In terms of that image, *having a truth-value* is connected to the possibility of *negation* as a reversal of "direction" (1982, 93–95). But an insight that has opposed to it nothing but confusion does not have the true-false reversibility that characterizes propositions. One image, Geach's, puts before us a logical characteristic of great importance in our thought; the other image, Anscombe's, provides a wider range of applications of "true," nevertheless taken (I think) to be univocal. Anscombe (in her discussions of truth and of the picture theory) emphasizes as clearly as does Geach the importance of reversibility in the case of propositions that have a negation and are such that both the proposition and its negation have the possibility of truth and of falsehood. It is not clear how the two images might fit together, but I think we may read Anscombe as holding *that* they do, in her lecture on Anselm and Wittgenstein on truth (2011d).

## 9. Conclusions

In many contexts it is useful to make a distinction between propositions that belong to a pair, both of which have the possibility of truth and of falsehood (and to both of which one and the same reality corresponds), and other propositions, which are not members of such pairs of propositions, and which do not have the possibility of truth and that of falsehood. Propositions of the latter sort are enormously various, and may be useful in all sorts of ways. Wittgenstein teaches us to look at that variety and at those uses; he should not be read as ruling out such propositions or as requiring us to treat them differently from the way they are treated in ordinary discourse. He had no theory, even in the *Tractatus*, that would have required them (or all of them except tautologies, or all of them except tautologies and equations) to be described as nonsensical.

Anscombe criticized the *Tractatus* for excluding things which shouldn't be excluded; and I have taken her interest to be focused on the exclusion of statements which can only be true and the negations of which are (as I would now put it) miscarryings of thought. I have tried to see how far Wittgenstein's *complications* of his *Tractatus* views allow for Anscombe's concerns. And my conclusion is: more than you might think. In reading Wittgenstein and Anscombe, we can see them thinking about *thinking,* and about the ways we may respond to thinking that has miscarried or gone astray. Anscombe thinks about thinking in a teleological way that links it to truth; but the linkages in Wittgenstein's thought about thinking are different. It is the grammar of "philosophy" that is linked to that of "thinking"—strikingly, for example, in the image of the philosopher as someone who is afflicted by *Krankheiten* of the understanding that he needs to remedy. That image is linked (through a double meaning of "*gesunden Menschenverstandes*") to an idea of healthy human understanding (Wittgenstein 1980a, 44).

Contemporary theorists of truth have different accounts of what it is that can be described as "true" or "false"; but in general they take it that these things come in pairs, so that negating one of them gives you another one of them. It is one of the supposed platitudes of truth that the negation of what is truth-apt is truth-apt. But Anscombe on responses to confusion rejects the platitude; and her view has an implicit generality: what can only be true need not have a significant negation. It may be a guide for thinking, something that opens up a path for thought, that warns of a path to be avoided, or that helps thought to move back to "the notions of the healthy human understanding." Thinking may be guided well or badly; and what guides it well can be described as true. Adrian Moore suggests that, when we listen to what philosophers of the past say to us, we should ask how we can appropriate what they say—a precept that is particularly important "when we cannot hear what they are saying to us as a contribution to any contemporary debate" (2012, xviii). So far as we take for granted that what is truth-apt can be significantly negated, Anscombe on what can only be true cannot be heard as a contribution to any contemporary debate; hence (following Moore's precept), we need to ask how we might appropriate what she says.[14]

14. An ancestor of this paper was presented at the Kirchberg Wittgenstein Symposium and at the Wittgenstein Workshop at the University of Chicago. I am very grateful to the members of the audience on both occasions, to Adrian Moore, Silver Bronzo, Jean-Philippe Narboux, Sophie Grace Chappell, Anselm Mueller, and to a reviewer for Harvard University Press for helpful comments and suggestions.

# PART III

# Going On to Think about Ethics

## 1. The Background to Essay 6: Two Questions Arising from the Essays in Part II

*The first question.* Essays 4 and 5 are about propositions that can only be true, and more generally about propositions that do not have an intelligible negation. So far as any of them count as thinkables, they are thinkables to which *there is no alternative.* When I was working on those essays, I wondered what connections, if any, there were with David Wiggins's ideas—for he too had written about thinkables to which there is no alternative. In explaining the form of moral cognitivism that he defends, he had given this account of what the moral cognitivist needs to make plausible, about the judgment "Slavery is unjust and insupportable":

> By drawing upon the full riches of our intersubjectivity and our shared understanding, such a wealth of considerations can now be produced, all bearing in some way or other upon the question of slavery, that, at some point in rehearsing these considerations, it will become apparent that there is *nothing else to think* but that slavery is unjust and insupportable. (Wiggins 1991a, 70)

Wiggins connects this understanding of the status of "Slavery is unjust and insupportable" with that of "$7 + 5 = 12$." He points to the way in which children are taught arithmetic (67). They learn to use calculating rules which enable them to see that *there is nothing else to think* but that $7 + 5 = 12$. In the case, then of "$7 + 5 = 12$" and of "Slavery is unjust and insupportable," we have propositions to which there is no thinkable alternative. There was apparently, then, a question for me how close Wiggins's ideas were to the ideas that I had been writing about in Essays 4 and 5.

*The second question.* Toward the end of Essay 5, I suggested that there were connections between Anscombe's thought about "'Someone' is not the name of someone" and her writings on ethics and action. In both kinds of case, Anscombe is concerned with a situation in which (as she sees it) our thinking has gone astray; and in both kinds of case, a statement that does not have the possibility of falsehood may be a helpful and illuminating response. But I did not, in Essay 5, do anything more than mention connections with Anscombe's writings on ethics. So, besides the specific question about Wiggins's ideas, there was a further unanswered question about what relation to ethics the ideas in Essays 4 and 5 might have.

I wanted to explore these questions, and took the opportunity of an invitation to give a talk at the Jowett Society at Oxford to do so. But it was clear that I could not talk about how the ideas in Essays 4 and 5 were connected with ethics in general or with David Wiggins's kind of moral cognitivism unless I started off with a summary of the material in those two essays. That explains the shape of Essay 6, which I gave as a talk at Oxford in the autumn of 2014. The essay is meant not to presuppose the arguments that I provide in more detail in Essays 4 and 5, and so it can serve as an introduction to the themes of all the essays after Part I of this volume.

## 2. More about Essay 6

When I began thinking about the topics of Essay 6, I did not at all see what the relation was between the kinds of thinkables-with-no-alternatives that David Wiggins was discussing and my sorts of cases—the ones discussed in Essays 4 and 5. I have come to think that there is a significant difference. The cases that had been central for me involved propositions that did not have an intelligible negation. In Anscombe's words, the contradictory (in the case she considers) "peters out into nothingness." But this is quite different from David Wiggins's cases as he understands them. Although, in these cases, there is nothing to think about some question but that thus-and-so, there is an opposed thought that is intelligible. If, however, you attend to the considerations bearing on the question, there is only the one answer to be reached, the answer to which those considerations lead; and it will then be possible for someone to explain why you came to think that *p* by reference to your awareness of considerations that leave no thinkable alternative to *p*. In both sorts of case, one could speak of *asymmetries in thinking about thought,* but there are two different sorts of asymmetries at stake. The distinction between the two sorts of case lies in whether we take the thinkable-that-has-no-alternative to have or to lack an intelligible contradictory. It's worth noting here that, although the two kinds of case are, as I take it, quite different, it is possible for one and the same statement to be taken by someone to have no intelligible negation, and by someone else to be a Wigginsian thinkable-with-no-alternative—that is, something that has an intelligible negation. An example would be arithmetical propositions like "$7 + 5 = 12$," which were taken (at least some of the time) by Wittgenstein to have no intelligible negation and by Wiggins (as far as I can see) to be opposed to intelligible but false propositions.

One aim, then, of Essay 6 was to bring out the two kinds of ways we can take there to be no alternative to thinking thus-and-so. But I also wanted to explore what the role might be within ethics of propositions that guide thinking by being either blockers of false paths or indications of open and useful ones. In Essay 6, I give examples of both sorts of path-indicators in ethics, and explain how they may enter into moral thought and discussion. In a variety of different sorts of cases, the structure of thought and debate may involve propositions the role of which is to block paths of thought, or to indicate their availability and significance. We won't, in philosophy, be able to get a clear idea of such stretches of thought, or of such discussions, if we don't see their complex structure and the shaping role that can be played by propositions that guide thought—path-indicators and path-blockers.

That last point developed into a criticism of David Wiggins. Although he does allow for some significant kinds of variety within moral thinking, it seemed to me he did not see the structural complexity that there may be within moral thinking—a complexity that can be found within the thinking-through of an issue by an individual and also within the thinking that goes on in discussions and debates. I took it to be a problem for Wiggins's account of the nineteenth-century debate about slavery, that he had not seen the role in it of the path-blocking moves made by both defenders and opponents of slavery.

When I was writing Essay 6, I was aware of how some defenders of slavery had argued against the whole business of debating slavery in abstract general terms. What had struck me particularly forcibly was the repudiation, by nineteenth-century pro-slavery thinkers like Thomas R. Dew, of the principles expressed in the Virginia Declaration of Rights and the Declaration of Independence. Both declarations state that all men are by nature equally free; and, not surprisingly, their broad claims were frequently appealed to in arguments against slavery. For Dew, these general abstract arguments from the natural liberty of mankind to the injustice of slavery manifested a wholly wrong kind of approach to political controversy. Real issues, embedded in social circumstances, cannot be thought about through such metaphysical abstractions as the supposed natural rights of men. Don't go down that path in political thinking! I didn't realize until somewhat later that the opponents of slavery had also held that there were profoundly wrong paths down which one shouldn't go in thinking about slavery. I argue in Essay 6 that David Wiggins's understanding of the nineteenth-century debate about slavery was flawed. The structure of the debate had a kind of complexity arising from the place in it of path-blocking arguments used by participants on both sides.

Those are the main topics that are introduced in Essay 6, and not covered at all in Parts I and II of this volume. There are also some topics that are not treated in the same way in Essay 6 as they were in Essays 4 and 5. I discuss two of those topics in the next two sections here, before turning to Essay 7. In summary of Part III: There are two sorts of asymmetry that I contrast in Essay 6, and Essay 7 is about one of them, Wigginsian asymmetry, as illustrated by Wiggins's own discussion of the question about the justice or injustice of slavery. Williams, whose criticism of Wiggins is discussed in Essay 7, defends a kind of "symmetry" between opposed moral points of view, which Wiggins rejects. Wiggins wrote, about his own sort of cognitivism, "Against the claim that, *whatever* conviction may be achieved, there will always be a tenable point of view that finds something inconsistent with our own best considered finding, its main defence will have to be to attack the insidious *presumption of symmetry* between points of view" (1991a, 78). Although Essay 7 is about Wigginsian asymmetry, the second half includes an account of the role of path-blocking arguments in the debate about slavery. This leads into a wider discussion of symmetry and asymmetry in such debates.

### 3. Anscombe on the *Tractatus* and Natural Theology

At the end of her exposition of the picture theory in *IWT*, Anscombe says that it is worth remarking that the theory would be "death to natural theology," because the propositions of natural theology are not ones "that happen to be true out of pairs of possibilities," nor are they logical or mathematical propositions (*IWT*, 78). For many of her readers, this would not have counted as any kind of objection to the theory; but it is a point that is plainly connected with the objection she does make, both in *IWT* and later, that the picture theory is incredible in the restrictions that it places on language.[1] In both of my essays in Part II, I argued that Anscombe reads the *Tractatus* as more restrictive than it genuinely is, but this left the question, discussed in Essay 5, whether she would still have objected to the kind of modified-but-still-*Tractatus*-like view that I was sketching. That view allowed for propositions like Anscombe's "'Someone' is not the name of someone," the contradictories of which are nothing but confusion. But would she have taken such a view still to have excluded the propositions of natural theology, and to be objectionable on that account? In Essay 5, I looked at a possible response based

---

1. See especially Anscombe 2011e, 229–230.

on Helmut Gollwitzer's description of the traditional proofs of God's existence in natural theology and what they are concerned to show—that, without God, "all thinking about the world ultimately goes astray" ("in die Irre geht," 1965, 213; 1963, 172). In Essay 6, I was not explicitly concerned with that objection, but I did have it in mind, and wanted to bring in an illustrative case from natural theology. Instead of taking Gollwitzer again, I considered Brian Davies's "Is God a Moral Agent?" (2008), an essay that draws on Aquinas's discussion of the simplicity of God. One reason I switched to a different example is simply that I wanted to block what I took to be a possible but irrelevant objection to the argument in Essay 5—that Gollwitzer was a Lutheran. (I take the objection to be irrelevant because I don't think Gollwitzer's description of the traditional arguments depends on specifically Lutheran or Barthian elements of his thought; but that's not something I wanted to get into!) The interest of having two different examples in Essays 5 and 6 is that Davies and Gollwitzer in slightly different ways bring out an important conceptual point that works in both essays to widen the discussion. In both essays, I start off by considering responses to confusion. But in both the essays, the theological case leads into a much broader understanding of what sorts of failures in thinking one might be responding to, and here I found particularly helpful Gollwitzer's phrase, about thought's going astray. The kinds of confusion that I had discussed before I got to Gollwitzer's remark could be connected, through the conceptual link provided by the idea of thought's going astray, with ideas in Anscombe's essays about other kinds of goings-wrong of thought, miscarryings of thought. The discussion of Brian Davies in Essay 6 leads into the idea there of blockings-off of paths down which thought goes wrong—the same idea, which then can be connected with Anscombe's aims in "Mr Truman's Degree," "Modern Moral Philosophy," and her discussions of intention and action. In both essays, then, the theological example leads into a more general discussion of thought as something vulnerable to going wrong, something that one might then try to lead back—and here there are connections with Wittgenstein on philosophy as leading words back, when we have gone wandering off and got ourselves lost, without realizing it, in our philosophical use of them. The idea of thought as vulnerable to going wrong, and as something that one might try to lead back, also goes with the connections I draw in Essays 5, 6, and 7 to a kind of Anscombean-Aristotelian idea of the guiding of thinking as part of the *ergon* of thinking.

## 4. Philosophical Method: A Theme

It might be suggested that the kinds of propositions that I focus on in Essays 4, 5, and 6, which do not come in pairs, are *rules*, and that this explains their differences from ordinary experiential propositions. In Essay 6, I suggest that this is less illuminating than it may seem. I don't doubt that there are cases in which pointing out that something is or isn't a rule, or that it is or isn't a referring expression, or that it is or isn't a bit of descriptive language, or whatever, can be helpful. But often the logic-words of ordinary language, and often enough also the logic-words of logicians, cannot bear the weight that we try to put on them in philosophical discussion. What does bear the weight is the way you lay out the kind of use of words that you want to focus on. In the case of the propositions-that-don't-come-in-pairs, which I discuss in Essay 6, some of them do have features in common with at least some sorts of rules, and it may indeed be very helpful to bring out these features—as Roger White does, in explaining the *Tractatus* view of mathematical equations (2006). He brings out the analogy between such equations and indicative sentences used in giving definitions, and then also with statements of the rules of a game. These analogies enable us to see "$7 + 5 = 12$" as a kind of rule permitting (for example) the substitution of "12 altogether" in statements in which we have spoken of seven of this and five of that. And this can then be philosophically helpful. But what is important here is seeing the differences between the use of such an equation and that of sentences that may look similar—sentences about, for example, what you will actually get if you put seven of these things together with five of those, say five pythons and seven rabbits.

The idea that the logical category-words in ordinary language and in logical talk may not bear much philosophical weight runs in various ways through many of the essays in this volume. In Essay 2, I argue that, if you are trying to help a person who has misunderstood the word "someone" by taking it to function as a name, you can lay out the differences between its use and that of names. If the person sees these differences, the use of the label "name" in connection with one use rather than the other is not what is significant. Anscombe's own point, that "'Someone' is not the name of someone," can sum up a helpful drawing out of differences, but then what bears the weight in such an account is the setting out of the differences.

The kind of weight that logical category-words have is a main topic of Essay 3, which I won't go into details about here. In Essays 3 and 4, I characterize Frege's aim in "On Concept and Object" as that of reaching a shared understanding of a kind of use of words or symbols, in the face of the varied and to some extent confused uses of "concept." The appropriation of the word "concept" for what he is trying to put before his readers is not the central thing. He isn't getting *concepts* right, as if Benno Kerry had got them wrong. I was concerned there with an idea that I think influences us—the idea that logical category-words of ordinary language already point us to a *kind,* which goes with the idea that identifying whether an expression picks out something of this or that kind (getting the right logical label on it) can be explanatory, in the same sort of way as getting right the class of things to which *whales* belong helps us to explain some of their features. Anscombe makes what I take to be a comparable point about "I," and the idea that we can explain the meaning of "I" by recognizing it to be a pronoun, the meaning of which involves the idea of reference. She notes that the problem then is to see what "reference" is here, and how it is accomplished. I want to emphasize the idea that we are not given anything useful in this context by being told that "I" is a referring term, unless we make clear *what counts as reference* in this case. The point I am making comes out in a different way in her essay as a whole. She is usually read as arguing that "I" is not a referring expression. But a better formulation of her conclusion is her own: "'I' is neither a name nor another kind of expression whose logical role is to make a reference, *at all*" (1981a, 32). And that conclusion is backed up by her looking in detail at various uses of expressions to speak of something or other. She looks carefully at what the use would be of "I" as a proper name by which each person could speak of herself or himself. She shows what it would be to have a word that functioned like that, and "I" does not work *like that*. She looks carefully at what the use would be of "I" as a kind of demonstrative, and shows how such a use would involve the possibility of a kind of failure of reference, which marks a difference from the use of "I." It isn't that we have some starting-off clear conception of what a referring expression is, and "I" isn't *that*. Anscombe's argument is rather: Here is one sort of use, which evidently we can take to be that of a referring expression (namely, a proper-name use); here is another sort of use, which can be taken to be that of a referring expression (namely, a demonstrative use); "I" doesn't have either of those uses. If we see that it is not used in either of those ways, and we still think of it as *referring to something*, "we are led to rave in consequence"—that is, to invent a something that we confusedly think will work as a thing-to-be-thus-referred-to. I am not here trying to defend her argument from the various kinds of objection that people have raised: I want only to bring out something about its structure, and the way we may mis-see the role in it of something's being or not being a "referring expression." That is, Anscombe isn't making an argument from some general feature that all referring expressions have, which allows us to make the philosophical move to ruling out "I" as a referring expression because it lacks the supposed general feature. The argument provides something one might be offered as what one wants and shows how one may be led to recognize that it is not what one wants; the argument then provides something else as a candidate for what one is after, and one is led to see that that isn't what one wants either . . . and ultimately one in this way can come to see that one hadn't meant *anything at all*. This is a kind of *reductio* argument, but it does not start from some clear notion of what it is we are assuming, which it then goes on to reduce to absurdity. (In Essay 6, I mention Anscombe's rejection of any conception of the semantic uniformity of declarative sentences that wouldn't allow for a *Tractarian* distinction between propositions that have the possibility of truth and of falsity and those that don't. But there is, in her discussion of the use of "I," a further kind of rejection of the supposed needs of semantic theory. The use of "I" can be assimilated in various ways to that of referring expressions as part of the development of a systematic account of a language; but so far as such an aim distorts the use of the word, *her* interest is in making clear how that would be a distortion.)

## 5. On Truth in Ethics: Essay 7

When I gave a version of Essay 6 as a talk for the Jowett Society, much of the discussion was about the dispute between Bernard Williams and David Wiggins about truth in ethics (which wasn't actually mentioned in the talk), and about the nineteenth-century debate between defenders of slavery and those who took it to be a great evil. This seemed to me a very rich topic, or more accurately, a pair of intertwined topics. Each of the topics is extremely extensive, and Essay 7, "Truth in Ethics," does not take on everything involved in the Williams-Wiggins disagreement, much less everything in the debate about slavery.

Williams had criticized Wiggins in a paper he gave at a conference in 1994 on truth in ethics. His conference paper and a reply by Wiggins were published in the December 1995 issue of *Ratio*, together with other papers from the conference and some further contributions. Williams had particularly in view the paper by Wiggins from which I quoted in the first part of this introduction. At the beginning of Essay 7, I summarize the dispute. It's important here to note that neither Williams nor Wiggins takes there to be a uniformity in the character of moral judgments. Wiggins thinks that truth is attainable in many moral questions, but there are other moral questions that lack such determinate answers. His discussion of the case of slavery should not be read as if it were being put forward as illustrative of the general nature of moral disagreement. And Williams, too, emphasizes that moral claims are not homogeneous, and that we shouldn't, as philosophers, think that the same things need to be said about all of them. In fact the issue of slavery has, I believe, particular features that set it off in significant ways from virtually any other issue, since it brings into question *who* are the addressees of the arguments about slavery, and *who* are the contributors to the debate—who, in short, are those who may be recognized to be concerned with justice and injustice. The role in the debate of the notion of *natural slaves* can't be narrowly confined to the content of the debate, but is inseparable from ideas, implicit or explicit, about who may be taken to be engaged in moral or political or juridical discussion and debate.[2]

I've just mentioned the notion of *natural slaves,* and this is a main theme in Essay 7. I take it to have been of central importance in the way thinking about slavery developed in the eighteenth and nineteenth centuries in Britain and America. Perhaps the most striking expression of its significance is in the so-called Cornerstone Speech of Alexander Stephens, the vice-president of the Confederacy. The speech set out the fundamental principles of the Confederacy, of which the most important, on Stephens's account, was that the nature of Africans justified their status as slaves. I suggest, in Essay 7, that the statement that men are by nature free and equal functioned as a path-blocker against looking for any kind of natural character of Africans (or any other group of people) that would justify their subjugation or enslavement. In addition, then, to the path-blocking considerations appealed to by pro-slavery thinkers, there were path-blocking considerations that played a role in anti-slavery thought. (Perhaps I should note that the idea of *naturally just subordination* has had a continuing history, and is hardly dead. I should also add that there are significant questions about gender in relation to eighteenth- and nineteenth-century claims about what supposedly holds of all men; and I can mention these issues only to say that I can't go into them.)

I do not, in Essay 7, explicitly consider racism, though I am discussing a racialized form of slavery, and a racialized notion of *natural slaves.* The reason for not considering racism is that it was common to almost all the white participants in the nineteenth-century debates about slavery in America, and was not limited to defenders of slavery. Most white anti-slavery thinkers, including many abolitionists, accepted some form of racism. Strong arguments against slavery—for example, those accepted by Lincoln—were compatible with common forms of racism.

2. From the point of view of many Southerners in the 1830s and later, it would have been taken to be insulting to be thought to be willing even to take up something purportedly put forward by slaves in a debate about slavery. See the suggestion, in the House of Representatives in 1837, that John Quincy Adams should be *punished* for trying to introduce a petition purportedly from slaves.

## 6. More about "Truth in Ethics"

Essay 7, "Truth in Ethics," is about whether there is only one tenable answer to the question about the justice or injustice of slavery. But three distinct questions come up in the essay, and it might be helpful to set them out here. One is the question confronted by people who were in one way or another engaged in the debate about slavery, who were thinking about such claims as that it was unjust. Imagine, perhaps, someone thinking about it in 1830 in Scotland, who doesn't know any slaves or anyone who has been a slave. But perhaps her son or her brother is a bookkeeper on a plantation in Barbados, and she has been asked to sign a petition to Parliament in favor of the abolition of slavery in the West Indies. We can think our way back into the question as such a person confronted it. She might, for example, have thought about what it would be to treat a human being as a piece of property—might have tried fully to take that in—or might have made connections with the Golden Rule, as she understood the Rule. And despite the family ties to the plantation system, she might have seen that the injustice of slavery is undeniable.

The second question is the one between Williams and Wiggins. Williams had insisted that there was a kind of relativism implicitly built into Wiggins's view, and that the recognition of this implicit relativism unfanged that view—undid the apparent compulsoriness suggested by Wiggins's presentation of it. Really (so Williams argues), Wiggins can't get moral conclusions to which there is no alternative, because the supposed absence of alternatives depends upon accepting the particular question itself (to which there is supposedly only the one thinkable answer), and the moral concepts with which it is expressed—but the question, and the vocabulary in which it is expressed, can be rejected, and the question might indeed not even be seen. So there are always tenable ways of thinking within which one doesn't have to accept the supposed thing-that-there-is-no-alternative-to-thinking. This Williamsian line of argument exemplifies what Wiggins had spoken of as "the insidious *presumption of symmetry*" in moral thought: the presumptive uncompulsoriness of everything, the presumptive availability of a tenable alternative to anything, to any moral point of view. And so, for Wiggins, there is a question about what *in a particular case* that presumption would come to. It may be that, when we see what the supposed alternative would come to, we can see that it is not a genuinely tenable scheme of moral thought. Such an argument would then undercut the generality of Williams's claim. The Wigginsian approach to the question between him and Williams involves arguing *from a particular case or particular cases* against the general Williamsian theoretical claim that one needn't accept the moral concepts that supposedly make some moral judgment one to which there is no alternative. What needs to be investigated in particular cases is what it would actually be to think, or to try to think, about ethical matters *without* the concepts or modes of thinking that lead to the judgment to which there is supposedly no alternative. That is, Wiggins disallows, as a philosophical move, the *general* move to saying that you can always have an alternative tenable mode of thought—the general move that does not examine what the supposedly tenable mode of thought would be in such a case as that of the injustice of slavery.

One can take Wiggins's response to Williams to be an argument of this form:[3]

(1) There is no genuinely tenable mode of thought about moral issues within which there is some alternative to taking slavery to be unjust.

(2) Williams's general meta-ethical claim is that, in ethics, statements of the form "There is nothing else to think but that thus-and-such" are always relative to some moral vocabulary. There is, on the Williams view, always some tenable alternative (which may involve a rejection of the question and of the moral vocabulary within which it is formulated).

(3) Williams's meta-ethical claim should be rejected.

The third question that I take up in Essay 7 is the *Wigginsian question* what the costs would be of taking up, or trying to take up, a mode of thought within which the sorts of consideration that weighed with the

3. See especially Wiggins 1995, 251–252.

Scotswoman in my example are outweighed or cannot even be formulated, and within which slavery passes as a tolerable or even desirable practice, or within which the question of its justice is not seen to be a question. What scheme of moral ideas would then be possible? What I am calling the Wigginsian question is the one that underlies the claim at (1) above. A "Wigginsian question" would be askable in the case of any moral judgment about which one might want to say: There is nothing to think but that thus-and-such. One could say that Wigginsian questions belong to reflections on ethics, not to meta-ethics, but one might add that they may be taken to be directly relevant to meta-ethical claims, as in Wiggins's reply to Williams. Or one might say that the significance of Wigginsian questions shows the artificial character of the supposed contrast between normative ethics and meta-ethics. In meta-ethics, we need to be aware that there may be nothing more to a supposedly possible point of view than an empty "it is always possible to say that . . . ," which ignores the impossibility of taking the supposed position to be, or to be any longer, or to be as it was once taken to be, a serious bit of human thinking.

When Wiggins considers what I am calling the Wigginsian question in regard to the injustice of slavery, he asks whether ethics itself is not at stake: Could one take up "the point of view that shall be common between one person and another," and not "subsume the institution of slavery under the concepts it is subsumed under in the argument to its injustice and insupportability"? What workable scheme of moral ideas could one have, if one did without such concepts as *justice* and *using human beings as means, not ends*? My argument is somewhat different from Wiggins's, because I differ with him about whether nineteenth-century defenders of slavery did want to hold on to the notion of justice; but I argue that the costs of the denial of the injustice of slavery are still extremely high: those who defended slavery were not able genuinely to keep hold of the notion of justice, although they took themselves to be able to do so.

What I try to do, and what Wiggins tried to do, is in a sense meta-ethical: he and I give alternative responses to Williams's meta-ethical argument. But we reject an essential feature of Williams's approach, exemplified in his 1995 essay by his appeal to the case of Oscar Wilde (as he remembered it).[4] Williams's Wilde avoids answering counsel's question whether the passage he has just read to Wilde is obscene, by saying "'Obscene' is not a word of mine." Williams's appeal to the case is part of his argument that there is a difference between different ethical cultures in the thick ethical concepts that they use. Because (as Williams reads Wiggins) every supposed Wigginsian thing-there-is-supposedly-no-alternative-to-thinking depends upon a particular ethical vocabulary, and because there are always alternatives to any such vocabulary, there are no genuine things-there-is-no-alternative-to-thinking. What Wiggins rejects in his response to this kind of approach, and what I reject, is the idea that you can ignore the particular case and argue from what is supposedly "always" available. You don't have to consider what would actually be involved, in the particular case, in taking up one of the supposedly available "alternatives." But it's in considering the costs of taking up this or that supposed alternative, that you see what the "insidious presumption of symmetry" involves ignoring. And what you can be ignoring as a cost may be *ethics* itself. The point is: it's not given in advance that taking up such a supposed alternative leaves a possibility of tenable thinking about human life and what matters in it. The picture provided by the case of Wilde rejecting the word "obscene," if it is taken to be generally applicable, obscures what actually may be involved in taking up a position in which slavery need not be recognized as unjust. The insistence that you look at the costs in the particular case, that you think about what moral thinking would actually come to in this supposed alternative, can be thought of as belonging to a kind of meta-ethics, but whether you call it meta-ethics or not, it avoids the characteristic generality of meta-ethical argument. It takes seriously that what it is for there to be an alternative to some moral claim can't be deduced from general theoretical ideas about moral thought or vocabulary—about there always being other modes of thought, other

4. Williams says that counsel read Wilde a passage from one of his works and asked Wilde whether he thought it was obscene. Counsel had in fact read Wilde a passage from a story by someone else, and asked repeatedly whether he took it to be blasphemous. Wilde said he thought the story horrible, and added that "the word 'blasphemous' is not a word of mine."

vocabularies. If one wanted to say that the examination of the particular case is not meta-ethics, the meta-ethical point would be: There can be cases *like this*—cases where the general Williamsian line about there always being a way not to have to think the Wigginsian thing-which-there-is-no-alternative-to-thinking amounts to no more than a skeptical insistence on a supposed theoretical possibility of thinking something, in the face of the utter failure or utter poverty of the thing in question as a genuine piece of human thinking. Wiggins connects his rejection of the "insidious *presumption of symmetry*" with the importance of the "enlightenment and refinement of moral conceptions." That it *may have been hard to see* that there is nothing to think but that slavery is unjust should not be taken to support general meta-ethical claims of the sort that Williams defended.[5]

I have set out here three questions that come up in Essay 7, the first and third of which might not be seen to be distinct. This is because in both cases, one might say of the person asking the question, that she comes to recognize that here there is only one thing to think. Thus, the person who thinks about the justice or injustice of slavery, in the context of 1830s Scotland and the decision to sign a petition to Parliament against slavery, may take there to be only one thing to think about slavery, after seeing what the considerations are. But think also of the person who is reflecting on the dispute about slavery itself, who may ask whether there is any "workable scheme of moral ideas" available, if one rejects the question about the justice of slavery, and in that way avoids recognizing its injustice. Or such a person might ask whether one deprives oneself of any "workable scheme of moral ideas" if one tries to keep hold of the notion of *justice,* but weakens it so far as to make it apparently compatible with taking slavery to be just. In the context of such reflection on the costs to tenable thinking about questions of human life, of any supposed alternative to recognizing the injustice of slavery, one might come to recognize that there is only one thing to think about the justice or injustice of slavery.

I wanted to make clear the several distinct questions that come up in Essay 7, because there are possibilities of confusion. What is relevant to

5. The last two sentences of this paragraph are based on Wiggins 1991a, 78.

the Wigginsian question may not play a role in the thinking of someone who wonders whether to sign the petition against slavery. She does not need to ask whether a scheme of moral ideas within which one could avoid the question about the injustice of slavery would be at all a tenable approach to thinking about ethics. She wants to grasp the considerations against slavery, and also to see what has been said on the opposite side. It is no necessary part of this to see where one would be if one tried to avoid whatever the conclusion is that those considerations point to, or if one gave up using the concepts involved in formulating the question. The considerations that show the costs of such avoidance would not be the considerations that would normally weigh with someone thinking about the injustice of slavery, or trying to discuss it with someone else. Since I am writing about both sorts of consideration in Essay 7, I wanted to try to head off the possibility of their being run together. I would not want to deny that there are discussions of slavery that encompass both the ordinary first-order question about the justice of slavery and the reflective question about the costs of supposed alternative points of view. (I was thinking in particular of some of Frederick Douglass's speeches.)

### 7. Dotty People, Cranks, and Fanatics: More on the Vulnerability of Thought to Going Wrong

Raimond Gaita has written about the significance of the word "cranks" in our assessments of how well or how badly someone is thinking. The fundamental point at issue is whether that person is unable (or apparently unwilling) properly to exercise the capacity to *rule some things out of consideration* (2000, xxvi–xxix, 157–186). Bernard Williams also spoke of the importance of the set of evaluative terms that includes "dotty" "crank" "eccentric," and "weird," terms for people whose "judgment is out" (Williams et al. 1999, 250–251). We can't get by, he said, without a sense of what's dotty, what's "off judgment." But he noted that satire, which depends on such a sense, may be extremely conservative, and his example was the ridicule of early defenders of women's rights as eccentric ladies in trousers. He emphasized also that a recognition of how the ideas of dottiness, crankiness, eccentricity, and so on are used in defense of conservative institutions may lead some social thinkers to reject such notions altogether, as reflective merely of prejudice. Nothing, they think, should ever be rejected because of its being supposedly utterly outside the way sensible people judge. Gaita, too, considers the arguments that appear to lead to the idea that "if we were perfectly rational, then there is nothing that we would fear to think." Gaita and Williams, in somewhat different ways, point to the human importance and the philosophical interest of the capacity to rule some things out of consideration, and of the evaluative terms we use in exercising that capacity, including such terms as "crank" and "fanatic." They both emphasize how a rejection of such evaluative terms as expressive of prejudice may get built into philosophical conceptions of rationality.

In Essays 5, 6, and 7, I discuss various attempts to block paths of thought that we may be inclined to take, but the path-blockers I discuss are not connected with the evaluative terms to which Gaita and Williams draw attention. Thus, for example, I discuss the attempt by conservative pro-slavery thinkers to block the kind of thinking that appealed to the natural equality and liberty of mankind. But although they repudiate such thinking, the nineteenth-century defenders of slavery do not regard Jefferson as dotty or as a crank. The people who were regarded as cranks were the abolitionists; but in Essay 7, when I discuss responses to various anti-slavery views, I do not take on the response to abolitionism. It had two quite distinct sorts of element. One was the calling into question of abolitionist views of the nature of slavery in the South, through such arguments as that the treatment of slaves was as good as it could be for any members of the laboring classes, and much better than the treatment of free workers in the industrial North or in England. The other was the attack on abolitionists as monomaniacal fanatics—as cranks and crackpots who endangered the fundamentally sound way of life of the Southern part of the country and thereby endangered the Union itself. Earlier in Britain, abolitionists there had been dismissed as fanatics, enthusiasts, and Methodists. Here I want simply to note that although Essays 5, 6, and 7 touch on the questions raised by Gaita and Williams, and Essay 7 itself skates very close to those questions as they arose in connection with abolitionism, none of the essays here gives those questions the attention they need.[6]

6. On these issues and Gaita's treatment of them, see also Glover 2011.

### 8. What about Wittgenstein?

In the first six essays of this book, connections with Wittgenstein's thinking are clear. What about Essay 7? There is some discussion of Wittgenstein in Sections 7 and 8 of Essay 7, but there are also connections with his thought that I don't explicitly set out. Here are two of them.

1. In *The Blue Book,* when Wittgenstein is criticizing the "craving for generality" in philosophy, he says that he could also have spoken of "the contemptuous attitude towards the particular case" (1964, 18–19). He gives as an example the case in which someone is trying to explain the concept of number, and argues that such and such a definition is inadequate because it applies only, say, to finite cardinals. Wittgenstein says that he would answer that the mere possibility of the *limited* definition is itself interesting and important. Why should what finite and transfinite numbers have in common be more interesting than what distinguishes them? And he adds that it *isn't,* and that this characterizes what he speaks of as "our" way of thinking. The particular case is important for itself, not (as he had said in the *Tractatus*) only because of what it can disclose about "the essence of the world." I am not sure what to say about the disclosure, by a particular case, of what the essence of the world *isn't*—its disclosure, or apparent disclosure, that a general philosophical claim *can't* be made. I take the case of the dispute about slavery, as it developed in the eighteenth and nineteenth centuries, to be philosophically interesting, in part because it does help us to recognize that a general philosophical claim can't be made—the general claim for which Williams argues in his criticism of Wiggins, about the availability of a tenable alternative to any moral point of view. But I take the dispute about slavery to be philosophically interesting also because of how deeply the human shape of the debate, including the social institution of ethics in a slave society, was entangled with its content, with what were taken to be the considerations relevant to the question of slavery. What ethics is, was entangled in the debate. And that this can happen is itself philosophically interesting (though I'd be inclined also to say that it does show something of the essence of the world, that a dispute about a particular moral question can so deeply be entangled with our understanding of what ethics is).

2. Here is part of §131 of *Philosophical Investigations* (1958):

> For we can avoid ineptness or emptiness in our assertions only by presenting the model as what it is, as an object of comparison—as, so to speak, a measuring-rod; not as a preconceived idea to which reality *must* correspond.

Williams, in his "Truth in Ethics" (1995), sets out a model of ethics, of the role of thin concepts and thick concepts in ethics, and of how ethical disagreement and difference are connected with the availability of distinct moral vocabularies. The model then provides an account of how far truth is available in ethical judgments. He sets out the model, using a couple of examples, and generalizes from those in his criticism of Wiggins. There is no mention of the case of slavery, or of what Wiggins actually had argued about slavery, anywhere in Williams's essay. He does not treat his model as an object of comparison. A philosophical model can be treated as an object of comparison, but used in that way, it would not back up the "insidious presumption of symmetry." My response to Williams, and Wiggins's response to Williams, can be seen as Wittgensteinian, in that they are attempts to bring out the "ineptness or emptiness" to which Williams's use of the model leads. (There is a striking contrast between Williams's approach in his 1995 essay and his most powerful writings about ethics, in which he immerses himself deeply in the details of the forms of thinking with which he is concerned, and in which the conclusions are expressed in a kind of invitational form.)[7]

7. The introduction owes a great deal to Raimond Gaita and Oskari Kuusela.

# Asymmetries in Thinking about Thought: Anscombe and Wiggins

~

In what kinds of case may there be no alternative to thinking that *so and so*? If I think that *p*, I am quite prepared, usually, to find that others may think the opposite, and indeed that they have what at least appear to be good reasons for what they think. There may be more than one tenable thought about what is in question. And, normally, if I think that *p*, I recognize that those who disagree (or who at any rate appear to disagree) are not *thinking nothing at all*. Are there cases, though, in which these symmetries do not hold?—that is, in which thoughts do not come along with opposed thinkables? Elizabeth Anscombe allows for some such cases, and so does David Wiggins. I here explore their ideas, beginning with a question to which we are led by Wiggins's views. I then explain Anscombe's quite different approach and some of the wider issues with which it is connected. That will then enable me to consider the relation between Wiggins's approach and Anscombe's.

## 1. Questions to Which We May Be Led by David Wiggins's Work

When Wiggins writes about the objectivity of ethics, he notes that first-order morality is very unlike elementary arithmetic, but he adds that there is an aspect in which they can usefully be compared.[1] In both cases—in ordinary moral thinking, and in ordinary arithmetical thinking—there are judgments about which we can say: "there is nothing else to think *but that so and so.*" He has used the examples of *judging that 7 + 5 = 12,* and *judging that slavery is wrong.* Thus, in the latter case, the idea would be that if you know what slavery is, and what "wrong" means, there are considerations that (working together) leave you no alternative but to think that slavery is wrong.[2] Wiggins calls into question "the insidious *presumption of symmetry*"—the presumption that, whatever moral view one takes to be true, there are tenable opposed views.[3] It is against this presumption, characteristically accepted by noncognitivists, that Wiggins argues for there being moral questions in response to which there is *nothing else to think* but that *so and so.* This is not the claim that there is nothing else *for us* to think but that *so and so,* but that there is nothing else to think on this matter. His formulation of the asymmetry here thus goes against the kinds of claim that various relativists may make, that, while there may be nothing else *for us* to think, a view inconsistent with ours may be taken by those to whom things appear differently.[4]

Wiggins himself is concerned with the role that *the truth of your belief* can have in explaining why you have that belief.[5] I want to look at a different sort of question. It comes up because, if you say that there is nothing else to think but *that so and so,* this looks as if it might be taken in two different ways. It might mean that, if you deny the so and so in question, the relevant considerations will speak conclusively against your judgment. There is, as it were, *a thought there*—there *is a thought*

1. Wiggins 2006, 330–331.

2. Ibid., 366–367.

3. Wiggins 1991a, 78.

4. For a discussion of what one might call "the symmetry of opposing appearances," and its relevance to arguments for relativism, see Burnyeat 1979. I am very grateful to Sabina Lovibond for bringing to my attention the relation between Burnyeat on philosophical appeals to conflicting appearances and Wiggins on the presumption of symmetry in metaethics.

5. Wiggins 1991a; see also Moore 1996.

opposed to what may be taken to be the only thing that one can think, or maybe there are several candidate thoughts in this region, but they are not thoughts that anyone would actually think, if paying attention to the issue and to the relevant considerations. So that is one way of taking a claim that there is nothing else to think but that so and so. The alternative way of taking the claim is as saying that there is no thought there *to think*. If you say the opposite, there is nothing to what you say but muddle. It is not that you are thinking something, and nothing speaks *for it*, but that there is really no *it*. It might be objected that there is no sharp distinction there; but I am going to take seriously the idea that there is a distinction.[6] But, in any case, there is another objection to the idea that there is no opposed thought. Wittgenstein said once that the negation of nonsense is nonsense,[7] which may be taken to suggest that the negation of muddle is muddle, and that you cannot turn muddle into something thinkable by negating it. But it is not clear what the range of that point should be taken to be. May what has the form of the negation of what one takes to be not an intelligible thought nevertheless be something helpful or illuminating? Or even true?

## 2. Anscombe on These Questions

In an entirely different sort of context, Anscombe leads us into closely related questions. When she discusses what is wrong with the picture theory, in her *Introduction to Wittgenstein's Tractatus*, one of her complaints is that there are statements which the *Tractatus* counts as nonsensical and which it excludes, although they are illuminating and may be true—indeed, "obviously true" (*IWT*, 85). The example on which she focuses comes from her criticism of Antony Flew, who had said that it was part of the logic of the word "somebody," unlike "nobody," to refer to somebody.[8] "If this were so," Anscombe said, "then, on being told

6. See also Wiggins 1991a, 67n7.

7. Wittgenstein 1995, 217.

8. The example comes from Flew's explanation of what philosophers have in mind when they speak of misunderstanding the logic of our language (Flew 1951, 7–8).

that everybody hates somebody, we could ask to be introduced to this universally hated person." Anscombe takes to be obviously true the sort of statement that one might then make in response to Flew: "'Somebody' does not refer to somebody" or "'Someone' is not the name of someone." Such a statement, she says, expresses an insight, the opposite of which is nothing but confusion. The contradictory of the statement, if examined, "peters out into nothingness." So she takes it that there can be statements that are true, but such that there is no opposing thought. The denial of the statement expresses nothing but muddle, not some alternative thinkable thing.

There is in the case as Anscombe describes it a striking sort of asymmetry, which contrasts with two closely related sorts of symmetry. The first sort of symmetry can be seen in discussions of what is truth-apt, where it is usually supposed that if something is truth-apt, it has a truth-apt negation.[9] The second can be seen in Wittgenstein's remark cited in Section 1, that the negation of nonsense is nonsense—which appears to rule out the kind of asymmetry in which there is nothing but sheer muddle opposed to some intelligible statement.

Thinking about Anscombe's case and her description of it leads into a great variety of issues in philosophy of language, philosophy of mind, and ethics. One of these issues is the relation between Wigginsian asymmetry and Anscombean asymmetry, both of which involve cases about which one can say: *there is nothing else to think but that so and so.* I shall be focusing first on Anscombean asymmetry. In Section 3, I look at some examples of cases like hers, which I shall call "solo propositions," simply meaning that they do not come in pairs. Solo propositions are then to be contrasted with ordinary propositions as these might, for example, be understood on the basis of the picture theory. Ordinary senseful propositions come in pairs, the proposition and its negation, with both members of the pair having the possibility of truth and the possibility of falsity.[10]

One might or might not believe in another kind of proposition which would also come in pairs: one member of the pair expresses something that must be the case, and has a negation that does not peter out into nothingness but expresses something that cannot be the case. This, then, is a conception of substantial necessities as also coming in pairs: a necessary truth paired with a necessary falsity, where both members of the pair are supposedly intelligible propositions.

There are questions about how to fit tautologies and contradictions into my idea of paired propositions and solo propositions. I am not sure how far Anscombe accepted the Tractarian account of logical propositions; but on that account a tautology does not say the opposite of what you get by negating it, since neither the tautology nor the contradiction says anything. What I am after with the idea of *solo propositions* is a contrast with pairs of propositions both of which say that something is the case; and you do not have that kind of pairing with logical propositions as understood in the *Tractatus*. A tautology may nevertheless be described as "opposed to" what you get by negating it, in that there is no proposition with a sense that affirms them both.[11] Tautology and contradiction can be taken as an anomalous case, or as a limiting case of paired propositions.[12]

When I introduced the contrast between solo propositions and paired propositions, I did not want to imply anything about whether solo propositions may be taken to be true. Anscombe plainly thought they could. Peter Geach, writing about a case like Anscombe's, denied that such propositions would have any truth-value.[13] Anscombe's view is also at odds with the idea referred to above, and accepted in virtually all contemporary philosophical discussion of truth, that truth-apt items come in pairs. To see more clearly what is involved in thinking about solo propositions, I turn now to some cases that might be put alongside Anscombe's example.[14]

---

11. See *TLP* 5.1241.
12. I am grateful to Steven Methven for discussion of these cases.
13. Geach 1991.
14. For more discussion of the examples, see Essay 4.

### 3. Solo Propositions: Some Examples

To start with, there are cases that resemble Anscombe's. There is, for example, a discussion by Sophie Grace Chappell of Bernard Williams on internal and external reasons.[15] Chappell says that, when Williams argues against there being "external reasons," what he is denying is "only a piece of confusion." Chappell provides a summary statement of Williams's view, but that statement itself has, Chappell says, nothing opposed to it but confusion. There isn't an intelligible thought expressed by the negation. I am not sure whether Chappell would say that the statement she provides of Williams's view is *true*—so I am not sure whether she would agree with Anscombe on the reasonableness of calling true a statement that has no intelligible negation. But whether or not she would call Williams's view true, there is a significant similarity between what she is doing and what Anscombe was doing: they both take there to be a kind of asymmetry between *what can be said in response to confusion* and *the confused statement itself.* What they say in response to confusion they take to be not muddle, although their responses (what they are saying in their own voice) are set out in the form of a negation of something they take to be mere confusion.

Another case would be Frege's response to Benno Kerry in "On Concept and Object."[16] Frege's response is similar in structure to Anscombe's and Chappell's. Frege takes Kerry's sentence "The concept 'horse' is a concept easily attained" to embody confusion; and Frege's statement "The concept *horse* is not a concept" is part of his response to confusion—and, despite its not being easy to characterize Frege's own statement, it is not itself muddle, or so I should say.—There is, then, a range of asymmetrically structured cases of responses to confusion: in each such case, the response to confusion is a proposition that is doing some work, but one might say of its negation that it "peters out into nothingness." I should note that it is often not entirely clear how phi-

---

15. Chappell 2010. The quoted words are in Chappell's earlier version, http://plato .stanford.edu/entries/williams-bernard/. This 2010 version was replaced by Chappell in 2013, with the same URL.

16. Frege 1984b.

losophers who are responding to what they take to be confusion conceive what they themselves are doing. A possible example would be David Wiggins's discussion of the confusion of thinking that there are no genuinely benevolent motives, because the pleasure the agent takes in achieving his aim is his own pleasure, and thus his pleasure is the point of his action.[17] That, Wiggins says, is muddle; but then what about the summary statements that Wiggins gives of the opposing view? Some of them are structured as negations of what he takes to be mere muddle; but *they* are not muddle; and he may well take them to be true.

The other kind of case I want to touch on here comes from two readings of the *Tractatus* on mathematical propositions, Michael Kremer's and Roger White's.[18] The basic picture that you get in Kremer's account is that we may do a calculation in the course of working out how to infer from some senseful propositions to a senseful proposition; and we may then make a record of the calculation. Such a *record-of-a-calculation* can then go on to have a significant kind of use in the language: we can continue using it to guide inference from senseful propositions to senseful propositions. This is, then, what equations are; so, on this view, an equation is a kind of record of a calculation, and serves as a shortcut for us in inferring; it helps us to see what paths in inferring are open. This account of the *Tractatus* view of equations treats them as structures resembling propositions in the narrow Tractarian sense, which have a use as part of the language, and which are not nonsensical. They do not come with negations that have any role in the language, and they are in that sense, then, a kind of solo proposition. Roger White, in his book on the *Tractatus,* gives a similar account of how Wittgenstein understood mathematical propositions. He explicitly takes Wittgenstein to treat mathematical propositions as having the function of rules. While mathematical propositions may resemble senseful propositions, their function is entirely different; it is to indicate the ways we can substitute signs for each other. For example, the equation "$7+5=12$" is a rule that allows us to move from the proposition "There are 7 books here and 5 there" to the proposition "There are 12 books here or there." Here, as in

17. Wiggins 2006, 41–43.
18. Kremer 2002; White, 2006, 106–111.

Kremer's account of the *Tractatus*, Wittgenstein is read as specifying the kind of use that mathematical propositions have. They are not nonsensical, but provide ways in which we can handle senseful propositions. Understood in this way, they could also be described as solo propositions in my sense. The account White gives of the *Tractatus* on mathematical propositions is quite close to things Wittgenstein in fact says about mathematical propositions later on, in the 1930s, when he compares them with rules, and takes them not to be propositions in a narrow sense, and not to have significant negations.

It may seem that the first group of examples, responses to confusion, are totally different from the second group, mathematical propositions as understood in the *Tractatus*. But that is not right: there are significant common features, which are the subject of Section 4.

### 4. Indicating Paths We Can Take, and Paths We Should Not Take: Two Similarities

1. In the cases of philosophical responses to confusion, there is a path of thought that people have taken, or that someone has taken, and some philosopher or philosophers may bring out why you should not take that path. When they have done that—when they have brought out what the confusion is, or at any rate take themselves to have done so—they may then provide some sort of summary statement of their response, and this is frequently explicitly negative in form, as with "'Someone' is not the name of someone," and "The concept *horse* is not a concept." In the concept-horse case, Frege had been trying to make plain the confusion in what Benno Kerry had said about the concept *horse*, and you could say that Frege wanted to block the road into the confusion. The point of Frege's own statement is, in large part, what it is *against*, and what Frege shows about how not to get *there*. I am suggesting that we can think of "The concept *horse* is not a concept" as a kind of roadblock, blocking a road to confusion. And, if we look at responses to confusion as roadblockers, we can bring out also a resemblance to mathematical propositions on the *Tractatus* view, which could be described as indicating paths that are open for us to take. I am suggesting, then, that my two groups of examples of solo propositions can be described as

*propositions that are indicators of paths:* paths for us to take in thinking, or paths not to take. There is an important kind of example that will bring out the similarity I am suggesting—the example of mathematical inequalities. Suppose, for example, we found ourselves frequently multiplying 2 times 24 and getting 46 (perhaps because we tended to slip from multiplying 2 times 4 to adding instead). So in this kind of case, an inequality, "$2 \times 24 \neq 46$," might come in handy. On Kremer's kind of reading of the *Tractatus,* if we wrote down that inequality and kept it handy, it could have a function as an indicator of ways we *should not* go in making inferences between senseful propositions. What I am suggesting, then, is that an inequality can be used to indicate a path we should not take: it can function as a *path-blocker.* This is, then, an account that fits closely with Kremer's and White's readings of the *Tractatus* on mathematical propositions, and that also resembles the account one can give of solo propositions that function as responses to confusion.[19]

2. There is a further similarity between my two groups of cases: Consider Frege's statement "The concept *horse* is not a concept." This comes, as I said, from his response to Benno Kerry; but you could not possibly get what Frege is after when he says "The concept *horse* is not a concept" if his statement were detached from the account he gives of how Kerry is confused. Or take Anscombe's description of "'Someone' is not the name of someone" as an insight. This comes after she spells out what she takes to be the confusion in what Flew had said about "somebody," and explains how it goes wrong. Detached from her account of the confusion, the statement "'Someone' is not the name of someone" would not convey the insight which, in context, it can convey. There is a kind of parallel here with the *Tractatus* view as Kremer explains it. An equation, on this view, is a record, a helpful record, of a calculation. On this view, then, we can say that its capacity to indicate an inferential path that we may go on to take depends upon the original calculation. And, again, if someone multiplies 2 times 24 and comes up with 46, you can go over the calculation with the person, and make clear the point at

19. Inequalities can also function as indicators of useful paths. This possibility is discussed in a footnote to Section 5 of Essay 4.

which it goes wrong; you do not merely state or write out the inequality that marks the rejection of "2 times 24 equals 46." The point here is that path-indicators—whether they indicate paths of thought that we should not take, *or* paths of thought that we can take—go with a story that shows why the path is blocked, *or* that show it to be an open path. That is, the solo propositions that I have considered are associated with a persuasive backstory; and their having such a connection is tied to the kind of use they are meant to have.

In response to the similarities I have noted, it might be said that really what these cases have in common is that they all involve rules, and that rules in general, while they may be expressed in indicative sentences, can be contrasted with genuine propositions. It is not, then, surprising that they do not come in pairs, or that they do not come with significant negations. That is explained by their being rules. An example that might be brought in here is Ramsey's discussion of the kinds of propositions he calls variable hypotheticals—propositions like "All men are mortal." These sorts of proposition had earlier been taken by Ramsey himself to be genuine propositions, in fact to be conjunctions. In an account based on that of the *Tractatus,* he had taken them to be capable of truth and falsity in the way any other genuine proposition is. In his late paper "General Propositions and Causality," he presented deep objections to that view, and set out an alternative account according to which these "variable hypotheticals" are not genuine propositions. "They are not judgments," he said, "but rules for judging: If I meet a ϕ, I shall regard it as a ψ." Ramsey added that "this cannot be *negated* but it can be *disagreed* with by one who does not adopt it."[20] (This view has some resemblances to the *Tractatus* view of mathematical propositions, as Roger White explains it, and also resembles Wittgenstein's own later view of mathematical propositions.) But the suggestion that solo propositions (like the ones I have looked at) are really *rules* is less illuminating than it may seem. Independently of any comparison with rules, what we have is the idea that solo propositions may function as indicators of paths that we can take in thinking, or that we should not take in thinking. There is not *more* in saying "Ah they are rules!" than that. It

20. Ramsey, 1931.

is not as if there were some clear understanding available of a contrast between genuine propositions and rules, and as if we therefore understand these path-indicators better, in terms of that existing contrast. Further, there are no conclusions one might draw from identifying path-indicators or other solo propositions as rules. Thus, for example, it is not as if you could settle whether solo propositions could be called true by taking such propositions to be rules. Even if we read Anscombe's "'Someone' is not the name of someone" as a rule specifying where we should not go, its being a rule *and* there being lots of rules that we might not consider true or false, would leave it unclear whether *her* case was indeed one in which something you could call a rule was or was not something you might describe as true.

## 5. Pursuing the Issues Here Further

There is another case that is worth considering here. It is an example of a path-blocker, but it is not entirely clear whether it is an example of a solo proposition. The case is that of Brian Davies's defense of the claim that *God is not a moral agent subject to moral praise or censure.*[21] Davies says that the kind of theology that he is doing "is sometimes called 'negative theology,'" and adds that it "puts up 'No Entry' signs . . . at the beginning of certain roads down which one might be tempted to wander." One of these roads at which he is posting a warning is the "God is a moral agent" road. Davies is doing something which is structurally like some of the cases I looked at earlier; that is, he does not just say "Do not go down this road" but explains in some detail what is the matter with it as a road. He does not say that "God is a moral agent" is a false proposition; he says that we have reason for *fighting shy of that formula*—a very striking remark, partly in that, in speaking of it as a *formula* we have reason to fight shy of, Davies is avoiding speaking of it as something fully coherent. He does not explicitly say this, but I am going to ascribe to him the view that, when people take God to be a moral agent, their thought has gone off the rails in a significant way.

---

21. Davies 2008, esp. 111 and 116.

(I should add that he thinks you have reason to "fight shy of the formula 'God is a moral agent'" whether or not you believe in God.)

There is a way of connecting what I have just said back to Anscombe. In her work on Aristotle and practical truth, she makes use of a very striking passage in the *Nicomachean Ethics,* beginning at 1139a, 21.[22] This is the passage where Aristotle says that truth is the business of everything intellectual. Doing well and doing badly in thinking are truth and falsehood, whether we are concerned with purely theoretical thinking or practical thought. Here we may ask: Might we take it to be— might *Anscombe* have taken it to be—part of the business of thinking, part of its job, to guide, or to help put back on track, the business of thinking? If you held that that *was* part of the business of thinking—*if you held that part of the business of thinking is to help along the business of thinking—and* if you worked with the Aristotelian idea that truth is what you have when the business of thinking is done well, then indeed statements that respond to confusion, and that help to put thinking back on track, help it to be done well, could indeed be described as *true,* even though such a statement might not have an intelligible negation. I do not know whether what I have just suggested was indeed Anscombe's view, but it is constructed with Anscombean material, and is meant to fit what she says in response to Flew's confusion.

I have, though, in making this move, changed my description of the cases. The Anscombe case I originally described as a response to confusion, in which the negation of what she puts forward is something that peters out into nothingness. I described the Brian Davies case as reflecting his view that, when people take God to be a moral agent, their thinking has gone off the rails—which is not the same as to say there is no thought there that they are thinking. But both of these ways of speaking reflect some notion of *failure of thought*—and this is not merely a notion of thinking something straightforwardly false. Here I should note something that has been implicit in my talk of "paths of thought." One's thinking may take one from this thought to something else, and then to something else, and one can speak of this as a path one's thought has taken. Speaking in this kind of way, one may describe the entire se-

22. Anscombe 1981g; Anscombe 2005.

quence as *thinking*. But in going down that path, one's thinking may have *gone astray as thinking*. One may have wound up in sheer muddle, or one's thinking may have miscarried in some other significant way. My use of the phrase "a path of thought" does not carry the implication that one is thinking in any full sense as one goes down the path. One's having apparently gone on thinking may nevertheless involve a *failure of thinking*, as in the case of apparent thinking that "peters out into nothingness."[23]

In my sketch of an Aristotelian-Anscombean conception of *guides to thinking*, I have worked myself into territory closer to my starting point, David Wiggins's views about ethics, as illustrated by his example of judging that slavery is wrong, and there not being anything else to think *but that*. But I want to postpone a while longer any attempt to bring questions about ethics or about David Wiggins's ideas into relation with what I have been saying about solo propositions. I need to look first at a kind of conceptual organization that can be found in both Frege and Wittgenstein.

### 6. Frege, Wittgenstein, and Where We Get by Thinking about Definitions

Frege had the idea that there is a phase in the development of a systematic science, prior to the system's actual use—a phase in which the expressions that will be used in the system are prepared for use. In what Frege speaks of as the propaedeutic, both complex notions and logically primitive elements can be clarified. The clarification of complex notions makes it possible to stipulate the sense of some signs to be used in the system, through definitions that will form part of the system. The proposition used initially to give a definition can then have a distinct and different sort of use as an assertion. Thus, a proposition used to establish the meaning of a proper name can be used afterward to express an assertion about the thing named. In general, if a proposition is used in the preparatory phase or propaedeutic, or if it is used as a definition

---

23. I am grateful to Steven Methven for drawing to my attention the problems in talk of "paths of thought."

within the system, it may look as if it is expressing an assertion about things that are named in it, but it may have, at that stage, a quite different sort of use. When Frege explains what he means by "concept," "function," and "object," these explanations belong to the preparatory phase; and I think we can take what Frege says, when he is trying to clear up misunderstandings of his remarks about concepts, as also belonging to the preparatory use of language.

Wittgenstein also worked with an idea of preparatory uses of language. In lectures in 1939, Wittgenstein made an analogy between the way definitions set things up for the later use of signs and the way mathematical propositions provide procedures you can use in handling experiential propositions. That was in 1939, but already in the *Tractatus,* he took a view of mathematical propositions that can be understood by connecting it with what he says about definitions. Mathematical propositions are *like definitions* in being helps to what we do with senseful propositions. So the germ of Wittgenstein's distinction between preparations for the use of language and engaged uses of language can be seen already in the *Tractatus.* There are similarities and differences between what Frege does with the idea of preparatory uses of language and what Wittgenstein does, but they both held that a proposition used in these ways can also have a different sort of use. They both also held that a proposition that has a preparatory use may be misread, if we take it, or try to take it, as asserting something about the things that are meant by the signs in it. There are, though, extremely significant differences between them on this whole business of preparatory uses of language. For Wittgenstein, many propositions that have this character *keep it.* Their use continues to be that of enabling other types of uses of propositions. And this is indeed at the heart of his treatment of mathematical propositions. What I have been trying to lead up to here is the importance for Wittgenstein, in many contexts, of thinking in terms of a contrast between *kinds of setting out of paths we can take in language,* and *engaged uses of language where we are taking these or those paths.* The notion of *preparation of language for its application* may then be philosophically useful to us, in that it draws to attention possible ways we may be using language that are not themselves engaged uses, but work as path-indicators and path-blockers for engaged uses. There is a very interesting remark of Wittgenstein about path-blockers:

> Language has the same traps ready for everyone; the immense network of easily trodden false paths. And thus we see one person after another walking down the same paths and we already know where he will make a turn, where he will keep going straight ahead without noticing the turn, etc., etc. Therefore, wherever false paths branch off I ought to put up signs to help in getting past the dangerous spots.[24]

My suggestion here is that the role of false-path markers is related to that of equations, thought of as indicating useful paths. Path-indicators—indicators of useful paths, on the one hand, and paths leading into confusion, on the other—belong in the general and varied group of "preparatory" propositions. And then the point is that propositions with a preparatory use may be misunderstood if one reads them without awareness of their differences from and their relations to the engaged uses of language that they are meant to respond to or to guide.[25]

In Section 7, I shall bring the discussion back to ethics, and then, in Section 8, to the views of David Wiggins and the relation between his views and Anscombe's.

### 7. Ethics: Indicating and Blocking Paths of Thought

One of the most striking features of practical reasoning is that it is beset with temptations, and this includes practical reasoning when it is philosophically reflective. So a second striking feature of thinking in the region of ethics is that there are responses to practical thinking, responses which come from seeing common kinds of practical reasoning as *thought's having gone astray:* we have gone down paths of thought that should be avoided but that may be profoundly tempting. Philippa

24. Wittgenstein 2005, 312.

25. For discussion of Frege and Wittgenstein on "preparatory" uses of language, see Essay 4.

Foot provides a good example of this kind of response. She says, "Something drives us towards utilitarianism . . . we must be going wrong somewhere." There is an easily trodden false path here. What she thinks is, indeed, that where we are going wrong is in "accepting the idea that there *are* better and worse states of affairs in the sense that consequentialism requires"; and at the end of her essay, she says that we should accustom ourselves to the thought that there is simply *a blank* where consequentialists see the phrase "the best state of affairs."[26] I read this as meaning that, where consequentialists think that there is a thought they are thinking, about the significance of the betterness of states of affairs, there is no thought, there is something with a blank in the middle of it. So I see her discussion of this case as a fine example of the significance in ethics of responses to temptation, to the tendencies in practical thinking to go down false paths. Another case of the attempt in ethics to block off paths of thought that may be found extremely tempting is Sabina Lovibond's, on the entertaining (in advance of any actual case) of questions about what we should do if faced with horrific dilemmas.[27] Lovibond was discussing ideas of Elizabeth Anscombe's; and it would be good to mention a quite different sort of example, from Anscombe herself—from the speech she gave against the awarding by Oxford of an honorary degree to Truman. In that speech (published as "Mr Truman's Degree"), she says that "choosing to kill the innocent as a means to your ends is always murder."[28] In its original context of her speech to Convocation, that statement was meant to indicate a path of thought of which her colleagues might not have been aware, or to which they might not have been attending, as they were deciding whether to vote for the degree. The path she wanted to draw plainly to their attention was the inferential path from "I am going to vote to give Truman the degree" to "I am going to vote to honor a murderer." That is, she wanted to draw to their attention a path of thought that would lead them to see *what it was they were doing*. It was easy not to see this; it was easy to take the giving of the degree to Truman to be utterly normal and rea-

26. Foot 2002, esp. 59, 62, 77.

27. Lovibond 2004.

28. Anscombe 1981d, 66; see also 64.

sonable; hence the value in the circumstances of a path-indicator that might change their conception of what they were doing.—My suggestion here is that, in various ways, in practical thinking, we may stand in need of, or find useful, many different sorts of path-indicators, both of the kind that block paths of thought we may be tempted to take, and also of the kind that indicate open paths of thought which it may be important for us to be aware of, but which habits of ease-in-thinking make invisible to us, or enable us to go on not seeing.

Suppose one of the members of Convocation heard Anscombe, and realized that voting in favor of the degree would be voting to honor a murderer, and suppose he came to think then that it would be a kind of moral failure to vote for the degree—a failure to take seriously the victims of the bombings that Truman had authorized. We can see what is going on there as having two stages. There is first the stage in which Anscombe's words (her characterization in general terms of *what it is* to choose to kill the innocent) indicate a significant kind of path for thinking; and secondly there is the stage in which the don who hears the speech takes the path, and judges that he should not vote for the degree and that to do so would be a moral failure. I am suggesting that what went on can be conceptualized in terms of the Wittgensteinian contrast between preparation for use of language and the engaged use of what is thus made available. The example is also meant to bring out a further point, about truth in ethics. In Section 5, I suggested that we could have a sort of Anscombean-Aristotelian account of truth, based on the idea that it is part of the business of thinking to guide the business of thinking, and that when this guiding is done well, we have truth. This would suggest that there may be importantly different kinds of cases of truth in ethics, depending on whether we have in view the guidance of thinking, or engaged thinking that may take or fail to take this or that path of thought.

## 8. Back to David Wiggins

I began, in Section 1, with David Wiggins's remark that there is an aspect in which elementary arithmetic and first-order morality may be compared: in both, there are judgments about which we can say

"There is nothing else to think but *that so and so*"; among his examples were "7 + 5 = 12" and "Slavery is wrong." The comparison is central in Wiggins's view of the kind of objectivity that moral judgments, understood as he understands them, do have. It is thus also part of his account of moral judgments as capable of truth. His account of moral judgments allows for there being many different sorts of thinking and judging that go on in ethics; but it does not allow for the kind of difference I have wanted to suggest—namely, the difference between ethical judgments that are guides to thinking (indicators of paths that can be taken and paths that should not be taken) and judgments that are not meant as such guides, but that are themselves takings of this or that path in thinking about some case, or kinds of case, and that may follow, or may ignore or flout, what one might regard as guides to thinking. I take the absence of attention to that difference to be a significant feature of Wiggins's approach to ethics; I believe it leads to his not getting into focus the structure of the nineteenth-century dispute about slavery. The dispute itself, especially after the cessation of the (legal) Atlantic slave trade, was at least in part a dispute about whether it was a false path in thinking about human affairs to treat such issues (including, in particular, slavery) in an abstract general way. Wiggins invites us to see the nineteenth-century dispute about slavery as capable of illuminating the issue of objectivity in ethics, and as helping us to see our way to rejecting the "insidious presumption of symmetry" in ethics. But in order to see the relevance of the dispute to the possibility of objectivity in ethics, we need to understand the kind of complexity the dispute actually had, and the role in it of attempts by pro- and anti-slavery thinkers alike to set up "No Entry" signs to paths of thought taken by their opponents.[29]

We can now look at the similarities and differences between the Anscombean approach that I have sketched and Wiggins's view. In Wiggins's remarks about the cases in which there is nothing else to think but that *so and so,* and in Anscombe's discussion of her example and of related sorts of case, there are ideas about the normativity of thinking—

---

29. See Essay 7 for a detailed discussion of the nineteenth-century dispute and its relevance to Wiggins's arguments about truth in ethics.

what is for thinking to be going as it should, and what it is for it to fail to do so. Their ideas about the normativity of thinking are closely tied, in both cases, to their rejection of familiar sorts of symmetry in philosophical thought about thinking. Wiggins rejects the "insidious presumption" that there is some tenable position opposed to any ethical judgment we take to be true; Anscombe rejects the idea that a thought must have, opposed to it, something that is thinkable. But their treatments of the normativity of thought are nevertheless deeply different. This deep difference arises, I think, out of their different ways of inheriting from Frege and Wittgenstein. Wiggins has his own version of a Davidsonian version of this inheritance, which places great emphasis on the connection between meaning and truth-conditions.[30] He holds that that connection can be worked up into a general account of linguistic meaning that itself can be elaborated to allow for the plain truth of moral judgments. The account he gives is intended to cover the relation between truth and meaning for declarative sentences in general.[31] Anscombe, on propositions that can only be true, represents a very different understanding of what we should inherit from Frege and Wittgenstein. In particular, she held that there were fundamental insights about truth and meaning in the picture theory—and a big question for her was how far one could keep hold of those insights in the light of Wittgenstein's later work. She took it that there was something basically right in the picture-theory account of the sorts of propositions that have the possibility of truth and the possibility of falsehood, and that there was also something right in the *Tractatus* contrast between such propositions and propositions that can only be true. What she objected to, and thought needed to be changed, was the narrowness of Wittgenstein's conception, in the *Tractatus,* of the second category. One can begin to see what she has in view from her example of "'Someone is not the name of someone," but that is not an isolated sort of case, and resembles other kinds of case of responses to what may be taken to be confusion or some other kind of going-wrong of thought. The intelligibility of what we may say in response to confusion, or to other kinds of

30. See especially Wiggins 1999.
31. See Wiggins 1991b.

ways in which thought miscarries, may depend on the context: on the confusions and miscarriages of thought themselves. Anscombe's treatment of her example goes, I think, with rejecting any conception of the semantic uniformity of declarative sentences that would *not take deeply enough* the distinction between propositions that have the possibility of truth and of falsity and propositions that do not. In allowing for solo propositions, for significant declarative sentences which lack significant negations, an Anscombean approach differs from that of Wiggins on what possible kinds of thinking may be involved in ethics, and thus also on what different possibilities there are for what truth in ethics might be. I have not tried to argue for an Anscombean approach as opposed to a Wigginsian one. I have wanted to show that there are possibilities here, there is a kind of approach—but it is an approach that has had no place in our picture of how we can think about thinking, about language and about ethics.[32]

32. An earlier version of this essay was read at a meeting of the Jowett Society in Oxford. I am very grateful to members of the audience for their questions and comments, to Steven Methven and John Haldane for their helpful suggestions, and to Adrian Moore for his clarification of David Wiggins's views on truth.

# Truth in Ethics: Williams and Wiggins

~

## 1. Introduction

This essay starts from a disagreement between Bernard Williams and David Wiggins—a disagreement which came out in the essays they wrote on truth in ethics, for the journal *Ratio* (Williams 1995; Wiggins 1995). Wiggins had earlier developed an account of truth in ethics, which included the claim that there were many moral questions about which truth can be attained.[1] In criticizing Wiggins, Williams drew on the distinction for which he is well known, between thick and thin ethical concepts—between ethical concepts like *good, right,* and *wrong* and concepts like *treacherous, cruel, brutal,* and *dishonest.* As Williams understands the distinction, there are also concepts which lie between the thick and the thin, like *justice.* In his contribution to *Ratio,* Williams uses that distinction as the basis of a criticism of Wiggins on truth in ethics. Two central ideas about thick concepts play a role in Williams's argument: the first idea is that the application of a thick ethical concept is determined by what the world is like (1985, 129), and the second idea is that people have different thick ethical concepts. As Williams puts it, "the vocabulary of thick concepts is not homogeneous in a pluralistic society, nor homogeneous over time or between different societies"

---

1. Wiggins 1991a, esp. 62.

(1995, 236). Williams's basic anti-Wiggins argument is that, in order to get the kind of substantial truth that Wiggins thinks we can get in ethics, there would have to be some thick concepts that were not local and particular but universal. But there aren't any; there is an irreducible plurality of thick concepts.

Williams did not directly attack Wiggins on truth. He focused instead on a formula that Wiggins uses. This is the formula: *there is nothing else to think but that p.* Wiggins's idea was that there are various subject-matters in which someone may consider a question, and may be given the reasons supporting *p* as the answer to the question—and may be able, on the basis of these reasons, to recognize that *there is nothing else to think in response to that question but that p.* For example, you can be given calculating rules, and shown how to use them, and then come to recognize that the answer to "What does 7 plus 5 come to?" is 12. You can come to see that, on that matter, there is nothing else to think but that 7 plus 5 is 12. Wiggins then argues that, within ethics, there are also cases in which there is nothing else to think but that such-and-such. Wiggins is not arguing that, on some matters, there is nothing else *for us* to think; he's making the stronger point that there are ethical matters about which there is nothing else *to think* but that so-and-so. The example he uses is: *there is nothing else to think, but that slavery is unjust and insupportable.* His point is that a "wealth of considerations can . . . be produced" that make it evident that there is *nothing else to think* but that slavery is unjust and insupportable. He says: "At some point in running through these considerations, . . . it will appear that the price of thinking anything at variance with the insupportability of slavery is to have opted out altogether from the point of view that shall be common between one person and another" (1991a, 70). Here you may want to ask, "Well, what if, when you say that there is nothing else to think but that *p*, there are people who think something else?" Wiggins did set out ways to explain what is happening in these cases. Anyway, it is that view of Wiggins's that Williams is criticizing.

Williams tried to show that Wiggins can't get what he wants: he isn't going to be able to come up with cases in ethics, where there is nothing else to think but that such-and-such. All Wiggins is going to be able to get, as Williams sees it, will be cases where there is nothing else for *us* to think but such-and-such, or nothing else for some other group of people to think but that such-and-such. When we take there to be nothing else *to think but that such-and-such,* this will depend upon some particular vocabulary of evaluation, and none of these is universal. So that is what Williams is trying to show. What Williams does when he tries to show this is fishy. But interestingly so. So now I want to turn to what he does.

## 2. Williams's Argument

Williams begins his argument by producing a formula of the same sort as Wiggins's—but using a quite different example. Wiggins's example was "There is nothing else to think but that slavery is unjust and insupportable." The case that Williams sets up is one in which some boys "do a wanton and hideous thing to the cat, [causing] the cat great pain" (1995, 237). Wiggins's view, Williams says, is that there is nothing else to think but that this was a cruel thing to do; but the boys may nevertheless not think that; they may think that it was fun. So this is meant to go against Wiggins. (Williams is here drawing on Wiggins's discussion of this sort of case in Wiggins 1987b.)

But there is already something peculiar going on here, since Wiggins's formula, "There is nothing else to think but that slavery is unjust and insupportable" should not rule out thinking various other things about slavery—for example, that it was profitable. When Wiggins gives the example, "there is nothing else to think *but that slavery is unjust and insupportable,*" he is concerned with what there is to think about the moral legitimacy of slavery. If someone thinks that *slavery is profitable,* this is not disagreeing about whether slavery is unjust. It wouldn't be a counterexample to Wiggins. Similarly, if we consider the boys who think that what they did was fun, it's not remotely clear that we have a case that counts against Wiggins. Unless you make clear what *question* is being asked, Wiggins's approach doesn't set up any kind of conclusion about what is the only thing to think.[2]

2. Miranda Fricker (2013) has a discussion of the dispute between Williams and Wiggins, which is marred by the same misunderstanding of Wiggins's argument—a misunderstanding about what would constitute a counterexample to his views. Her account draws on Williams's remarks about the ancient Greek view of slavery. She

Wiggins has a reply to Williams on this issue (1995, 250–252), in which he allows for cases where someone thinks, about slavery, that it is profitable. But Wiggins makes his reply to Williams on this point depend on the person's categorizing the institution in some way other than as *slavery*. That is, on the Wiggins view, you might categorize the institution as both slavery and as a commercial practice, and then you could say of the commercial practice that it was profitable. But this is an unnecessary detour. There is no reason not to categorize the practice as slavery and say of it, of slavery described as such, that it is profitable. You don't need to attach the property of profitableness to something described in some other way than as slavery. I believe that Wiggins himself is not clear about this, but it seems to me that what he should hold, given his overall account, is that people can call slavery profitable, without its being even apparently inconsistent with saying that there is nothing else to think, *about the moral and political issue of slavery,* but that slavery is unjust and insupportable. Compare saying that the slave trade, besides being unjust and inhumane, was detrimental to British commercial and strategic interests.[3]

Back to Williams's argument against Wiggins. He says that, if you use the concept *cruel,* if it is in your vocabulary of thick concepts, then indeed there is nothing else to think but that what the boys did was

---

says that he presents a "robust historical case," which she takes to provide a counterexample to Wiggins. Williams had said that, because the Greeks, on the whole, took the institution of slavery to be a necessity, there was "no space, effectively, for the question of its justice to be raised" (1993, 124). Since this implies that you don't have to think that slavery is unjust and insupportable, Fricker takes it that the case thus counts against Wiggins. But this sort of case is no objection to Wiggins. He was not suggesting that people in any set of historical circumstances, who had (or knew about) the institution of slavery, would have been in a position to consider the question of its justice or injustice, and would then have been able to recognize its injustice. He was arguing that, if the question of the rightness or wrongness of slavery "*has come into focus,*" there is only one thing to be thought about that question. He was at no point suggesting that it had to come into focus. He would not have said that the description of a slave society within which supposedly there was no space for the question to be thought about constituted an objection to his argument.

3. See Farrell 2007.

cruel. So Williams's picture of the situation is one in which the boys aren't users of the concept *cruel,* and this is reflected in their thinking that what they did was fun. But, with this move, Williams's approach gets even fishier. After all, maybe these boys are users of the concept *cruel*—they may use it, for example, to criticize some teacher, whom they take to be horribly cruel. They've seen movies with cruel villains, and they understand and go along with what people say in the movie when the villain is described as cruel. If the concept *cruel* is in their evaluative vocabulary, it is nevertheless perfectly possible for them to avoid thinking of what *they themselves are doing,* as cruel. This sort of thing happens all the time: you may use some evaluative concept in many circumstances, but may avoid thinking about whether it applies to something you are doing. There is no inference from the boys' describing what they did as fun (and their evading any question of its cruelty) to their not being users of the concept *cruel.* In fact, the evasion of the question may indeed be an indication that they do use the concept. The main point here, then, is that, in various ways, people may *turn off* the issue of the application to themselves (or to particular others) of some concept that they do use in an ordinary way in other circumstances.[4]

Williams goes on, and things get fishier still. After he has given us his picture of the situation as one in which the boys do not yet use the concept *cruel,* he says: "This draws our attention to an extremely important form of ethical difference—namely that between those who do and those who don't use a certain concept" (1995, 237). And he then gives us the case of Oscar Wilde's saying that "obscene" is not a word of his, as an illustration of the difference.[5] He is suggesting, then, that we take the idea of there being an important ethical difference between those who do and those who don't use a particular concept, and see that difference as exemplified both in the case of boys who haven't got the concept of cruelty, and Oscar Wilde, who is deliberately repudiating the use

4. See Williams's discussion of thick concepts (1985, 141). So far as he is committing himself to the idea that, in a nonmarginal case, those who have mastered the use of a thick concept will agree on its application, his account is unrealistic.

5. See the Introduction to Part III. Williams had misremembered the case, which involved the word "blasphemous," not "obscene."

of a concept. Those who don't use some thick concept may nevertheless have a kind of nonuser's understanding of it: it isn't part of their own evaluative language, but they may be able to pick up the use well enough to apply the concept themselves in the way it is applied by the users of the concept. The reason Williams has been leading up to the case of Oscar Wilde is that it illustrates particularly well the differences there are, between people and between cultures, in the thick concepts that people use. His basic argument against Wiggins is, then, that there is no set of thick concepts that we all share. *If* there were some underlying canonical, homogeneous set of thick concepts, then we might be able to get some kind of truth in ethics that went beyond the appropriate application of the thick concepts of this or that culture, but the idea of such a canonical homogeneous set of thick concepts is utterly unrealistic. And so, therefore, is the idea of getting any kind of substantial truth in ethics, anything beyond truth as tied to this or that particular evaluative language. Thus, there is no nonrelative truth in ethics. What is fishy here is that Williams has an idea of what the best prospect for substantial truth in ethics *would be:* you'd get it if there were some universal set of thick concepts. But what is striking about his whole approach is that in his argument, he moves further and further at each step from what Wiggins was actually trying to do, and specifically further and further from the kind of case that Wiggins gave as his example. So in the next section I want to turn to Wiggins's example, to bring out how far it is from anything that Williams is discussing.

### 3. There Is Nothing Else to Think but That Slavery Is Unjust and Insupportable

The first move that Williams made was to replace Wiggins's example of the injustice of slavery with the case of the cruelty of what the boys did. The reason Williams changed the example is that he wanted the focus to be on a case where a thick concept plainly applies to something, in the way the concept of cruelty plainly applies to the wanton thing the boys did, which caused the cat great pain. Williams wanted an example using a concept with much tighter connections to how the world is than the concept of injustice. In the case of injustice, there can be serious disagreement about what the concept does or doesn't apply to. *Justice* had indeed been Williams's example of a concept that is neither thick nor thin but in between (1995, 234); and Williams's argument against Wiggins depends upon switching to an example involving the application of a thick concept to a nonmarginal case, and then showing that that thick concept won't be part of some people's vocabulary. I want to argue that Wiggins's example is extremely interesting and important, just the way it is, because it brings out that Wiggins is not doing what Williams thinks you have to do if you are trying to set out a substantial notion of truth in ethics. When Williams moves away from Wiggins's example of slavery to the example of the cruelty of what the boys did, he obscures important features of the case of slavery.

Think about slavery. Institutions of slavery have been very various; and have involved many kinds of cruelty and brutality. *Cruel* and *brutal* are thick concepts, and the application of these thick concepts to slavery is important, as is that of *degradation;* but there is a further issue, of a different kind, at the heart of what makes slavery odious, on many people's view. A central thing in the various institutions of slavery is *property in human beings.* If there are considerations that can be brought to bear on thought about slavery—considerations that will leave you with nothing to think but that it is odious, unjust, an intolerable evil—these often involve showing what is appalling about a man or woman being owned and used and disposed of as a piece of property; they involve showing what is wrong with using another human being as a kind of extension of your own will.[6] The issue about slavery, as it has been thought about, doesn't in any straightforward way depend on thick concepts of the sort that Bernard Williams discussed. It's not an accident that the original form of Wiggins's example does not use any thick con-

6. See, for example, Haven 1859, 121–125. See also Corbin 1787. In a deed in which he freed twenty-one of his slaves, George Corbin said, "It is Repugnant to Christianity and even common Honesty to live in Ease and affluence by the Labour of those whom fraud and Violence have Reduced to Slavery; (altho' sanctifyed by General consent, and supported by the law of the Land)." Although *dishonest* is a thick concept, what emerges in this deed is that it is given a perceptive kind of application to the case of slavery, an application that many users of the concept might have rejected.

cept. (I should note here that some defenders of slavery in the American South denied that slavery involved property in human beings, and claimed that it merely involved a property right to their labor—and that it was therefore entirely consistent with respecting the human nature of the slaves, their rationality and their moral agency. This is a piece of double-think, as can be seen from such characteristic features of American slavery as the disallowing of testimony from slaves in court, and the treatment of harm done to a man's slave as legally in the same category as harm done to his horse.[7] In fact, the Confederate Constitution explicitly established property *in slaves.* I would argue that the institutions we think of as slavery, while they can be thought of as systems of *property in labor,* distinctively involve one or another form of *property in human beings.* It's important, too, to note how particularly deeply felt can be the slave's hatred of slavery as a system in which he is deprived of his self in being the property of another human being. This is something that Frederick Douglass especially sought to convey in his speeches.)

I don't at all want to deny the significance of thick concepts applying to slavery, but these are not concepts that those who defended slavery lacked or repudiated; and further, I want to keep in the center here the idea that it is *property in human beings* that is an abomination. (I will also discuss below the importance of a feature of pro-slavery arguments—namely, their insistence that anti-slavery thought frequently treats as essential features of slavery what they claim are features only of bad slave-owners or bad systems of slavery.)

I am going to look more at Wiggins and his reply to Williams, but here now, at the end of Section 3, my conclusion so far is that what Williams does when he reads Wiggins is impose *his model* of what you'd have to do if you were putting forward an account of ethical statements as capable of substantial truth. Williams thinks that the best you can get, if you are looking for truth in ethics, is the kind of truth that you get with the application of thick concepts, belonging to this or that particular vocabulary. Although this is the best you can get, this truth has an irremovable kind of relativity—relativity to particular vocabularies

---

7. See Gross 2000.

of evaluation. This model, then, of what the best is that you can get, under-lies Williams's idea that Wiggins's account of truth in ethics cannot get further than a kind of relativism. I have wanted to suggest that Williams, by imposing this model, misses what Wiggins was doing in his discussion of truth in ethics, and also misses what is at stake in the debate about slavery. I turn in Section 4 to Wiggins's reply.

Many anti-slavery thinkers did make use of the concept of natural rights, which some pro-slavery thinkers rejected. But *violation of natural right* would not be an example of what Williams thinks of as a "thick concept." It is much more like *unjust* than like *cruel* or *deceitful*. Further, in at least some cases when the notion of natural rights was used in arguments about the wrongness of slavery, it was not actually doing serious work. See, for example, Haven 1859. None of the considerations which Haven takes to show that slavery is invariably grievously wrong needs to be tied to a notion of natural rights. That point would lend support to Williams's claim, questioned by Richard Kraut, that considerations making possible a recognition of the injustice of slavery were "basically available" to the Greeks.[8] In any case, the notion of natural rights, as applied to a supposed right to property, was used by some pro-slavery thinkers. I would not want to deny the force of natural rights arguments as used against those who upheld slavery while celebrating the American Revolution as a defense of natural rights, and in particular of the natural right to liberty.

## 4. Wiggins's Reply

Wiggins's reply can be seen in three places. He had anticipated Williams's kind of response when he originally set out his view (Wiggins 1991a). Then he replied directly to Williams in his contribution to *Ratio* (Wiggins 1995), and there is a more developed reply in his book *Ethics* (Wiggins 2006).

Wiggins's central idea is that, if you refuse to subsume the institution of slavery under the concepts it is subsumed under in the argument

8. For Williams's view, see his 1993, 124; for Kraut's discussion, see his 1994, esp. 180. For more about this disagreement, see note 28 below.

for its injustice and insupportability, you are at risk of depriving yourself, at the same time, of any workable scheme of moral ideas. You need to consider what would be involved in having a workable system of moral ideas that dispensed, in the face of phenomena like the slave trade and its historical effects, with ideas like *justice, slavery,* and *using human beings as means, not ends* (1991a, 78; 2006, 369).

I want to see where Wiggins's argument leads us, but first I shall try to remove from his argument a couple of features that I think are distractions, things that make it hard to see what is genuinely significant in the argument.

1. Wiggins asks us to think about what would be involved in not granting the injustice and insupportability of slavery in the face of such things as the slave trade and its historical effects. It isn't clear whether Wiggins means the transatlantic trade, or whether instead he means the slave trade more generally. I think he had in mind the transatlantic trade in African slaves; and if so, that puts a distracting feature into his argument. Many American slave-owners condemned that trade, and many American defenses of slavery after the end of the (legal) transatlantic trade were intended to be entirely compatible with condemning the brutality and cruelty of the trade.[9] These defenses of slavery also emphasize the distinctive features that American slavery developed after the end of the legal transatlantic trade.[10] So I want to have in view, not Wiggins's actual argument, but a Wigginsian argument that does not appeal to features of the transatlantic trade and the way its existence shaped the treatment of slaves (especially in the West Indies). The issues here will come out more clearly if we don't suggest that criticism of slavery is tied to such things as the character of the transatlantic trade. If you want to claim that there is nothing else to think but that slavery is an evil, a wide focus is important. Otherwise it can be argued that the

9. The transatlantic trade could not be constitutionally ended by the federal government until 1808, but in fact every state except South Carolina enacted a ban on the transatlantic trade before that—and even in South Carolina, when the trade was re-opened, there was considerable controversy.

10. See especially Ford 2009 on the development of paternalism in the ideology of slaveholders.

evils to which you have drawn attention are not tied to slavery *as such*. Defenders of slavery have themselves insisted that slavery as practiced in many cases has involved terrible brutality and cruelty. But compare John Stuart Mill, in *The Subjection of Women* (1870, 62–63): "Whether the institution to be defended is slavery, political absolutism, or the absolutism of the head of a family, we are always expected to judge of it from its best instances; and we are presented with pictures of loving exercise of authority on one side, loving submission to it on the other— superior wisdom ordering all things for the greatest good of the dependents, and surrounded by their smiles and benedictions. All this would be very much to the purpose if anyone pretended that there are no such things as good men. Who doubts that there may be great goodness, and great happiness, and great affection, under the absolute government of a good man? Meanwhile, laws and institutions require to be adapted, not to good men, but to bad." Joseph Haven, in his antebellum moral philosophy textbook, also contrasts the essential points of wrongness of slavery with accidental ones (1859, 125). Haven's discussion of slavery is a good example of what Wiggins had in mind: Haven provides considerations that are meant to rule out thinking anything about the moral character of slavery but that any and every system of slavery is grievously wrong (126).[11]

It may be that Wiggins, in referring to "the slave trade," meant to include, not just the transatlantic trade, but also (for example) the trade within the United States, the cruelties of which were legion. "For slaves it was the trade, more than the plantation, that bared the essence of a system that made the slave into a commodity, 'a person with a price.'"[12] The character of the domestic trade in the United States does, I think, make possible an argument about the failure of attempts to defend slavery by portraying it in paternalistic terms. The point would be that paternalistic defenses of slavery as practiced in the American South had either to ignore the incompatibility of any such defense with the

11. Compare also Moncure Conway's description of slavery in its "best" form, in his 1864.

12. J. William Harris, 2014, 345. The last four words are taken by Harris from Walter Johnson.

continued significance of a trade that constituted a threat to every slave or to pretend that slaves did not feel in the way white people would about the breakup of their marriages, families, and communities. I cannot discuss this issue here.

2. The other distracting feature of Wiggins's argument is his taking the concept of *slavery* as a thick concept which is important for the condemnation of slavery, and which it will be found extremely hard to dispense with, if we want to have a workable system of moral ideas. So Wiggins's idea is that the concept of *slavery* does significant work when we try to show that slavery is an evil. The anti-slavery argument, as he sees it, involves recognizing that there is no other way to categorize slavery than as slavery, and that *therefore* various further moral considerations take hold. The trouble with Wiggins's idea is that almost all *defenders* of slavery had no problem at all about categorizing slavery as slavery. You don't get anywhere in a discussion of the moral character of slavery by insisting that it be characterized as slavery. Your opponents may perfectly well agree, and may argue in response (as, for example, in the American South), that slavery as they practiced it was not unjust.[13]

Although the concept of *slavery* is not a thick concept, it has some resemblances to thick concepts; and it may be helpful here to set out some elements of the use of the words "slave" and "slavery." There are contexts in which the application of these words may be disputed, as when a foreign diplomat (for example, in the United States or the United Kingdom) is accused of having kept a native of her country as a slave, and the diplomat denies that she has been keeping the girl in slavery.[14] There have also been a few defenders of this or that particular form of slavery who have wanted to deny that it was really *slavery*.[15] And, further, some abolitionists have denied that a person can, properly

---

13. See, e.g., Harper 1838.

14. The categorization of such cases as slavery may have significant legal consequences. See especially Scott 2012.

15. A well-known case is that of Henry Hughes (1854), who described the antebellum South as having an institution, not of slavery, but of "warrenteeism"; see also the introduction to Elliott 1860; also, for an English / Barbadian example, see Samuel Estwick 1773.

speaking, be said to own another person; and some freed slaves denied that anyone ever had a property right in them. But these disputes about categorization are not relevant to the question whether there is anything else to think but that slavery is unjust and insupportable. Further, there were social contexts within American slave society, and within the post-bellum South, in which various other expressions were preferred to the word "slave," including "servant," "hand," and "negro," as in "Five of Smith's negroes have run away." But these forms of expression were never meant to suggest that the people spoken about in these terms were not slaves. These are not cases of not categorizing someone as a slave, or of not categorizing an institution as slavery, but of not using the explicit term in contexts in which it could be avoided. (The use of these euphemisms persisted for over a century after the abolition of slavery; "servant" is still used in some tours of historic plantations, and on websites and brochures for these plantations.) A further context within which the word "slave" was avoided was that of constitution-writing. The word is omitted from the U.S. Constitution and from the constitution voted on in 1790 by the Constituent Assembly of France. The point of avoiding the word is that of not granting what might seem to follow about the legitimacy of slavery from the extent to which the constitution, in both cases, does provide protection for the interests of slave-owners.[16] I do not want to deny here that categorization of some practice as "slavery" can be significant in various political and legal contexts.[17]

Back, then, to Wiggins's argument: the argument that, if you claim that there is something else to think about the moral and political question of slavery, other than that slavery is unjust and insupportable, you are at risk of depriving yourself of the possibility of putting together a workable system of moral ideas. Pressure can be put on you, in the form of considerations about slavery, which you can avoid taking to show that slavery is unjust and insupportable only by depriving yourself of such

16. See Drescher 2009, 131–132, 157–158; also Oakes 2013, 19–20; Sumner 1856. On the connection with the Somerset case, see Oakes 2013, 9. For a different view of why the U.S. Constitution does not use the words "slave" or "slavery," see Van Cleve 2010, 178–179.

17. See Allain 2012; also Drescher 2009, 387 and 409.

moral concepts as *justice* and *treating human beings as mere means*. And what kind of system of moral ideas will then be available to you? (This is the argument that is at the heart of Wiggins's denial of the "presumption of symmetry" on the part of noncognitivists about ethics, the presumption that, in the case of any moral view that one takes to be true, there is a tenable opposed moral point of view).—What I think is great about Wiggins's argument is that it leads us into an examination of what we need in order to be able to think about ethical matters. What do we need, in order to be able to think, in order to be able to think well, about such an extraordinarily significant human matter as slavery?

Here we need to have before us some idea of what was actually argued by those who were defending slavery, and who were therefore apparently thinking something that (at least according to Wiggins) isn't there to think. This is the subject of Section 5.

I should note that Wiggins did look into this issue, but what he looked at, the parliamentary debate about slavery in 1833, was not a good sample of debate about slavery. Reading through the parliamentary debate left Wiggins with the impression that the defenders of slavery could not come up with any sustainable position in favor of slavery. He emphasizes that the main thought that they did come up with was "Though men may be generous with their own property, they should not be so with the property of others" (1991a, 71). But if one wants to see what serious attempts were made to develop a "sustainable position" by proslavery thinkers, the parliamentary debate was the wrong place to look. The parliamentary defense of the West Indian interest, in the 1833 debates, was directed toward minimizing and postponing as far as possible the effects that emancipation was likely to have. There was no doubt, among the participants in the parliamentary debate, that slavery in the West Indies was going to be brought to an end—the questions being rather whether this was going to be done immediately or gradually, what sort of compensation the slave-owners might get, and what system of labor would replace the slave system.[18] The limited range of considerations

18. On there not being any real question about whether slavery was going to be brought to an end, see Edward Stanley's speech on introducing the government's plan, May 14, 1833.

involved in the parliamentary debate should be contrasted with the full range of pro-slavery arguments developed in other contexts. See, for example, Drew Gilpin Faust on the significance of American defenses of slavery within the "effort to construct a coherent southern social philosophy" (1981, 1). The failure of the pro-slavery participants in the 1833 parliamentary debate to put forward any "sustainable position" in favor of slavery does not enable one to draw any conclusion about the possibility of a sustainable pro-slavery position, and hence does not provide support for Wiggins's denial of the "presumption of symmetry" by noncognitivists. Because Wiggins himself looked at the 1833 debate, I have focused in what follows on defenses of slavery from roughly the same period.

### 5. Wiggins's Argument, Seen in Relation to Pro-Slavery Thought

Wiggins's idea was that denying that slavery is evil puts you at risk of having no workable system of moral ideas, because you will be working *without* such central moral ideas as justice and the significance of treating human beings not as mere means. In much moral thinking about slavery, there is the idea of a deep incompatibility between recognizing someone as a human being and treating him or her as a piece of property; and Wiggins's argument takes this seriously. He said that the issue about whether slavery is indeed evil can be joined only if one compares the system of moral ideas that we have, including notions like justice and respect for humanity, with a system of moral ideas dispensing with such notions.[19] Once you've got justice and respect for humanity on board, you've got (so he is arguing) considerations that will lead to recognition of the evil of slavery. So what system do you have without such notions? That's the question Wiggins wants us to ask.

Pro-slavery writers, though, did not in general dispense with such notions; they rather understood them not to lead to a condemnation of slavery. One source of such pro-slavery thought is Aristotle's *Politics,* where Aristotle defended slavery against the charge, by some unnamed

---

19. Wiggins 1991a, 78–79; also Wiggins 1995, 252.

people, that holding and using human beings as slaves was contrary to nature.[20] Centuries later, those defending the subjugation of American Indians and the enslavement of Africans made use of various forms of the idea that there are *natural slaves,* whom it is no injustice to subjugate or enslave. I want to emphasize what's going on here: the issue of the injustice of slavery, about which (according to Wiggins) there is only one thing to think, comes up in Aristotle's *Politics,* in a passage that was echoed (and in some cases directly appealed to) by defenders of slavery in the Americas.[21] There is, however, a significant difference between Aristotle's claims about there being people who are slaves by nature (and who therefore may be owned and used by other people without injustice) and defenders of the enslavement of Africans (and some earlier defenders of the treatment by the Spanish of American Indians). Aristotle held that there is no straightforward way to distinguish those who have the internal character of being naturally slaves; you can't tell by looking because nature has not made this obvious (*Politics* bk. 1, 1254b). But pro-

20. In his 2006 book, Wiggins touches on Aristotle on "natural slavery" as something we might try to forget if that is indeed possible (276). He clearly doesn't take there to be a "sustainable position" on the justice of slavery to be found in Aristotle. He may have held that the question which Aristotle was answering had a sense fixed by the "historical context and circumstances," which are very different from ours, and hence that Aristotle cannot be read as giving an answer with which we may disagree to a question which he and we have in common. (See Wiggins 1987b, 162). On the importance of Aristotle for the issues here, see Blackburn 2006.

21. The Aristotelian view of "natural slaves" was used early in the sixteenth century by John Major, who said that American Indians could justly be ruled by whoever first conquers them, because they are by nature slaves; in the mid-sixteenth century, Sepúlveda gave a similar defense of Spanish treatment of the Indians. (On what specifically was being defended, see Marenbon 2015, 250n50.) On Aristotle's defense of slavery, in relation to Southern pro-slavery thought, see Millett 2007, 179; Monoson 2011. Bernard Williams has claimed that Aristotle's defense of slavery played a secondary role in nineteenth-century defenses of slavery, in comparison with scriptural defenses (1993, 115). He got this from Finley 1980, but what there is in Finley is a dogmatic assertion which appears not to have much behind it. Finley cites Bledsoe 1856, but there is no evidence that Finley read Bledsoe with any care, that he read any other pro-slavery work, or that he had any familiarity with the development of pro-slavery thought in America.

slavery writers of the eighteenth and nineteenth centuries frequently held that Africans, identifiable by racial characteristics, were naturally fitted to be slaves;[22] they also made use of a conception which is either based on Aristotle's, or very close to Aristotle's, of how slavery benefits a person who is a "natural slave."[23]

There is a huge disagreement about ethical things that is coming up at just this point. And Wiggins's discussion is important for leading us into such issues. We need to see what kind of disagreement there is here. There are disagreements about ethics where one group of people thinks that the other side has got things wrong, but there are also, I think, disagreements in which people take some way that other people are thinking about ethics *not just to be wrong,* not just to be something they disagree with—but to be a case of *the other people's thinking having gone off the rails.* I'm suggesting that the dispute about slavery involves a disagreement of that sort. That is, one response to all ideas that take some group of people to be natural slaves is: *thinking that way is thinking that has gone off the rails, it is not merely mistaken.* There's a road that you are going down, and thought that goes down that road has gone profoundly astray. Signs ought to be put up saying: "Don't go down that road." And indeed there was such a sign that was put up, the statement that men are by nature equal, or the statement that all men are created equal. This was a road sign for how to think, a road sign that says: "Don't go in search of, or think that you have found, an essential nature that some group of people have—an essential nature that makes it perfectly in keeping with justice to turn them into slaves, to keep them and use

22. See, for example, Bledsoe 1856, 53–54. After formulating a version of the argument that Africans are naturally fitted for slavery, he remarks that the argument is "prominently set forth" by every defender of slavery in the South. The idea also has a central place in Alexander Stephens's "Cornerstone Speech"—a statement of the fundamental political ideas of the Confederacy. On debate about the supposed natural fitness of Africans for slavery, see also Gates 1989, 72; for criticism (from an Aristotelian-Thomist point of view) of the possibility of identifying a *race* of natural slaves, see Las Casas 1974.

23. See especially Kraut 2002, chap. 8, esp. 297–299; also Lockwood 2007. On the arguments about how slavery, in its American form, supposedly benefited the slaves, see Anderson 2014, esp. 10–11.

them as slaves." I'm suggesting, then, that we should take statements like "All men are created equal" to have, as part of their meaning, something like this: There are all kinds of differences and inequalities of talents and intelligence and reasonableness and character between human beings, but none of these can be taken to indicate an inbuilt natural distinction in virtue of which some people may *justly* be owned by others, and may justly be treated merely as means by which others make *their* wills effective.[24] See, for example, Francis Hutcheson:

> No endowments, natural or acquired, can give a perfect right to assume power over others, without their consent. This is intended against the doctrine of Aristotle, and some others of the antients [sic], 'that some men are naturally slaves.' . . . The natural sense of justice and humanity abhors the thought.[25]

I am trying to draw a contrast between two kinds of disagreement in ethics: on the one hand, the kind of disagreement I've just been talking about, where one group of people believes that the thinking of the people they disagree with has gone off the rails, and, on the other hand, disagreements where you merely believe that what the other people think is wrong, but you don't take their thinking to have gone deeply astray. A good example of the more ordinary sort of disagreement would be over the question whether owning slaves is itself corrupting. There is a very clear statement of that view by Thomas Jefferson; he said that a child of a slave-owner would have to be a kind of prodigy for his manners and morals not to be depraved by witnessing members of his family trampling the rights of the black members of

24. It should be noted that the issues of natural subordination of some people to other people include questions about women. I have used formulae involving the equality of all men, because anything else would be anachronistic. I cannot discuss how the questions about slavery and the status of women were seen to be connected, in Aristotle or in the eighteenth and nineteenth centuries.

25. Hutcheson 1755, 1:300–301. For a sixteenth-century version of this point, see Las Casas 1974. There is a legal use of the idea of "natural equality" against the legitimacy of slavery, in the decision of Lord Kames in Knight v. Wedderburn, 1778.

the household. The child of a slave-owner learns from an early age to be a tyrant.[26] Quite a number of pro-slavery thinkers argued against this view of slave-owning as incompatible with virtue, and believed that the master-slave relation should be analogous to the relation of a good father to his children.[27]

I wanted to emphasize the contrast between ordinary moral disagreements and disagreements where one group believes that the thinking of the others has gone totally astray, that it is a kind of misuse of our thinking capacity. But this is not just the way critics of slavery may treat apologists for slavery: many *pro*-slavery thinkers believed that anti-slavery thinking had gone off the rails, had gone profoundly astray as thinking. This is now what I want to get to: how defenders of slavery took abolitionist and other anti-slavery thought not just to be mistaken but to have gone off the rails, to have gone down a path of disastrously tempting but utterly confused thought. If they had been able to read Wiggins, they'd have taken *his* thinking also to have gone down just such a path.

Wiggins was using as his example the general claim that there is no alternative to thinking that *slavery is unjust and insupportable.* He connects that claim with the idea that human beings should not be treated merely as means. Many, many people would agree that slavery is unjust and insupportable, full stop, total generality. I think this. Further, many people also would, like Wiggins, connect the general claim with ideas about respect for humanity. One main strand in pro-slavery thinking argues that thinking in those abstract general terms about slavery is thinking that has gone astray. It's thinking about social and political life in a way that utterly ignores our nature and capacities. It's exactly the kind of thinking that leads to revolutionary destruction of workable though flawed institutions. William Harper, for example, argues this way:

---

26. Compare Mill 1870, 66: "The relation of superiors to dependents is the nursery of these vices of character, which, wherever else they exist, are an overflowing from that source."

27. See, e.g., Dew 1832.

It is no less a false and shallow than a presumptuous philosophy, which theorizes on the affairs of men as of a problem to be solved by some unerring rule of human reason. . . . Man is born to subjection. . . . To say that there is evil in any institution, is only to say that it is human. (1838, 7)

A few years later, James Hammond, the former governor of South Carolina, wrote:

Every attempt which has been made by fallible man to extort from the world obedience to his "abstract" notions of right and wrong, has been invariably attended with calamities. . . . On slavery in the abstract, then, it would not be amiss to have as little as possible to say. (1845, 7)

Hammond and Harper, like other pro-slavery thinkers, repudiated many of the ideas associated with the American Revolution: the ideas expressed in the Declaration of Independence, of equality and liberty as human rights.[28] What I'm suggesting now is that many defenders of slavery believed that there is a path of thinking which may be found attractive, but it is a path down which thought is led fundamentally astray—down that path, *thinking goes adrift from all sense of our limits and fallibility as human beings.* Any general critique of slavery as inconsistent with justice and what is due to human beings has been tempted down that false path.[29]

28. The issues here are connected with a point raised by Bernard Williams in his 1993 and by Richard Kraut, in response, in 1994. Williams claimed that the Greeks had concepts which would have enabled them to see the injustice of slavery. Kraut replied that they did not have the concept of human rights, which plays a role in the kind of way we would explain why slavery is insupportable. Kraut takes this to indicate a kind of impoverishment of Greek thought in relation to modern thought. Nineteenth-century defenses of slavery bring out how this shift in the resources available for political thought could be taken to be a kind of deterioration. For the history of these ideas about liberty and equality in relation to the institution of slavery, see Honoré 2012.

29. See O'Brien 2004, 2:962, on the abandonment, by later pro-slavery thinkers, of the attack on thinking about the rights and wrongs of slavery in abstract terms. Eu-

Where are we now? That's the question to which I turn in Section 6.

## 6. Four Issues I Want to Think about, and Six That I Can Merely Mention

1. Wiggins had argued that there are categorizations of (the practices of) slavery that make it impossible to deny that slavery is unjust and insupportable; and you are landed with these categorizations when you utilize notions that cannot easily be dispensed with in any workable system of moral ideas. He later put the issue this way: "the only way to think anything at variance with the insupportability and injustice of slavery is to opt out altogether from any moral viewpoint that can make sense of asking the question 'what is one to think of the supportability or justice of slavery?'"[30] The problem with that line of argument is that defenses of slavery do not usually dispense with the notions that Wiggins thinks lead to the conclusion that slavery is unjust and insupportable. From Aristotle on, defenders of various forms of slavery have insisted that certain forms of enslavement are just. Again, there is a problem with Wiggins's point that you can't think anything at variance with the insupportability and injustice of slavery without opting out of any moral viewpoint that can even make sense of the question whether slavery is just or supportable. The problem there, at first sight anyway, is that defenders of slavery do apparently make sense of the question whether slavery is just, and provide what they take to be good reasons for the answer that they give. Further, the defenses of slavery that I have been discussing not only take the enslavement of at least some people to be just, they also include ideas about human nature and what is appropriate treatment given the forms that they take human nature to have. Their defenses of slavery contain arguments, formulated from what purports

---

gene Genovese has argued that, although Southern intellectuals explicitly attacked the idea that the rights and wrongs of slavery should be discussed in abstract terms, really and truly they were committed to a view of the sort they apparently rejected— namely, the view that slavery in the abstract was a human good. I cannot discuss Genovese's claim here, but see Daly 2002, 36; also Harris 2014.

30. Wiggins 2004, 108.

to be the moral point of view, that there is no disrespect for human nature inherent in slavery, but rather a realism about the forms that human nature takes.

I've just disputed Wiggins's claims, but I think that he is on to something; and the claims that I have been disputing can be pushed further, against the sort of response that I just gave. Isn't there something right in Wiggins's belief that, if you take "the moral point of view," there is no alternative to the condemnation of slavery? Do the defenders of slavery really have an alternative system of moral ideas? Do they really have an alternative answer to the question whether slavery is just? Does it all come apart? Does their thinking come apart? Is it a kind of miscarriage of thinking?—But I've also suggested in Section 5 that defenders of slavery see a kind of miscarriage of thinking in anti-slavery writings. This sort of issue is one that needs to be argued: if you believe that there is a miscarriage of thinking in the ideas of those who disagree with you, *that* needs to be shown. But what this all does mean is that Wiggins's example of slavery, which he tries to use as a case where there are concepts through which we can categorize a practice, concepts the application of which can make clear that there is only one thing to think about its injustice—that example is problematic. People who defend slavery do not give up the concept of justice; they hold on to the concept but put it to very different work.

2. One reason I went into the details of what Wiggins says about slavery is that it brings out the inadequacy of Bernard Williams's treatment of truth in ethics. His general account takes as central the application of thick concepts, and the idea that there is no basic shared human vocabulary of thick concepts. Possibly one could reformulate some of the dispute about slavery in Williams's sort of terms. One would then see the dispute as a matter of pro-slavery people and anti-slavery people having different vocabularies of thick concepts. Anti-slavery thinkers totally reject the concept of *natural slaves,* and one can say that that is a thick concept of pro-slavery thinkers that we don't use. So far as Williams draws that kind of difference to attention, that's fine.[31] But

31. Williams does not himself present the nineteenth-century dispute about slavery in terms of his account of thick ethical concepts. He says very little about that dis-

the objection to Williams's kind of presentation of the issue is that the anti-slavery people don't just reject the concept of *natural slaves;* they don't just work with some different evaluative concepts. The disagreement goes deeper. And here I think Wiggins points us in the right direction. The pro-slavery people and the anti-slavery people have very different systems of moral ideas, and to understand what is involved in their disagreement about slavery, it's not enough to see the heterogeneity of moral vocabulary. You have to see how their systems of moral ideas as a whole work against each other, despite sharing—in some sense sharing—such crucial notions as that of justice. They both *want* the concept of justice; they both take there to be something that is thinking well about justice in relation to slavery; they both want to make plain how they, as opposed to the people they disagree with, are thinking rightly about the justice of slavery.

3. I have made use of the idea that there are disagreements in ethics, in which one side or the other or both hold that the thinking of their opponents is a kind of *miscarriage* of thought. There are two sorts of question about this. First, couldn't one say that, whenever someone disagrees with you about anything, her thinking is miscarrying?[32] That is, one might question what I have said so far, and ask whether it is helpful to conceptualize ethical disagreements as in *some* cases involving claims about other people's thought having gone off the rails, miscarried or failed as thought, in contrast with *other* ethical disagreements where we merely take other people to be holding a wrong view, but still to be engaged in *thinking.* I'm suggesting that it *is* helpful, because it is a significant

---

agreement, and is concerned instead to contrast the context of ancient thought about slavery with that of the nineteenth century. At no point does he suggest that the concept of "natural slave" played a significant role in the nineteenth century, which I think may reflect his taking much of his story about the nineteenth-century dispute from Moses Finley.

32. One could appeal to Frege for a similar sort of point: any science can be regarded as providing rules about how to think, if our judgments are to be true (1979a, 145). So it might look as if any time you think something that is not true, you have broken some rule about how to think about the particular subject matter, and it might then look as if the "miscarriage of thought" accusation might be made against your judgment.

feature of ethics that we may want to think of there being tempting paths of thought in ethics, paths that tempt us onward—and we may believe that *thought going down those paths has got lost, or gets lost*. Ethics works with *ideas of temptation,* ideas of there being tempting but terribly misleading paths of thought; and I think such ideas shape our understanding of many of our disagreements.[33] The other question that comes up is how this all connects with Wiggins's defense of nonrelative truth in ethics. When we take his own example of slavery, and follow it up, we can see disagreements between different systems of moral ideas, where each side may want to characterize the other as having gone totally astray in its thinking; but then *can there be truth and falsity about such a matter?* Or is each side just berating the other?

4. I want not to let drop a quotation that I had from Wiggins in Section 1:

> At some point in running through these considerations, . . . it will appear that the price of thinking anything at variance with the insupportability of slavery is to have opted out altogether from the point of view that shall be common between one person and another. (1991a, 70)

One way in which the idea of some people as being "natural slaves" and of slaves as being a kind of property plays out in practice is that the moral point of view, as understood by pro-slavery thinkers, is not a point of view that can be shared "between one person and another," but a point of view that can be shared only between some persons and others, not including slaves. Slaves have no point of view that need be taken into account; they have no voice that need be heard. From the pro-slavery point of view, there is nothing unjust in excluding any "slave

---

33. Williams himself is indeed aware of exactly this issue, as it comes up in connection with ethical thinking about animals, some of which he takes to be *dotty*—and he takes *dottiness* (and similar concepts) to express an important kind of criticism of moral views. (See Williams et al. 1999.) Other terms in the critical vocabulary for thought that has gone fundamentally astray include *fanatic* and *corrupt*.

point of view," in treating them as not addressed in any discussion of slavery, and as having nothing to say in it.[34] There is an echo here of the Aristotelian conception of the natural slave as defective in his or her capacity to reason: the natural slave is someone whose use of reason goes no further, at most, than being able to appreciate someone else's rationality. What I want to bring out here is that *what the moral point of view is,* is itself one of the things that is in dispute, in the dispute about slavery. (The exclusion of any slave point of view was one of the things that underlay the disputes in the South about slave literacy and the anxieties about making the Bible available to slaves, since the central story in the Old Testament takes seriously the point of view on slavery of an enslaved people. The story is not presented as an assault on the property rights of Egyptians.) You cannot separate the question about the justice of slavery from the question what the moral point of view supposedly is, the question who can have something to say from that point of view, and whom one is taking oneself to address if speaking from this point of view.[35]

34. See also the post–Civil War edition of R. H. Rivers's moral philosophy text, *Elements of Moral Philosophy,* which is explicitly addressed solely to members of the "Caucasian race" (1883, 330). The antebellum conception of slavery as beneficial to slaves becomes, after the War, a conception of subordination as essential to the welfare of those of African descent. The "moral point of view" here is understood to include inculcating a recognition by members of the Caucasian race of their obligations to keep the members of the other race from reverting to barbarism (330–332).

35. Related questions come up in connection with MacIntyre's account of truth and rationality. See, e.g., Grant 2002. Grant argues that a MacIntyrean view can explain "how all persons have the potential to know through the activity of rational justification, even if some initially inhabit traditions whose standards of justification support false beliefs" (116); but this account runs into trouble in connection with traditions that hold that not all, but only some, persons have the potential to know through the activity of rational justification. A normative conception of the equality of persons—in their capacity for thought from "the moral point of view," or in relation to the "common human potency to be informed by reality"—is important for both a MacIntyrean and a Wigginsian conception of thinking as capable of being informed by reality.

Wiggins's example of there not being anything else to think but that slavery is unjust and insupportable was meant to support his general claim against noncognitivists in ethics, that they are making a questionable presumption of symmetry between moral points of view. He believed that there was only one sustainable position on slavery, and he read the 1833 parliamentary debate about slavery as illustrating the failure of the pro-slavery side to come up with any sustainable position. The problem is that the issue of symmetry doesn't go away so easily, given that Wiggins seems not to have considered a significant range of pro-slavery thinkers, many of whom believed that there was only one sustainable position on slavery—namely, their own. The view that there is no symmetry, and that there is only one sustainable view, can be symmetrically held. Wiggins ends his discussion of the "insidious" presumption of symmetry by remarking that "unless the non-cognitivist or the error theorist can show that there is an incoherence in the very idea of enlightenment and of refinement of moral conceptions, it is simply question-begging to make this presumption" (1991a, 78). His reference there to "enlightenment" is particularly striking in relation to the debate over slavery, since many pro-slavery thinkers were concerned to reject central Enlightenment ideas. Their criticisms of Jeffersonian thinking reflect the view that there are tempting and deeply misleading impressions of "enlightenment" in regard to moral thinking. I am not here presuming symmetry, but suggesting that the debate about slavery doesn't deliver any easy defeat to the "symmetry" view, but rather raises deep questions about what "the moral point of view" is, and suggests at the same time that there is a danger of a too-easy defeat for the presumption of symmetry if one reads the pro-slavery view out of moral thought altogether.

The six points that follow are the ones that I am merely mentioning.

5. Many of those involved in the debate about slavery took to be absolutely central the consistency, or the inconsistency, of slavery in the New World with Christianity. I don't mean to suggest that such considerations can be separated from the issue of justice, which, following Wiggins, I have emphasized. On the contrary, the issue of the justice or injustice of slavery was tied directly to what was taken to be condemned, or not, by God. Wiggins also used the term "insupportable" of slavery;

and slavery was taken, by many of those involved in missionary work with slaves, and by the societies supporting such work, to be something they had to take to be "supportable," given the greater importance, as they saw it, of bringing the Gospel to slaves. But what I want to note here is that Wiggins's reference to "considerations" relevant to the question about slavery has only a partial overlap with what were taken to be relevant considerations within the late-eighteenth- and nineteenth-century contexts. Wiggins was concerned specifically with *the moral point of view*, but what that is, was not in general separated (by those engaged in arguing about slavery) from seeing in the light of God's love toward all human beings, and thus seeing human beings as brethren. Though obviously this language of "brethren" was profoundly significant in anti-slavery thought, pro-slavery thinkers used it as well. Besides not discussing the role of Christianity in debate about slavery, I am also not discussing debates about slavery within Islam. (This is relevant also to point 6, below.)

6. The issue of what we are calling "the moral point of view" also comes up when views like those that Wiggins thinks are "the only thing to think about slavery" are described as "a European discourse about slavery" that has been imposed on African and Asian societies that were colonized by European countries or dominated by them. I cannot discuss this issue here, since it would take another essay; but it should be mentioned.

7. I have focused on strands in American pro-slavery thought, in order to work with Wiggins's idea that you need to see the denial that slavery is unjust within the system of moral ideas to which it may belong. Another case in which the legitimacy of slavery was long maintained is that of Catholic moral theology. Here too the idea of slavery as capable of legitimacy (if abuses were avoided) was part of a system of moral thinking. For a detailed account of the history of Catholic teaching on the legitimacy of slavery, see Maxwell 1975. Kieran Setiya remarked that "deep mistakes about the content of morality entail mistakes about how to engage in moral reasoning that will obstruct any rational improvement in one's moral views."[36] Maxwell provides a fas-

36. Marshall and Setiya 2014, 88.

cinating account of the relation between the false Catholic teaching on the legitimacy of slavery and those features of the institutional treatment of slavery by the Church that "obstructed any rational improvement" (1975, 13–21).

8. An important element in Wiggins's thought is that, in some cases, the explanation why someone believes that $p$ will include reference to the fact that there is nothing else to think but that $p$, and that the person who has the belief came to it by recognizing considerations that make it clear that there is nothing else to think but that $p$. The belief that slavery is unjust and insupportable came to be widely accepted in parts of the English-speaking world during the late eighteenth century; and groups began to work to end the slave trade and to abolish slavery itself. Historians have debated what the best explanation is of these changes; they may, for example, be taken to be part of the development of the ideology of emergent capitalism. I leave as another unsettled question that of the relation between Wigginsian "vindicatory" explanations of why people may think that slavery is unjust and insupportable and the debate among historians about the explanation of these changes.[37]

9. I cannot here discuss the defense of slavery, or at least what appears to be such a defense, on the part of Nietzsche. Nietzsche's uses of the notion of slavery have ramified connections with the issues raised by Wiggins.

10. I have included in the pro-slavery views that I have presented their criticism of what might now be labeled "the Enlightenment meta-narrative." I have not wanted to suggest that anti-slavery thinking depends on that "meta-narrative," although certainly there are forms of anti-slavery thinking which involve characteristic Enlightenment conceptions of rationality and progress. Wiggins's views on slavery and the Wigginsian Wittgensteinianism that I discuss in Sections 7 and 8 do not involve such a conception.

Sections 7 and 8 are about Wigginsian, Wittgensteinian, and Anscombean responses to the questions in Section 6.

---

37. See Bender 1992; also Drescher 1993 and Brown 2006. On the Scottish abolitionists, see Rice 1979, and the reply in Whyte 2006, esp. 250–254.

## 7. Wigginsian and Wittgensteinian Things to Think about in Response to the Questions in Section 6

A Wigginsian point. Wiggins's point about slavery wasn't that there was nothing else *for us* to think but that slavery is unjust and insupportable, but that there is nothing else *to think* but that. But he then distinguished between there being a *real disagreement* about an issue and there being a *difference* between people—a difference in how they conceptualize and think about some kind of practical situation. You don't have real disagreement about something merely in that different people, in different times and places, conceptualize things differently and apply different maxims from those used by people at other times or in other places. So Wiggins has the idea of there being a difference between, on the one hand, *mere difference* between your evaluative or practical thinking and someone else's and, on the other, real disagreement between your thought and someone else's, where you both have in focus the same question, but you think two opposed things in response to that question. So, given what appears at first to be two different answers that pro-slavery and anti-slavery thinkers have given to the question of the justice of slavery, a Wigginsian move might be to say there was there no *real disagreement;* there was *mere difference.* Well, *was* it a real disagreement? My answer would be that there are things that support saying that they did disagree—that they meant to disagree, and they did, about the question whether slavery is just.[38] But there are things that support saying that their conceptions of what it is to engage a moral question diverged deeply from each other, and hence that they were not really disagreeing with each other: they were taking vastly different views, but not genuinely disagreeing. Wiggins takes engaging the question about slavery to involve speaking from a point of view that can be "common between

---

38. See Gaita 2000, 12–13: "It matters to us, as individuals and as members of political communities, that we are just and honourable, that our institutions are decent in ways that are not explicable entirely by other things that matter to us—safety, security and happiness, for example." Gaita's remark suggests a kind of explanation of why we might take pro-slavery and anti-slavery thinkers to be genuinely disagreeing, and not merely holding different views expressed through different conceptions of justice.

one person and another"; but pro-slavery writers plainly do not engage in the dispute about slavery from such a point of view. And both sides of the dispute provide reasons for holding that the thought of the other side has, as thought, utterly gone off the rails. Each side, then, appears to repudiate the idea that the other side has a genuine point of view.—And yet: the intention is to express a genuinely contrary point of view.

Another Wigginsian point, but this one is Wittgensteinian as well. When Wiggins first works out his example of there not being anything else to think but that slavery is unjust and insupportable, he treats it as analogous to the case of there not being anything else to think but that 7 plus 5 is 12. He had earlier worked out a more detailed connection between the kind of objectivity there can be in ethics and objectivity in mathematics; and he had drawn on Wittgenstein, on the *Remarks on the Foundations of Mathematics*. He had said:

> For someone who wanted to combine objectivity with a doctrine of qualified cognitivism or of underdetermination, there might be no better model than Wittgenstein's normative conception of the objectivity of mathematics; and no better exemplar than Wittgenstein's extended description of how a continuing cumulative process of making or constructing can amount to the creation of a shared form of life that is constitutive of rationality itself, furnishing proofs that are not compulsions but procedures to guide our conceptions, explaining, without explaining away, our sense that sometimes we have no alternative but to infer this from that.[39]

In that passage, Wiggins invites us to treat Wittgenstein on mathematics as a model for the kind of objectivity available in ethics; and I think we can usefully look further at this *Wigginsian Wittgenstein* as a model for what is going on in the dispute about slavery.

1. One thing we get from the Wigginsian Wittgenstein is the idea of procedures that *guide our conceptions*. Mathematical activities—of

39. Wiggins, 1987a, 128. Wiggins gives a citation to the first edition of *Remarks on the Foundations of Mathematics* (Wittgenstein 1956, pt. 3, §30).

giving proofs and working over proofs—can be seen as procedures that *guide our conceptions,* our conceptions of how we have to infer, how we have to think. Moving over to the case of slavery, and using Wiggins's Wittgenstein as our model, we can think of the arguments given by anti-slavery thinkers as *meant to guide our conceptions,* meant to guide our thinking, away from any paths of thought that allow for there being people whose nature makes it just and proper to use them as slaves; we can also think of the arguments by pro-slavery thinkers as meant to guide our conceptions, meant to guide our thinking, away from any paths of thought that introduce notions of the natural equality and natural liberty of human beings. The pro-slavery arguments are meant also to guide us away from attempts to treat social and political life as subject to universal rational principles.

2. On the Wigginsian Wittgensteinian view, the business of giving and working over mathematical proofs has two features. One we have already seen: these proofs guide our conceptions. The second is that this is a cumulative process, a process through which we construct a form of life, including how we understand what is and isn't rational. In this way, we develop the capacity to judge, in particular cases, *that we have no alternative to inferring this from that—to moving this way, not that, in our thinking.* The idea of a cumulative process through which we shape what we take to be rational involves there being new principles or arguments that we come to take as guides to how we think; but the cumulative process may also involve taking principles or propositions or arguments that we already had, and coming to see their force in new ways. This is, indeed, particularly relevant to the case of statements like "All men are by nature equal," which I was treating as guides to thinking, as warnings against thinking that such-and-such people can justly be enslaved. The statement that all men are created equal has a history: it *comes to be* understood as a standing rebuke to justifications of slavery—where this, then, is one of the things that feeds into the cumulative process of shaping rationality, shaping how we think *thinking* needs to go.[40]

40. In speaking of the statement that all men are created equal as a "rebuke" to justifications of slavery, I am drawing on Lincoln's speech on the Dred Scott decision.

3. The model of Wittgenstein on mathematics is useful but has its limits when we think of it as a model for objectivity in ethics, as Wiggins suggests. The model suggests that there is something we might think of as the shared form of moral life, within which we may sometimes have a sense that we have to go this way, not that, in our thinking. But I don't think that the notion of a shared form of life goes very far when we think about the debate about slavery, and ask whether pro-slavery thinkers and anti-slavery thinkers were or weren't answering *the same question,* or whether they were or weren't, some of them, opting out of the moral point of view. Were they or weren't they genuinely disagreeing, genuinely contradicting each other, genuinely addressing each other? Where there are the kinds of deep disagreements that there were over slavery—where these disagreements even included disagreements about what color skin you had to have, to have a voice in the disagreement—*Wittgenstein on forms of life provides no answers.* The idea that you have in some readings of Wittgenstein, that he provides a kind of theoretical picture of what there has to be for there to be genuine disagreement about something, seems to me to be a gross distortion of what he was attempting to enable us to do. He wasn't giving us anything to plug in to answer such questions.

4. Wiggins suggests taking Wittgenstein on the objectivity of mathematics as a model for our thinking about the objectivity of ethics. He recommends Wittgenstein's idea of mathematical proofs, as being not compulsions but procedures that guide our conceptions. But I am not sure how far Wiggins goes with Wittgenstein. The proved propositions that we take and keep as guides, Wittgenstein thinks of as *like rules,* and as being in some ways very unlike experiential propositions. But I think Wiggins might reject this, given his understanding of the workings of

---

On the history of how the statement was understood, see Maier 1999. There are also pro-slavery readings of the statement; and important later uses of the statement by W. E. B. DuBois and by Martin Luther King. The idea that such statements of the natural equality of men or of their equal natural freedom are inconsistent with slavery can be seen in eighteenth-century manumission documents in Virginia, which frequently refer to the Virginia Declaration of Rights (one of the sources of the Declaration of Independence). On unfolding the meaning of the Declaration of Independence, see also Burt 2013.

language. I can't discuss Wigginsian semantics, but I take it that Wiggins would not go along with Wittgenstein's conception of mathematical propositions as being *like rules.*

In Section 8, I'll take a different sort of approach to the questions I've been discussing, and there too I'll be dropping Wigginsian semantics (what I take to be Wigginsian semantics).

## 8. An Anscombean-Aristotelian but Not Entirely UnWittgensteinian Approach

In the remark of Wiggins's that I quoted in Section 7, he is talking about proofs that guide our conceptions by enabling us to see a path we *need to take* in our reasoning. But in the dispute about slavery, it appears that each side was trying to indicate a path of thought that we *should not take.* And that is different from the cases of mathematical proof that Wittgenstein has centrally in mind. But despite the differences, I want to work with the idea that, in both kinds of case, we have *guides to thinking,* or, at any rate, what purport to be guides to thinking. Here I want to develop a kind of Anscombean view about propositions that guide thinking. Anscombe, in writing about practical truth, appeals to a passage in Aristotle's *Ethics,* where Aristotle says that truth is the business of everything intellectual. Doing well and doing badly in thinking are truth and falsehood, whether we are concerned with purely theoretical thinking or practical thought.—The Anscombean view I want to suggest here is not something Anscombe herself puts forward. I want to go on from what she does say to ask whether we might take it to be part of the business of thinking, part of its job, to guide, or to help put back on track, the business of thinking. If you held that that *was* part of the business of thinking—*if you held that part of the business of thinking is to help along the business of thinking*—and if you worked with the Aristotelian idea that truth is what you have when the business of thinking is done well—then statements that guide thinking, or that put thinking back on track, that help it to be done well, could themselves be described as *true,* if they are indeed doing their guiding-job well, if they get right how to guide thought well.[41]

41. See also Essays 5 and 6.

There is a kind of *asymmetrical structure* in the cases in which we say something in response to what someone else has said, which we think of as involving a kind of miscarriage of thought. What we are responding to is *thinking that has gone off course,* and what we say gets its point from the confusion or miscarriage of thinking. So if the situation is as we think it is, what we say may be thinking done well, while what we are responding to is a kind of muddle or confusion or miscarriage of thought. Here there are not two opposed thoughts, *p* and *not-p,* but failed thought, on the one hand, and what we hope is a kind of thinking that guides thought well, on the other hand. Thinking is getting something right, here, but its rightness is that of a right and helpful response to a failure of thought. Because there are not here two opposed thoughts, but *failed thought,* on the one hand, and what we hope is *thinking that guides thought well* on the other, there are the problems we saw about whether the two sides in a debate like that over slavery are actually disagreeing with each other. Where there is, as we may think, some kind of failure of thought on the part of those with whom we disagree (or with whom we may appear to disagree), there is no easy or straightforward story about the semantics of what we may say in response, especially if the response has explicitly the form of a denial of what is supposedly muddle or confusion or miscarriage of thought. The response has its sense, its point, from being a response to thought that has failed. We get it, we get what it means, in seeing it as pointful response to something we take to be meant as proper thought, but which is *not that.*[42]

There is a further point here that we can get from Wiggins's Wittgenstein, of there being a kind of cumulative process, as we shape *what thinking is,* what counts as *thinking,* by working our way to this or that thought-guide, and recognizing its usefulness. In this cumulative process, we are making or constructing a shared form of life that is constitutive of rationality. Wiggins's discussion of truth in ethics, focusing on the idea that *there is nothing to think but that slavery is unjust and insupportable,* does, I think, significantly reflect the idea of there being a cumulative process within which we have shaped a form of life consti-

---

42. I am indebted to Jean-Philippe Narboux for the shape of my argument in this paragraph.

tutive of moral rationality. Within the way this form of life has developed, we can see to be blocked off, as *failed thought,* any conception of justice that *excludes from justice-thought* some group of human beings. What I am trying to get at is Wiggins's belief that if you keep hold of justice, you will find that there is nothing to think but that slavery is unjust; hence I'm ascribing to Wiggins a conception of the opposition here as having *lost hold of justice.* Thinking has a teleology that is shaped (and may be shaped *well*) in what we come to be able to recognize as failures of thought; and there are ways of apparently thinking about justice, which are central in pro-slavery thought, and which we have come to be able to recognize as non-thought, failed thought. Some such idea as this underlies, I think, Wiggins's criticism of the "presumption of symmetry." A presumption of symmetry in ethics involves failing to see that thought has a teleology, and that, although what belongs to that teleology is shaped by us, we may get the job of such shaping done well or badly. Losing hold of justice, as pro-slavery thought did, was shaping thought badly. Here we can see a Wigginsian response to the question "What about Aristotle? Doesn't he illustrate that there isn't just one thing to think about the injustice of slavery?" The answer is that *it can become clear* (though it may not always have been clear) that there is only one thing to think here.

There are connections between Wiggins's attack on "the insidious *presumption of symmetry*" and Anscombe on Wittgenstein and *On Certainty* (Anscombe 1981e). She was thinking about cases where you are confronted with a system of knowledge that you reject. She asks: "If one calls something error which *counts as knowledge* in another system, the question arises: has one the right to do that? Or has one to be 'moving within the system' to call anything error"? (1981e, 131). In such cases, there may be the possibility of *persuading* those who accept that other system to change, but *can there be right and wrong here?* She herself pretty plainly believed that there can be right and wrong in such cases; and she thought that one shouldn't read Wittgenstein as denying it.[43] The Wigginsian Wittgensteinian view is, I think, similar. Wiggins takes over for ethics the idea of a cumulative process within which we shape

43. See Diamond 2013 for discussion of Anscombe's view.

what we take to be rational; and he sees this as allowing him to deny "the presumption of symmetry," the idea that there is always a tenable alternative to any moral view. Against that view, Wiggins insists that there is the possibility of "enlightenment and refinement of moral conceptions"—that is, *we can get something right, which we hadn't got right before.* So this is indeed an answer to Anscombe's question. Anscombe and Wiggins, in their different ways, are arguing that the philosophical appearances here can be deeply misleading. The philosophical appearances here seem to lead to forms of relativism or idealism. Bernard Williams's argument against Wiggins, from the plurality of evaluative concepts, is itself one example of how the presumption of symmetry can work to make truth appear always relative. My argument has been that following out Wiggins on slavery can help us see the issues here.[44]

44. When I read an early version of Essay 6 at the Jowett Society in Oxford, members of the audience raised questions about the slavery debate and its bearing on the dispute between Williams and Wiggins, which I had mentioned in the lecture. The force and philosophical interest of those questions were what led me to write this paper, and I am very grateful for the suggestions and the provocation.

REFERENCES

ACKNOWLEDGMENTS

INDEX

# References

Allain, Jean, ed. 2012. *The Legal Understanding of Slavery: From the Historical to the Contemporary.* Oxford: Oxford University Press.

Anderson, Elizabeth. 2014. "The Quest for Free Labor: Pragmatism and Experiments in Emancipation." *The Amherst Lecture in Philosophy.* Lecture 9. *http://www/amherstlecture.org/anderson2014/anderson2014 _ALP.pdf.*

Anscombe, G. E. M. 1958. "Modern Moral Philosophy." *Philosophy* 33, 1–19. Reprinted in *Ethics, Religion and Politics* (Oxford: Blackwell, 1981), 26–42. Reprinted also in *Human Life, Action and Ethics: Essays by G. E. M. Anscombe,* edited by Mary Geach and Luke Gormally (Exeter, UK: Imprint Academic, 2005), 169–194.

———. 1963a. *An Introduction to Wittgenstein's Tractatus.* London: Hutchinson University Library.

———. 1963b. *Intention.* Oxford: Blackwell.

———. 1965. "War and Murder." In *Nuclear Weapons and Christian Conscience,* edited by Walter Stein, 43–62. London: Merlin. Reprinted in *Ethics, Religion and Politics* (Oxford: Blackwell, 1981), 51–61.

———. 1981a. "The First Person." In *Metaphysics and the Philosophy of Mind,* 21–36. Oxford: Blackwell. Originally published in *Mind and Language,* edited by Samuel Guttenplan, 45–65. Oxford: Oxford University Press, 1975.

———. 1981b. "The Intentionality of Sensation: A Grammatical Feature." In *Metaphysics and the Philosophy of Mind,* 3–20. Oxford: Blackwell.

———. 1981c. "Introduction." In *From Parmenides to Wittgenstein,* vii–xi. Oxford: Blackwell.

———. 1981d. "Mr Truman's Degree." In *Ethics, Religion and Politics,* 62–71. Blackwell: Oxford.

———. 1981e. "The Question of Linguistic Idealism." In *From Parmenides to Wittgenstein,* 112–133. Oxford: Blackwell. Originally published in *Essays on Wittgenstein in Honour of G. H. von Wright, Acta Philosophica Fennica* 28 (1976): 188–215.

———. 1981f. "The Reality of the Past." In *Metaphysics and the Philosophy of Mind,* 103–119. Oxford: Blackwell. Originally published in *Philosophical Analysis,* edited by Max Black, 38–59 (Ithaca, NY: Cornell University Press, 1950).

———. 1981g. "Thought and Action in Aristotle: What Is 'Practical Truth'?" In *From Parmenides to Wittgenstein,* 66–77. Oxford: Blackwell.

———. 1989. "The Simplicity of the *Tractatus.*" *Critica* 21, no. 63 (December): 3–16. Reprinted in Anscombe 2011a, 171–180.

———. 1995. "Ludwig Wittgenstein." *Philosophy* 70:395–407. Reprinted in Anscombe 2011a, 157–169.

———. 2005. "Practical Truth." In *Human Life, Action and Ethics: Essays by G. E. M. Anscombe,* edited by Mary Geach and Luke Gormally, 149–158. Exeter, UK: Imprint Academic.

———. 2011a. *From Plato to Wittgenstein: Essays by G. E. M. Anscombe.* Edited by Mary Geach and Luke Gormally. Exeter, UK: Imprint Academic.

———. 2011b. "Ludwig Wittgenstein." In Anscombe 2011a, 157–169. Originally published in *Philosophy* 70:395–407.

———. 2011c. "The Simplicity of the *Tractatus.*" In Anscombe 2011a, 171–180. Originally published in *Critica* 21, no. 63 (December): 3–16.

———. 2011d. "Truth: Anselm and Wittgenstein." In Anscombe 2011a, 71–76.

———. 2011e. "Was Wittgenstein a Conventionalist?" In Anscombe 2011a, 217–230.

———. 2011f. "Wittgenstein's 'Two Cuts' in the History of Philosophy." In Anscombe 2011a, 181–186.

Ayer, A. J. 1962. *Language, Truth and Logic.* London: Gollancz.

Bender, Thomas, ed. 1992. *The Antislavery Debate: Capitalism and Abolitionism as a Problem in Historical Interpretation.* Berkeley: University of California Press.

Blackburn, Simon. 2006. Review of David Wiggins. *Ethics: Twelve Lectures on the Philosophy of Morality.* http://www2.phil.cam.ac.uk/~swb24 /reviews/Wiggins.htm.

Bledsoe, Albert Taylor. 1856. *An Essay on Liberty and Slavery.* Philadelphia: J. B. Lippincott and Co.

Broadie, Sarah. 1991. *Ethics with Aristotle.* Oxford: Oxford University Press.

Bronzo, Silver. 2011. "Context, Compositionality and Nonsense in Wittgenstein's *Tractatus.*" In *Beyond the Tractatus Wars: The New Wittgenstein Debate,* edited by Rupert Read and Matthew A. Laverty, 84–111. London: Routledge.

Brown, Christopher Leslie. 2006. *Moral Capital: Foundations of British Abolitionism.* Chapel Hill: University of North Carolina Press.

Burnyeat, Myles. 1979. "Conflicting Appearances." *Proceedings of the British Academy* 65:69–111. Reprinted in Myles Burnyeat, *Explorations in Ancient and Modern Philosophy* (Cambridge: Cambridge University Press, 2012), 1:276–315.

———. 2006. "Introduction." In Bernard Williams, *The Sense of the Past: Essays in the History of Philosophy,* edited by Myles Burnyeat. Princeton, NJ: Princeton University Press.

Burt, John. 2013. *Lincoln's Tragic Pragmatism: Lincoln, Douglas, and Moral Conflict.* Cambridge, MA: Harvard University Press.

Candlish, S. 1999. "Identifying the Identity Theory of Truth." *Proceedings of the Aristotelian Society* 99:233–240.

Chappell, Sophie Grace. 2010. "Bernard Williams." In *Stanford Encyclopedia of Philosophy.* http://plato.stanford.edu/entries/williams-bernard/. Replaced by Chappell in 2013 with the same URL.

Conant, James, and Cora Diamond. 2004. "On Reading the *Tractatus* Resolutely: Reply to Meredith Williams and Peter Sullivan." In *Wittgenstein's Lasting Significance,* edited by Max Kölbel and Bernhard Weiss, 46–99. London: Routledge.

Conway, M. D. 1864. *Testimonies concerning Slavery.* London: Chapman and Hall.

Corbin, George. 1787. Deed of manumission, in *Accomack County Deeds,* No. 6, 1783–1788. The deed is in the document collection *Slavery and Emancipation,* edited by Rick Halpern and Enrico Dal Lago, 91–92. Malden, MA: Blackwell.

Crary, Alice. 2007. *Wittgenstein and the Moral Life.* Cambridge, MA: MIT Press.

Crary, Alice, and Rupert Read. 2000. *The New Wittgenstein.* London: Routledge.

Daly, John Patrick. 2002. *When Slavery Was Called Freedom: Evangelicalism, Proslavery, and the Causes of the Civil War.* Lexington: University Press of Kentucky.

Davies, Brian. 2008. "Is God a Moral Agent?" In *Whose God? Which Tradition? The Nature of Belief in God,* edited by D. Z. Phillips, 97–122. Aldershot, UK: Ashgate.

Dew, Thomas Roderick. 1832. "Abolition of Negro Slavery." *American Quarterly Review* 12:189–265.

Diamond, Cora. 1991. "What Does a Concept Script Do?" In *The Realistic Spirit: Wittgenstein, Philosophy, and the Mind,* 114–144. Cambridge, MA: MIT Press. Originally published in *Philosophical Quarterly* 34 (1984): 158–183.

———. 2002. "Truth before Tarski: After Sluga, after Ricketts, after Geach, after Goldfarb, Hylton, Floyd, and Van Heijenoort." In Reck 2002, 252–279.

———. 2005. "Logical Syntax in Wittgenstein's *Tractatus.*" *Philosophical Quarterly* 55:78–89.

———. 2010. "Inheriting from Frege: The Work of Reception as Wittgenstein Did It." In *The Cambridge Companion to Frege,* edited by Michael Potter and Tom Ricketts, 550–601. Cambridge: Cambridge University Press.

———. 2011. "The *Tractatus* and the Limits of Sense." In *The Oxford Handbook to Wittgenstein,* edited by Marie McGinn and Oskari Kuusela, 240–275. Oxford: Oxford University Press.

———. 2012. "What Can You Do with the General Form of Proposition?" In *Wittgenstein's Early Philosophy,* edited by José Zalabardo, 151–194. Oxford: Oxford University Press.

———. 2013. "Criticising from 'Outside.'" *Philosophical Investigations* 36:114–129.

———. 2014a. "Addressing Russell Resolutely?" *Philosophical Topics* 42, no. 2 (Fall): 13–43.

———. 2014b. "The Hardness of the Soft: Wittgenstein's Early Thought about Skepticism." In *Varieties of Skepticism: Essays after Kant, Wittgenstein, and Cavell,* edited by James Conant and Andrea Kern, 145–181. Berlin: De Gruyter.

———. Unpublished. "Murdoch Off the Map, or Taking Empiricism Back from the Empiricists."

Drescher, Seymour. 1993. "Review Essay: *The Antislavery Debate: Capitalism and Abolitionism as a Problem in Historical Interpretation.*" *History and Theory* 32:311–329.

———. 2009. *Abolition: A History of Slavery and Antislavery.* Cambridge: Cambridge University Press.

Dummett, Michael. 1973. *Frege: Philosophy of Language.* London: Duckworth.

———. 1999. "Of What Kind of Thing Is Truth a Property?" In *Truth,* edited by S. Blackburn and K. Simmons, 264–281. Oxford: Oxford University Press.

———. 2000. "Sentences and Propositions." In *Logic, Cause and Action: Essays in Honour of Elizabeth Anscombe,* edited by R. Teichmann, 9–23. Cambridge: Cambridge University Press.

Elliott, E. N., ed. 1860. *Cotton Is King and Pro-Slavery Arguments.* Augusta, GA: Pritchard, Abbott and Loomis.

Estwick, Samuel. 1773. *Considerations on the Negroe Cause, Commonly So Called.* London: J. Dodsley.

Farrell, Stephen. 2007. "'Contrary to the Principles of Justice, Humanity and Sound Policy': The Slave Trade, Parliamentary Politics and the Abolition Act, 1807." *Parliamentary History* 26, issue supplement S1:141–202.

Faust, Drew Gilpin. 1981. Introduction. In *The Ideology of Slavery: Proslavery Thought in the Antebellum South, 1830–1860,* edited by Drew Gilpin Faust, 1–20. Baton Rouge: Louisiana State University Press.

Finley, M. I. 1980. *Ancient Slavery and Modern Ideology.* London: Chatto and Windus.

Flew, Antony, ed. 1951. *Logic and Language,* first series. Oxford: Blackwell.

Floyd, Juliet. 1995. "On Saying What You Really Want to Say: Wittgenstein, Gödel, and the Trisection of the Angle." In *From Dedekind to Gödel: Essays on the Foundations of Mathematics,* edited by J. Hintikka, 373–426. Dordrecht: Kluwer.

———. 2000. "Wittgenstein, Mathematics, Philosophy." In Crary and Read 2000, 232–261.

———. 2007. "Wittgenstein and the Inexpressible." In Crary 2007, 177–234.

———. 2010. "On Being Surprised: Wittgenstein on Aspect-Perception, Logic, and Mathematics." In *Seeing Wittgenstein Anew,* edited by W. Day and V. J. Krebs, 314–337. Cambridge: Cambridge University Press.

Foot, P. 2002. "Utilitarianism and the Virtues." In *Moral Dilemmas and Other Topics in Moral Philosophy,* 59–77. Oxford: Clarendon Press. Originally published in *Mind* 94 (1985): 196–209.

Ford, Lacy. 2009. *Deliver Us from Evil: The Slavery Question in the Old South.* New York: Oxford University Press.

Frascolla, P. 2007. *Understanding Wittgenstein's Tractatus.* Abingdon, UK: Routledge.

Frege, Gottlob. 1974. *The Foundations of Arithmetic.* Translated by J. L. Austin. Oxford: Blackwell.

———. 1979a. "Logic." In Gottlob Frege, *Posthumous Writings,* edited by Hans Hermes et al., translated by Peter Long et al., 126–151. Oxford: Blackwell.

———. 1979b. "Logic in Mathematics." In Gottlob Frege, *Posthumous Writings,* edited by Hans Hermes et al., translated by Peter Long et al., 203–250. Oxford: Blackwell.

———. 1979c. "Notes for Ludwig Darmstaedter." In Gottlob Frege, *Posthumous Writings,* edited by Hans Hermes et al., translated by Peter Long et al., 253–257. Oxford: Blackwell.

———. 1980. Letter to Anton Marty. In Gottlob Frege, *Philosophical and Mathematical Correspondence,* edited by Gottfried Gabriel et al., 99–102. Oxford: Blackwell.

———. 1984a. *Collected Papers on Mathematics, Logic, and Philosophy.* Edited by Brian McGuinness. Translated by Max Black et al. Oxford: Blackwell.

———. 1984b. "On Concept and Object." In Frege 1984a, 182–194.

Fricker, Miranda. 2013. "Styles of Moral Relativism: A Critical Family Tree." In *The Oxford Handbook of the History of Ethics,* edited by Roger Crisp, 793–817. Oxford: Oxford University Press.

Gaita, Raimond. 2000. "Introduction: Take Your Time." In *A Common Humanity: Thinking about Love and Truth and Justice,* 1–16. London: Routledge.

Gates, Henry Louis, Jr. 1989. *Figures in Black: Words, Signs, and the "Racial" Self.* New York: Oxford University Press.

Geach, P. T. 1964. *Mental Acts.* London: Routledge and Kegan Paul.

———. 1976. "Saying and Showing in Frege and Wittgenstein." In *Essays on Wittgenstein in Honour of G. H. von Wright,* edited by J. Hintikka, *Acta Philosophica Fennica* 28:54–70.

———. 1979. "Kinds of Statement." In *Intention and Intentionality: Essays in Honour of G. E. M. Anscombe,* edited by C. Diamond and J. Teichman, 221–235. Brighton, UK: Harvester Press.

———. 1982. "Truth and God." *Proceedings of the Aristotelian Society,* suppl. 56:83–97.

———. 1991. "Philosophical Autobiography." In *Peter Geach: Philosophical Encounters,* edited by H. A. Lewis, 1–25. Dordrecht: Kluwer.

Glover, Jonathan. 2011. "Insanity, Crankiness and Evil—And Other Ways of Thinking the Unthinkable." In *Philosophy, Ethics and a Common Humanity: Essays in Honour of Raimond Gaita,* edited by Christopher Cordner, 37–48. London: Routledge.

Goldfarb, Warren. 2002. "Wittgenstein's Understanding of Frege: The Pre-Tractarian Evidence." In Reck 2002, 185–200.

———. 2011. "Das Überwinden: Anti-metaphysical Readings of the *Tractatus.*" In *Beyond the Tractatus Wars: The New Wittgenstein Debate,* edited by Rupert Read and Matthew A. Lavery, 6–21. London: Routledge.

———. Unpublished. "Objects, Names, and Realism in the *Tractatus*."

Gollwitzer, Helmut. 1963. *Die Existenz Gottes im Bekenntnis des Glaubens*. Munich: Chr. Kaiser Verlag.

———. 1965. *The Existence of God as Confessed by Faith*. Translated by James W. Leitch. Philadelphia: Westminster Press.

Grant, W. Matthews. 2002. "Thomist or Relativist? MacIntyre's Interpretation of *adaequatio intellectus et rei*." In *Jacques Maritain and the Many Ways of Knowing*, edited by Douglas A. Ollivant, 102–119. Mishawaka, IN: American Maritain Association.

Griffin, James. 1964. *Wittgenstein's Logical Atomism*. Oxford: Clarendon Press.

Gross, Ariela J. 2000. *Double Character: Slavery and Mastery in the Antebellum Southern Courtroom*. Princeton, NJ: Princeton University Press.

Gustafsson, Martin. 2006. "Nonsense and Philosophical Method." In *Wittgenstein and the Method of Philosophy*, edited by S. Pihlstrom. *Acta Philosophica Fennica* 80:11–34,

———. 2014. "Wittgenstein and 'Tonk': Inference and Representation in the *Tractatus* (and Beyond)." *Philosophical Topics* 42:75–99.

———. 2017. "Wittgenstein, Language and Chess." In *Finding One's Way through Wittgenstein's Philosophical Investigations: New Essays on §§ 1–88*, edited by Emmanuel Bermon and Jean-Philippe Narboux, 77–93. Cham, Switzerland: Springer International.

Hacker, P. M. S. 2000. "Was He Trying to Whistle It?" In Crary and Read 2000, 353–388.

Hammond, J. H. 1845. *Two Letters on Slavery in the United States, Addressed to Thomas Clarkson, Esq*. Columbia, SC: Allen, McCarter and Co.

Harper, William. 1838. *Memoir on Slavery*. Charleston, SC: James S. Burges.

Harris, J. William. 2014. "Eugene Genovese's Old South: A Review Essay." *Journal of Southern History* 80:327–372.

Haven, Joseph. 1859. *Moral Philosophy: Including Practical and Theoretical Ethics*. Boston: Gould and Lincoln.

Hertz, Heinrich. 1899. *The Principles of Mechanics Presented in a New Form*. Translated by D. E. Jones and J. T. Walley. London: Macmillan and Co.

Honoré, Antony. 2012. "The Nature of Slavery." In Allain 2012, 9–16.

Hornsby, J. 1999. "The Facts in Question: A Response to Dodd and to Candlish." *Proceedings of the Aristotelian Society* 99:241–245.

Hughes, Henry. 1854. *Treatise on Sociology: Theoretical and Practical*. Philadelphia: Lippincott, Grambo & Co.

Hutcheson, Francis. 1755. *A System of Moral Philosophy*. Privately published by his son, Francis Hutcheson, MD, through a Glasgow printer.

Hylton, Peter. 1990. *Russell, Idealism, and the Emergence of Analytic Philosophy*. Oxford: Clarendon Press.

———. 2005a. "Frege and Russell." In *Propositions, Functions, and Analysis: Selected Essays on Russell's Philosophy*, 153–184. Oxford: Clarendon Press.

———. 2005b. "Functions, Operations, and Sense in Wittgenstein's *Tractatus*." In *Propositions, Functions, and Analysis: Selected Essays on Russell's Philosophy*, 138–152. Oxford: Clarendon Press. Originally published in *Early Analytic Philosophy, Frege, Russell, Wittgenstein: Essays in Honor of Leonard Linsky*, edited by W. W. Tait, 91–105. Chicago: Open Court.

Ishiguro, Hidé. 1969. "Use and Reference of Names." In *Studies in the Philosophy of Wittgenstein*, edited by Peter Winch, 20–50. London: Routledge and Kegan Paul.

Jolley, Kelly Dean. 2007. *The Concept "Horse" Paradox and Wittgensteinian Conceptual Investigations*. Ashgate, UK: Farnham.

———. 2015. "Once Moore unto the Breach! Frege, Concepts, and the Concept 'Horse.'" *Philosophical Topics* 43, nos. 1–2: 113–124.

Kenny, A. 1973. *Wittgenstein*. Harmondsworth, UK: Penguin Books.

Kerry, Benno. 1887. "Ueber Anschauung und ihre psychische Verarbeitung," part 4, *Vierteljahrsschrift für wissenschaftliche Philosophie* 11:249–307.

Kienzler, Wolfgang. 2011. "Wittgenstein and Frege." In *The Oxford Handbook of Wittgenstein*, edited by Oskari Kuusela and Marie McGinn, 79–104. Oxford: Oxford University Press.

Klement, Kevin C. 2004. "Putting Form before Function: Logical Grammar in Frege, Russell, and Wittgenstein." *Philosophers' Imprint* 4, no. 2: 1–47.

Koethe, John. 2003. "On the 'Resolute' Reading of the *Tractatus*." *Philosophical Investigations* 26:187–204

Kraut, Richard. 1994. Review of Bernard Williams, *Shame and Necessity*. *Ethics* 105:178–181.

———. 2002. *Aristotle: Political Philosophy*. Oxford: Oxford University Press.

Kremer, Michael. 1997. "Contextualism and Holism in the Early Wittgenstein: From *Prototractatus* to *Tractatus*." *Philosophical Topics* 25, no. 2: 87–120.

———. 2001. "The Purpose of *Tractarian* Nonsense." *Nous* 35:39–73.

———. 2002. "Mathematics and Meaning in the *Tractatus*." *Philosophical Investigations* 25:272–303.

———. 2007. "The Cardinal Problem of Philosophy." In Crary 2007, 143–176.

———. 2012. "Russell's Merit." In *Wittgenstein's Early Philosophy*, edited by José Zalabardo, 195–240. Oxford: Oxford University Press.

Las Casas, Bartolomé de. 1974. *In Defense of the Indians*. Translated by Stafford Poole. DeKalb: Northern Illinois University Press.

Lockwood, Thornton C., Jr. 2007. "Is Natural Slavery Beneficial?" *Journal of the History of Philosophy* 45:207–221.

Lovibond, Sabina. 2004. "Absolute Prohibitions without Divine Promises." In *Modern Moral Philosophy*, edited by Anthony O'Hear, 141–158. Cambridge: Cambridge University. Reprinted in Lovibond, *Essays on Ethics and Feminism* (Oxford: Oxford University Press, 2015), 146–161.

Maier, Pauline. 1999. "The Strange History of 'All Men Are Created Equal.'" *Washington and Lee Law Review* 56:873–888.

Malcolm, Norman. 1986. *Nothing Is Hidden: Wittgenstein's Criticism of His Early Thought*. Oxford: Blackwell.

Marenbon, John. 2015. *Pagans and Philosophers: The Problem of Paganism from Augustine to Leibniz*. Princeton, NJ: Princeton University Press.

Marshall, Richard, and Kieran Setiya. 2014. "Kieran Setiya: What Anscombe Intended and Other Puzzles." An interview in Richard Marshall, in *Philosophy at 3:AM: Questions and Answers with 25 Top Philosophers*, 80–90. New York: Oxford University Press.

Maxwell, John Francis. 1975. *Slavery and the Catholic Church: The History of Catholic Teaching concerning the Moral Legitimacy of Slavery*. Chichester, UK: Barry Rose.

McGinn, Marie. 1999. "Between Metaphysics and Nonsense: Elucidation in Wittgenstein's *Tractatus*." *Philosophical Quarterly* 49:491–513.

———. 2002. "Wittgenstein et l'a priori: Y a-t-il une continuité entre le *Tractatus* et *De la Certitude*?" In *Wittgenstein, dernières pensées*, edited by J. Bouveresse et al., 29–47. Marseille: Agone.

———. 2006. *Elucidating the Tractatus*. Oxford: Clarendon Press.

McGuinness, B. F. 1981. "The So-Called Realism of Wittgenstein's *Tractatus*." In *Perspectives on the Philosophy of Wittgenstein*, edited by Irving Block, 60–73. Oxford: Blackwell.

McManus, Denis. 2006. *The Enchantment of Words*. Oxford: Clarendon Press.

Mill, John Stuart. 1843. *A System of Logic*. London: John W. Parker.

———. 1870. *The Subjection of Women*, 3rd edition. London: Longmans, Green, Reader, and Dyer.

Miller, H., III. Unpublished. "Discussions of Wittgenstein's N Operator Notation, and Correspondence with P. T. Geach."

Millett, Paul. 2007. "Aristotle and Slavery in Athens." *Greece and Rome* 54:178–209.

Monoson, S. Sara. 2011. "Recollecting Aristotle: Proslavery Thought in Antebellum America and the Argument of *Politics* Book I." In *Ancient*

*Slavery and Abolition: From Hobbes to Hollywood,* edited by Edith Hall
et al., 247–277. Oxford: Oxford University Press.

Moore, Adrian W. 1996. "On There Being Nothing Else to Think, or Want, or
Do." In *Essays for David Wiggins: Identity, Truth and Value,* edited by
Sabina Lovibond and S. G. Williams, 165–184. Oxford: Blackwell.

———. 2007. "Wittgenstein and Transcendental Idealism." In *Wittgenstein
and His Interpreters,* edited by Guy Kahane et al., 174–199. Oxford:
Blackwell.

———. 2012. *The Evolution of Modern Metaphysics: Making Sense of Things.*
Cambridge: Cambridge University Press.

Moore, G. E. 1959. "Wittgenstein's Lectures in 1930–33." In G. E. Moore,
*Philosophical Papers,* 252–324. London: George Allen and Unwin.
Originally published in *Mind* 63 (1954): 289–316; 64 (1955): 1–27.

Moyal-Sharrock, Daniele. 2007. "The Good Sense of Nonsense." *Philosophy*
82:147–177.

Narboux, Jean-Philippe. 2014. "Showing, the Medium Voice, and the Unity
of the *Tractatus.*" *Philosophical Topics* 42, no. 2: 201–262.

Oakes, James. 2013. *Freedom National: The Destruction of Slavery in the
United States, 1861–1865.* New York: W. W. Norton.

O'Brien, Michael. 2004. *Conjectures of Order: Intellectual Life in the American South, 1810–1860.* 2 volumes. Chapel Hill: University of North
Carolina Press.

Pears, David. 1987. *False Prison: A Study of the Development of Wittgenstein's
Philosophy.* Oxford: Clarendon Press.

Railton, Peter. 2000. "A Priori Rules: Wittgenstein on the Normativity of
Logic." In *New Essays on the A Priori,* edited by P. Boghossian and
C. Peacocke, 170–196. Oxford: Oxford University Press.

Ramsey, Frank P. 1931. "General Propositions and Causality," in Frank
Ramsey, *The Foundations of Mathematics,* edited by R. B. Braithwaite,
237–255. London: Routledge and Kegan Paul.

Rayo, Agustin. 2015. "A Compositionalist's Guide to Predicate-Reference."
http://web.mit.edu/arayo/www/ch.pdf.

Reck, E. H. 2002. *From Frege to Wittgenstein: Perspectives on Early Analytic
Philosophy.* Oxford: Oxford University Press.

Rhees, Rush. 1970. "Miss Anscombe on the *Tractatus.*" In Rush
Rhees, *Discussions of Wittgenstein,* 1–15. London: Routledge and
Kegan Paul. Originally published in *The Philosophical Quarterly*
10 (1960): 21–31.

Rice, C. Duncan. 1979. "Controversies over Slavery in Eighteenth- and
Nineteenth-Century Scotland." In *Antislavery Reconsidered: New*

*Perspectives on the Abolitionists,* edited by Lewis Perry and Michael Fellman, 24–48. Baton Rouge: Louisiana State University Press.

Ricketts, Thomas. 1986. "Objectivity and Objecthood: Frege's Metaphysics of Judgment." In *Frege Synthesized,* edited by L. Haaparanta and J. Hintikka, 65–95. Dordrecht: Reidel.

———. 1996. "Pictures, Logic, and the Limits of Sense in Wittgenstein's *Tractatus.*" In *The Cambridge Companion to Wittgenstein,* edited by Hans Sluga and David G. Stern, 59–99. Cambridge: Cambridge University Press.

———. 2002. "Wittgenstein against Frege and Russell." In Reck 2002, 227–251.

———. 2010. "Concepts, Objects, and the Context Principle." In *The Cambridge Companion to Frege,* edited by Thomas Ricketts and Michael Potter, 149–219. Cambridge: Cambridge University Press.

Rivers, R. H. 1883. *Elements of Moral Philosophy.* Nashville, TN: Southern Methodist Publishing House.

Ruffino, Marco Antonio. 1994. "The Context Principle and Wittgenstein's Criticism of Russell's Theory of Types." *Synthese* 98:401–414.

Russell, Bertrand. 1932. "Knowledge by Acquaintance and Knowledge by Description." In *Mysticism and Logic,* 209–232. London: Allen and Unwin.

———. 1937. *The Principles of Mathematics,* 2nd edition. London: Allen and Unwin.

———. 1956. "On Denoting." In *Logic and Knowledge,* edited by R. Marsh, 41–56. London: Allen and Unwin.

———. 1967. *The Problems of Philosophy.* Oxford: Oxford University Press.

———. 1992. *Theory of Knowledge: The 1913 Manuscript.* Edited by Elizabeth Ramsden Eames, with Kenneth Blackwell. London: Routledge.

———. 1996. *The Principles of Mathematics.* 4th edition. New York: W. W. Norton.

Scott, Rebecca J. 2012. "Under Color of Law: Siliadin v. France and the Dynamics of Enslavement in Historical Perspective." In Allain 2012, 152–164.

Shanker, Stuart G. 1987. *Wittgenstein and the Turning Point in the Philosophy of Mathematics.* Albany: SUNY Press.

Shieh, Sanford. 2014. "In What Way Does Logic Involve Necessity?" *Philosophical Topics* 42, no. 2: 289–337.

Strawson, P. F. 1962. "Freedom and Resentment." *Proceedings of the British Academy* 48:187–211.

Sullivan, Peter. 2001. "A Version of the Picture Theory." In *Ludwig Wittgen-stein: Tractatus Logico-Philosophicus,* edited by Wilhelm Vossenkuhl, 89–110. Berlin: Akademie Verlag.

———. 2004. "'The General Propositional Form Is a Variable' (*Tractatus* 4.53)." *Mind* 113:43–56.

———. 2011. "Synthesizing without Concepts." In *The Tractatus Wars: The New Wittgenstein Debate,* edited by Rupert Read and Matthew Lavery, 171–189. London: Routledge.

Sumner, Charles. 1856. "Freedom National; Slavery Sectional." Speech in the Senate of the United States, 26th August 1852. In *Recent Speeches and Addresses,* 69–171. Boston: Ticknor and Fields.

Tejedor, Chon. 2015. *The Early Wittgenstein on Metaphysics, Natural Science, Language and Value.* London: Routledge.

Thompson, Michael. 2008. *Life and Action: Elementary Structures of Practice and Practical Thought.* Cambridge, MA: Harvard University Press.

Urmson, J. O. 1956. *Philosophical Analysis: Its Development between the Two World Wars.* Oxford: Clarendon Press.

Van Cleve, George William. 2010. *A Slaveholders' Union.* Chicago: University of Chicago Press.

Walker, R. C. S. 1997. "Theories of Truth." In *A Companion to the Philosophy of Language,* edited by B. Hale and C. Wright, 309–330. Oxford: Blackwell.

Weiner, Joan. 1999. *Frege.* New York: Oxford University Press.

———. 2008. "Preface to the Paperback Edition." In *Frege in Perspective.* Paperback edition. Ithaca, NY: Cornell University Press.

White, Roger. 2006. *Wittgenstein's Tractatus Logico-Philosophicus.* London: Routledge.

Whitehead, Alfred North, and Bertrand Russell. 1962. *Principia Mathematica to *56.* Cambridge: Cambridge University Press.

Whyte, Iain. 2006. *Scotland and the Abolition of Black Slavery, 1756–1838.* Edinburgh: Edinburgh University Press.

Wiggins, David. 1987a. "Truth, Invention, and the Meaning of Life." In *Needs, Values, Truth,* 87–137. Oxford: Blackwell. Earlier version published in *Proceedings of the British Academy* 62 (1976): 331–378.

———. 1987b. "Truth, and Truth as Predicated of Moral Judgments." In *Needs, Values, Truth,* 139–184. Oxford: Blackwell.

———. 1991a. "Moral Cognitivism, Moral Relativism and Motivating Moral Beliefs." *Proceedings of the Aristotelian Society* 91:61–85.

———. 1991b. "Truth, and Truth as Predicated of Moral Judgments." In *Needs, Values, Truth,* 139–184. Oxford: Blackwell.

———. 1995. "Objective and Subjective in Ethics, with Two Postscripts on Truth." *Ratio,* n.s., 8:243–258.

———. 1999. "Meaning and Truth Conditions: From Frege's Grand Design to Davidson's." In *A Companion to the Philosophy of Language,* edited by Bob Hale and Crispin Wright, 3–28. Oxford: Blackwell.

———. 2004. "Reflections on Inquiry and Truth Arising from Peirce's Method for the Fixation of Belief." In *The Cambridge Companion to Peirce,* edited by Cheryl Misak, 87–126. Cambridge: Cambridge University Press.

———. 2006. *Ethics: Twelve Lectures on the Philosophy of Morality.* Cambridge, MA: Harvard University Press.

Williams, Bernard. 1985. *Ethics and the Limits of Philosophy.* Cambridge, MA: Harvard University Press.

———. 1993. *Shame and Necessity.* Berkeley: University of California Press.

———. 1995. "Truth in Ethics." *Ratio,* n.s., 8:227–242.

———, et al. 1999. "Seminar with Bernard Williams." *Ethical Perspectives* 6:243–265.

Williams, Patricia. 2006. Preface. In Bernard Williams, *The Sense of the Past: Essays in the History of Philosophy,* ed. Myles Burnyeat. Princeton, NJ: Princeton University Press.

Winch, Peter. 1987. "Language, Thought and World in Wittgenstein's *Tractatus.*" In *Trying to Make Sense,* 3–17. Oxford: Blackwell.

Wittgenstein, Ludwig. 1956. *Remarks on the Foundations of Mathematics.* Edited by G. H. von Wright et al. Translated by G. E. M. Anscombe. Oxford: Blackwell.

———. 1958. *Philosophical Investigations.* Translated by G. E. M. Anscombe. Oxford: Blackwell.

———. 1961a. "Notes on Logic." Appendix I in *Notebooks, 1914–1916,* edited by G. H. von Wright and G. E. M. Anscombe, translated by G. E. M. Anscombe, 93–106. Oxford: Blackwell.

———. 1961b. "Notes Dictated to G. E. Moore in Norway." Appendix II in *Notebooks, 1914–1916,* edited by G. H. von Wright and G. E. M. Anscombe, translated by G. E. M. Anscombe, 107–118. Oxford: Blackwell.

———. 1963. *Tractatus Logico-Philosophicus.* Translated by D. F. Pears and B. F. McGuinness. London: Routledge and Kegan Paul.

———. 1964. *The Blue and Brown Books.* Oxford: Blackwell.

———. 1967. *Zettel.* Edited by G. E. M. Anscombe and G. H. von Wright. Translated by G. E. M. Anscombe. Oxford: Blackwell.

———. 1969. *On Certainty.* Edited by G. E. M. Anscombe and G. H. von Wright. Translated by D. Paul and G. E. M. Anscombe. Oxford: Blackwell.

———. 1971. *Prototractatus*. Edited by B. F. McGuinness, T. Nyberg, and G. H. von Wright. Translated by D. F. Pears and B. F. McGuinness. London: Routledge and Kegan Paul.

———. 1973. *Letters to C. K. Ogden*. Edited by G. H. von Wright. Oxford: Blackwell.

———. 1975. *Philosophical Remarks*. Edited by R. Rhees. Translated by R. Hargreaves and R. White. Oxford: Blackwell.

———. 1976. *Wittgenstein's Lectures on the Foundations of Mathematics: Cambridge, 1939*. Edited by C. Diamond. Ithaca, NY: Cornell University Press. Reprinted 1989, Chicago: University of Chicago Press.

———. 1979. *Wittgenstein's Lectures, Cambridge, 1932–1935*. Edited by A. Ambrose. Oxford: Blackwell.

———. 1980a. *Culture and Value*. Edited by G. H. von Wright, with H. Nyman. Translated by P. Winch. Oxford: Blackwell.

———. 1980b. *Wittgenstein's Lectures, Cambridge, 1930–1932*. Edited by D. Lee. Oxford: Blackwell.

———. 1995. *Ludwig Wittgenstein: Cambridge Letters*. Edited by Brian McGuinness and G. H. von Wright. Oxford: Blackwell.

———. 2000. *Wittgenstein's Nachlass: The Bergen Electronic Edition*. Oxford: Oxford University Press.

———. 2005. *The Big Typescript: TS 213*. Edited and translated by C. G. Luckhardt and M. A. E. Aue. Oxford: Blackwell.

Wright, Crispin. 1992. *Truth and Objectivity*. Cambridge, MA: Harvard University Press.

# Acknowledgments

I am deeply grateful to Lindsay Waters for his encouragement, and for the persistence and enthusiasm with which he expressed it. I want also to thank Volker Munz for what I can call the Kirchberg side of this volume. More than half of the book grew from my two stays in Kirchberg am Wechsel, in 2013 and 2015, when James Conant and I taught the fifth and then the seventh Wittgenstein Summer Schools and participated in the Wittgenstein Symposia. It was Volker who invited us to teach in the Summer Schools, Volker who arranged my stay in Kirchberg each time, and Volker who, along with Margret Kronaus, attended to countless details. I am very grateful to have had the chance to spend time in Kirchberg, and I profited enormously from the philosophical discussions at the Summer Schools and at the Symposia. The Austrian Ludwig Wittgenstein Society made both those summer stays in Kirchberg possible, and I want to thank them as well.

The essays in Parts II and III benefited greatly from discussion at the Wittgenstein Workshop at the University of Chicago in 2013 and at the Jowett Society in Oxford in 2014. My thanks go to Nic Koziolek and Gilad Nir for handling all the details for the talk in Chicago, and to Michael Price for arranging everything for my visit to the Jowett Society.

I have been helped in many ways by comments and suggestions and criticism from other philosophers, whom I have thanked in the individual essays, but there are three people whose comments were particularly important in the shape of the book as a whole. One is Jean-Philippe Narboux, who altogether changed my understanding of the problems into which my work on Anscombe and Wittgenstein was leading me. Warren Goldfarb's remarks during the Wittgenstein Workshop at the University of Chicago enabled me to see how deeply relevant the ideas of Frege were to the issues that I was exploring. The third person whose comments shaped the volume is a reviewer for Harvard University Press. His criticisms led me to rethink the organization of the book as a whole, and many of the topics within it.

Two friends who have contributed in innumerable ways to this book are James Conant and Alice Crary. I have been discussing with them the kinds of questions that come up in this book for more than twenty-five years. They have read through countless drafts of things I've written, and have enabled me to see all kinds of ways in which what I'd written—and what I'd thought—needed to be improved. Here I want simply to acknowledge my great debt to them.

I am grateful also to Deborah Grahame-Smith and Wendy Nelson, at Westchester Publishing Services, for their help in preparing the manuscript, and to Dan Boscov-Ellen and Gilad Nir, who reconstructed old files for me. I am greatly indebted also, for their patience and helpfulness, to Joy Deng, Scarlett Wilkes, Jeff Dean, Anne Zarrella, Lisa Roberts, and Stephanie Vyce at Harvard University Press.

The six previously published essays in this volume appear here with permission from the publishers, which is gratefully acknowledged. The essays originally appeared in the places listed.

Essay 1: "Finding One's Way Into the Tractatus," *SATS - Northern European Journal of Philosophy*, Vol. 4, No. 2 (January 2003), 165–182. © Philosophia Press, 2003. Copyright and all rights reserved. Material from this publication has been used with the permission of Walter De Gruyter GmbH, Berlin.

Essay 2: "Saying and Showing: an Example from Anscombe" in Post-Analytic *Tractatus*, ed. Barry Stocker (Farnham, Surrey: Ashgate Publishing Limited, 2004), 151–166. © Barry Stocker, 2004. Reproduced by permission of Taylor and Francis Group, LLC, a division of Informa plc.

Essay 3: "Reading the Tractatus with G.E.M. Anscombe" in The Oxford Handbook of the History of Analytic Philosophy, ed. Michael Beaney

(Oxford: Oxford University Press, 2013), 870–905. Reprinted by permission of Oxford University Press.

Essay 4: "Wittgenstein and What Can Only Be True," *Nordic Wittgenstein Review*, Vol. 3, No. 2, eds. Martin Gustafsson, Lars Hertzberg, and Yrsa Neuman (December 2014): 9–40, (CC-BY-NC-SA).

Essay 5: "Disagreements: Anscombe, Geach, Wittgenstein," *Philosophical Investigations: Special Issue on the Work of Elizabeth Anscombe and Peter Geach*, Vol. 38, No. 1-2 (January / April 2015), 1–24. © 2015 John Wiley & Sons Ltd. Reproduced by permission of John Wiley & Sons Ltd.

Essay 6: "Asymmetries in Thinking About Thought: Anscombe and Wiggins," *American Catholic Philosophical Quarterly*, Vol. 90, No. 2 (Spring 2016), 299–315. Reproduced by permission of the American Catholic Philosophical Association.

The versions of these essays published here incorporate some changes and new material.

# Index

Anscombe, Elizabeth: on Antony Flew, 37, 72, 79, 89–91, 163, 202, 253–254; on Aristotle and practical truth, 162–163, 214, 226, 262, 303; context principle, 17, 32–35, 43, 106–107, 109, 111, 113, 118–119, 121–122, 150; "empiricist" readings of *Tractatus*, 3, 46, 99–100, 110; on first person, 74n2, 217–218, 238–240; Frege's *Begriffsschrift*, 54; on its looking as if the sun goes round the earth, 41–42, 55–58, 62, 66–67; on limits, 41–43; logical chemistry, 52–53, 105, 115, 150; negation, 4, 22, 23, 46–49, 51–52, 106; philosophical clarification, 37, 39, 51n6, 52, 53, 55, 75, 78–79, 85, 115–122; on "Red is a color," 31–35, 39, 42, 56–58, 58–59n11, 66–68, 135–137, 165, 204–205; reversibility of sense, 23, 46n1, 47, 106–107, 227; Russell, 8, 9, 48, 62–64, 98–101, 103–104, 109, 111, 151; on sentences of the form "'p' says that p," 59–60; on "'Someone' is not the name of someone," 31, 37–38, 57, 58–59n11, 61, 71–76, 77, 85, 91–93, 158–161, 173n1, 186, 188, 193, 200, 202–204, 208–209, 218, 219, 226, 232, 238, 253–254, 258, 259, 261, 269; on signs and symbols, 54, 58–59n11, 92–93, 112–113; on thinking that has gone wrong, 162–163, 226–228, 236, 269–270; *Tractatus* not combination of picture theory and theory of truth-functions, 46–48, 100, 104, 171–172; on Truman's degree, 225–226, 266–267; on Wittgenstein and idealism, 305–306; on Wittgenstein and what shows itself, 31, 34, 36–37, 71–96, 165, 203; on Wittgenstein's relation to Frege, 8, 23, 26, 46, 50, 98, 99–104, 105, 109, 115, 149–150, 169. *See also* picture theory